WOOD HOUSES

LE BOIS EN ARCHITECTURE – INNOVATIONS & ESTHÉTIQUE

HÄUSER AUS HOLZ

VAN HOUT GEBOUWD

CASAS DE MADERA

CASE IN LEGNO

CASAS DE MADEIRA

TRÄHUS

KÖNEMANN
is an imprint of Frechmann Kolón GmbH
www.frechmann.com

Editorial project:
LOFT Publications
Barcelona, Spain
Tel.: +34 932 688 088
Fax: +34 932 687 073
loft@loftpublications.com
www.loftpublications.com

Editorial coordinator:
Simone K. Schleifer

Assistant to editorial coordination:
Aitana Lleonart

Editor:
Francesc Zamora Mola

Art director:
Mireia Casanovas Soley

Design and layout coordination:
Claudia Martínez Alonso

DTP Designer:
Ignasi Gracia Blanco, Juan Prieto

Translations:
Equipo de Edición, Barcelona
Denis-Armand Canal (French)

Published in the United States in 2014 by:

Skyhorse Publishing
307 West 36th Street, 11th Floor
New York, NY 10018, USA
T: +1 212 643 6816
info@skyhorsepublishing.com
www.skyhorsepublishing.com

ISBN 978-3-86407-359-5 (GB)
ISBN 978-3-86407-357-1 (D)
ISBN 978-3-86407-360-1 (NL)
ISBN 978-3-86407-358-8 (E)
ISBN 978-3-86407-361-8 (PORT)
ISBN 978-3-86407-362-5 (SWE)
ISBN 978-1-63220-596-4 (Skyhorse, USA)

Printed in Spain

Wood is a natural resource that has been available to man through history. It has provided fuel, tools, and shelter. It has left traces that show its presence in many human activities. The advance of technology has provided a growing variety of wood derived products that are adapted to modern times and usages. The availability of this resource, which had always seemed inexhaustible, is now a concern for the entire world. The solution for its preservation lies in the balance between how quickly we use it up against how fast it regenerates: sustainable management of the resource.

Trees grow thanks to the activity of a single layer of cells called vascular cambium between the phloem and the xylem. The vascular cambium wraps the living parts of the tree and divides to produce secondary xylem cells and secondary phloem cells resulting in the increase in the girth of the plant's root or stem, rather than of its length, during active growth periods. Wood presents two different qualities: one peripheral, soft and porous, called sapwood where the hardening process is incomplete. Another in the interior called heartwood, which has reached the maximum strength and density. The proportion of sapwood versus heartwood varies on different species: For instance, pines and Holm oaks have considerably thick sapwood while chestnut and elm hardly have any. The quality of the sapwood is always inferior to that of the heartwood. Generally, sapwood is much lighter in color that the heartwood.

Each species of wood has its own physical and mechanical properties such as hardness, weight, shrinkage or flexibility, and other properties that provide color, luster and odor. Following are some of the most important physical properties of wood:

- Hardness is defined by the level of difficulty when in working the wood. Hard woods, for instance, include ebony, oak, or boxwood while softwoods include poplar, willow or balsa amongst others.
- Flexibility is the property that some woods have to bend in the longitudinal direction without breaking. Examples are the ash or the elm. The least flexible are the oak or the maple, for instance.
- Luster is the quality of the wood that is best achieved with hard woods such as the walnut, cherry or pear wood because fibers don't separate.
- Density is the relation between the wood's weight and its volume.
- Porosity is the ratio of the volume of all the pores in the wood to the volume of the whole.
- Homogeneity is defined by a uniform structure and composition of the wood fibers.
- Color is different with different species: poplar and maple are characterized by their whitish wood, oak wood is yellow-brownish, mahogany is reddish, rosewood is purplish and ebony is black.
- Figure is the textural pattern formed by wood fibers. Some woods like larch and walnut show a very visible figuring.
- Odor often serves to differentiate the various species.
- Durability determines the natural resistance of wood species to decay.

All these properties have been exploited throughout the centuries so that the various species have come to be used for their specific properties. To obtain the best wood quality, the tree should be harvested when it has reached full development. Younger trees produce soft wood and trees that are too old may show a deteriorated inner part. The wood also lacks good quality if the tree is left dead while still in the ground. In this case the wood will have lost its elasticity and consistency. The optimal age for trees to be cut depends on the species.

The best time for logging is in winter. During this period the sap activity is nonexistent and the bark easily separates from the sapwood. But summer is the season when the sapwood is filled with sap, which contains substances vulnerable to the attack of destructive organisms.

Once the logging phase is over the timber is taken to manufacture plants where the transformation phase begins, becoming fuel, construction material or household goods.

Throughout history, wood has been used as fuel and is at present a major source of energy derived from a solid fuel biomass. Wood fuel is available as logs, charcoal, chips, sheets, pellets and sawdust. It can be used for cooking and heating, and also to generate electricity. But beyond the utilitarian aspects of this resource, its warmth and aroma radiating from a fireplace or a furnace adds an undeniably pleasant atmosphere to a home.

Wood has always been used extensively in domestic settings for furniture, tools, and for other utensils. Wood furniture is warm, comforting and appealing, as well as suitable for both outdoor and indoor applications. While many people prefer the rustic aesthetic of handcrafted wooden furniture, contemporary design has much to offer without diminishing the character of wood.

While wood has been an important construction material for millenniums, researchers keep developing innovative new construction systems and solutions to mitigate the problems of durability, and strengthen the role of wood in construction as a sustainable material. Engineered wood products are becoming a bigger part of the construction industry whether used as structural or aesthetic materials.

Wood used in construction includes products such as glued laminated timber (glulam), laminated veneer lumber (LVL), parallam and I-joists. These engineered wood products have proved to be more environmentally friendly, and sometimes cheaper, than building materials such as steel or concrete.

Wood that is grown in sustainable forests, whether it is used for furniture or large-scale construction, is an environmentally friendly material. Other manufactured construction materials generate more pollution while consuming more energy and non-renewable natural resources. Additionally, wood is biodegradable, recyclable and relatively durable.

Forests are most effectively sustained through natural regeneration and the practice of eco friendly techniques that ensure a sustainable supply of timber for wood products. A good example of this is selective harvesting. Instead of clear cutting areas of forest specific, mature trees are designated for harvest, which minimizes the impact on the forest ecosystem.

Le bois a toujours été une ressource naturelle à la disposition des hommes, tout au long de leur histoire. Il leur a fourni – et continue de leur fournir – du combustible, des outils, des abris. Il a laissé des traces qui témoignent de sa présence dans de multiples activités humaines. Les progrès de la technologie ont fourni une gamme de plus en plus vaste de produits dérivés du bois, adaptés aux besoins et aux usages de la vie moderne. Toutefois, la disponibilité de cette ressource – qui avait toujours paru inépuisable – pose aujourd'hui un problème de préservation à l'échelle mondiale. La solution ? Une gestion raisonnée et durable des forêts, en équilibrant soigneusement la cadence de la consommation et le temps indispensable à leur régénération.

Les arbres croissent grâce à l'activité d'une seule assise ou couche de cellules régénératrices, le cambium vasculaire, entre le phloème (ou liber) et le xylème. Le cambium enveloppe les parties vivantes de l'arbre et se subdivise pour produire des cellules secondaires de phloème et de xylème, dont la combinaison fait croître la circonférence de la racine ou de la tige de la plante – plutôt que leur longueur – lors des périodes de croissance.
Le bois présente deux qualités différentes : l'aubier à la périphérie, tendre et poreux, où le processus de durcissement n'est pas achevé ; le cœur ou duramen, à l'intérieur, qui a atteint le maximum de solidité et de densité. Les proportions respectives de cœur et d'aubier varient selon les espèces : par exemple, les pins et les chênes de Holm ont un aubier très épais alors que le châtaignier et l'orme n'en ont pratiquement pas. La qualité de l'aubier est toujours inférieure à celle du cœur ; l'aubier est généralement beaucoup plus clair que le cœur.
Chaque espèce de bois a des propriétés physiques et mécaniques spécifiques : dureté, poids, retrait ou flexibilité, mais aussi couleur, lustre et odeur. Les propriétés physiques les plus importantes d'un bois sont les suivantes :

- la dureté est définie par le niveau de difficulté rencontré dans le travail du bois. Parmi les bois durs figurent par exemple l'ébène, le chêne ou le buis ; on range au nombre des bois tendres le peuplier, le saule ou le balsa.
- la flexibilité est la faculté qu'ont certains bois de se plier longitudinalement sans se briser. Le frêne et l'orme sont de ceux-là ; en revanche, les moins flexibles sont par exemple le chêne ou l'érable.
- le poli est une qualité qui s'obtient au mieux avec les bois durs comme le noyer, le merisier ou le poirier, dont les fibres sont très serrées.
- la densité est la relation entre le poids du bois et son volume.
- l'homogénéité est définie par la structure et la composition des fibres du bois.
- la couleur varie elle aussi en fonction des espèces : le peuplier et l'érable sont blanchâtres, le chêne brun clair, l'acajou rougeâtre, le bois de rose violâtre, l'ébène noir.
- la figure est le schéma de texture dessiné par les fibres, le fil et le grain du bois. Des essences comme le mélèze et le noyer ont une figure très visible.
- l'odeur sert souvent à distinguer les diverses espèces.
- la durabilité traduit la durée de résistance d'un bois au pourrissement.

Toutes ces propriétés ont été plus ou moins reconnues et exploitées au fil des siècles, si bien que l'usage spécialisé des es-sences s'est peu à peu perfectionné. Pour obtenir le meilleur bois, l'arbre doit être coupé lorsqu'il a atteint son plein développement : les arbres trop jeunes donnent du bois trop tendre, les arbres trop vieux peuvent receler des parties intérieures en mauvais état. Un bois coupé perd aussi de ses qualités s'il est laissé trop longtemps sur le sol après abattage : il risque en effet de perdre de son élasticité et de sa consistance. L'âge optimal de coupe varie selon les essences.
Le meilleur moment pour l'abattage est l'hiver : pendant cette période, l'activité de la sève est inexistante ou très ralentie et l'écorce se détache facilement de l'aubier. En été, au contraire, l'aubier est gorgé de sève qui contient des substances vulnérables aux attaques des organismes destructeurs.
Une fois l'abattage terminé, le bois coupé est acheminé à l'usine où se fait la phase de transformation : il devient alors combustible, matériau de construction ou mobilier.

Tout au long de l'histoire, le bois a d'abord servi de combustible ; il constitue toujours une source majeure d'énergie tirée de la biomasse solide. Il est utilisé sous forme de bûches, de charbon, de copeaux, de plaquettes et de sciure. On peut l'employer pour la cuisine et le chauffage, mais aussi pour fabriquer de l'électricité dans une centrale thermique. Au-delà des aspects utilitaires de cette ressource, la chaleur et les parfums qui se dégagent d'une cheminée ou d'un fourneau en fonctionnement donnent toujours une atmosphère plaisante à un intérieur.
Le bois est également utilisé depuis toujours pour le mobilier, l'outillage et d'autres ustensiles domestiques. Le mobilier en bois est chaud, confortable et séduisant ; on peut l'employer avec le même succès à l'intérieur comme à l'extérieur de la maison. Et si beaucoup préfèrent l'esthétique rustique du mobilier en bois ouvré artisanalement, le design contemporain propose aussi nombre de créations qui ne retirent rien au caractère du bois.

Si le bois a également servi de matériau de construction traditionnel pendant des millénaires, les chercheurs continuent à développer des systèmes et des solutions de construction innovants, afin de pallier les problèmes de durabilité et renforcer le rôle du bois dans la construction en tant que matériau renouvelable. Les produits usinés à partir du bois tendent aujourd'hui à prendre une part croissante dans l'industrie de la construction, aussi bien comme éléments structurels que comme éléments de décoration.

Le bois qui pousse dans les forêts renouvelables, qu'il serve pour le mobilier ou pour des constructions à grande échelle, est un matériau écologique. D'autres matériaux de construction manufacturés engendrent davantage de pollution tout en consommant plus d'énergie au détriment de ressources naturelles non renouvelables. De plus, le bois est biodégradable, recyclable et relativement durable. Les forêts sont très efficacement renouvelées par régénération naturelle et par l'application de techniques favorables à l'environnement : cette combinaison harmonieuse assure une fourniture durable de bois pour tous les usages. Un bon exemple de cette gestion intelligente est l'abattage sélectif : au lieu de dégarnir en coupe claire des secteurs entiers d'une forêt, on n'abat que les arbres arrivés à maturité, ce qui minimise l'impact de l'abattage sur l'écosystème et préserve du même coup la ressource.

Holz ist ein natürlicher Rohstoff, der dem Menschen seit Anbeginn der Geschichte zur Verfügung steht. Es wurde als Brennstoff genutzt sowie um Werkzeuge herzustellen und Behausungen zu errichten. In vielen Bereichen menschlicher Tätigkeit sind seine Spuren erkennbar. Der technische Fortschritt hat eine wachsende Anzahl verschiedenster Produkte aus Holzderivaten mit sich gebracht, die den Anforderungen der modernen Zeit und neuen Verwendungszwecken entsprechen. Die Verfügbarkeit dieser bisher unerschöpflich scheinenden Ressource erregt nun weltweite Besorgnis. Die Lösung liegt in einem ausgewogenen Verhältnis zwischen Nachwachsen und Verbrauch, mit anderen Worten, in einem nachhaltigen Umgang mit dem Rohstoff Holz.

Für das Wachstum von Bäumen ist das vaskuläre Kambium verantwortlich, eine einfache Zellschicht, die zwischen dem Phloem und dem Xylem liegt. Diese Schicht umhüllt die lebenden Teile des Baumes. In aktiven Wachstumsperioden entstehen durch die Teilung der Kambiumzellen sekundäre Phloem- und Xylemzellen, die für das Dickenwachstum der Wurzeln oder des Stamms, also für das Dicken- nicht das Höhenwachstum, verantwortlich sind. Holz kann zwei verschiedene Qualitäten aufweisen: Man unterscheidet zwischen dem weichen und porösen Splintholz an der Peripherie des Stammes, dessen Verkernung noch nicht abgeschlossen ist, und dem innen liegenden Kernholz, das seine maximale Härte und Dichte erreicht hat. Das Verhältnis zwischen Splintholz und Kernholz variiert bei den verschiedenen Baumarten: So haben zum Beispiel die Kiefer und die Steineiche eine beeindruckend dicke Splintholzschicht, während der Walnussbaum und die Ulme fast gar keine aufweisen. Splintholz weist immer eine geringere Qualität als Kernholz auf und ist im Allgemeinen viel heller als Kernholz.

Jede Holzart zeichnet sich durch bestimmte physische und mechanische Eigenschaften aus, wie zum Beispiel Härte, Gewicht, Schwindung oder Biegsamkeit und andere Merkmale wie Farbe, Glanz oder Geruch. Im Folgenden werden einige der wichtigsten physikalischen Eigenschaften von Holz erörtert:

- Die Härte wird an dem Schwierigkeitsgrad gemessen, den die Bearbeitung des jeweiligen Holzes erfordert. Zu den harten Hölzern zählen zum Beispiel Ebenholz, Eiche und Buchsbaum, zu den weichen gehören Pappel, Weide und Balsaholz.
- Die Biegsamkeit eines Holzes bezeichnet, wie stark es längsseitig gekrümmt werden kann, ohne zu brechen. Gute Biegeeigenschaften besitzen zum Beispiel das Holz der Esche und der Ulme. Die geringste Biegsamkeit weisen Eiche und Ahorn auf.
- Der Glanz von Holz ist eine Eigenschaft, die am besten bei harten Hölzern zum Ausdruck kommt, wie zum Beispiel beim Walnuss-, Kirsch- oder Birnbaum, weil ihre Fasern eng zusammen liegen.
- Die Dichte beschreibt das Verhältnis zwischen Gewicht und Volumen des Holzes.
- Die Porosität beschreibt das Verhältnis zwischen dem Volumen der Holzporen und dem Gesamtvolumen des Holzes.
- Die Homogenität bezieht sich auf die Gleichmäßigkeit der Struktur und der Maserung eines Holzes.
- Die Farbe ist je nach Art unterschiedlich: Pappel und Ahorn zeichnen sich durch ihr weißliches Holz aus, Eichenholz ist braun-gelblich, Mahagoniholz rötlich, Rosenholz leicht violett und Ebenholz schwarz.
- Die Zeichnung bezeichnet die von den Holzfasern gebildete Oberflächenstruktur. So zeichnen sich manche Holzarten, wie zum Beispiel Lärche und Walnuss, durch eine besonders ausgeprägte Zeichnung aus.
- Die verschiedenen Arten werden oft auch an ihrem Geruch unterschieden.
- Die Haltbarkeit ist die dem Holz eigene Widerstandsfähigkeit gegen den Verfall.

Alle diese Eigenschaften werden seit vielen Jahrhunderten genutzt, und die verschiedenen Holzarten je nach Verwendungszweck gezielt eingesetzt. Um eine optimale Holzqualität zu erzielen, muss der Baum geschlagen werden, wenn er völlig ausgewachsen ist. Jüngere Bäume liefern ein weiches Holz und bei zu alten Bäumen kann der innere Teil verdorben sein. Das Holz ist ebenso qualitativ minderwertig, wenn der Baum vor der Abholzung, also noch am Boden, abstirbt. In diesem Fall verliert das Holz seine Elastizität und Konsistenz. Der optimale Zeitpunkt für die Abholzung hängt von der jeweiligen Art ab.

Die beste Zeit für die Abholzung ist der Winter. In dieser Zeit zirkuliert der Baumsaft nicht, und die Rinde lässt sich leicht vom Splintholz trennen. Im Sommer hingegen ist das Splintholz mit Baumsaft gefüllt, der Substanzen enthält, die für Schädlinge anfällig sind.

Nach der Abholzung wird das Nutzholz in Holzfabriken zu Brennholz, Baumaterial und Haushaltsgütern weiterverarbeitet.

Der Mensch hat sein Beginn seiner Geschichte Holz als Brennmaterial genutzt, in der Gegenwart stellt es eine bedeutende Energiequelle dar, die sich aus einer festen brennbaren Biomasse nährt. Holz steht in Form von Klötzen, Holzkohle, Hackschnitzeln, Latten, Pellets und Sägespänen zur Verfügung. Es kann zum Kochen und Heizen, und auch zur Gewinnung von Strom verwendet werden. Über seine nützlichen Aspekte hinaus strahlt ein mit Holz beheizter Kamin oder Ofen eine Wärme und einen Geruch aus, die unserem Zuhause eine besonders angenehme Atmosphäre verleihen.

Holz dient in unserem häuslichen Lebensraum verschiedenen Zwecken, es wird für Möbel, Werkzeuge oder andere Utensilien genutzt. Holzmöbel sind warm, behaglich und ansprechend, und zudem sowohl für den Außen- wie auch den Innenraum geeignet. Die rustikale Ästhetik handgefertigter Holzmöbel erfreut sich großer Beliebtheit, doch auch zeitgenössische Designer wissen den Grundcharakter des Holzes innovativ zu nutzen.

Holz stellt seit Jahrtausenden ein wichtiges Baumaterial dar, doch wird weiterhin an innovativen Bausystemen und -lösungen geforscht, um die Haltbarkeit zu verbessern und die Rolle von Holz als nachhaltigem Material zu stärken. Verarbeitete Holzprodukte gewinnen in der Bauindustrie zunehmend an Bedeutung, und zwar sowohl mit tragender als auch mit schmückender Funktion.

Das beim Bau verwendete Holz umfasst Produkte wie Brettschichtholz, Furnierschicht- und Furnierstreifenholz und I-Balken. Diese technischen Holzprodukte haben sich als umweltfreundlicher und oftmals billiger erwiesen als Baumaterialien wie Stahl oder Beton.

Das in nachhaltig bewirtschafteten Wäldern heranwachsende Holz stellt ein umweltfreundliches Material dar und kann zur Fertigung von Möbeln oder in der Großbauindustrie verwendet werden. Andere industriell gefertigte Baumaterialien verursachen mehr Umweltverschmutzung und verbrauchen zudem mehr Energie und nicht erneuerbare natürliche Ressourcen. Außerdem ist Holz biologisch abbaubar, wieder verwertbar und relativ lange haltbar. Die Nachhaltigkeit der Wälder wird am besten durch natürliche Regeneration und die Anwendung umweltfreundlicher Methoden gewährleistet, die den nachhaltigen Vorrat an Bauholz sicherstellen. Ein gutes Beispiel dafür ist die selektive Abholzung. Anstatt einer großflächigen Abholzung werden dabei bestimmte, ausgereifte Bäume gefällt, wodurch das Ökosystem des Waldes erheblich weniger belastet wird.

Hout is natuurlijk materiaal dat door de eeuwen heen beschikbaar is geweest voor de mens. Hout voorziet in brandstof, gereedschap en onderdak. Het heeft sporen nagelaten waaraan te zien is wat de mens er allemaal mee heeft gedaan. Door de ontwikkeling van de technologie zijn er steeds meer van hout afgeleide producten gekomen die aangepast zijn aan de moderne tijd. Inmiddels is de hulpbron die onuitputtelijk leek een bron van zorg geworden. Om ook in de toekomst over hout te kunnen beschikken moet het gebruik duurzaam zijn, dat wil zeggen aangepast aan de snelheid waarmee het natuurlijk reservoir weer aangroeit.

Bomen groeien dankzij de activiteit van één enkele laag cellen. 'Vasculair cambium' is de benaming van dit weefsel, dat zich tussen het floëem (de bast) en het xyleem (het hout) bevindt. Het omhult de levende delen van de boom en groeit naar twee kanten door zich op te delen in secundaire hout- en bastcellen. Daardoor neemt tijdens de groei vooral de omvang van de wortel of de stam toe en niet zozeer de lengte. Hout wordt naar binnen toe steeds harder. Het zachte en poreuze hout onder de bast heet 'spint'. Binnenin zit het kernhout, dat veel sterker, dichter en zwaarder is. De verhouding tussen de aandelen spint en kernhout is bij elke boomsoort verschillend. Zo hebben dennen en steeneiken een dikke spintlaag, terwijl kastanjes en iepen bijna helemaal geen spint hebben. Spint is altijd van lagere kwaliteit dan kernhout en meestal ook lichter van kleur.

Elke houtsoort heeft zijn eigen fysieke en mechanische kenmerken, zoals hardheid, gewicht, krimping en buigzaamheid, en andere eigenschappen die bepalend zijn voor de kleur, glans en geur.
De belangrijkste fysieke eigenschappen zijn:

- De hardheid, die bepaalt hoe gemakkelijk of moeilijk het hout te bewerken is. Harde houtsoorten zijn ebben, eiken en bukshout. Voorbeelden van zachte houtsoorten zijn populieren-, wilgen- en balsahout.
- De buigzaamheid is de mate waarin het hout in de lengte kan buigen zonder te breken. Het hout van essen of iepen is bijvoorbeeld veel buigzamer dan dat van eiken of esdoorns.
- Glans is een eigenschap die vooral bij harde houtsoorten, zoals walnoten-, kersen- en perenhout, naar voren treedt, omdat de vezels van dit hout niet splijten.
- Het soortelijk gewicht is de verhouding tussen het gewicht en het volume van het hout.
- De poreusheid is de verhouding tussen het volume aan poriën in het hout en het totale volume.
- Homogeniteit staat voor eenvormigheid in de structuur en samenstelling van de houtvezels.
- Kleur is een belangrijk onderscheidend kenmerk: populieren- en esdoornhout is bijna wit, eiken is geelbruin, mahonie is roodachtig, palissander is paarsig en ebben is zwart.
- De tekening is het structuurpatroon dat de houtvezels vormen. Sommige houtsoorten, zoals lariks en walnoot, zijn opvallend mooi getekend.
- De geur dient vaak om te bepalen om welke houtsoort het precies gaat.
- Duurzaamheid is de mate waarin het hout van nature bestand is tegen verval.

In de loop der eeuwen heeft de mens al deze eigenschappen van hout leren kennen en de verschillende houtsoorten voor verschillende doeleinden leren gebruiken. Om hout van de beste kwaliteit te krijgen moet de boom gekapt worden wanneer hij volledig is uitgegroeid. Het hout van jongere bomen is zacht en te oude bomen zijn vanbinnen soms vermolmd. De kwaliteit van het hout gaat ook achteruit als een dode boom in de grond blijft staan. Dan wordt het minder soepel en verbrokkelt het. Op welke leeftijd een boom het best geveld kan worden, hangt af van de soort.
De winter is de beste tijd om een boom om te hakken. Dan is de sapstroom opgehouden en komt de bast makkelijk los van het spinthout. In de zomer zit het spinthout vol sap, dat stoffen bevat die vatbaar zijn voor aantasting door schadelijke organismen.
Na het kappen gaat het hout naar fabrieken, waar het wordt omgezet in brandstof, bouwmateriaal of huishoudelijke artikelen.

Sinds mensenheugenis is hout als brandstof gebruikt. Nog steeds is het een belangrijke bron van energie die uit vaste biomassa wordt gehaald. Brandhout is verkrijgbaar in de vorm van houtblokken, houtskool, snippers, platen, korrels en zaagsel. Het kan gebruikt worden voor het koken en de verwarming of om elektriciteit op te wekken. Afgezien van het nut vormt hout vooral een bron van gezelligheid. De behaaglijke warmte en de prikkelende geur van een open haard verhogen de sfeer in huis.
Hout is altijd gebruikt voor de vervaardiging van meubels, gereedschap en andere gebruiksvoorwerpen. Hout doet warm aan. Houten meubels zijn gerieflijk en kunnen zowel buiten als binnen staan. Veel mensen kiezen voor de rustieke schoonheid van handgemaakte meubels, maar modern design dat het karakter van hout intact laat, heeft ook veel te bieden.

Sinds duizenden jaren is hout een van de belangrijkste bouwmaterialen. Onderzoekers blijven innovatieve bouwmethoden ontwikkelen en oplossingen bedenken om de milieuonvriendelijke aspecten aan te pakken en de rol van hout als duurzaam materiaal in de bouw te vergroten. Bewerkte houtproducten worden steeds belangrijker in de bouwindustrie, zowel voor constructieve als decoratieve doelen.
In de bouw worden onder andere de volgende producten gebruikt: gelijmd laminaat (glulam), gelamineerd fineer (LVL), Parallam® en I-balken. Deze bewerkte houtproducten bleken milieuvriendelijker en soms goedkoper te zijn dan bouwmaterialen als staal en beton.

Duurzaam verbouwd hout is milieuvriendelijk materiaal, of het nu voor meubels of voor gebouwen wordt gebruikt. Andere in de fabriek vervaardigde bouwmaterialen zijn vervuilender, omdat er voor de productie meer energie nodig is en er een beroep wordt gedaan op hulpbronnen die niet hernieuwbaar zijn. Hout gaat lang mee, is biologisch afbreekbaar en geschikt voor recycling. Duurzaam onderhoud van bossen draait om natuurlijke regeneratie en de toepassing van ecologisch verantwoorde technieken om hout te winnen. Een van deze methoden is selectief kappen. In plaats van een heel stuk bos te rooien, wijzen de beheerders een beperkt aantal volgroeide bomen aan voor de kap, met minimale gevolgen voor het bos als ecosysteem.

La madera es un recurso natural que siempre ha estado a disposición del hombre a lo largo de la historia, proporcionándole combustible, herramientas y cobijo y dejando rastros que muestran su presencia en muchas actividades humanas.
Gracias al avance de la tecnología, disponemos de una creciente variedad de productos derivados de la madera que se adaptan a los tiempos y usos modernos. La disponibilidad de este recurso, que hasta ahora nos parecía inagotable, se ha convertido en una gran preocupación en todo el mundo. La solución para su preservación radica en el equilibrio entre el tiempo en que lo agotemos y la rapidez con que se regenera, o lo que es lo mismo, en la gestión sostenible del mismo.
Los árboles crecen gracias a la actividad de una única capa de células llamada cámbium vascular situada entre el floema y el xilema. El cámbium envuelve las partes vivas del árbol y se fragmenta para producir las células del xilema secundario y las del floema, gracias a lo cual aumenta la circunferencia de la raíz o del tallo de la planta -más que de su longitud- durante los periodos de crecimiento activos. La madera presenta dos cualidades diferentes: una periférica, blanda y porosa llamada albura, en que el proceso de endurecimiento es incompleto, y otra interior llamada duramen, caracterizada por poseer una densidad y una resistencia máximas. La proporción entre albura y duramen varía según sean la especie; por ejemplo, mientras el pino y la encina tienen una albura de grosor considerable, el castaño y el olmo prácticamente carecen de ella. La calidad de la albura es siempre inferior a la del duramen y, por lo general, presenta un color mucho más claro que este último.
Las propiedades físicas y mecánicas como la dureza, el peso, la contracción o la flexibilidad, así como otras que proporcionan el color, el brillo y el olor, dependerán siempre del tipo de madera.
A continuación se enumeran algunas de las principales propiedades físicas de la madera:
– La dureza se establece a partir de las dificultades que plantea durante su trabajo y transformación. Entre las maderas duras o nobles, podríamos citar el ébano, el roble o el boj y entre las blandas, el álamo, el sauce y el balso.
– La flexibilidad es la propiedad que poseen algunas maderas para doblarse longitudinalmente sin llegar a romperse. Sería el caso del fresno y del olmo. Los menos flexibles son, por ejemplo, el roble y el arce.
– El brillo es una cualidad presente sobre todo en las maderas duras como el nogal, el cerezo o el peral ya que sus fibras no se separan.
– La densidad es la relación entre el peso de la madera y su volumen.
– La porosidad es la proporción del volumen de todos los poros en la madera en relación con el volumen del todo.
– La homogeneidad equivale a una composición y una estructura uniformes de las fibras de la madera.
– El color varía en función de las especies: el álamo y el arce tienen una madera blanquecina, el roble amarilla tirando a marrón, la caoba rojiza, el palisandro violácea y el ébano negra.
– La figura es el dibujo que forman las fibras de la madera. Algunas maderas como la del alerce y el nogal muestran una veteado muy visible.
– El perfume es con frecuencia un elemento que nos permite diferenciar las especies.
– La durabilidad determina la resistencia natural de los tipos de madera a la descomposición o al deterioro.

Todas estas propiedades han sido explotadas durante mucho tiempo, gracias a lo cual la experiencia nos ha enseñado a utilizar las diferentes especies en función de sus propiedades específicas. Para conseguir una madera de máxima calidad, el árbol deberá ser talado cuando haya alcanzado su pleno desarrollo: ni muy joven, pues su madera es blanda, ni muy viejo pues puede presentar una parte interna deteriorada. La madera también puede ser de mala calidad si se deja morir el árbol en el terreno; en este caso, la madera perderá su elasticidad y consistencia. La edad óptima para talar un árbol dependerá de la especie.
La mejor estación para la tala es el invierno. Durante este periodo, la actividad de la savia es inexistente y la corteza se separa fácilmente de la albura; el verano, en cambio, es la estación en que la albura está rebosante de savia, que contiene sustancias vulnerables al ataque de organismos destructivos.
Una vez concluida la fase de tala, la madera se traslada a la fábrica o al aserradero en donde será cortada y transformada, convirtiéndose en combustible, en material para la construcción o en artículos para el hogar.
A lo largo de la historia, la madera ha sido empleada como combustible y en la actualidad es una de las principales fuentes de energía derivada de un biocombustible sólido. La leña está disponible como leños, carbón, virutas, chapas, gránulos y serrín. Puede usarse para cocinar y calentar, pero también para generar electricidad; pero más allá de los aspectos utilitarios de este recurso, su calor y su aroma, cuando se consume en una chimenea o en un horno, crea en el hogar una atmósfera realmente agradable.
La madera se ha utilizado ampliamente en escenarios domésticos para la fabricación de muebles, herramientas y otros utensilios. El mobiliario de madera es cálido, confortable y atractivo, además de ser apropiado para espacios exteriores e interiores. Mientras muchas personas prefieren la estética rústica de los muebles de madera hechos a mano, el diseño contemporáneo tiene mucho que ofrecernos sin por ello mermar el carácter de la madera.
Aunque durante milenios este preciado recurso ha sido un importante material de construcción, los investigadores siguen aún desarrollando nuevos sistemas y soluciones de construcción innovadores a fin de mitigar los problemas relacionados con la durabilidad y de potenciar el papel de la madera en el ámbito de la construcción por ser un material sostenible. Los productos de madera prefabricados están ganando terreno en el sector de la construcción, ya sea en la realización de materiales estructurales ya estéticos.
La madera empleada en la construcción incluye productos tales como la madera laminada encolada, el tablero laminado, el parallam y la vigueta en T. Estos productos prefabricados de madera han demostrado ser más ecológicos y a veces incluso más económicos que materiales como el acero o el hormigón.
La madera que está creciendo en bosques sostenibles, tanto si va a ser empleada para la fabricación de muebles como para la construcción a gran escala, es un material que no daña el medio ambiente. Otros materiales utilizados en la construcción, además de aumentar en grado de contaminación, consumen más energía y recursos naturales no renovables. Además, la madera es biodegradable, reciclable y relativamente duradera.
Las selvas y los bosques se preservan de forma más efectiva a través de la regeneración natural y de la práctica de técnicas ecológicas que aseguran un suministro sostenible de madera para la fabricación de productos lignarios. Un buen ejemplo de ello es la tala selectiva. En lugar de amplias áreas de desmonte, se seleccionan cuidadosamente los árboles maduros destinados a la tala, algo que minimiza el impacto sobre el ecosistema forestal.

Il legno è una risorsa naturale che è sempre stata sempre a disposizione dell'uomo nel corso della sua storia, e gli ha fornito combustibile, strumenti e riparo. Ha lasciato tracce che dimostrano la sua presenza in svariate attività umane.
Grazie al progresso tecnologico, abbiamo alla nostra portata sempre più prodotti derivati dal legno che si adattano ai tempi e agli usi moderni. La disponibilità di questa risorsa, che finora ci sembrava inesauribile, è però divenuta oggi motivo di una grande preoccupazione in tutto il mondo. La soluzione per la sua salvaguardia consiste nel raggiungere un equilibrio tra i tempi in cui lo consumiamo e la velocità con cui si rigenera o, in altri termini, in una gestione sostenibile di tale risorsa.
La crescita degli alberi è dovuta all'attività di un solo strato di cellule chiamato cambio vascolare localizzato tra il floema e lo xilema. Il cambio vascolare circonda le parti vive dell'albero e si frammenta per produrre le cellule dello xilema secondario nonché quelle del floema, e grazie a ciò aumenta la circonferenza della radice o del fusto della pianta -più che la loro lunghezza- durante i periodi di crescita attiva. Il legno presenta due diversi stadi: uno periferico, tenero e poroso chiamato alburno, nel quale il processo d'indurimento non è ancora completo, e l'altro interno, denominato durame, caratterizzato dal fatto di possedere una densità e una resistenza massime. La proporzione tra alburno e durame cambia in base alla specie; per esempio, mentre il pino e la quercia possiedono un alburno di spessore considerevole, il castagno e l'olmo ne sono quasi privi. La qualità dell'alburno è sempre inferiore a quella del durame e, in genere, presenta un colore più chiaro di questo.
Le proprietà fisiche e meccaniche quali la durezza, il peso, la contrazione o la flessibilità, così come altre che forniscono il colore, la lucentezza e l'odore, dipenderanno sempre dal tipo di legno.
Qui sotto riportiamo alcune delle principali proprietà fisiche del legno:

– La durezza si definisce in base alle difficoltà affrontate durante la sua lavorazione. Tra i legni duri o nobili, potremmo citare l'ebano, la quercia o il bosso e tra quelli dolci, il pioppo, il salice la balsa.
– La flessibilità è la proprietà posseduta da alcuni legni di piegarsi in senso longitudinale senza arrivare a rompersi. Sarebbe il caso del frassino e dell'olmo. I meno flessibili sono, per esempio, la quercia e l'acero.
– La lucentezza è una qualità presente soprattutto nei legni duri come il noce, il ciliegio o il pero, giacché le loro fibre non si separano.
– La densità è il rapporto tra il peso del legno e il suo volume.
– La porosità è la proporzione del volume di tutti i pori del legno rispetto al volume complessivo.
– L'omogeneità equivale a una composizione e a una struttura uniformi delle fibre del legno.
– Il colore varia in base alle specie: il pioppo e l'acero presentano un legno biancastro, la quercia giallo tendente al marrone, il mogano rossiccio, il palissandro violaceo e l'ebano nero.
– La figura è il disegno che formano le fibre del legno. Alcuni tipi di legno come quello del larice e del noce presentano venature molto visibili.
– Il profumo è spesso un elemento che grazie al quale riusciamo a differenziare le specie.
– La durabilità determina la resistenza naturale dei vari tipi di legno alla decomposizione o al deterioramento.

Tutte queste proprietà sono state sfruttate nel corso di molti secoli, pertanto l'esperienza ha insegnato a utilizzare le differenti specie in funzione delle loro proprietà specifiche. Per ottenere un legno di massima qualità, l'albero deve essere tagliato quando ha raggiunto il suo pieno sviluppo: né molto giovane, poiché il suo legno sarebbe ancora dolce, né troppo vecchio perché potrebbe avere una parte interna deteriorata. Il legno può essere di cattiva qualità se si lascia morire l'albero sul terreno; in questo caso, il legno perde la sua elasticità e la sua consistenza. L'età ottima per tagliare un albero dipende dalla specie.
La migliore stagione è l'inverno. Durante questo periodo, l'attività della linfa è assente e la corteccia si separa facilmente dall'alburno; d'estate, invece, l'alburno è pieno di linfa, che contiene sostanze vulnerabili all'attacco di organismi distruttivi.
Una volta terminata la fase del taglio degli alberi, il legno viene trasportato nella fabbrica o nella segheria dove viene tagliato e lavorato, diventano combustibile, materiale per l'edilizia o articoli per la casa.
Nel corso della storia, il legno è stato utilizzato come combustibile e attualmente è una delle principali fonti d'energia derivata dalla biomassa combustibile. La legna da ardere è disponibile sotto forma di ciocchi, carbone, trucioli, fogli, granuli e segatura. Può essere utilizzata per cucinare e riscaldare, ma anche per produrre elettricità. Tuttavia, oltre agli aspetti utilitari di questa risorsa, il suo calore e il suo profumo, quando si consuma in un camino o in un forno, crea nella casa un'atmosfera veramente gradevole.
Il legno è stato ampiamente utilizzato in ambito domestico per fabbricare mobili, strumenti da lavoro e altri utensili. L'arredamento di legno è caldo, confortevole e attrattivo, oltre a essere appropriato per spazi esterni e interni. Se, da un lato, molte persone preferiscono l'estetica rustica dei mobili di legno fatti a mano, dall'altro, il design contemporaneo ci può offrire molto senza snaturare il carattere del legno.
Sebbene per millenni questa pregiata risorsa sia stata ampiamente utilizzata come materiale edile, i ricercatori continuano a sviluppare nuove e innovative soluzioni di costruzione allo scopo di limitare i problemi legati alla sua durevolezza e di potenziare il suo ruolo nell'ambito dell'edilizia, in quanto materiale sostenibile. I prodotti prefabbricati a base di legno stanno guadagnando terreno nel settore della costruzione, sia nella realizzazione di materiali strutturali sia in quella di elementi estetici.
Il legno utilizzato nell'edilizia comprende prodotti quali il legno lamellare, il pannello stratificato di sfogliati (LVL), il parallam e le travi a T composte. Questi prodotti prefabbricati di legno hanno dimostrato di essere più ecologici e a volte perfino più economici di materiali quali l'acciaio o il calcestruzzo.
Il legno che sta crescendo in boschi sostenibili, se deve essere utilizzato per la produzione di mobili quanto o per la costruzione su grande scala, è un materiale che non danneggia l'ambiente. Altri materiali impiegati nell'edilizia, oltre ad aumentare il livello di inquinamento, consumano più energia e risorse naturali non rinnovabili. Inoltre, il legno è biodegradabile, riciclabile e relativamente durevole.
Le foreste e i boschi si tutelano in maniera più efficace attraverso la rigenerazione naturale e la pratica di tecniche ecologiche che garantiscono un rifornimento sostenibile di legno per la fabbricazione di prodotti lignei. Un ottimo esempio di ciò è il taglio selettivo. Invece di disboscare aree intere, si scelgono con cura gli alberi maturi da tagliare, il che riduce al minimo l'impatto sull'ecosistema forestale.

A Madeira é um recurso natural ao qual o Homem recorreu ao longo dos tempos. Serviu como material de combustão, para fabricar instrumentos e providenciar abrigo. Deixou marcas que atestam a sua presença em múltiplas actividades humanas.

O progresso da tecnologia tem-nos garantido um conjunto diversificado de aplicações de derivados da Madeira, adaptados à modernidade e aos seus usos. A procura deste matéria-prima, que por muito tempo parecia inesgotável, é hoje um problema global. A solução para a sua preservação está no equilíbrio resultante do uso que dela fazemos e da sua capacidade de regeneração: assenta, em suma, numa gestão sustentável deste recurso.

As árvores crescem graças à actividade de uma única camada de células radicada entre o xilema e o floema e à qual se chama tecido vascular. O tecido vascular envolve as partes vivas da árvore e divide-se produzindo células secundárias do xilema e do floema, daí resultando um avolumar da cilha da raiz ou do caule da planta, mais do que o crescimento desta, durante os períodos de medra. A madeira apresenta duas qualidades distintas: uma periférica, macia e porosa, chamada alburno, em que o processo de desenvolvimento está incompleto. A outra é interior, dá pelo nome de cerne, quando atingiu o máximo desenvolvimento e densidade. A proporção entre o alburno e o cerne varia de espécie para espécie: por exemplo, os pinheiros e os carvalhos apresentam um alburno relativamente espesso, mas os castanheiros e os ulmeiros têm-no muito fino. A qualidade do alburno é sempre inferior à do cerne. Geralmente, o alburno ostenta uma cor mais clara do que o cerne.

Cada espécie de madeira tem as suas específicas propriedades físicas e mecânicas, entre as quais se conta a resistência, o peso, a flexibilidade e a capacidade de retracção, e um conjunto de outras propriedades que definem a cor, o brilho e o cheiro.

Apresentam-se, seguidamente, algumas das mais importantes propriedades físicas da madeira:

- A resistência é definida pelo grau de dificuldade com que a madeira se deixa trabalhar. As madeiras duras, por exemplo, integram o ébano, o carvalho e o buxus, contando-se entre as madeiras macias o álamo, o salgueiro e a balsa, entre outros.
- A flexibilidade é a propriedade que apresentam algumas madeiras de se poderem dobrar longitudinalmente sem se partirem. São dela exemplos o freixo e o ulmeiro. As madeiras menos flexíveis são as do carvalho e as do bordo.
- O brilho é especificidade das madeiras duras, entre as quais se distingue a da nogueira e a da cerejeira, uma vez que as fibras não se separam.
- A densidade é a relação entre o peso da madeira e o seu volume.
- A porosidade é o rácio do volume de todos os poros da madeira em relação ao volume total daquela.
- A homogeneidade é definida pela estrutura e composição uniformes das fibras da madeira.
- A cor é diferente de espécie para espécie: o álamo e o bordo caracterizam-se por uma madeira esbranquiçada, o carvalho tem um tom amarelo-acastanhado, o mogno é avermelhado, o palissandro é púrpura e o ébano é negro.
- Os veios são o padrão de texturas formado pelas fibras da madeira. Algumas madeiras, como o lariço e a nogueira, apresentam veios bem visíveis.
- O odor serve frequentemente para diferenciar as várias espécies.
- A durabilidade determina a resistência natural das espécies de madeira à passagem do tempo.

Todas estas características foram exploradas ao longo dos séculos, de tal modo que as diferentes espécies arborícolas têm vindo a ser usadas em função das suas propriedades específicas. Para se obterem as melhores madeiras, as árvores devem ser cortadas quando atingem o seu máximo desenvolvimento. As árvores jovens proporcionam madeiras macias, as velhas podem apresentar um interior deteriorado. A madeira também perde qualidades se a árvore for cortada e permanecer presa ao solo. Nestes casos, a madeira perderá elasticidade e consistência. A idade ideal para o corte depende da espécie arborícola.

A melhor altura para cortar e recolher a madeira é o Inverno. Nessa época, a actividade do borne é quase inexistente, separando-se facilmente a casca do lenho. É no Verão que o alburno fica cheio de seiva, seiva essa que contém substâncias vulneráveis ao ataque de organismos destrutivos.

Uma vez terminada a fase de corte e recolha, a madeira é levada para a fábrica, onde começa a sua transformação, que pode ser em combustível, em material de construção ou em mobiliário.

Através da História, a madeira sempre foi usada como combustível, constituindo presentemente uma importante fonte energética derivada de uma biomassa combustível sólida. Podemos encontrar madeira combustível sob a forma de toros, carvão, bastões, lâminas, pastilhas e serrim. Pode ser usada para cozinhar e como fonte de aquecimento, bem como geradora de energia. Mas para além dos aspectos utilitários desta matéria-prima, o calor e o aroma que proporciona quando arde numa lareira ou braseiro, acrescenta um inegável toque de bem-estar ao ambiente de qualquer casa.

A madeira foi sempre muito usada em contextos domésticos, sob a forma de mobiliário e de uma vasta panóplia de utensílios. O mobiliário de madeira é aconchegante, quente e apelativo, podendo ser utilizado no interior como no exterior. E se muitos preferem os acabamentos rústicos do mobiliário em madeira trabalhado artesanalmente, também o design moderno tem muito para oferecer, sem desvirtuar em nada o carácter da madeira.

Muito embora a madeira tenha servido como material de construção ao longo de milénios, os investigadores continuam a desenvolver sistemas e soluções construtivas com vista a mitigar os problemas de durabilidade, e fortalecer o papel desempenhado pela madeira na construção enquanto material sustentável. Produtos industrialmente desenvolvidos à base de madeira assumem um papel de crescente relevância no contexto da construção, quer em aplicações estruturais, quer em aplicações estéticas.

A madeira utilizada na construção inclui produtos como o contraplacado, os lamelados de madeira folheada (LVL), a madeira laminada e as lajes de madeira. Estes produtos industrialmente transformados, têm-se revelado mais amigos do ambiente, e, frequentemente, mais baratos, do que os materiais de construção tradicionais, como o aço e o cimento.

A madeira que cresce em florestas sustentáveis, quer seja usada para mobiliário, quer o seja para a construção em grande escala, é um material não agressivo para o ambiente. Outros materiais utilizados na construção são bem mais poluentes, uma vez que consomem mas energia e recursos naturais não renováveis. Além disso, a madeira é biodegradável, reciclável e relativamente duradoura.

A melhor forma de garantir a sustentabilidade florestal reside na regeneração natural e na aplicação de técnicas não agressivas que garantam uma sustentável produção de madeira. Uma técnica bem representativa deste tipo de actividade é o abate selectivo. Por vez de se cortar a direito a madeira de determinada área, apenas se seleccionam para o corte as árvores adultas, assim minimizando o impacto do abate no ecossistema.

Trä är en naturtillgång som har varit tillgänglig för människan under historiens gång. Det har tillhandahållit bränsle, verktyg och skydd. Det har lämnat spår som visar på dess närvaro i många mänskliga aktiviteter. Teknikens framsteg har medgivit en växande variation av produkter framställda ur trä som är anpassade till modern tid och moderna användningsområden. Tillgängligheten på denna resurs, som alltid ansågs vara outtömlig, är nu en angelägenhet för hela världen. Lösningen för dess bevarande ligger i balansen mellan hur snabbt vi använder det och hur snabbt det förnyas: hållbar drift av tillgången.

Träd växer på grund av aktiviteten hos ett enda skikt av celler kallade vaskulär kambium mellan floem och xylem. Vaskulärt kambium omlindar de levande delarna av trädet och delar sig för att producera sekundära xylemceller och sekundära floemceller, vilket resulterar i en ökning i omfång av plantans rot eller stam snarare än dess längd under aktiva växtperioder. Trä representerar två olika kvaliteter: en perifer, mjuk och porös, så kallad vitved, där förhårdningsprocessen är ofullbordad. En annan i det inre kallas kärnvirke, detta har nått maximal styrka och densitet. Proportionen mellan vitved och kärnvirke varierar mellan olika arter: exempelvis har tallar och stenekar mycket tjock vitved medan kastanj och alm knappt har någon alls. Kvaliteten på vitveden är alltid sämre än på kärnvirket. Generellt är vitved mycket ljusare i färgen är kärnvirket.
Varje träsort har sina egna fysiska och mekaniska egenskaper såsom hårdhet, vikt, krympning eller flexibilitet, och andra egenskaper som ger färg, lyster och doft. Följande är några av de viktigaste fysiska egenskaperna hos trä:

- Flexibilitet är den egenskap en del träsorter har att kunna böjas longitudinellt utan att gå av. Exempel på detta är ask och alm. De minst flexibla är exempelvis ek och lönn.
- Lyster är den av träets kvaliteter som bäst uppnås av de hårda träsorterna såsom valnöt, körsbär eller päronträ, eftersom fibrerna inte delar sig.
- Densitet är relationen mellan träets vikt och volym.
- Porositeten är förhållandet mellan volymen på alla porerna träet och volymen på helheten.
- Homogenitet definieras av en enhetlig struktur och komposition på träfibrerna.
- Färg är olika hos olika arter: poppel och lönn karaktäriseras av sitt vitaktiga trä, ekträ är gulaktigt brunt, mahogny är rödaktigt, rosenträ är lilaaktigt och ebenholts är svart.
- Mönster är det strukturella mönster som skapas av träfiber. Vissa träsorter såsom lärk och valnöt uppvisar ett mycket synligt mönster.
- Doft används ofta för att skilja de olika arterna åt.
- Hållbarhet fastställer träsortens naturliga resistens mot förruttnelse.

Alla dessa egenskaper har exploaterats genom seklerna så att de olika sorterna har kommit att användas för deras specifika egenskapers skull. För att få bästa träkvalitet bör trädet avverkas när det är färdigutvecklat. Yngre träd producerar mjukt trä och träd som är för gamla kan uppvisa ett försämrat inre. Träet saknar också bra kvalitet om trädet tillåts dö medan det fortfarande står på rot. I detta fall har träet tappat sin elasticitet och fasthet. Den optimala åldern för att hugga träden varierar beroende på art.
Bästa tiden för avverkning är vintertid. Under denna tid är savningen ickeexisterande och barken delar sig lätt från vitveden. Sommaren är den säsong då vitveden är full av sav, som innehåller substanser som är sårbara för anfall av nedbrytande organismer.
När avverkningsfasen är över tas timret till industriplantor där förvandlingsfasen börjar, och det blir bränsle, byggmaterial eller hushållsvaror.

Genom historien har trä använts som bränsle och är i nuläget en mycket stor energikälla framställd ur en solid bränslebiomassa. Träbränsle finns som ved, träkol, träflis, träplattor, pellets och sågspån. Det kan användas till matlagning och uppvärmning och till att framställa elektricitet. Bortom nyttoaspekterna ger dess värme och doft som strålar ut från en eldstad eller värmepanna en oförnekligt trevlig atmosfär till ett hem.
Trä har alltid använts i stor utsträckning i bosättningar till möbler, verktyg och andra nyttoföremål. Trämöbler är varma, behagliga och tilltalande, lämpliga för ändamål såväl utomhus som inomhus. Även om många människor föredrar det rustika utseendet hos handgjorda trämöbler, har modern design mycket att erbjuda utan att minska träets karaktär.
Även om trä har varit ett viktigt byggmaterial i årtusenden, fortsätter forskare att utveckla innovativa nya byggsystem och lösningar för att lindra problemen med livslängd och för att stärka träets roll inom byggnation som ett hållbart material. Behandlade träprodukter håller på att bli en större del av byggnadsindustrin antingen det används till stomme eller till estetiska material.
Trä använt i byggnation inkluderar produkter såsom limlaminerat virke (limträ), laminerat fanervirke (LVL), parallam och I-balkar. Dessa behandlade träprodukter har visat sig vara mer miljövänliga och ibland billigare än byggmaterial som exempelvis stål eller betong.

Trä som har växt i hållbara skogar, antingen det används till möbler eller byggnation i stor skala, är ett miljövänligt material. Andra framställda byggmaterial genererar mer utsläpp samtidigt som de konsumerar mer energi och icke förnybara naturtillgångar. Utöver detta är trä biologiskt nedbrytbart, återvinningsbart och relativt hållbart. Skogar underhålls allra mest effektivt med naturlig föryngring och genom användning av ekovänliga tekniker som säkerställer en hållbar virkestillgång till träprodukter. Ett bra exempel på detta är gallring. Istället för kalhuggna områden väljs vissa vuxna träd ut för gallring, vilket minimerar inverkan på skogens ekosystem.

Schwebt Ihnen als perfektes Ferienhaus eine einfache Blockhütte an einem Bach oder ein malerisches Landhaus mit Schindelwänden vor? Holzhäuser - egal ob ein handgefertigtes Blockhaus mit nostalgischer, rustikaler Atmosphäre oder ein Fertigteilhaus - strahlen eine Wärme aus, die in anderen Häusern für gewöhnlich nicht zu finden ist.

Hoe ziet uw ideale vakantiewoning eruit? Is het een blokhut aan een beek of een met planken betimmerd sprookjeshuisje? Houten huizen stralen warmte uit, wat bij andere bouwtypen lang niet altijd het geval is. Ze hebben meer te bieden, of het nu om een zelfgebouwde rustieke blokhut gaat of om een modulaire prefabwoning.

WOOD HOMES MAISONS EN BOIS HOLZHÄUSER HOUTEN HUIZEN

Is your idea of the perfect vacation home a simple log cabin by a brook or a quaint cottage with shingle-clad walls? Wood homes provide a warmth not typically found with other types of construction, whether it is a handcrafted log cabin home offering a nostalgic and rustic atmosphere or a prefabricated modular home.

Désirez-vous une délicieuse thébaïde de vacances sous la forme d'une simple cabane en rondins près d'un ruisseau, ou bien un pittoresque chalet aux murs revêtus de bardeaux ? Les maisons en bois dégagent une chaleur que l'on ne trouve pas habituellement avec d'autres types de construction – qu'il s'agisse d'une cabane artisanale au charme rustique et nostalgique ou d'un chalet modulaire préfabriqué.

¿Su idea de la perfecta casa de vacaciones es una cabaña de troncos de madera cercana a un arroyo o una casita pintoresca con paredes revestidas de guijarros? Las casas de madera crean un ambiente cálido difícil de encontrar en otros tipos de construcciones, tanto si es una cabaña de madera hecha a mano envuelta en una atmósfera rústica y nostálgica como si es una casa modular prefabricada.

La nostra idea della perfetta casa di vacanze è un rifugio di tronchi di legno vicina a un ruscello o una casetta pittoresca con pareti rivestite di pietre? Le case di legno creano un ambiente caldo che difficilmente potremmo trovare in costruzioni di altro tipo, tanto se si tratta di una casupola di legno fatta a mano immersa in un'atmosfera campestre e nostalgica quanto se è una casa modulare prefabbricata.

A sua casa de Verão perfeita é uma simples cabana de troncos de madeira junto a um riacho, talvez com paredes de tabuinhas? As casas de madeira proporcionam um aconchego reconfortante raramente presente nos outros tipos de construção, quer se trate de uma rústica cabana de troncos envolvida em nostalgia, quer se trate de uma casa construída em módulos.

Är din bild av det perfekta semesterhuset en enkel timmerstuga vid en bäck eller en pittoresk stuga med spånklädda väggar? Hem av trä bidrar med en värme som vanligtvis inte återfinns hos andra byggnadstyper, oavsett om det är en handtimrad stuga som erbjuder en nostalgisk och rustik känsla, eller ett prefabricerat modulhus.

CASAS DE MADERA

CASE DI LEGNO

CASAS DE MADEIRA

HEM AV TRÄ

CONVERCEY HOUSE

BERNARD QUIROT ARCHITECTE ET ASSOCIÉS

This house pays homage to the landscape that surrounds it. While the long sides are mostly opaque only punctuated with small openings, the plan of the house is opened at both ends to frame the long views of the Saône plain. This accentuates the horizontality of the plan, reinforced by the uniformity of the larch exterior cladding.

Cette maison rend hommage au paysage environnant. Si les longs côtés ne sont percés que de petites ouvertures, le plan de la demeure s'ouvre aux deux extrémités pour encadrer les vastes perspectives sur la plaine de la Saône. Cette conception accentue l'horizontalité du plan, renforcée par l'uniformité du revêtement extérieur en mélèze.

Die Gestaltung des Hauses zollt der umliegenden Landschaft Anerkennung. Während die Längsseiten fast völlig undurchsichtig und nur mit wenigen kleinen Öffnungen ausgestattet sind, ist das Haus an beiden Enden offen gestaltet, um Ausblick über die Tiefebene der Saone zu gewähren. Dadurch wird die Horizontalität des Projekts noch betont, zu der auch die Einheitlichkeit der in Lärchenholz ausgeführten Außenfassade das Ihre beiträgt.

Dit huis is een eerbetoon aan het omringende landschap. Terwijl in de lange zijden alleen kleine openingen zitten, zijn de korte zijden opengewerkt om het uitzicht over de vlakte van de Saône te omlijsten. In het ontwerp ligt de nadruk op het horizontale, wat versterkt wordt door de eenvormigheid van de bekleding met lariks.

Esta casa rinde homenaje al paisaje que la rodea. Si bien sus largos laterales son bastante opacos, salpicados sólo con pequeñas aberturas, la planimetría de la casa está abierta en ambos extremos para enmarcar las amplias vistas de la llanura del Saona. Esta característica, sumada a la uniformidad del revestimiento exterior de alerce, acentúa la horizontalidad de la estructura.

Questa casa vuole essere un omaggio al paesaggio che la circonda. Sebbene le lunghe parti laterali siano abbastanza scure, intercalate solo da piccole aperture, la planimetria della casa prevede che entrambe le estremità siano completamente aperte per incorniciare le ampie viste della pianura del Saona. Questa caratteristica, sommata all'uniformità del rivestimento esterno di larice, risalta ancor di più l'orizzontalità della struttura.

Esta casa presta homenagem à paisagem que a rodeia. Enquanto os lados mais compridos são sobretudo opacos, pontuados apenas por pequenas aberturas, a planta da casa é aberta nas duas extremidades de forma a emoldurar a ampla vista da planície de Saone. Esta configuração acentua a horizontalidade da planta, reforçada pela uniformidade do revestimento exterior em lariço.

Detta hus hedrar landskapet som omger det. Medan långsidorna mestadels är opaka och endast punkterade med små öppningar är planlösningen öppen i båda kortsidorna för att rama in utsikten över Saône-slätten. Detta accentuerar planlösningens horisontalitet förstärkt av enhetligheten i den exteriöra panelen i lärkträ.

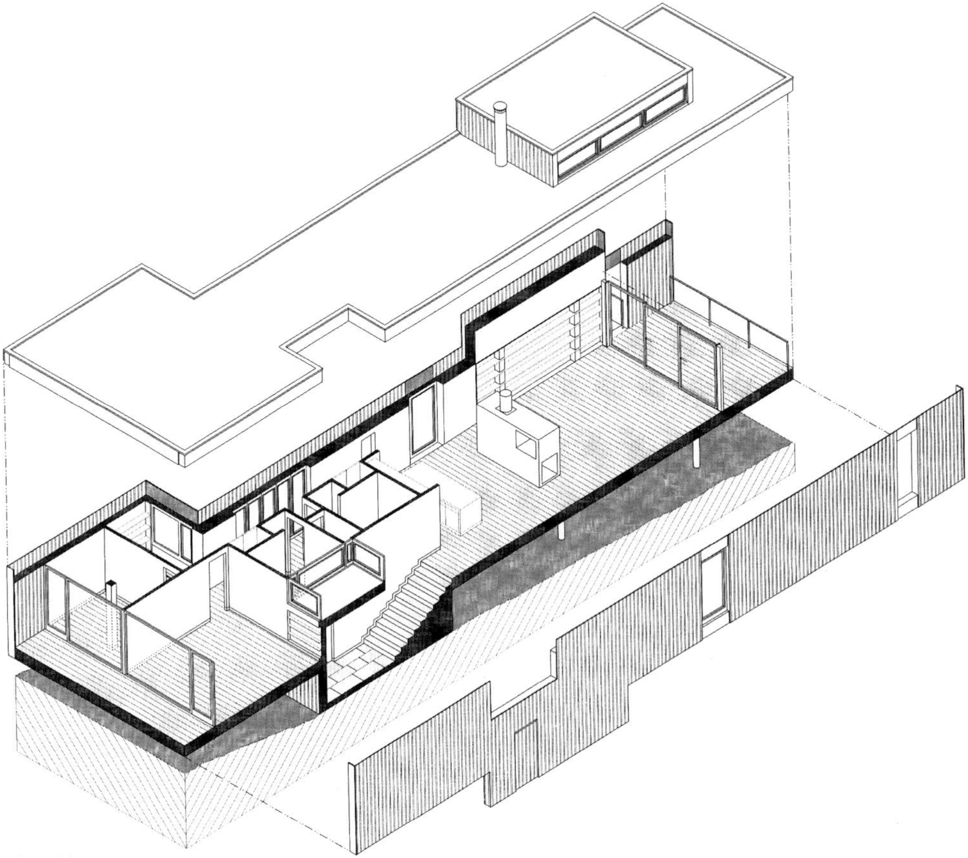

Axonometric

CHEN HOUSE

C-LABORATORIO

The house is built on an old Japanese cherry orchard in the Datun Mountains. The rectangular mahogany wood construction is raised above the ground in order to let the flood waters run under it. The kitchen and a small bathroom act as a kicker to stabilize the wooden structure during the frequent typhoons and earthquakes.

Cette maison est bâtie sur le terrain d'un ancien verger de cerisiers, dans les monts Datun. La construction en acajou, de plan rectangulaire, est surélevée au-dessus du sol pour permettre le libre écoulement des eaux de ruissellement. La cuisine et une petite salle de bains servent de butée pour stabiliser la structure de bois lors des typhons et des séismes, assez fréquents dans la région.

Das Haus wurde in einem alten japanischen Kirschgarten in der Bergregion von Datun errichtet. Die rechteckige Holzkonstruktion steht erhöht über dem Boden, um das Regenwasser unterhalb ablaufen zu lassen. Die Küche und das kleine Badezimmer erfüllen während der häufigen Taifune und Erdbeben eine Stützfunktion für die gesamte Holzstruktur.

Dit huis is gebouwd in een oude kersenboomgaard in het Datungebergte. De rechthoekige constructie van mahoniehout is boven de grond verheven, zodat het wassende water eronderdoor kan stromen. De keuken en een kleine badkamer fungeren tijdens de veel voorkomende tyfoons en aardbevingen als stootkussens: ze stabiliseren het huis.

La casa, una construcción rectangular de madera de caoba, fue construida en un viejo huerto de cerezas japonés en las Montañas Datun. Los arquitectos, a fin de que el torrente de agua presente en el terreno corriese por debajo, decidieron levantarla con respecto al nivel del terreno. La cocina y el pequeño baño contribuyen a estabilizar la estructura de madera durante los frecuentes tifones y terremotos.

La casa è un edificio di legno di mogano a base rettangolare ed è costruita in un antico giardino di ciliegi giapponese sui monti Datun. Gli architetti, hanno deciso di alzarla da terra per fare in modo che il torrente che scorre nel giardino vi passasse sotto. La cucina e il piccolo bagno contribuiscono a rendere più stabile la struttura di legno durante i frequenti tifoni e terremoti.

A casa foi construída num antigo cerejal japonês, nas montanhas de Datun. A construção rectangular, em madeira de mogno, foi elevada acima do solo de forma a permitir a passagem das águas das inundações. A cozinha e a casa de banho funcionam como uma parede mestra, para estabilizar a estrutura de madeira durante os frequentes tufões e terramotos.

Huset är byggt på en gammal japansk körsbärsträdgård i Datunbergen. Den rektangulära konstruktionen av mahognyträ är höjd ovanför marken så att flodvattnet kan rinna under den. Köket och ett litet badrum fungerar som stabilisatorer för att hålla träkonstruktionen stabil under de ofta förekommande tyfonerna och jordbävningarna.

Site plan

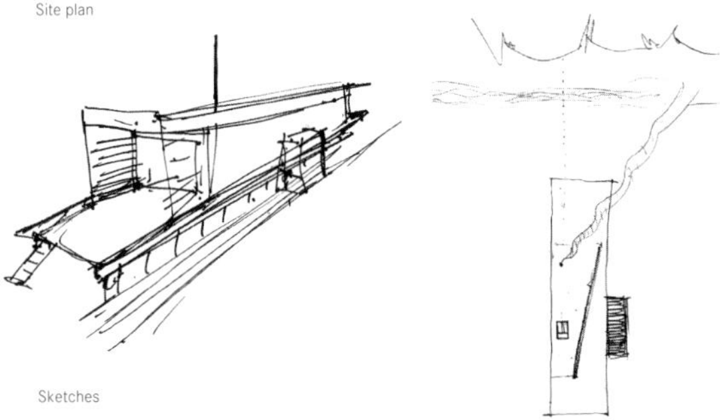

Sketches

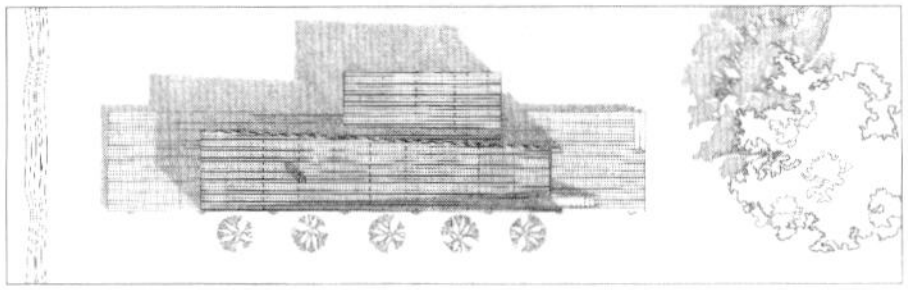

Roof plan

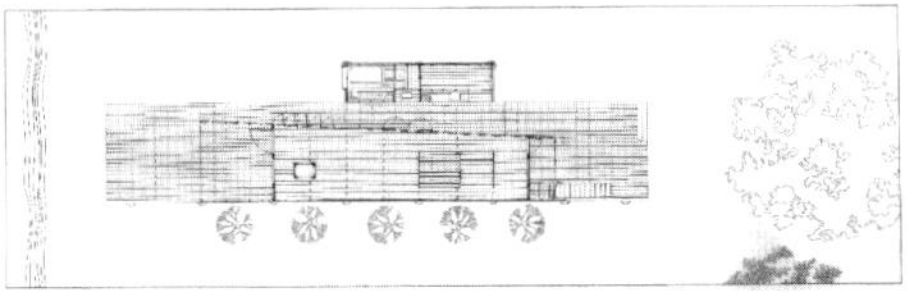

Ground floor

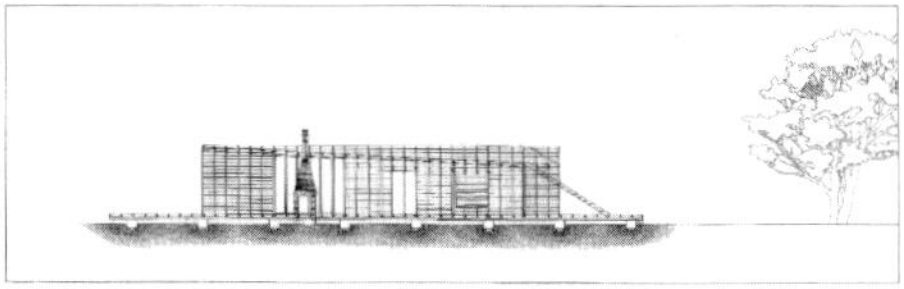

Section

THE HUMELGÅRD HOUSE AND LOGSAUNA

FRIMAN.LAAKSONEN ARKKITEHDIT OY
© Rauno Träskelin

The house is placed on a hill with its north corner facing the northern winds. A traditional log sauna is located to the east of the house with views of Degersjön Lake. Traditional and natural choices were made in materials: wood and wood fiber boards, glulam beams, plywood combined with galvanized corrugated steel, glass and concrete.

La maison est implantée sur une colline, son angle nord face aux vents de cette aire. Un sauna traditionnel en rondins est situé à l'est de la maison, avec une vue sur le lac Degersjön. On a privilégié un choix de matériaux naturels et traditionnels : planches de bois et de fibres de bois, poutres de glulam (bois lamellé-collé) et contreplaqué, utilisés en combinaison avec la tôle ondulée d'acier galvanisé, le verre et le béton.

Das Haus befindet sich auf einem Hügel, seine Nordecke ist den starken Nordwinden ausgesetzt. Eine traditionelle Holzsauna befindet sich auf der Ostseite des Hauses und bietet Ausblick auf den Degersjönsee. Man hat sich für natürliche und traditionelle Materialien entschieden: Holz und Holzfaserplatten, Brettschichtholzplatten, Sperrholz in Kombination mit verzinktem Wellstahl, Glas und Beton.

Het huis staat op een heuvel, met zijn noordelijke hoek in de noordenwind. Aan de oostkant van het huis, die uitziet op het meer Degersjön, staat een sauna van houtblokken. Er is gekozen voor natuurlijk bouwmateriaal: hout en houtvezelplaten, glulambalken en gelaagd hout, in combinatie met gegalvaniseerde stalen golfplaten, glas en beton.

La casa está situada en una colina con su ángulo norte expuesto a los vientos del norte. Al este de la casa, se levanta una cabaña para saunas tradicional con vistas al Lago Degersjön. La elección de los materiales se basó en criterios tradicionales y naturales: madera y tablas de fibra de madera, vigas de madera laminada, madera contrachapada combinada con acero galvanizado ondulado, cristal y hormigón.

La casa si trova su una colina con il suo angolo nord esposto ai venti settentrionali. A est della casa, sorge il tradizionale capanno per la sauna con vista sul Lago Degersjön. La scelta dei materiali è stata compiuta in base a criteri di tradizione e natura: legno e assi di fibra di legno, travi di legno laminato, legno compensato e acciaio galvanizzato ondulato, vetro e calcestruzzo.

A casa encontra-se numa colina com um dos lados exposto ao vento norte. A tradicional sauna de madeira está localizada a leste da casa, com vista sobre o Lago Degersjön. O tradicional e o natural ditaram a escolha dos materiais: madeira e tábuas de fibra de madeira, vigas Glulam, contraplacado combinado com aço ondulado e galvanizado, vidro e cimento.

Huset är placerat på en kulle med nordhörnet mot nordanvinden. En traditionell vedbastu är placerad öster om huset med utsikt över Degersjön. Traditionella och naturliga val gjordes gällande material: Trä och spånplattor i trä, bjälkar i glulam, plywood kombinerat med galvaniserat korrugerat stål, glas och betong.

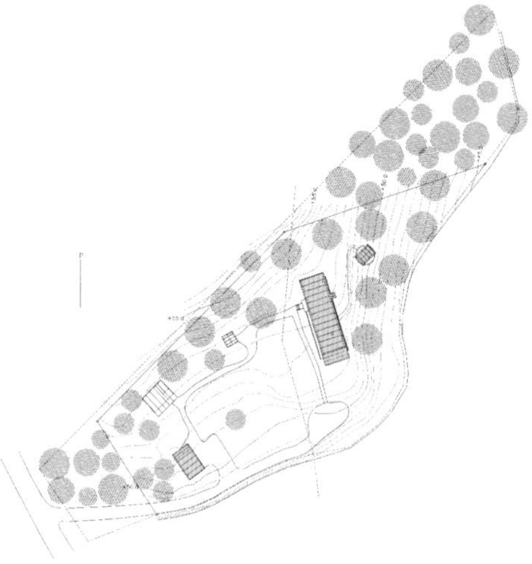

Site plan

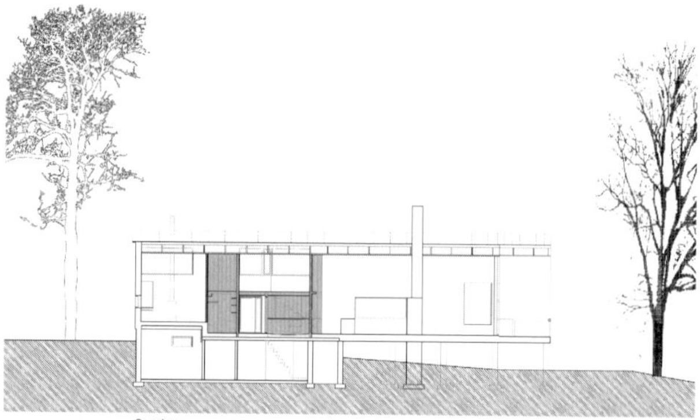

Section

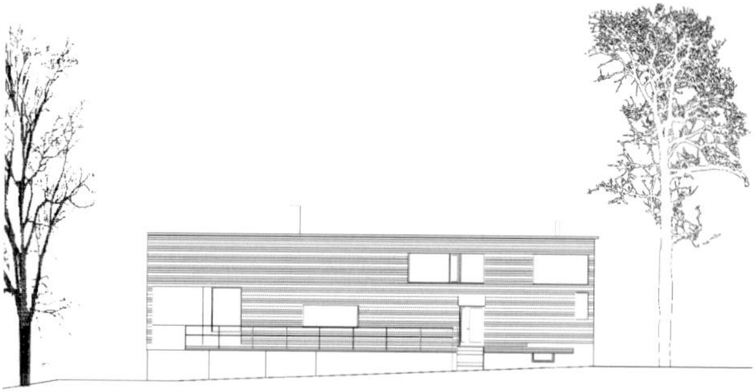

Elevation

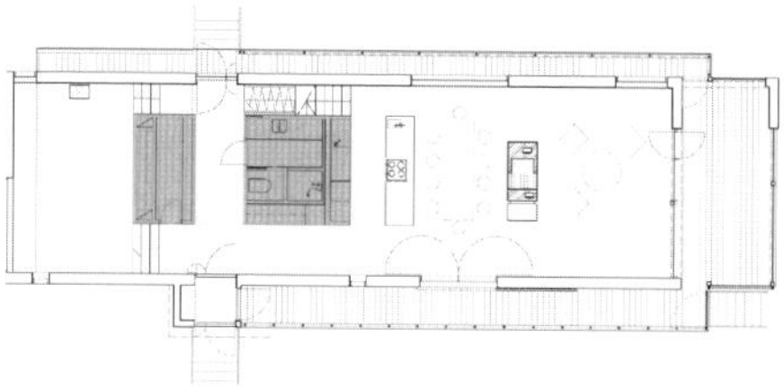

Lower floor

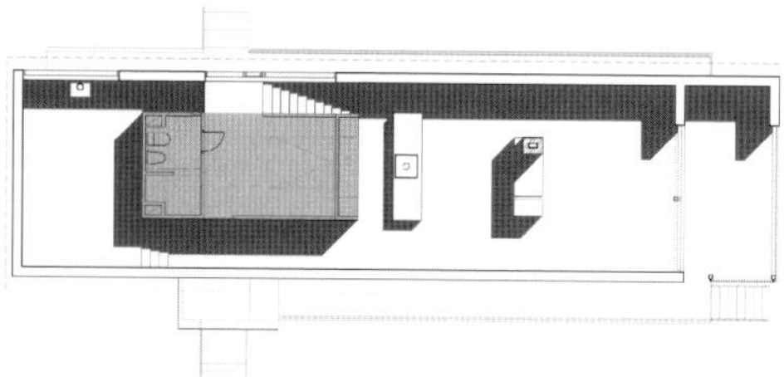

Upper floor

KILTRO HOUSE

JUAN PABLO CORVALÁN/SUPERSUDAKA
© Supersudaka

Made with a metallic structure covered entirely with wood and glass, the house integrates a patio and roof terrace. The rooms are organized around a glass box that lets light in and contains the stairs to the ground level. The house is topped by a wooden deck linked to one side by a long ramp that wraps the house.

Constituée d'une structure métallique entièrement habillée de bois et de verre, cette maison intègre un patio et un toit en terrasse. Les pièces sont distribuées autour d'une boîte en verre qui apporte la lumière et sert de cage d'escalier. La maison est coiffée d'un plafond de bois rattaché sur un côté à une longue rampe qui s'enroule autour de la maison.

Das Projekt besteht aus einer ganzheitlich mit Holz und Glas bedeckten Metallstruktur. Es umfasst einen Innenhof und eine Dachterrasse. Die Räume sind um eine lichtdurchlässige Glasbox angeordnet, an der die ins Untergeschoss führende Treppe ansetzt. Das Haus ist mit einem Holzdach ausgestattet, das an einer Seite in eine Rampe übergeht, die das gesamte Haus umläuft.

Het huis heeft een metalen skelet, dat helemaal bekleed is met hout en glas. Er is een patio in opgenomen en het heeft een dakterras. De kamers liggen rond een glazen trappenhuis, dat licht binnenlaat. Op het huis ligt een houten dek, dat aan de ene kant is verbonden met een aflopende strook die zich om het huis wikkelt.

Construida a partir de una estructura metálica cubierta completamente con madera y cristal, la casa integra un patio y una azotea. Las habitaciones están organizadas alrededor de una caja de cristal que permite la entrada de luz natural y contiene la escalera que conduce a la planta baja. La casa está coronada por una plataforma de madera comunicada por uno de los lados a través de una larga rampa que rodea la casa.

Realizzata con una struttura di metallo ricoperta completamente di legno e vetro, la casa possiede anche un cortile e una terrazza. Le stanze sono organizzate intorno a un parallelepipedo di vetro grazie al quale passa la luce naturale e contenente la scala che porta al pianterreno. La casa è coronata da una piattaforma di legno connessa su uno dei suoi lati mediante una lunga rampa che circonda l'edificio.

Constituída por uma estrutura metálica inteiramente coberta de madeira e vidro, a casa integra um pátio e um terraço no telhado. As divisões foram organizadas em redor de uma caixa de vidro que deixa passar a luz e onde se situam as escadas para o nível térreo. A casa é encimada por uma esplanada de madeira ligada, num dos lados, a uma longa rampa que envolve a casa.

Huset, gjort av en metallkonstruktion helt täckt med trä och glas, integrerar en uteplats och en takterrass. Rummen är organiserade runt en glaslåda som släpper in ljus och som hyser trapporna till markplanet. Huset är toppat av ett trädäck, på ena sidan förbundet av en lång ramp som omfamnar huset.

Design evolution

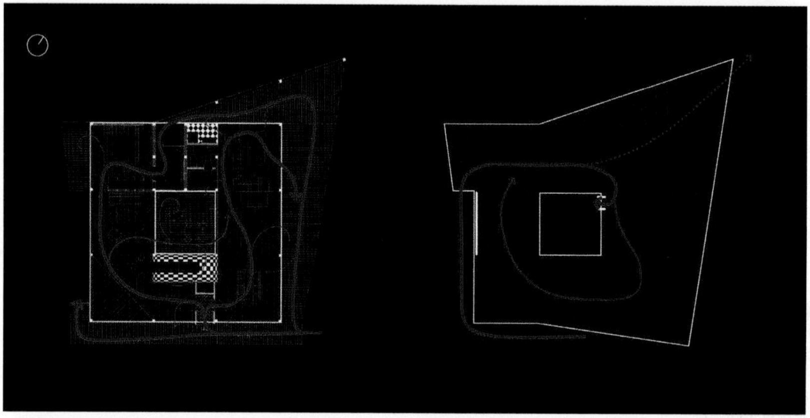

Floor plans

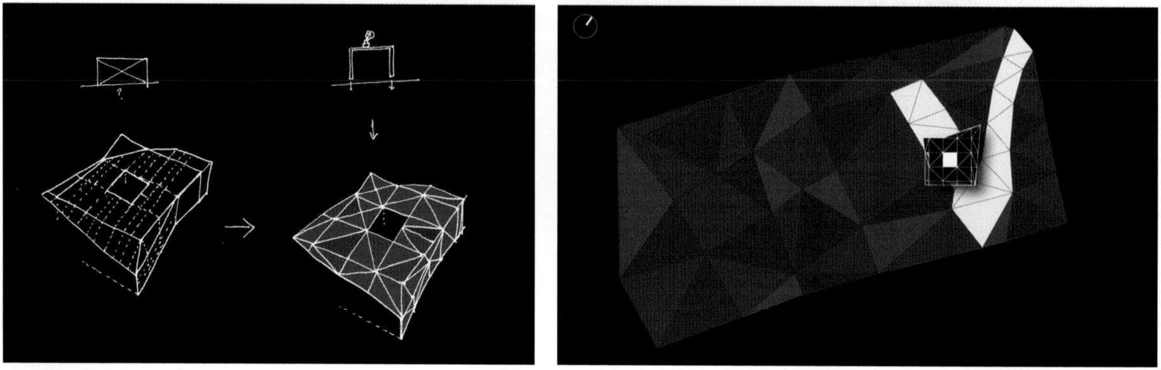

Structural diagrams

TOTAL MAKE-OVER OF **HOUSE B**

VBM ARCHITECTS (now Bogdan & Van Broeck Architects and Lava Architects)
© Toon Grobet, VBM Architects

This project is an extreme make-over of an existing house by means of a new wooden skin, a new entrance through a bridge, and strategically placed openings that offer magnificent views and provide abundant light. This smart, low energy house satisfies the need for privacy while establishing a more direct relationship with the surroundings.

Ce projet est la transformation radicale d'une maison existante, moyennant un nouveau revêtement de bois, un pont pour servir d'entrée, et des ouvertures disposées stratégiquement qui offrent des vues magnifiques tout en procurant une lumière abondante. Cette délicieuse maison, peu gourmande en énergie, satisfait le besoin d'intimité tout en établissant une relation plus directe avec l'environnement.

Dieses Projekt besteht in einer radikalen Umgestaltung des ursprünglichen Gebäudes, das man mit einer neuen Holzverkleidung, einer Brücke statt des bisherigen Eingangs und strategisch angebrachten Öffnungen mit herrlichem Ausblick und reichlichem Lichteinfall ausgestattet hat. Dieses intelligente, energiesparende Haus bietet die notwendige Privatsphäre und schafft zugleich eine unmittelbarere Beziehung zu seiner Umgebung.

Een bestaand huis krijgt een heel ander uiterlijk. Het wordt voorzien van een nieuwe houten bekleding, een nieuwe ingang over een brug en strategisch geplaatste openingen, die een schitterend uitzicht bieden en veel licht binnenlaten. Dit slimme, energiezuinige huis biedt privacy en bezit een directe relatie met de omgeving.

Este proyecto consiste en la reforma total de una casa a través de un revestimiento de madera nuevo, una nueva entrada a través de un puente y unas aberturas estratégicamente ubicadas a fin de ofrecer unas espléndidas vistas y un gran flujo de luz natural. Esta casa inteligente de baja energía satisface la necesidad de intimidad a la vez que establece una relación más directa con el paisaje circundante.

Questo progetto consiste nella completa ristrutturazione di una casa mediante un nuovo rivestimento di legno, un nuovo ingresso su un ponte e aperture strategicamente situate allo scopo di offrire splendide viste e un grande flusso di luce naturale. Questa casa intelligente e a basso consumo energetico soddisfa il bisogno d'intimità e crea, nel contempo, un rapporto più diretto con il paesaggio circostante.

Este projecto consiste numa transformação radical de uma casa já existente através do recurso a um novo revestimento de madeira, uma nova entrada por uma ponte e aberturas estrategicamente dispostas que permitem desfrutar de vistas magníficas e disponibilizam luz em abundância. Esta casa energeticamente eficiente estabelece, deste modo, uma relação mais directa com o espaço envolvente, não deixando de assegurar a necessária privacidade.

Detta projekt är en helombyggnad av ett existerande hus med hjälp av ett nytt yttre av trä, en ny entré genom en bro och strategiskt placerade öppningar som erbjuder storslagen utsikt och förser huset med rikligt med ljus. Detta smarta lågenergihus tillfredsställer behovet av avskildhet, samtidigt som det skapar ett mer direkt förhållande med omgivningarna.

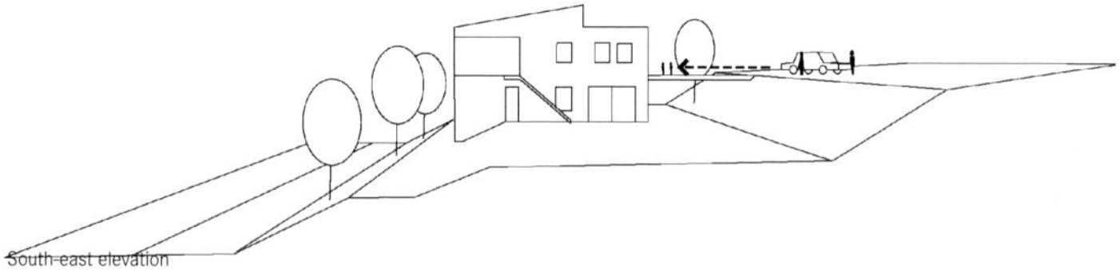

South-east elevation

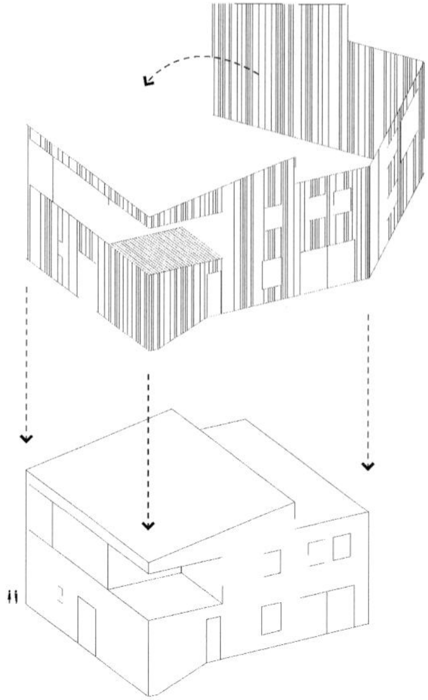

Axonometric view of intervention

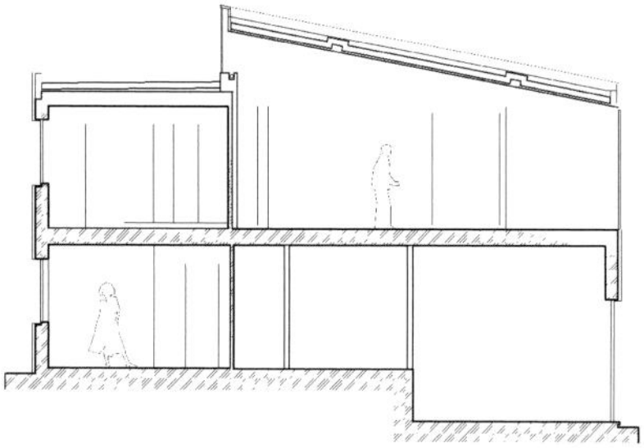

Section

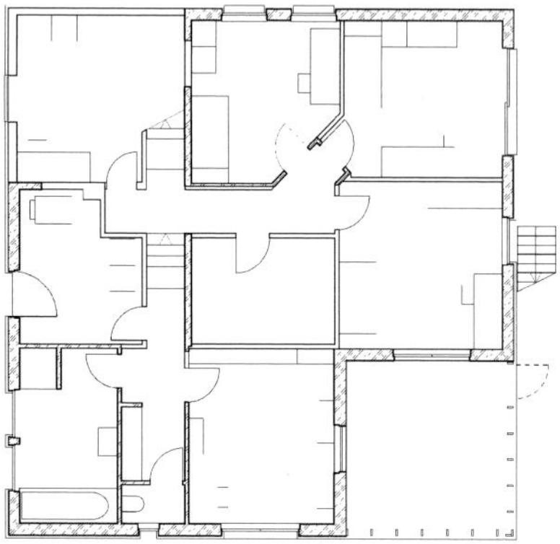

Lower floor plan

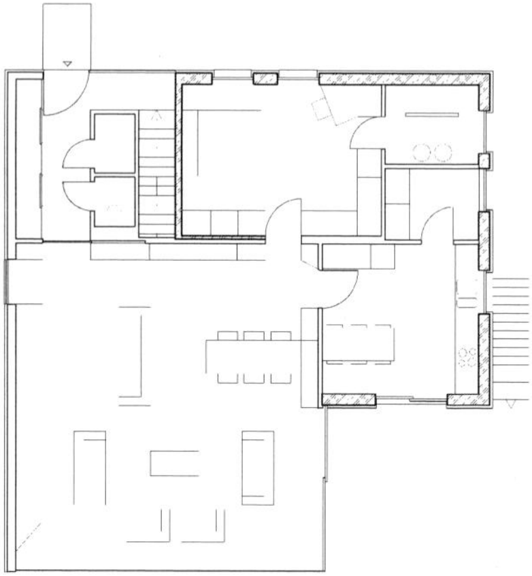

Upper floor plan

PATIO **VILLAS**

CASANOVA & HERNANDEZ ARCHITECTEN
© Ger van der Vlugt

The site incorporates three patio villas, one of which accommodates a 17 m tall spruce in its garden. The proposal consists of a continuous spruce wall that bends to define the new intervention. The same material used to build the fence is applied on the houses, the garage, and the shed, providing unity to the overall construction.

Le site comporte trois villas avec patio, dont l'une avec un épicéa de 17 m dans le jardin. Le projet consiste en un mur continu en épicéa destiné à définir le tout. Le même matériau est utilisé en revêtement pour les maisons, les garages et les remises, donnant ainsi une unité à l'ensemble.

Zu dem Projekt gehören drei Villen mit Innenhöfen. Eine der Villen beherbergt eine 17 Meter hohe Fichte in ihrem Garten. Der Entwurf zeichnet sich durch eine durchlaufende Wand aus Tannenholz aus, die den Umriss des Hauses und seine Formen definiert. Das für den Zaun verwendete Material wird auch für das Haus, die Garage und den Schuppen verwendet, es verleiht dem Bauwerk ein einheitliches Erscheinungsbild.

In dit project werden drie patiovilla's verenigd. In een van de tuinen rijst een 17 m hoge spar op. Het voorstel was een muur van sparrenhout tussen de villa's door te laten lopen. Het materiaal waarvan de schutting werd opgetrokken, is ook op de huizen, garage en schuur aangebracht om de eenheid te versterken.

En el solar se levantan tres casas con patio, una de las cuales cuenta en su jardín con una pícea de 17 metros de altura. La propuesta consiste en una pared de pícea continua que se dobla para definir la nueva intervención. El mismo material empleado para construir la valla se ha utilizado en las casas, el garaje y el cobertizo, armonizando de esta forma el conjunto de la construcción.

Il complesso comprende tre case con cortile, una delle quali he nel suo giardino un abete rosso di 17 metri. La proposta consiste in una parte di abete rosso continua che si piega per definire il nuovo intervento. Lo stesso materiale utilizzato per costruire lo steccato si trova anche nelle case, nel garage e nella tettoia, rendendo così armonico l'insieme delle costruzioni.

O local engloba três vilas com pátios, uma das quais acomoda, no seu jardim, um espruce com 17 metros de altura. A proposta consiste numa parede de espruce contínua, cuja forma curva define a zona da nova intervenção. O mesmo material usado para construir a vedação foi aplicado nas casas, na garagem e no telheiro, assegurando a unidade de toda a construção.

Platsen inkorporerar tre villor med uteplatser varav en hyser en 17 meter hög gran i sin trädgård. Förslaget består av en sammanhängande granvägg som böjer sig för att definiera detta nya ingrepp. Samma material som användes till staketbygget har använts till husen, garaget och skjulet och ger enhetlighet till den totala konstruktionen.

DESIGN STRATEGY

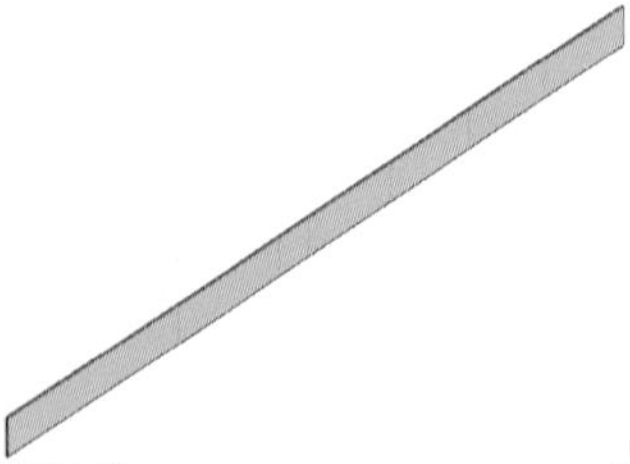

Unfolded wall

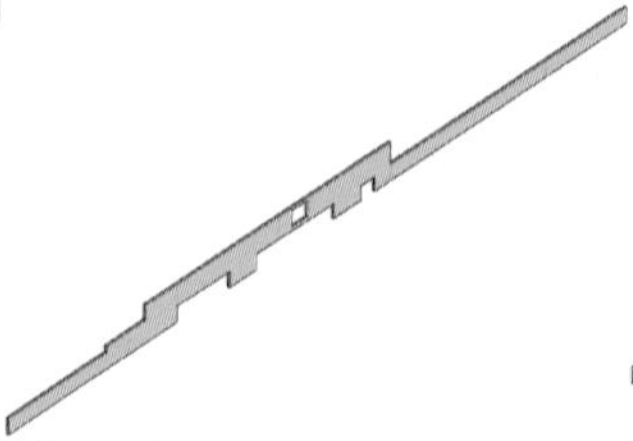

Unfolded cut wall

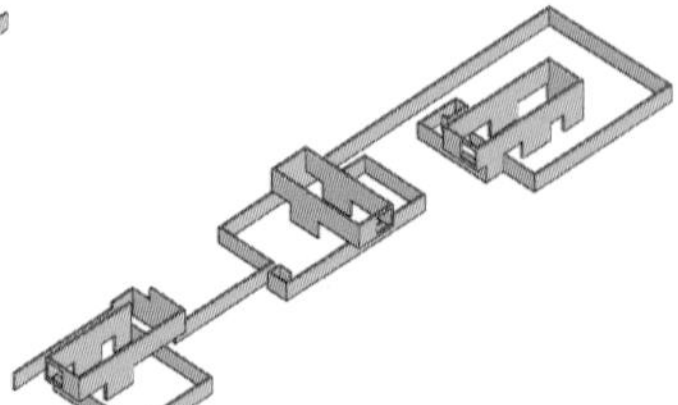

Folded and cut wall

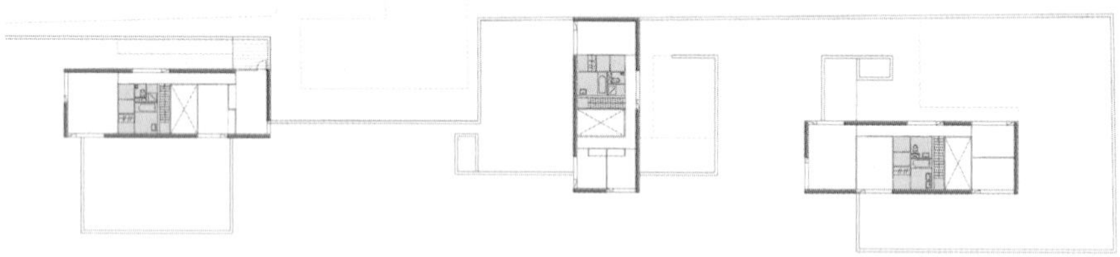

Second floor

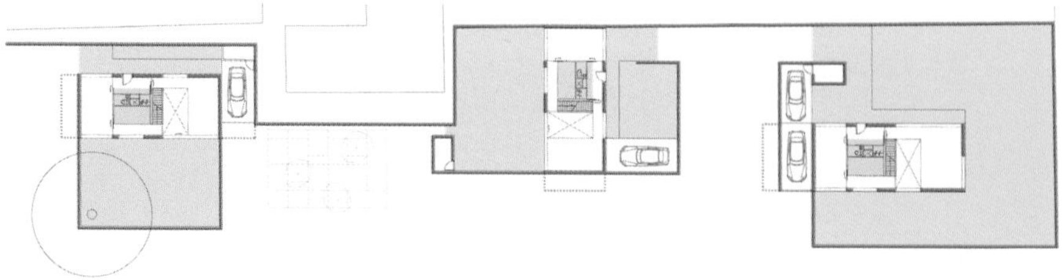

Ground floor

HOUSE **J2**

3LHD ARCHITECTS
© Damir Fabijanic

Located on a steep hill and bordered on two sides by a street and a tall building, the house is given an L shaped layout that protects it from the street while orienting all the rooms towards the newly designed garden. The common areas on the lower floor are glassed-in while the two upper floors containing the bedrooms are clad in wood.

Située sur une colline escarpée, entre une rue et un bâtiment élevé, cette maison est conçue selon un plan en L qui la protège de la rue, tout en ouvrant les pièces en direction du nouveau jardin. Les parties communes du rez-de-chaussée sont vitrées, tandis que les deux étages avec les chambres sont habillés de bois.

Dieses Projekt steht auf einem Steilhang und wird an zwei seiner Seiten von einer Straße bzw. einem hohen Gebäude begrenzt. Sein L-förmiger Grundriss schirmt es von der Straße ab. Alle Räumlichkeiten sind auf den neu gestalteten Garten ausgerichtet. Die Gemeinschaftsräume im Untergeschoss sind verglast, während die beiden Obergeschosse mit den Schlafzimmern mit Holz verkleidet sind.

Het huis ligt op een steile helling en wordt begrensd door een straat en een hoog gebouw. Het is in de vorm van een L gebouwd om het van de straat af te schermen en alle kamers uitzicht op de tuin te geven. De gemeenschapsruimten op de begane grond zijn in glas gevat. De twee verdiepingen erboven, met de slaapkamers, zijn met hout bekleed.

Situada en una colina empinada y lindante en dos de sus lados con una calle y un alto edificio, la casa tiene una distribución en forma de L que la protege de la calle al mismo tiempo que orienta todas sus habitaciones hacia el jardín recién diseñado. Las zonas comunes del piso inferior están acristaladas mientras los dos pisos superiores que albergan los dormitorios están revestidos de madera.

Sita su una scoscesa colina e con due lati che confinano con una strada e un alto edificio, la casa presenta una distribuzione a forma di L che la protegge dalla strada e, nel contempo, fa in modo che tutte le stanze siano orientate verso il nuovo giardino. Le zone comuni del piano inferiore sono a vetri, mentre i due piani superiori che ospitano le camere da letto sono ricoperti di legno.

Localizada numa colina íngreme e delimitada, em dois lados, por uma rua e um edifício alto, a casa apresenta uma disposição em L que a protege da rua, orientando, simultaneamente, todas as divisões para o jardim redesenhado. As áreas comuns, no rés-do-chão, são envidraçadas, enquanto os dois andares superiores, onde se encontram os quartos, são revestidos a madeira.

Huset, beläget på en brant kulle och avgränsat på två sidor av en gata och en hög byggnad, har givits en L-formad utformning som skyddar det från gatan medan alla rum är placerade mot den nydesignade trädgården. Gemensamhetsutrymmena på det nedre planet är inglasade medan de två övre planen, som hyser sovrummen, är klädda med trä.

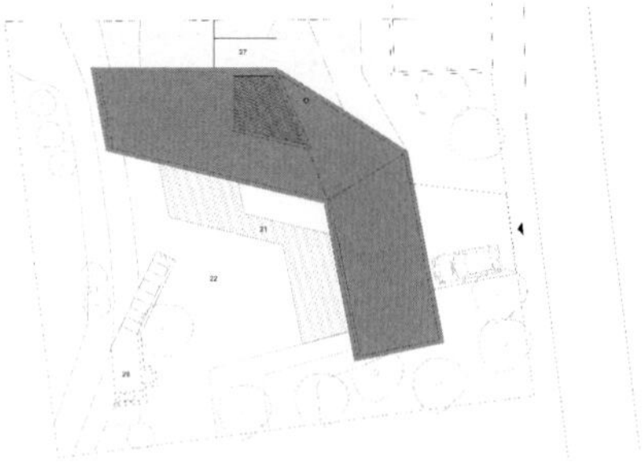

Site plan

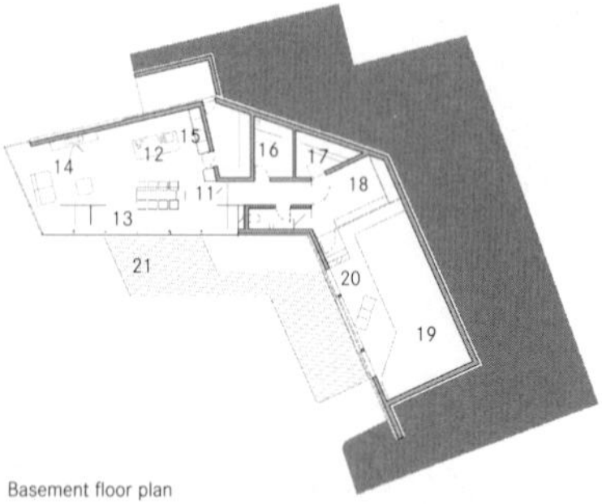

Basement floor plan

Ground floor plan

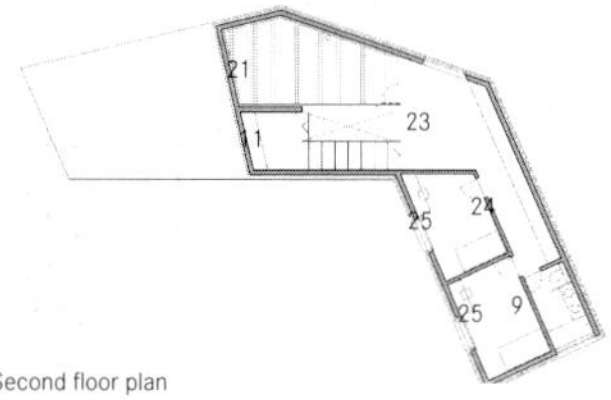

Second floor plan

1. Covered parking
2. Garage
3. Storage
4. Entrance
5. Wardrobe
6. WC/shower
7. Guest room
8. Master bedroom
9. Bathroom
10. Gallery
11. Staircase
12. Kitchen
13. Dining room
14. Living room
15. Storage
16. Laundry/boiler room
17. Sauna
18. Trim
19. Pool
20. Pool deck
21. Garden
22. Terrace
23. Utility terrace
24. Barbecue
25. Bedroom

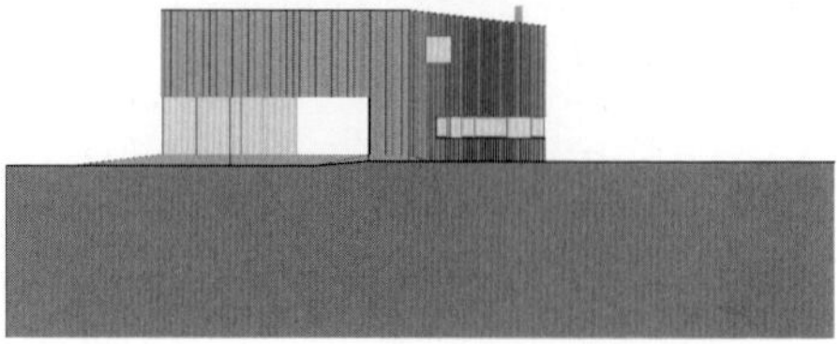

North-east elevation

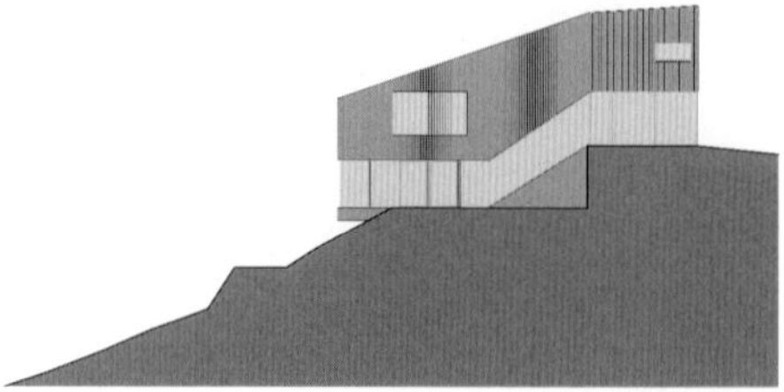

South-east elevation

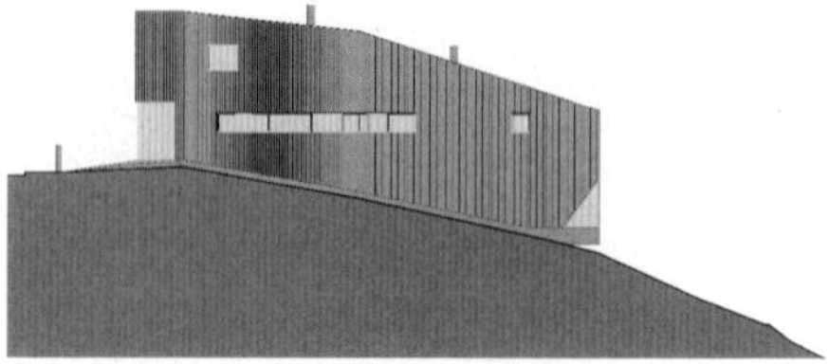

North-west elevation

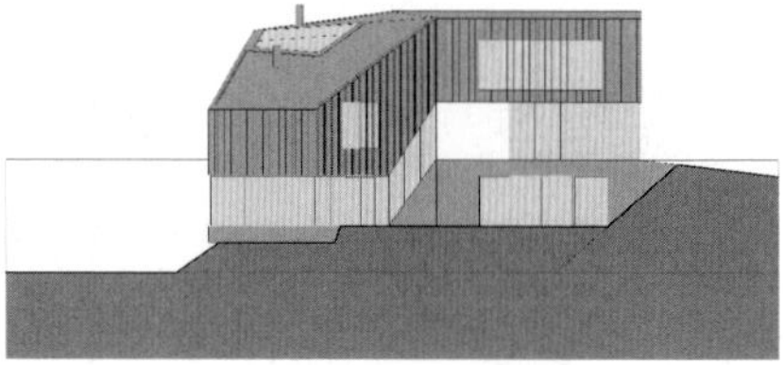

South-west elevation

BERNIER-THIBAULT HOUSE

PAUL BERNIER ARCHITECTE

Two volumes made of glass and wood were added to an existing house. One box was placed on the roof of the house becoming the parents room. Like a tree house, it is a space lined with wood from where one can see the city and the sunrise. The other box, with a green roof, is in the garden and serves as playroom for the children.

Deux volumes de bois et de verre ont été ajoutés à une maison existante. L'un deux a été installé sur le toit de la maison, pour devenir la chambre des parents. À l'instar d'une maison perchée dans un arbre, c'est un espace revêtu de bois d'où l'on peut contempler la ville et le lever du soleil. L'autre « boîte », dotée d'un toit de verdure, se trouve dans le jardin et sert de salle de jeu pour les enfants.

Dem ursprünglichen Haus wurden zwei aus Glas und Holz gefertigte Einheiten hinzugefügt. Eine davon wurde auf dem Dach des Hauses angebracht und dient als Elternschlafzimmer. In diesem aus Holz gefertigtem Raum, der an ein Baumhaus erinnert, kann man den Sonnenaufgang und den Ausblick auf die Stadt bewundern. Die zweite Einheit, mit einem begrünten Dach, steht im Garten und wurde als Spielraum für die Kinder konzipiert.

Aan een bestaand huis werden twee 'dozen' van glas en hout toegevoegd. De ene doos werd op het dak geplaatst. Deze voor de ouders bestemde ruimte is met hout bekleed en lijkt erg op een boomhut. Van hieruit zijn de stad en de zonsopgang te zien. De andere doos, met een groen dak, staat in de tuin en dient als speelkamer.

La casa existente fue ampliada con dos volúmenes de cristal y madera. En el tejado, se colocó un cubo que funcionaría como dormitorio de matrimonio. Al igual que una casa de árbol, es un espacio revestido de madera desde donde es posible deleitarse con las vistas de la ciudad y el amanecer. El otro cubo, con un tejado verde, se encuentra en el jardín y sirve como cuarto de juegos para los niños.

La casa preesistente è stata ampliata con due volumi di vetro e legno. Sul tetto è stato posto un cubo all'interno del quale è stata sistemata una camera da letto matrimoniale. Esattamente come una casa su un albero, si tratta qui di uno spazio ricoperto di legno da cui è possibile ammirare magnifiche viste della città all'alba. L'altro cubo, con un tetto verde, si trova nel giardino e serve da stanza dei giochi per i bambini.

Foram acrescentados dois volumes feitos de vidro e madeira a uma casa já existente. Foi colocada uma caixa sobre o telhado da casa, dando origem ao quarto dos pais. Tal como uma casa da árvore, é um espaço delimitado pela madeira, a partir do qual se pode ver a cidade e o nascer do sol. A outra caixa, com um telhado verde, situa-se no jardim e serve de sala de brincar para as crianças.

Två volymer gjorda av glas och trä lades till ett befintligt hus. En låda placerades på husets tak och blev föräldrarnas rum. Precis som ett trädhus är det ett utrymme kantat av skog, varifrån man kan se staden och soluppgången. Den andra lådan, med grönt tak, ligger i trädgården och fungerar som barnens lekrum.

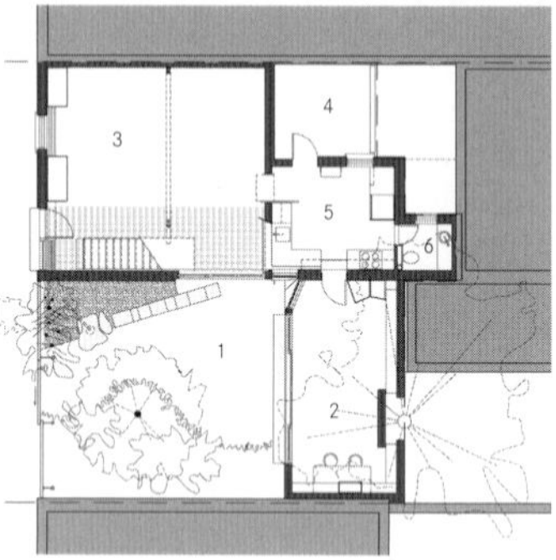

Ground floor

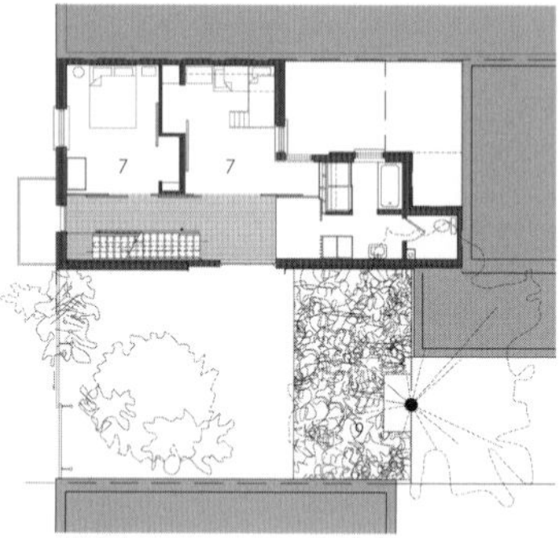

Second floor

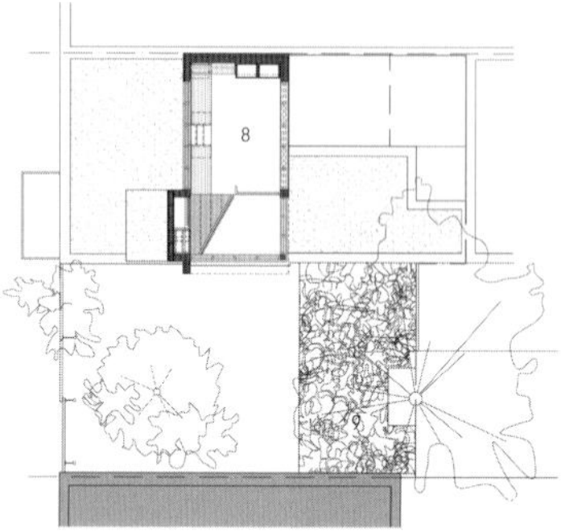

Third floor

1. Garden
2. Play room
3. Living room
4. Patio
5. Kitchen
6. Bathroom
7. Bedroom
8. Office
9. Green roof

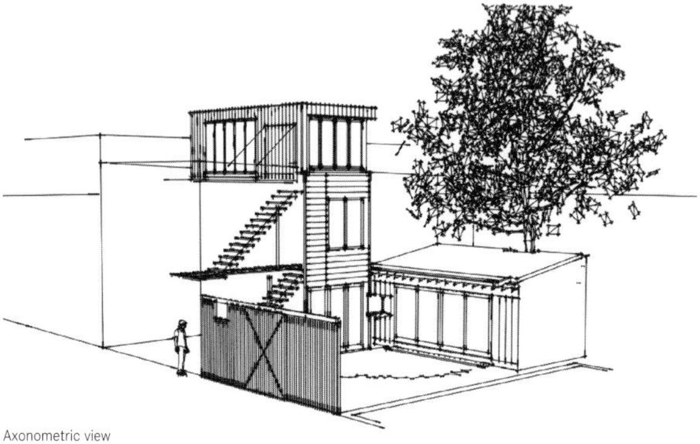

Axonometric view

GRANARY HOUSE

CAZÚ ZEGERS

A wooden skin establishes a discrete relationship with the natural surrounding. It does not interfere but it becomes a part with its traditional construction in the South of Chile. The siding of the walls and the roof generates a continuous shell containing a spacious double height interior with mezzanines and balconies to the exterior.

Un revêtement de bois établit une relation discrète avec l'environnement naturel sans interférer avec lui et devient ainsi partie intégrante d'une construction traditionnelle dans le sud du Chili. L'habillage des murs et du toit engendre une coquille continue, contenant un intérieur spacieux à double hauteur avec des mezzanines, et des balcons à l'extérieur.

Eine Holzhaut stellt eine dezente Verbindung zwischen dem Haus und der umliegenden Natur her. Es wirkt nicht störend, sondern ist mit seiner für den Süden Chiles typischen Bauart harmonisch in die Landschaft eingebunden. Die verkleideten Wände bilden gemeinsam mit dem Dach eine scheinbar nahtlose Umschalung, die einen geräumigen, doppelgeschossigen Innenraum mit einem Halbgeschoss beherbergt und mit Außenbalkonen ausgestattet ist.

Een houten huid verbindt het huis met de natuur in zijn omgeving. De houten bekleding van de muren en het dak is een integraal onderdeel van deze traditionele constructie in het zuiden van Chili. Als een naadloze schelp omhult ze het ruime, twee verdiepingen hoge binnenhuis, dat voorzien is van mezzanines en balkons.

La casa, recubierta completamente de madera, establece una discreta relación con el entorno natural; en lugar de interferir, se convierte en una parte más del mismo pues sigue los cánones constructivos tradicionales del sur de Chile. El revestimiento exterior de las paredes y el tejado forman una estructura continua que contiene un espacioso interior de altura doble con entresuelos y balcones al exterior.

La casa, completamente ricoperta di legno, instaura un rapporto discreto con l'ambiente naturale; invece d'interferire, ne diviene parte grazie al fatto che rispetta le regole costruttive tradizionali del sud del Cile. Il rivestimento esterno delle pareti e il tetto creano una struttura continua che contiene uno spazioso interno a doppia altezza con ammezzati e balconi verso l'esterno.

O revestimento de madeira estabelece uma relação discreta com o meio envolvente natural. Não interfere, antes se torna uma parte dele, com a sua construção tradicional do Sul do Chile. O revestimento exterior das paredes e do telhado cria uma concha contínua que engloba o espaçoso interior de pé duplo com mezaninos e varandas para o exterior.

Ett träskinn etablerar en diskret relation till den naturliga omgivningen. Det inkräktar inte utan blir en integrerad del med dess traditionella konstruktion i södra Chile. Väggbeklädnanden och taket bildar ett sammanhängande skal som innehåller en rymlig interiör av dubbel höjd med mezzaniner och balkonger mot exteriören.

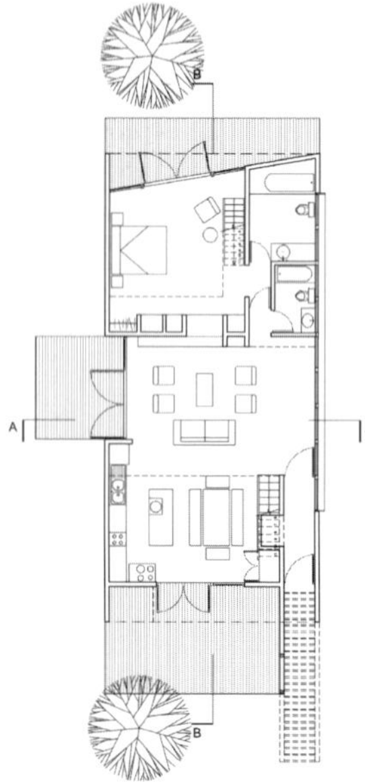

Ground floor

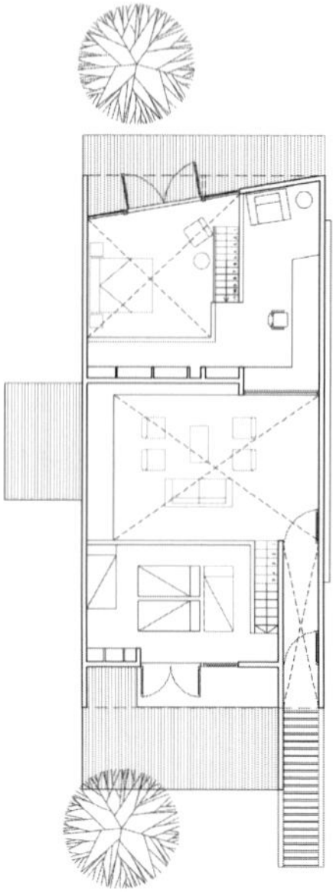

Second floor

North elevation

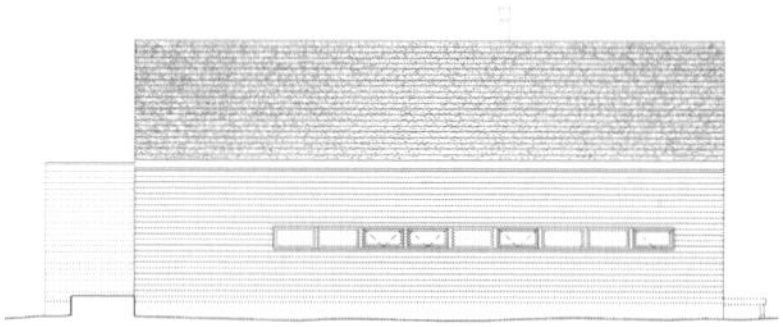

East elevation

Section A-A'

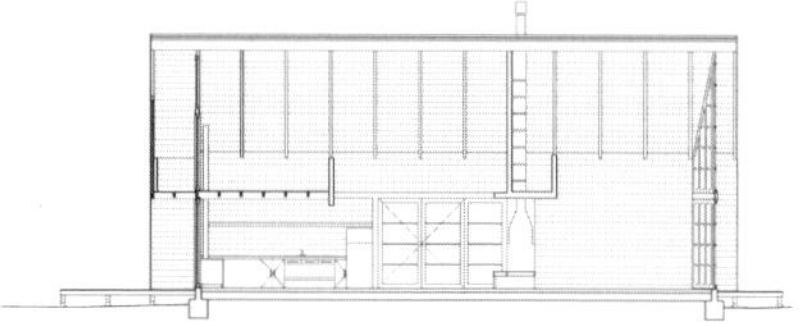

Section B-B'

FARM HOUSE **VOGES REDUX**

ARCHITEKTURBÜRO MATTHIAS LOEBERMANN
© Olaf Baumann

This project explores the possibilities of updating the vernacular residential architecture of northern Germany: the half-timbered house. The need for open space and natural light led to a renovation that opened up the ground floor. New glass walls on three sides add depth to the building and emphasize the original wood structure.

Ce projet explore les possibilités de mettre au goût du jour l'architecture résidentielle typique de l'Allemagne du Nord : la maison à colombages. Le besoin d'espace ouvert et de lumière naturelle a conduit les concepteurs à « ouvrir » le rez-de-chaussée. De nouveaux murs en verre sur trois côtés ajoutent de la profondeur au bâtiment et mettent en valeur la structure en bois originelle.

Bei diesem Projekt wurde versucht, das für die einheimische Wohnarchitektur Norddeutschlands typische Fachwerkhaus an die neuere Zeit anzupassen. Das Bedürfnis nach Raum und natürlichem Licht führte zu einer sehr offenen Neugestaltung des Erdgeschosses. Die an drei Hausseiten neu eingebauten Glaswände verleihen dem Gebäude Tiefe und unterstreichen die Wirkung der ursprünglichen Holzstruktur.

Dit project onderzoekt de mogelijkheden om het traditioneel Noord-Duitse vakwerkhuis aan te passen aan de moderne tijd. Voor meer ruimte en licht werd de benedenverdieping 'opengebroken'. Door de nieuwe glaswanden, aan drie kanten, lijkt het huis dieper en springt de oorspronkelijke structuur van hout en steen in het oog.

Este proyecto explora las posibilidades de modernizar la típica arquitectura residencial del norte de Alemania: la casa con entramado de madera y ladrillo. La necesidad de espacios abiertos y de luz natural condujo a una renovación que abrió al exterior la planta baja. Las nuevas paredes acristaladas en tres de sus lados aportan profundidad al edificio y realzan la estructura de madera original.

Questo progetto esplora le possibilità di modernizzare la tipica architettura residenziale del nord della Germania: la casa in legno e muratura. Il bisogno di avere spazi aperti e luce naturale ha fatto sì che la ristrutturazione aprisse il pianterreno all'esterno. Le nuove pareti di vetro lungo tre dei suoi lati conferiscono profondità all'edificio e mettono in risalto l'originale struttura lignea.

Este projecto explora as possibilidades de actualização da arquitectura residencial tradicional do Norte da Alemanha, representada pelas casas cuja metade está revestida a madeira. A necessidade de espaços abertos e de luz natural esteve na origem de uma remodelação que implicou a abertura do piso térreo. As novas paredes de vidro, instaladas em três dos lados, conferem mais profundidade ao edifício e realçam a estrutura original em madeira.

Detta projekt utforskar möjligheterna att uppdatera den lokala husarkitekturen från norra Tyskland: det halvtimrade huset. Behovet av ett öppet utrymme och naturligt ljus ledde till en renovering som öppnade upp markplanet. Nya glasväggar på tre sidor ger djup till byggnaden och framhäver den ursprungliga trästrukturen.

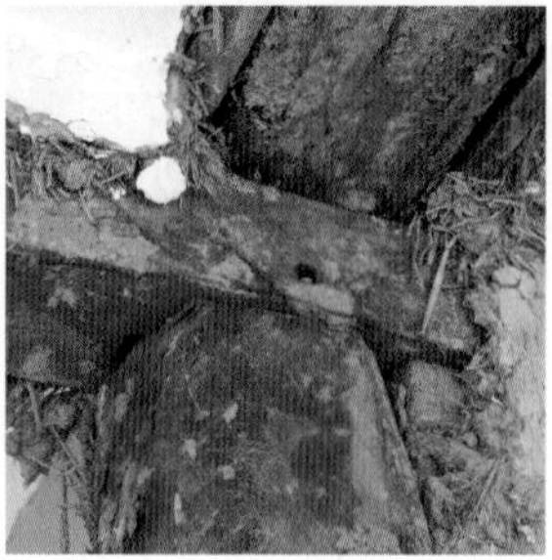

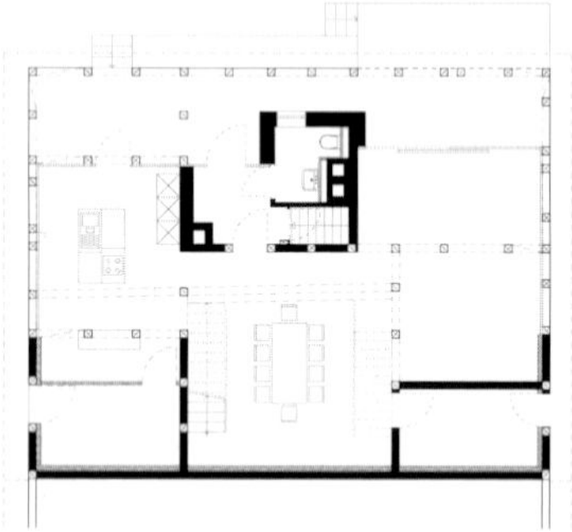

Ground floor

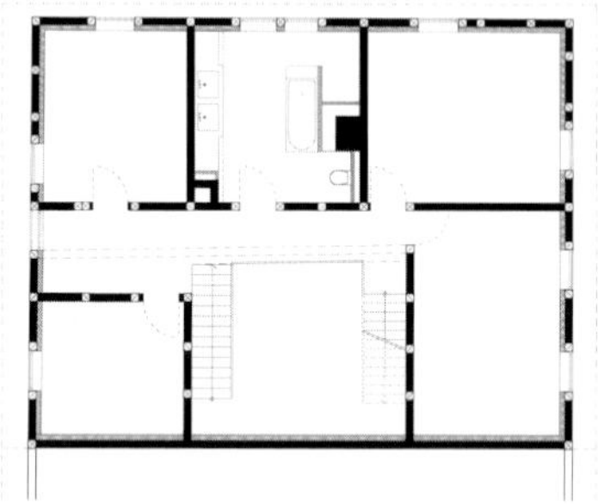

Second floor

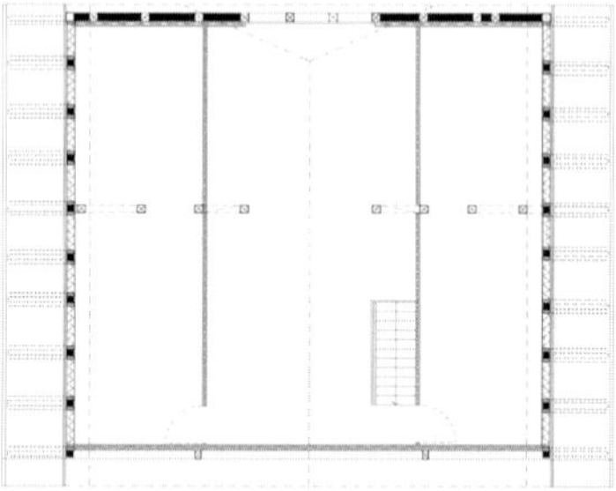

Third floor

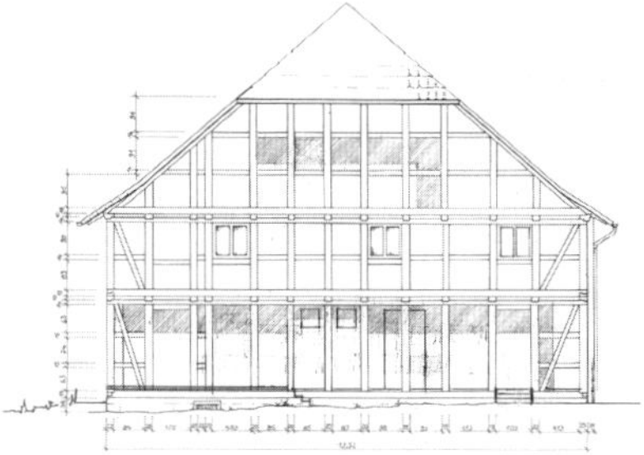

North elevation

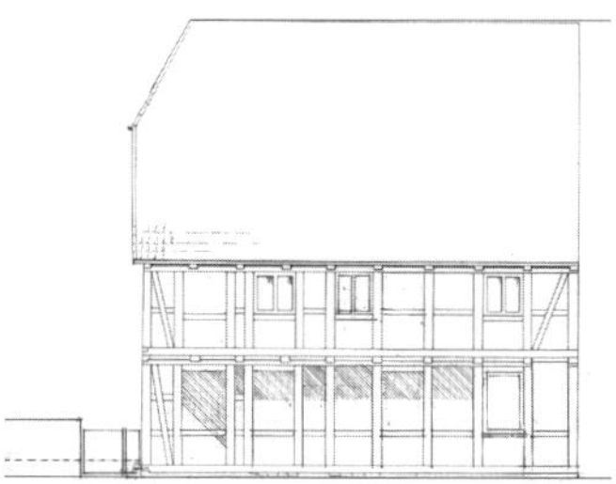

West elevation

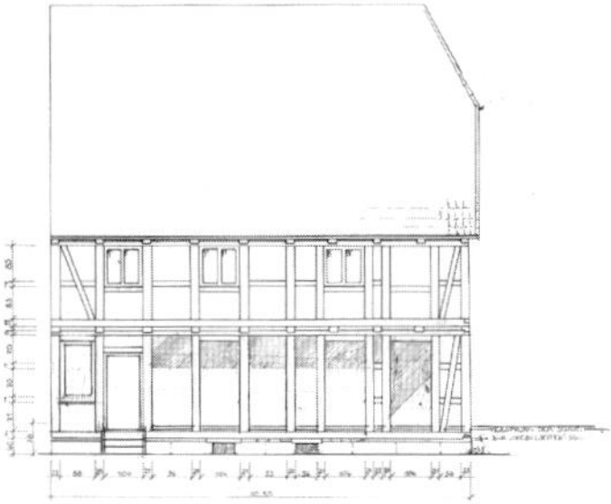

East elevation

HOUSE **R**

BEVK PEROVIČ ARCHITEKTI
© Miran Kambič

The architects designed this cottage in a settlement near Lake Bohinj. It is inspired by the vernacular alpine chalet and its traditional forms, such as the steep pitched roof and boxy base. The house, entirely sided with vertical wood planks, presents sliding panels that reveal different size openings and the stark white interior.

Les architectes ont conçu cette maison de campagne dans un lotissement, près du lac Bohinj. Elle s'inspire du chalet alpin vernaculaire et de ses formes traditionnelles telles que toit pointu et base cubique. La maison, entièrement revêtue de planches disposées verticalement, est dotée de panneaux coulissants qui dissimulent des ouvertures de différentes tailles et un intérieur tout blanc.

Die Architekten planten dieses Haus für eine in der Nähe des Bohinjsees gelegene Siedlung. Für seine Gestaltung inspirierten sich die Planer an der traditionellen Alpenhütte und ihren typischen Formen, zu deren Merkmalen das Steildach und die kastenförmige Grundstruktur gehören. Das durchgehend mit senkrechten Holzlatten verkleidete Haus ist mit Schiebepaneelen ausgestattet, die verschieden große Öffnungen freigeben und Einblick in den nüchternen weißen Innenraum gewähren.

De architecten ontwierpen dit huis voor een dorpje bij het Bohinjmeer. Het is geïnspireerd op de chalets in die streek en bezit een puntdak en een blokvormige basis. Het huis, dat aan alle zijden betimmerd is met verticale houten planken, heeft schuifpanelen, die door openingen van diverse grootte het witte interieur tonen.

Los arquitectos diseñaron esta casita de campo en un poblado cercano al Lago Bohinj y se inspiraron en el típico chalet alpino y en sus formas tradicionales, como la cubierta empinada de dos aguas y la base con forma de caja. La casa, totalmente revestida con tablas verticales de madera, dispone de paneles correderos que dejan al descubierto diferentes tamaños de aberturas y los sobrios interiores pintados de blanco.

Gli architetti hanno progettato questa casetta di campagna in un villaggio nei pressi del lago Bohinj; per farlo si sono ispirati al tipico chalet alpino e alle sue forme tradizionali, come il tetto spiovente a due falde e la base a forma di scatola. La casa, completamente rivestita con tavole verticali di legno, possiede pannelli scorrevoli che rivelano aperture di varie dimensioni nonché i sobri interni bianchi.

Os arquitectos desenharam esta pequena casa de campo, numa povoação perto do lago Bohinj. Foi inspirada no vernacular chalé alpino e nas suas formas tradicionais, com o telhado fortemente inclinado e a base quadrada. A casa, cujos lados são inteiramente feitos de tábuas de madeira verticais, apresenta painéis deslizantes que revelam aberturas de diferentes tamanhos e expõe o interior de um branco perfeito.

Arkitekterna designade denna stuga i en bosättning nära Bohinjsjön. Den är inspirerad av den inhemska fjällstugan och dess traditionella former såsom det branta toppade taket och den lådformade basen. Huset, som är helt klätt med vertikala träplankor, uppvisar förskjutna paneler som avslöjar öppningar av olika storlek och den rent vita interiören.

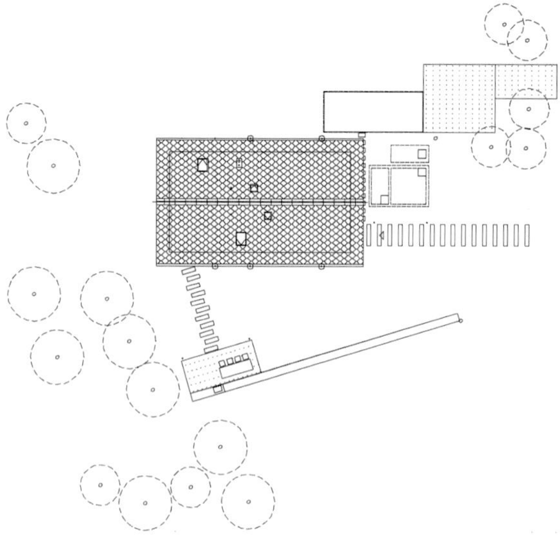

Site plan

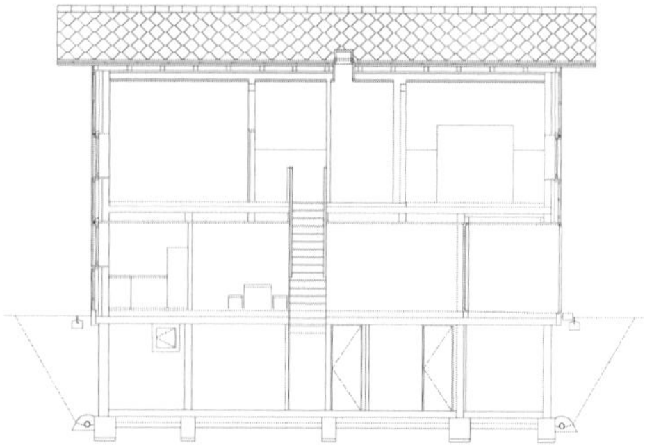

Section

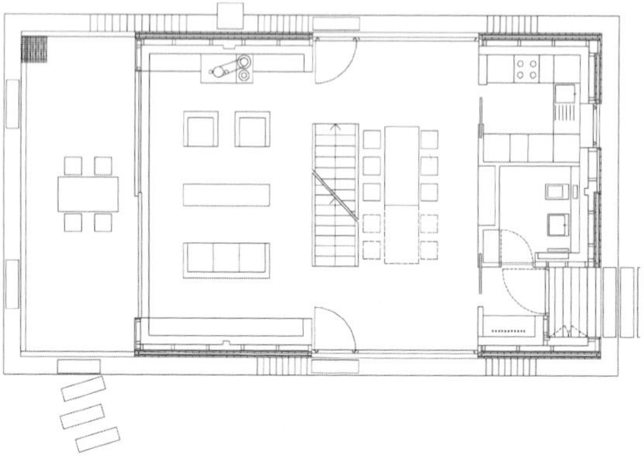

Ground floor

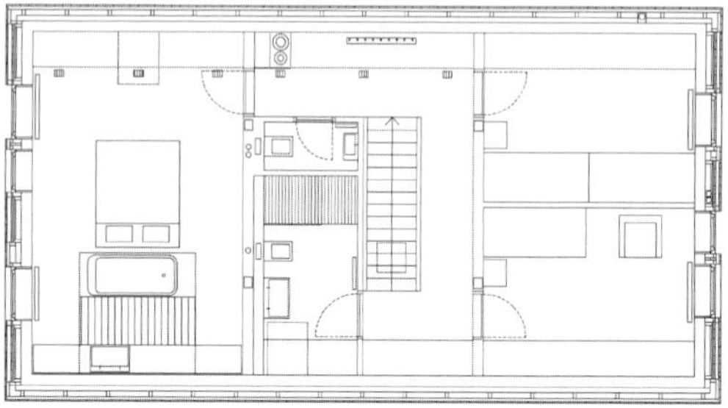

Second floor

POB 62 : PROTOTYPE OF PRECAST WOODEN HOUSE

COUNSON ARCHITECTES
© Laurent Brandajs

The POB 62 is a modular construction that allows any increase of the surface without affecting the overall design. POB 62 is built out of wood or wood products. Its skeleton is made of OSB panels fixed to a spruce frame. The facades and roof are a continuous skin of larch shingles: a contemporary interpretation of the traditional form

Le POB 62 est une construction modulaire permettant d'agrandir la surface sans affecter le *design* d'ensemble d'une structure ; il est constitué de bois ou de produits dérivés du bois. Le squelette est fait de panneaux d'OSB fixés sur une ossature en épicéa. Les façades et le toit ont reçu un revêtement continu de bardeaux de mélèze : c'est une interprétation contemporaine des formes traditionnelles.

POB 62 ist eine modular aufgebaute Konstruktion, bei der eine Flächenerweiterung möglich ist, ohne den Gesamtentwurf zu beeinflussen. POB 62 wird aus Holz oder Holzprodukten gebaut. Sein Rohbauskelett besteht aus OSB-Platten die an einem Gerüst aus Fichtenholz befestigt wurden. Die Fassaden und das Dach werden mit einer durchlaufenden Verkleidung aus Lärchenschindeln versehen. Es handelt sich somit um eine zeitgenössische Interpretation der traditionellen Bauweise.

De POB 62 is een modulaire constructie waarmee de oppervlakte vergroot kan worden zonder het ontwerp aan te tasten. Het skelet is gemaakt van OSB-platen op een frame van sparrenhout. De gevels en het dak bestaan uit latten van lariks. Deze houten 'huid' is een moderne interpretatie van de traditionele vorm.

El POB 62 es una construcción modular que permite la ampliación de la superficie sin afectar el diseño general. POB 62 está construido con madera o productos derivados de la madera. Su armazón está hecho de paneles OSB fijados a una estructura de pícea. La fachada y el tejado presentan un revestimiento continuo de placas de alerce: una interpretación contemporánea de la forma tradicional.

Il POB 62 è una costruzione modulare che è possibile ampliare senza modificare il progetto generale. È fatto di legno o prodotti derivati dal legno. La struttura è costituita da pannelli OSB fissati a una struttura di abete rosso. La facciata e il tetto presentano un rivestimento continuo fatto di scandole di larice: si tratta di un'interpretazione contemporanea della forma tradizionale.

O POB 62 é um módulo que permite o aumento da superfície sem que o *design* geral seja afectado. O POB 62 é construído em madeira ou derivados de madeira. O esqueleto é constituído por painéis de OSB fixados a uma estrutura em espruce. As fachadas e o telhado são uma estrutura contínua de ripas de lariço: uma interpretação contemporânea de uma forma tradicional.

POB 62 är en modulär konstruktion som tillåter alla typer av ökning av ytan utan att helhetliga designen påverkas. POB 62 är byggt av trä eller träprodukter. Dess skelett är gjort av OSB-paneler fästade vid en ram av granträ. Fasaderna och taket har ett sammanhängande skinn av lärkskivor: en modern tolkning av den traditionella formen.

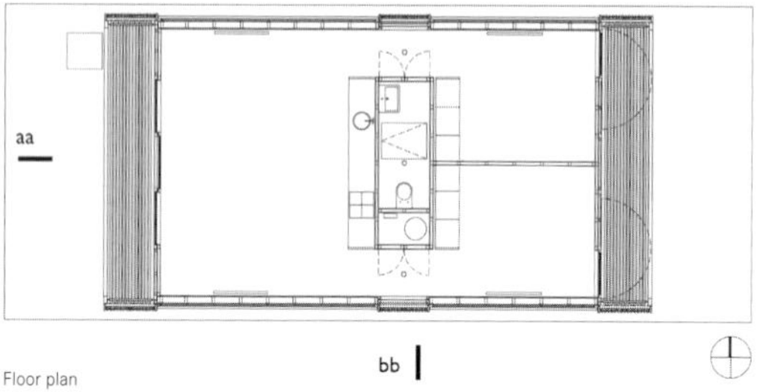

Floor plan

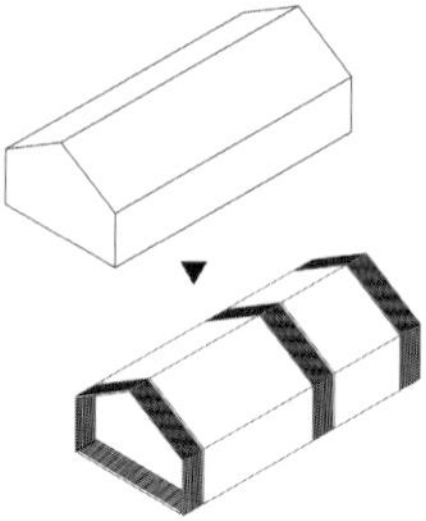

From archetype to prototype

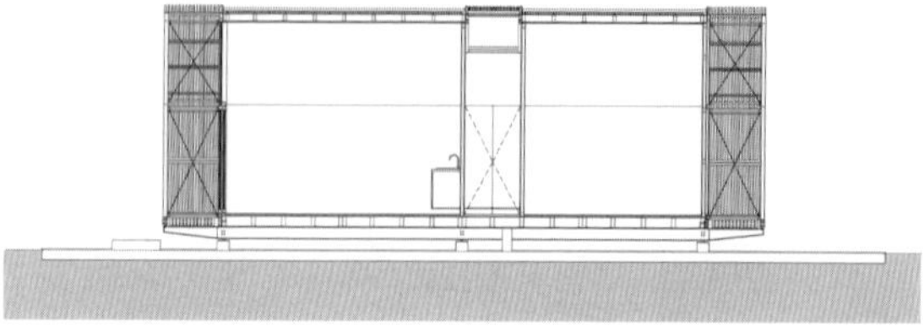

Section aa

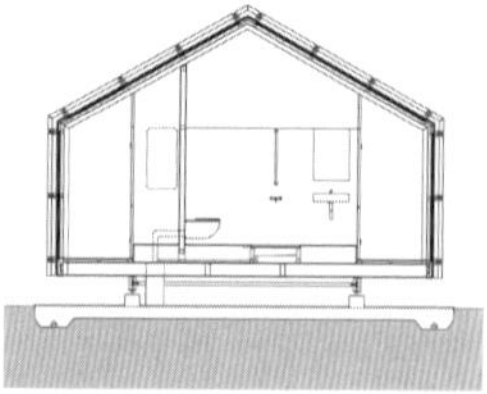

Section bb

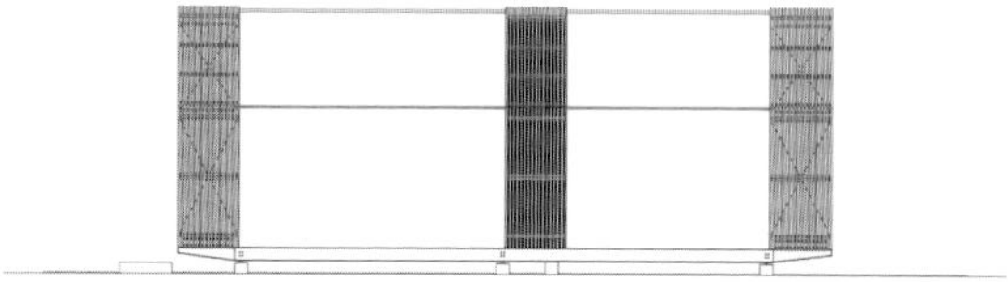

North elevation

SHELL HOUSE

CAZÚ ZEGERS

This dwelling appears to be protected by a wooden "rind" that transitions at both ends into horizontal louvers made out of 1×2 in slats. This strong architectural element is then perforated to create the entrance. The profound poetic concept of this architecture is materialized in wood and the handcrafted work.

Cette habitation semble être protégée par une « écorce » de bois qui se transforme aux deux extrémités en volets abat-vent faits de lattes de 2,5×5 cm. Cet élément architectural fort est ensuite perforé pour créer l'entrée. Le concept profondément poétique de cette architecture est matérialisé dans le bois et le travail artisanal.

Dieses Projekt scheint von einer schützenden hölzernen Schale umhüllt zu sein, die an beiden Enden in Jalousien übergeht, die aus waagrecht verlaufenden Latten (1×2 Zoll) bestehen. Dieses eindrucksvolle architektonische Element wird nur unterbrochen, um einen Eingang zu schaffen. Diesem Bauwerk liegt ein tiefgründiges poetisches Konzept zugrunde, das sich in den Holzmaterialien und den in Handarbeit gefertigten Elementen ausdrückt.

Het is alsof dit huis wordt beschermd door een houten schelp, die aan de beide uiteinden overgaat in horizontale jaloezieën, gemaakt van 25 mm dikke en 50 mm brede latten. Voor de ingang is er een gat in het omhulsel geboord. De idee van geborgenheid is verwezenlijkt in hout en volmaakt uitgevoerd handwerk.

Esta vivienda parece estar protegida por una "corteza" de madera que la circunda completamente con una especie de persiana horizontal realizada con listones de 2,5×5 cm. Este fuerte elemento arquitectónico ha sido perforado para crear la entrada. El profundo concepto poético de esta arquitectura se materializa en la madera y en el trabajo artesanal.

Questa dimora sembra essere protetta da una "scorza" di legno che la circonda completamente con una sorta di persiana orizzontale fatta di stecche da 2,5×5 centimetri. Questo elemento architettonico con carattere è stato perforato per creare l'ingresso. Il profondo concetto poetico di questa soluzione architettonica risiede nel legno e nel lavoro artigianale.

Esta moradia parece estar protegida por uma "casca" de madeira que se transforma, em ambas as extremidades, em venezianas horizontais feitas de ripas de 2,5×5 cm. Este forte elemento arquitectural foi, depois, perfurado para criar a entrada. O profundo conceito poético desta arquitectura materializa-se na madeira e no trabalho manual.

Denna boning förefaller skyddad av ett "träskal" som i båda ändar övergår i horisontella ventilationsgaller vilka är gjorda i 2,5×5 cm stora lattor. Detta starkt arkitektoniska element har sedan perforerats för att skapa entrén. Det djupa poetiska konceptet i denna arkitektur uttrycks i träet och hantverket.

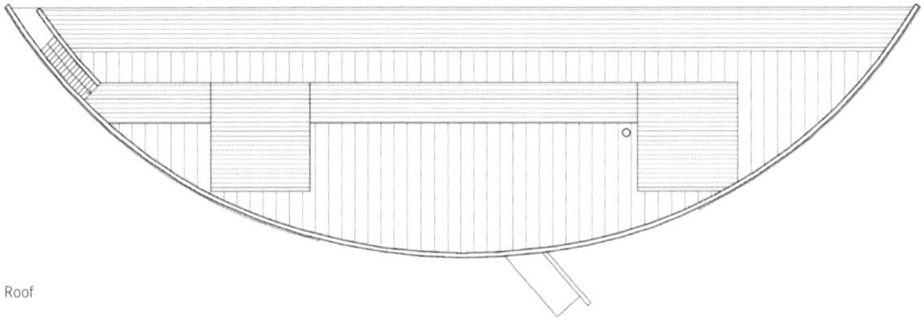

Roof

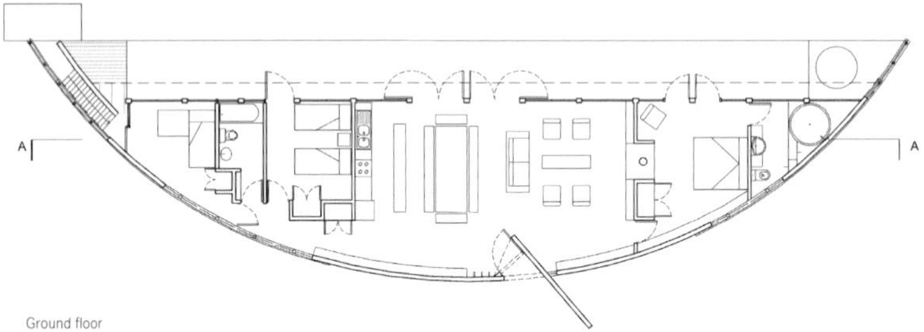

Ground floor

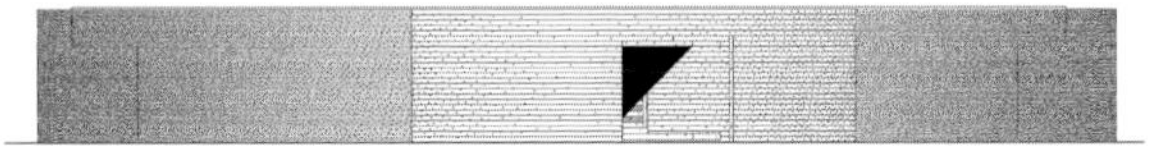

North elevation

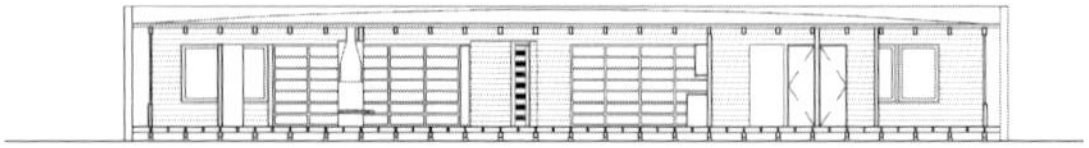

Section A-A'

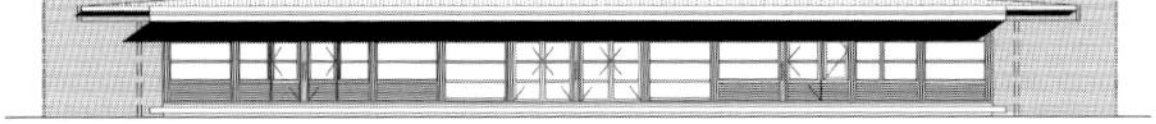

South elevation

WOOD HOUSE **IN CAVIANO**

MARKUS WESPI JÉRÔME DE MEURON ARCHITEKTEN

The house is located in an area of new buildings outside the historical center of Caviano. With its silver gray color and simple shape, the house takes on a subdued appearance that connects with the stone walls of the surroundings. In the interior, the raw wood elements are painted the same silver grey color that is used on the wood clad exterior.

La maison est située dans un secteur de nouveaux bâtiments, en dehors du centre historique de Caviano. Avec sa couleur gris argenté et sa forme simple, la maison revêt une allure modeste qui s'harmonise avec les murs de pierre des environs. À l'intérieur, les éléments de bois brut sont peints de la même couleur gris clair utilisée pour le revêtement de bois extérieur.

Das Haus befindet sich in einer neuen Bausiedlung außerhalb des historischen Zentrums von Caviano. Die silbergraue Farbe und die einfache Form verleihen dem Haus ein dezentes Erscheinungsbild, das mit den Steinmauern der Umgebung harmonisiert. Auch im Innenraum wurden die groben Holzelemente im silbergrauen Ton der holzverkleideten Fassade gestrichen.

Dit huis ligt in een wijk met nieuwe gebouwen buiten het historisch centrum van Caviano. Met zijn zilvergrijze kleur en eenvoudige vorm oogt het bescheiden. Het past bij de stenen muren in de buurt. In het interieur zijn de ruwhouten delen in dezelfde tint grijs geschilderd als die van de houten bekleding van de muren.

La casa está situada en una zona de edificios nuevos fuera del centro histórico de Caviano. Con su color gris plateado y su forma simple, la casa presenta un aspecto sobrio que armoniza con las paredes de piedra del entorno. En el interior, los elementos de madera sin tratar están pintados del mismo color gris plateado utilizado en el revestimiento de madera exterior.

La casa si trova in una zona di nuovi edifici fuori del centro storico di Caviano. Con il suo colore grigio argentato e la sua semplice forma, la casa presenta un aspetto sobrio che entra in armonia con le pareti di pietra del contesto ambientale. All'interno, gli elementi di legno non trattato sono dipinti dello stesso colore grigio argentato usato per il rivestimento ligneo esterno.

A casa está localizada numa zona de edifícios novos, fora do centro histórico de Caviano. De um cinzento prateado e forma simples, a casa assume uma aparência subjugada que se liga às paredes de pedra das cercanias. No interior, os elementos em madeira crua estão pintados na mesma tonalidade de cinzento prateado usada no revestimento de madeira exterior.

Huset är beläget i ett område med nya byggnader utanför Cavianos historiska centrum. Med dess silvergrå färg och enkla form framstår huset som tillbakadraget och förenas med omgivningarnas stenmurar. I interiören har de råa träelementen målats i samma silvergrå färg som använts på den träklädda exteriören.

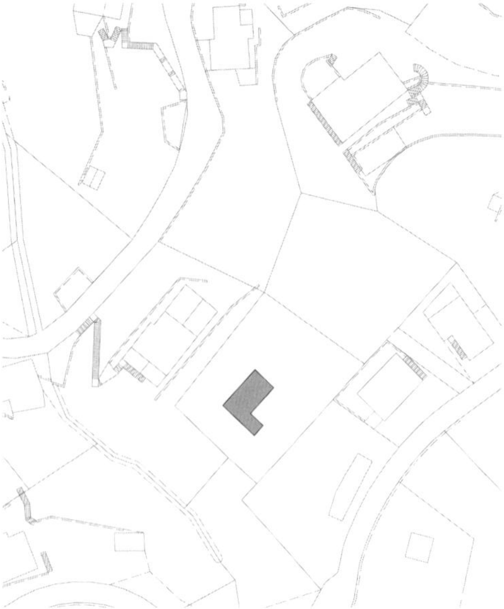

Site plan

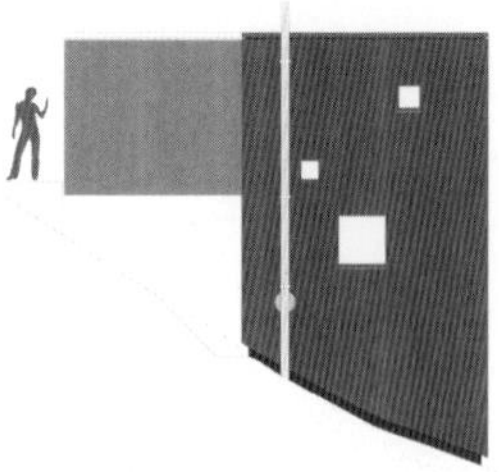

North-east elevation

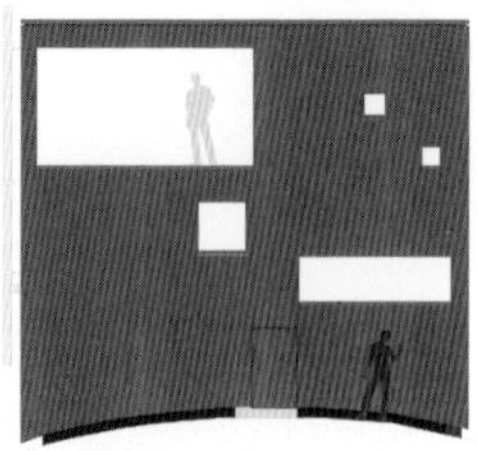

North-west elevation

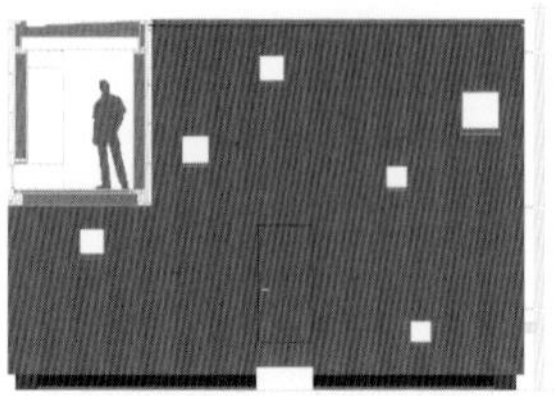

South-east elevation

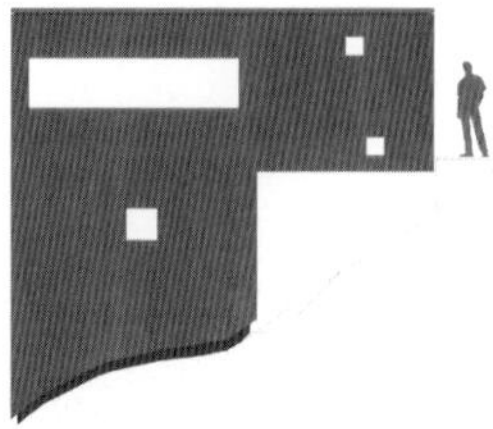

South-west elevation

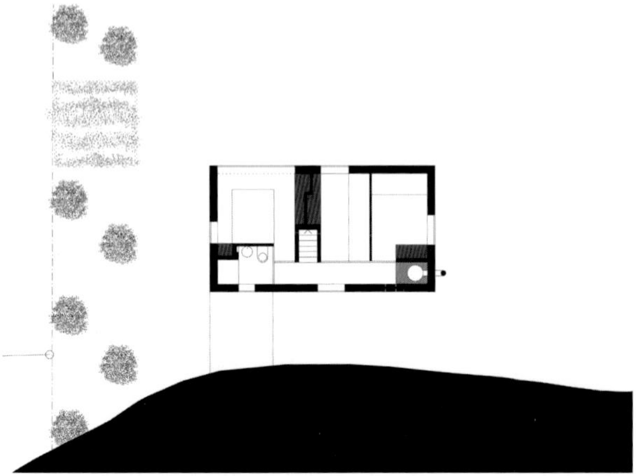

Upper floor

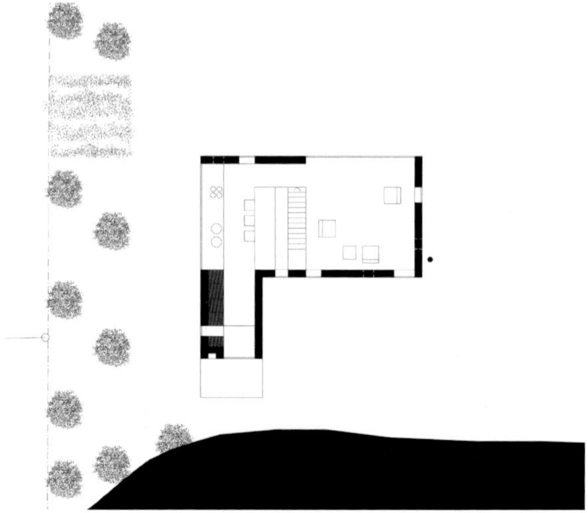

Lower floor

THE FINAL(LY) HOUSE

ROTHSCHILD SCHWARTZ ARCHITECTS

Green elements are integral to the overall design principles and ultimate expression of the house. The post-and-beam structure supports the living roof. Minimal and honest use of materials and simplicity of construction result in a modern form, which is clad in a combination of glass and 100¶year-old locally reclaimed redwood.

Les éléments de verdure font partie intégrante des principes généraux de la conception et déclinent l'expression ultime de la maison. La structure à pilier-linteau supporte le toit qui est aussi un espace à vivre. Un usage minime et mesuré des matériaux et la simplicité même de la construction assurent la modernité de la forme ; le tout est revêtu d'une combinaison de verre et de bois de séquoia centenaire, récupéré localement.

Die Grünelemente sind für die Gesamtgestaltung dieses Projekts entscheidend und verleihen ihm sein besonderes Erscheinungsbild. Eine Stützen-Balken-Konstruktion trägt das lebende Dach. Die moderne Form ergibt sich aus den mit minimalem Aufwand eingesetzten Materialien und der Einfachheit des Bauwerks, dessen Außenverkleidung aus einer Kombination von Glas und 100 Jahre altem, heimischem, wieder verwertetem Mammutbaumholz gefertigt wurde.

Groene elementen zijn essentieel in dit ontwerp. Ze geven het huis de gewenste expressie. Palen en balken ondersteunen het dak van de woonkamer. Minimaal en eerlijk gebruik van materialen en eenvoud van constructie leidden tot een moderne vorm in een omhulsel van glas en hout. Het hout is minstens honderd jaar oud redwood.

Los elementos verdes están integrados en los principios generales del diseño y de la expresión fundamental de la casa. La estructura de postes y traviesas soporta el peso de la azotera ajardinada. El uso minimalista y sencillo de los materiales y la simplicidad de la construcción dan como resultado una forma moderna, la cual está revestida con cristal y madera de secoya de cien años de antigüedad recuperada.

Gli elementi verdi sono perfettamente integrati nei principi generali del progetto e del concetto fondamentale della casa. La struttura a gabbia sopporta il peso del tetto vivente. L'uso sobrio e minimalista dei materiali e la semplicità della costruzione permettono di ottenere una forma moderna, che è ricoperta con vetro e vecchio legno di sequoia recuperato.

Os elementos verdes são parte integrante dos princípios gerais do design e da derradeira expressão da casa. A estrutura de postes e vigas suporta o telhado. O uso mínimo e honesto dos materiais e a simplicidade da construção resulta numa forma moderna, que está revestida por uma combinação de vidro e pau-brasil com 100 anos reutilizado.

Gröna element är grundläggande i den övergripande designprincipen och det slutgiltiga uttrycket hos huset. Stolp- och balkstrukturen stöttar upp det levande taket. Minimalt och uppriktigt användande av olika material resulterar i en modern form vilken är klädd i en kombination av glas och 100-årig lokalt återvunnen redwood.

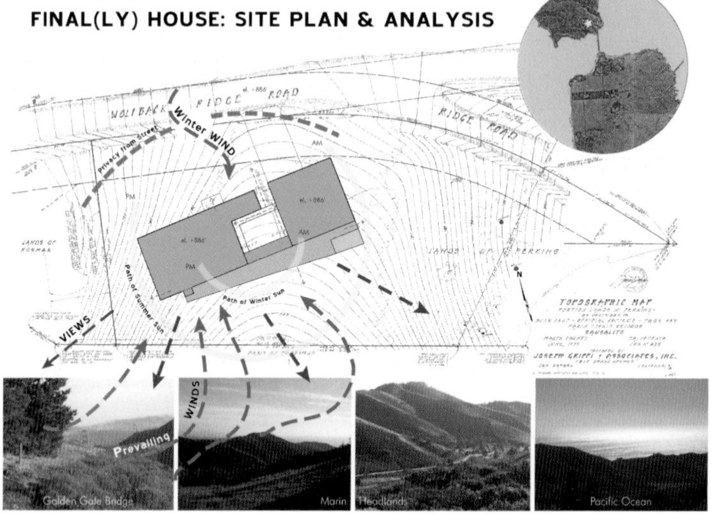

Site plan

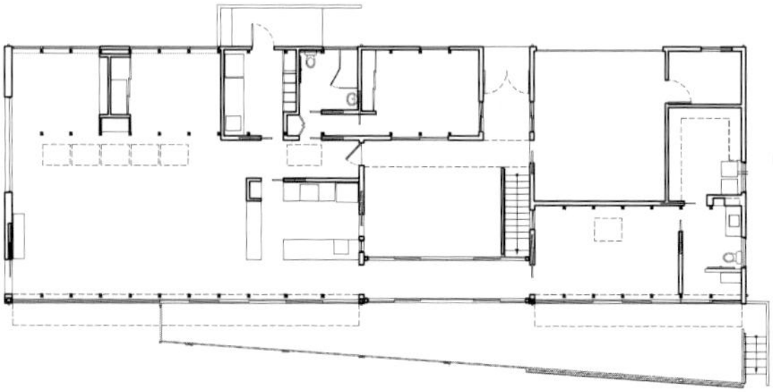

Ground floor

Roof detail

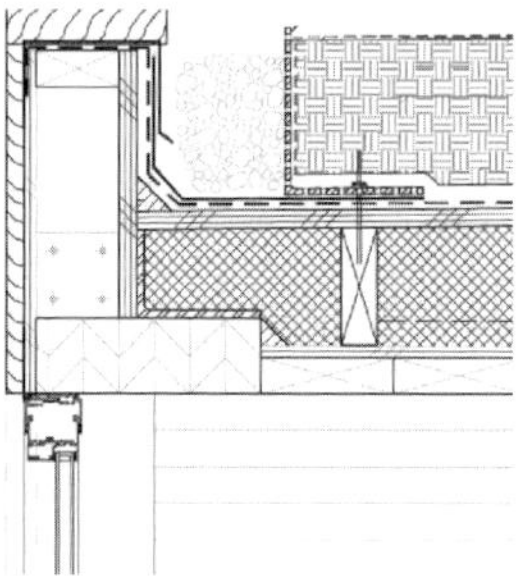

HOUSE **FOR A CARPENTER**

CUKROWICZ NACHBAUR ARCHITEKTEN

This new house for a carpenter and his family is made up of a small store on the ground floor and the living quarters on the two upper floors. In accordance with the regional building tradition, untreated local white fir is used exclusively for the walls, ceilings and floors. The degree of openness varies by adjusting the shutters.

Cette maison destinée à un charpentier et à sa famille comporte une petite boutique-atelier au rez-de-chaussée et deux étages de quartiers d'habitation. En accord avec les traditions de construction locales, on a utilisé exclusivement du sapin blanc pour les murs, les sols et les plafonds. Le degré d'ouverture se fait à l'aide des volets.

Dieser Neubau, der für einen Tischler und seine Familie konzipiert wurde, besteht aus einem kleinen Geschäft im Erdgeschoss und den Wohnbereichen in den beiden Obergeschossen. Im Stil der regionalen Bautradition wurde für Wände, Böden und Decken ausschließlich weißes, unbehandeltes einheimisches Tannenholz verwendet. Die beliebig einstellbaren Jalousien lassen das Haus als völlig oder halb geschlossen oder aber offen erscheinen.

Dit nieuwe huis voor een timmerman en zijn gezin bestaat uit een winkeltje op de begane grond en woonvertrekken op de twee verdiepingen erboven. Naar de traditionele bouwtrant is voor de wanden, plafonds en vloeren wit sparrenhout uit de streek gebruikt. Door de stand van de blinden oogt het huis open of juist ontoegankelijk.

Esta nueva casa para un carpintero y su familia consta de un pequeño almacén en la planta baja y de cuartos y salas de estar en los dos pisos superiores. Conforme a la tradición constructora regional, el abeto blanco local no tratado se utiliza única y exclusivamente en las paredes, techos y suelos. Es posible cambiar el grado de apertura regulando las persianas.

Questa nuova casa realizzata per un falegname e la sua famiglia è costituita da un piccolo magazzino al pianterreno e da stanze abitabili nei due piani superiori. In base alla tecnica di costruzione tradizionale della regione, l'abete bianco locale non trattato è utilizzato per pareti, soffitti e pavimenti. Il grado di apertura può essere modificato regolando le gelosie.

Esta casa nova, criada para um carpinteiro e a sua família, é constituída por uma pequena loja, no nível térreo, e pela residência nos dois pisos superiores. De acordo com a tradição de construção regional, foi usada apenas madeira de abeto branco não tratada para as paredes, tecto e chão. O grau de exposição ao exterior varia de acordo com o ajuste das portadas.

Detta nya hus för en snickare och hans familj består av en liten affär på bottenvåningen och bostad på de två övre våningarna. I enlighet med den lokala byggnadstraditionen används endast obehandlad lokalt växande rödgran till väggar, tak och golv. Graden av öppenhet varierar genom justerande av fönsterluckor.

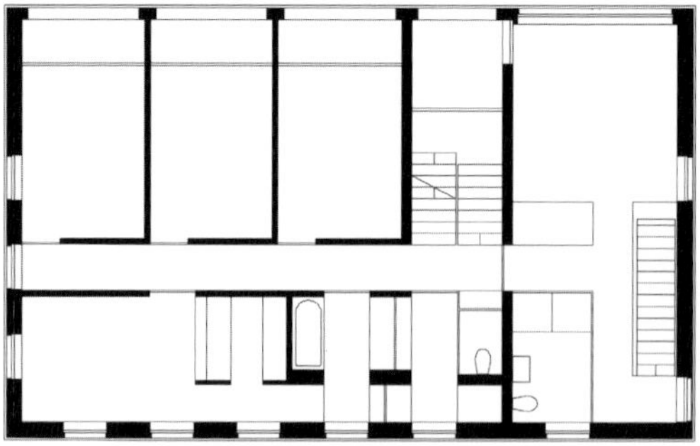

Third floor

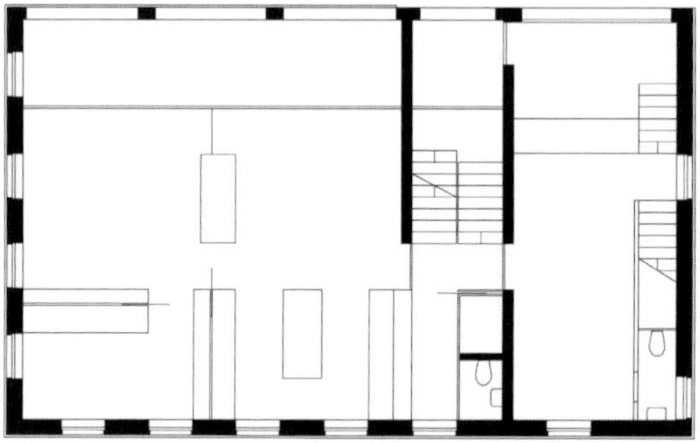

Second floor

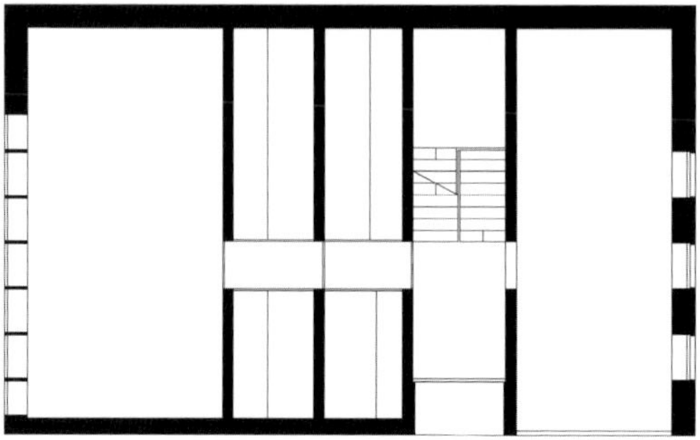

Ground floor

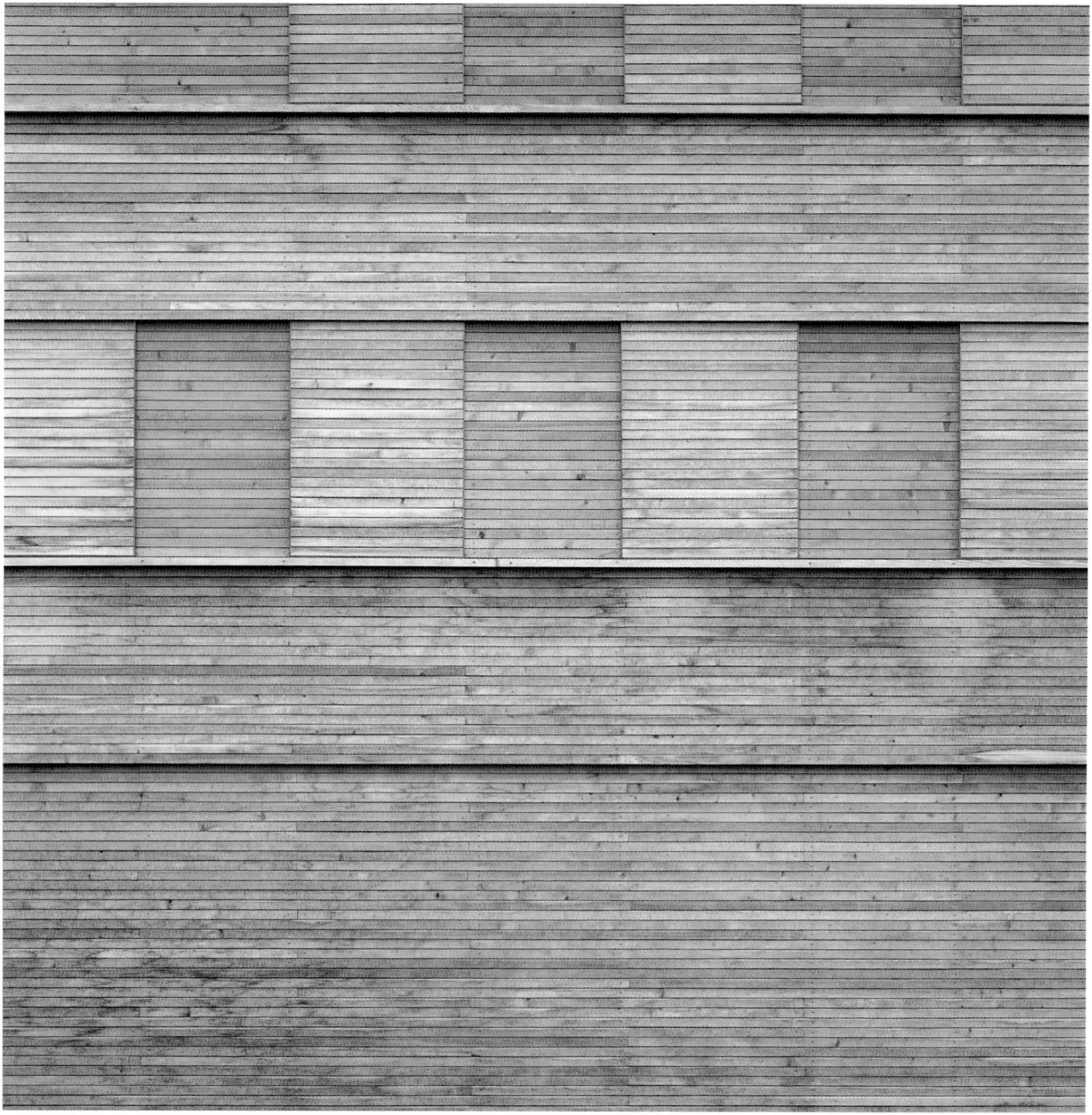

CARABANCHEL SOCIAL HOUSING

FOREIGN OFFICE ARCHITECTS

A parallelogram block contains tube-like units that offer a double orientation. The terraces are enclosed with bamboo louvers mounted on folding frames that provide the necessary protection from the strong East and West sun exposures. They also procure security for the units, or open entirely to a private garden when desired.

Un bloc parallélépipédique contient des unités d'habitation en forme de tube, dotées d'une double exposition. Les terrasses sont bordées d'abat-vent en bambous montés sur des cadres pliants, qui fournissent une protection indispensable contre la chaleur. Ils assurent aussi la sécurité de l'ensemble ou bien s'ouvrent entièrement sur un jardin privé, si on le désire.

Der parallelogrammförmige Block umfasst schlauchähnliche Einheiten mit zwei Ausrichtungen. Die Terrassen sind mit Bambusjalousien versehen, die auf faltbare Rahmen gespannt sind und den notwendigen Schutz vor dem starken Sonneneinfall im Westen und im Osten bieten. Zudem gewähren sie im geschlossenen Zustand Sicherheit und bieten in geöffnetem Zustand Ausblick auf den privaten Garten.

De naar twee zijden gerichte appartementen lijken als buizen in het woonblok geschoven te zijn. De terrassen zijn afgesloten met bamboe jaloezieën, die de woningen beschermen tegen de felle zon aan de oost- en westkant. Ze geven de bewoners een gevoel van geborgenheid. En wie naar de tuin wil, schuift of klapt ze gewoon open.

Se trata de un bloque paralelogramo compuesto de unidades con forma de tubo que ofrecen una doble orientación. Las terrazas han sido cerradas con persianas de bambú montadas en marcos plegables a fin de proteger de manera idónea del fuerte sol oriental y occidental. También aportan seguridad a las unidades o pueden abrirse por completo a un jardín privado cuando se desee.

Si tratta di un parallelogrammo contenente unità a forma di tubo con una duplice orientazione. Le terrazze sono state chiuse mediante persiane di bambù montate su cornici pieghevoli, allo scopo di fornire un'adeguata protezione dal forte sole dell'esposizione est-ovest. Danno anche un maggiore senso di sicurezza alle unità oppure, se si vuole, possono aprirsi completamente su un giardino privato.

Este bloco com a forma de um paralelogramo contém unidades de aparência tubular que oferecem uma dupla orientação. Os terraços são fechados com venezianas montadas sobre molduras desdobráveis que asseguram a necessária protecção da forte exposição solar, tanto a Este como a Oeste. Além disso, podem garantir a segurança das unidades ou abrir-se por inteiro para um jardim privado, conforme se pretenda.

Ett parallelogramblock innehåller tubliknande enheter som erbjuder dubbla riktningsmöjligheter. Terrasserna är omgärdade med ventilationsgaller i bambu monterade på vikskärmar som ger nödvändigt skydd mot den starka solen från öst och väst. De bidrar också till att säkra enheterna eller kan öppnas mot en privat trädgård när så önskas.

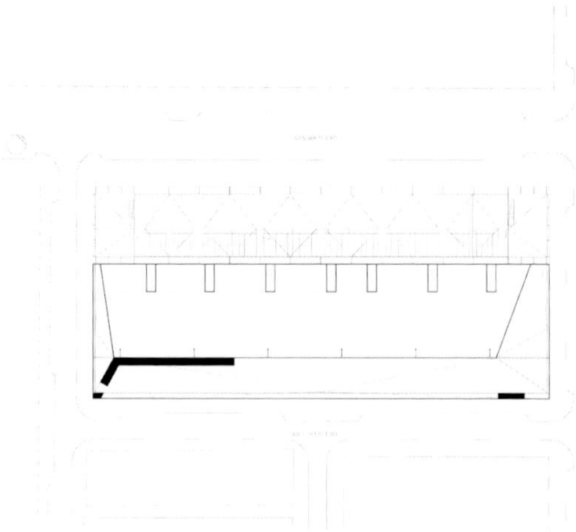

Site plan

Ground floor plan

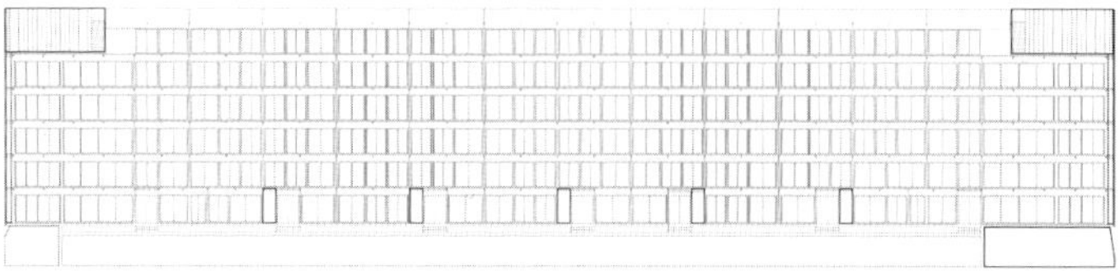

Longitudinal section

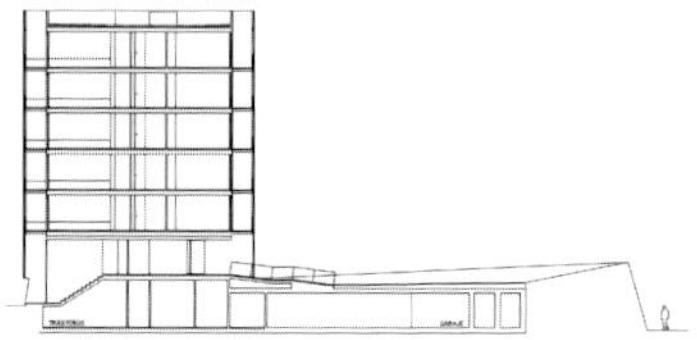

Transversal section

SURFSIDE

STELLE ARCHITECTS
© Jeff Heatley

Architecture and nature have been fully integrated in this light-saturated compound perched on top of an ocean side sand dune to maximize the views. The remodel includes a guest house, a two-car garage, a free form un-chlorinated pool and a two-story house clad in wood and cement panel rain screens with anodized aluminum windows.

Architecture et nature ont été totalement intégrées dans cet ensemble saturé de lumière, perché au sommet d'une dune de sable dominant l'océan pour offrir la plus belle vue. Le remaniement inclut une maison d'hôte, un garage pour deux voitures, une piscine (non chlorée) de forme libre et une résidence sur deux niveaux, revêtue de panneaux en bois et en ciment contre la pluie, avec des fenêtres en aluminium anodisé.

Bei diesem lichtdurchfluteten Gebäude wurden Architektur und Natur perfekt integriert: Es steht auf einer Sanddüne an der Küste, um einen optimalen Ausblick aufs Meer zu gewähren. Im Zuge der Neugestaltung wurden ein Gästehaus, eine Garage mit zwei Parkplätzen, ein chlorfreier Freiform-Swimmingpool und ein doppelstöckiges, mit Holz und wasserdichten Betonplatten verkleidetes Haus mit eloxierten Aluminiumfenstern hinzugefügt.

Architectuur en natuur versmelten in dit lichte complex boven op een duin met uitzicht op de oceaan. De verbouwing betrof een gastenverblijf, een dubbele garage, een zwembad met vloeiende vormen en een huis van twee verdiepingen, bekleed met hout en voorzien van regenschermen van cementpanelen en vensters van geanodiseerd aluminium.

A fin de potenciar al máximo las vistas, la arquitectura y la naturaleza se han integrado por completo en este complejo habitacional repleto de luz encaramado a la cima de una duna de arena junto al océano. La reforma incluye la casa de invitados, un garaje para dos coches, una piscina de forma libre con agua no clorada y una casa de dos pisos revestida de paneles de madera y cemento contra la lluvia con ventanas de aluminio anodizadas.

Architettura e natura sono state perfettamente integrate in questo complesso traboccante di luce, sito in cima a una duna di sabbia accanto all'oceano, per valorizzare al massimo le viste. La ristrutturazione comprende la casa per gli ospiti, un garage per due auto, una piscina dalla forma fantasiosa con acqua non clorata e una casa di due piani ricoperta di pannelli contro la pioggia di legno e cemento con finestre d'alluminio anodizzato.

A arquitectura e a natureza foram admiravelmente integradas neste complexo inundado de luz, empoleirado no topo de uma duna de areia, junto ao oceano, para maximizar a vista. A remodelação incluiu uma casa de hóspedes, uma garagem para dois carros, uma piscina de forma livre, sem cloro, e uma residência de dois andares, revestida de madeira e painéis de cimento especialmente desenhados para fachadas ventiladas, com janelas de alumínio anodizado.

Arkitektur och natur har blivit fullt integrerade i detta ljusfyllda hus beläget på en sanddyn för att maximera utsikten. Ombyggnationen inkluderar ett gästhus, ett tvåbilsgarage, en friliggande oklorerad pool och ett tvåvåningshus klätt i trä och cementpanelade regnskärmar med anodiserade aluminiumfönster.

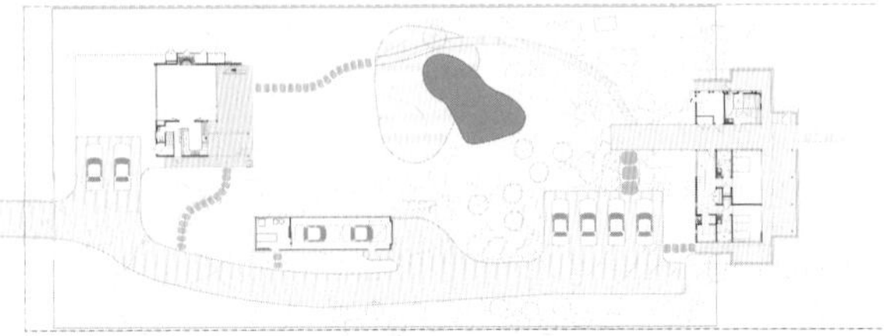

Site plan

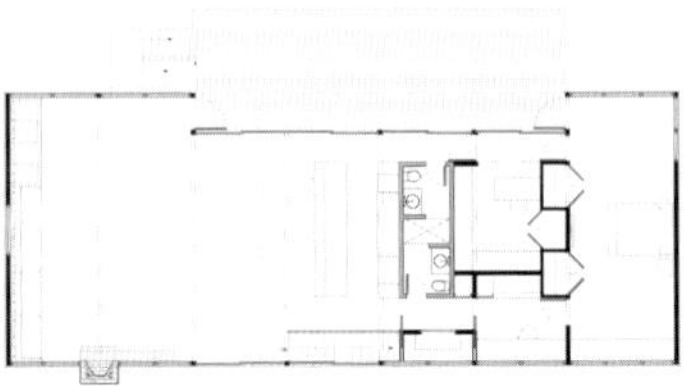

First floor

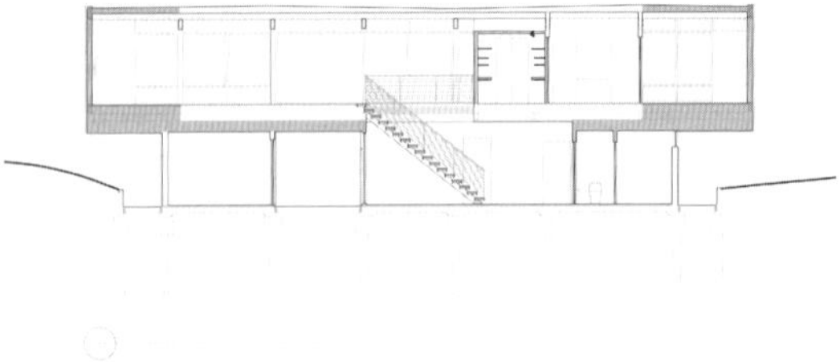

Longitudinal section

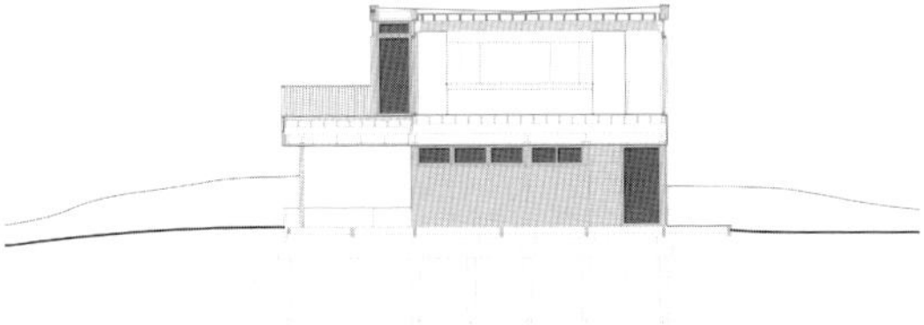

Transversal section

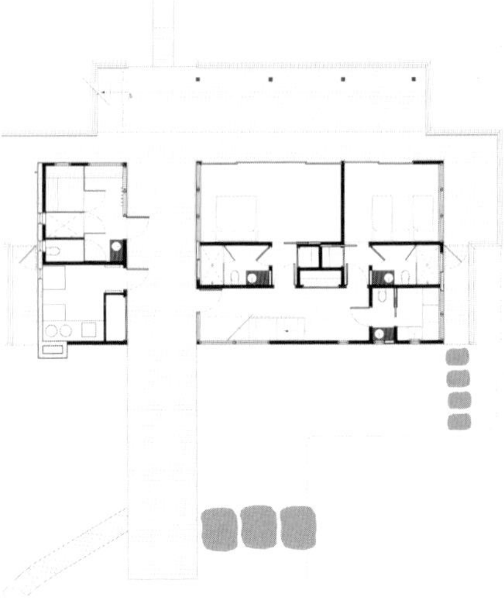

Ground floor

GHAUS

ARBAU STUDIO

Located in a rural area near Treviso, the Ghaus is built with an X-Lam bearing structure made of fir panels and wooden fiber insulation. The panels are exposed to the interior and clad with larch boards on the exterior. While the north wall presents few small openings, the south wall has large windows and timber louvers.

Situé dans une zone rurale près de Trévise, le *Ghaus* est construit avec une structure porteuse « X-Lam » faite de panneaux en sapin et d'une isolation en fibres de bois. Disposés sur l'intérieur, ces panneaux sont revêtus de grandes planches de sapin à l'extérieur. Le mur nord n'offre que quelques petites percées, tandis que le mur sud est doté de grandes baies et de persiennes en bois.

Dieses Projekt befindet sich in einer ländlichen Gegend in der Nähe von Treviso und besteht aus einer X-Lam-Tragstruktur, die mit Paneelen aus Tannenholz gefertigt und mit einer Holzfaserdämmung ausgestattet wurde. Die Paneele sind auf der im Innenraum liegenden Seite sichtbar und auf der Außenseite mit Lärchenbrettern verkleidet. Während die nach Norden gerichtete Wand nur wenige kleine Öffnungen aufweist, ist die südliche Seite mit großen Fenstern und Holzblenden ausgestattet.

Het Ghaus staat in een landelijk gebied bij Treviso. De dragende structuur bestaat uit vurenhouten panelen met een isoleatielaag van houtvezels. De panelen zijn aan de binnenkant onbekleed en aan de buitenkant bekleed met larikshout. In de noordmuur zitten een paar kleine openingen, maar in de zuidmuur zitten grote ramen en jaloezieën.

Situada en una zona rural cercana a Treviso, la Ghaus está construida con una estructura portante concebida mediante el sistema X-Lam hecha de paneles de abeto y dotada de un aislamiento térmico de fibra de madera. Mientras la pared norte presenta pocas aberturas, en su mayoría pequeñas, la pared sur tiene amplias ventanas protegidas por pantallas de láminas de madera verticales.

Sita in una zona rurale nei pressi di Treviso, la casa Ghaus è stata costruita con una struttura portante concepita mediante sistema X-Lam, fatta di pannelli d'abete e dotata di isolamento termico di fibra di legno. Mentre la parete settentrionale presenta poche aperture e per di più piccole, la parete esposta a sur possiede ampie finestre protette da schermi a lamine di legno verticali.

Localizada numa zona rural próximo de Treviso, a Ghaus foi erigida numa estrutura de X Lam constituída por painéis de abeto e isolamento de fibra de madeira. Os painéis estão expostos, no interior, e revestidos com tábuas de lariço, no exterior. Enquanto a parede norte tem aberturas escassas e pequenas, a parede sul apresenta grandes janelas e venezianas de madeira.

Ghaus är beläget i ett lantligt område nära Treviso och är byggt i X-Lam bestående av granpaneler och fiberisolering gjord på trä. Panelerna är exponerade mot insidan och klädda med skivor i lärkträ på utsidan. Medan den norra väggen har få öppningar finns det stora fönster och ventilationsgaller av timmer på södra väggen.

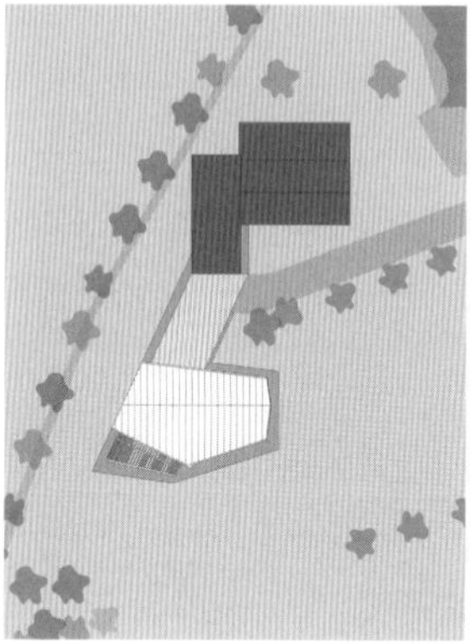

Site plan

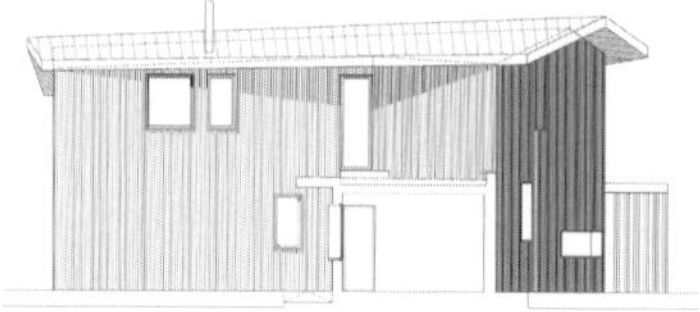

North elevation

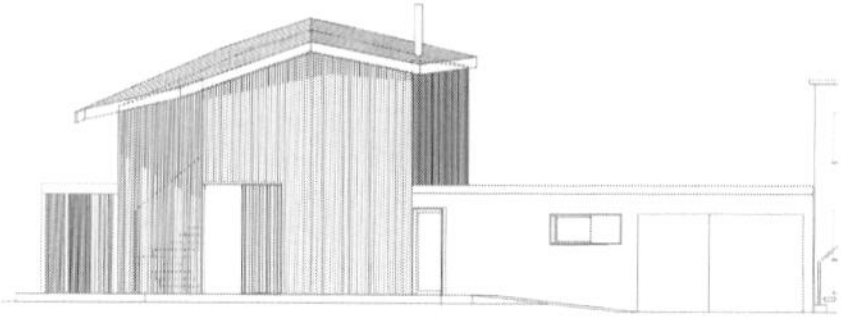

East elevation

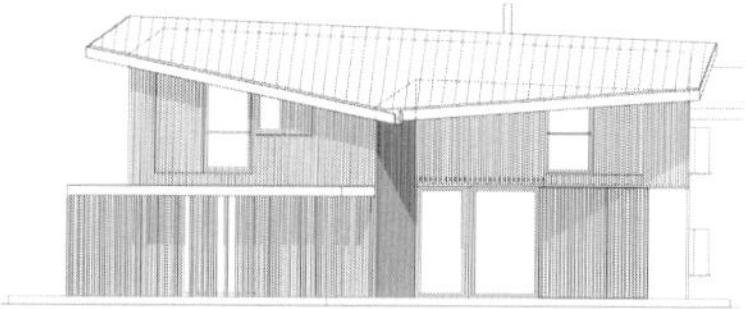

South elevation (open)

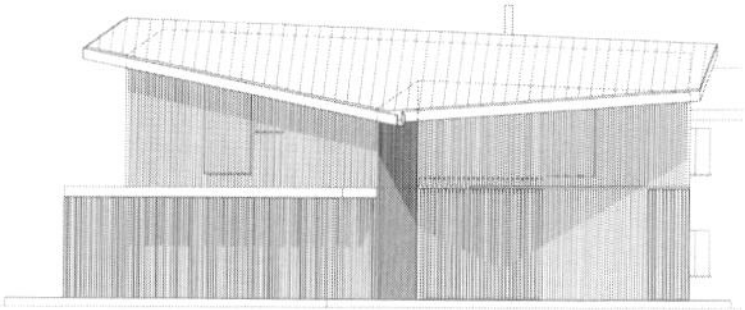

South elevation (closed)

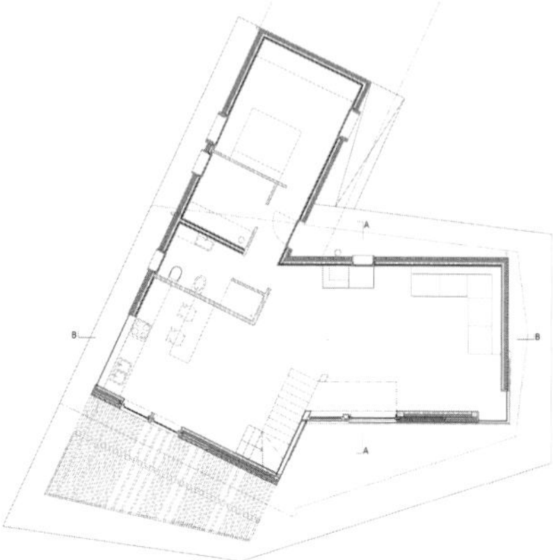

Ground floor

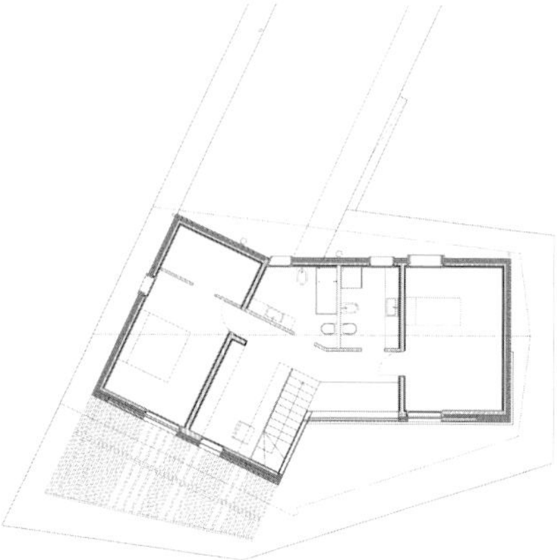

Second floor

TENT HOUSE

CAZÚ ZEGERS

The house is located in a valley along a river flanked by tall cliffs. It is conceived as a wooden canopy that protects the single space house. The area in front of the house is landscaped with terraces formed around fallen trees. The structure, designed to bear the heavy weight of snow, allows the walls to be built separately as infill.

La maison est située dans une vallée bordée de hautes falaises, le long d'une rivière. Elle est conçue comme une voûte en bois protégeant l'espace intérieur unique. Le secteur devant la maison est paysagé avec des terre-pleins qui se sont formés autour d'arbres tombés. La structure – conçue pour supporter le poids de la neige – permet de construire les murs séparément, par remplissage.

Das Haus liegt in einem Tal an einem Fluss und ist von steilen Klippen umgeben. Auffallend ist sein einem Baldachin gleichendes Holzdach, welches das Einraumhaus bedeckt. Die landschaftliche Gestaltung im Bereich vor dem Haus zeichnet sich durch Terrassen aus, die um umgestürzte Bäume herum errichtet worden sind. Die Struktur des Projekts wurde so ausgelegt, dass sie schwere Schneelast tragen kann, sodass man die Wände separat wie bei einer Ausfachung hochziehen konnte.

Dit huis staat in een dal, bij een rivier die tussen hoge rotsen door stroomt. Het is ontworpen als een houten overkapping van een eenkamerwoning. Vóór het huis zijn terrassen aangelegd rond omgevallen bomen. De kap kan een zware last sneeuw dragen. De constructie liet toe dat de wanden apart werden opgetrokken.

La casa está situada en un valle a lo largo de un río flanqueado por altos riscos. Fue concebida como una marquesina a fin de proteger el espacio individual de la vivienda. El área situada frente ha sido diseñada con terrazas formadas alrededor de los árboles caídos. Gracias a la estructura, proyectada para resistir el fuerte peso de la nieve, las paredes pudieron construirse por separado como elementos de relleno.

La casa è stata costruita in una valle lungo un fiume fiancheggiato da alti dirupi, ed è concepita come una tettoia di legno che protegge lo spazio dell'abitazione. L'area prospiciente alla costruzione è stata abbellita con terrazze formate intorno ad alberi caduti. Grazie alla sua struttura, progettata per resistere al grande peso della neve, è stato possibile costruire ogni singola parete come materiale da riempimento.

A casa fica localizada num vale ao longo de um rio flanqueado por altos penhascos. Foi concebido um dossel de madeira que protege a casa estúdio. A área em frente à casa foi trabalhada com terraços formados em redor de árvores caídas. A estrutura, concebida para aguentar o grande peso da neve, permite que as paredes sejam construídas separadamente como enchimento.

Huset är beläget i en dalgång längs med en flod kantad av höga klippor. Det är konstruerat som en träbaldakin som skyddar enrumshuset. Området framför huset är anlagt med terrasser formade runt nedfallna träd. Konstruktionen, designad för att bära den tunga vikten av snö, gör det möjligt att bygga väggarna separat som utfyllnad.

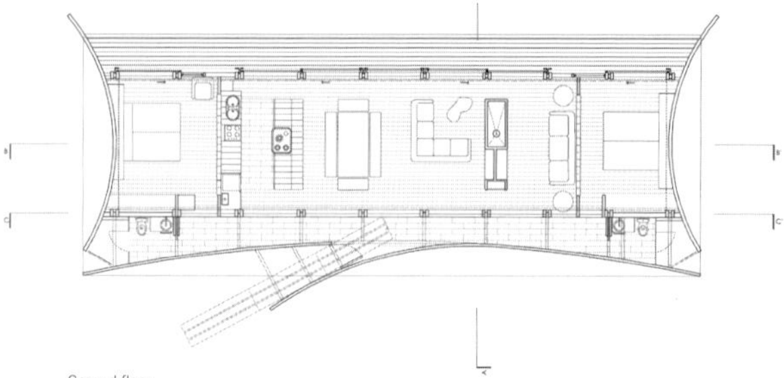

Ground floor

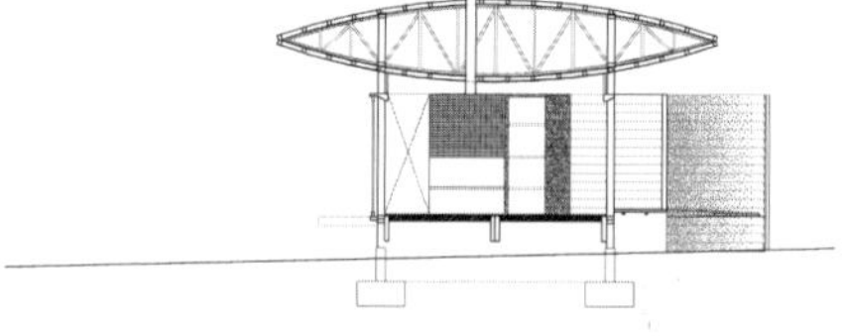

Section A-A'

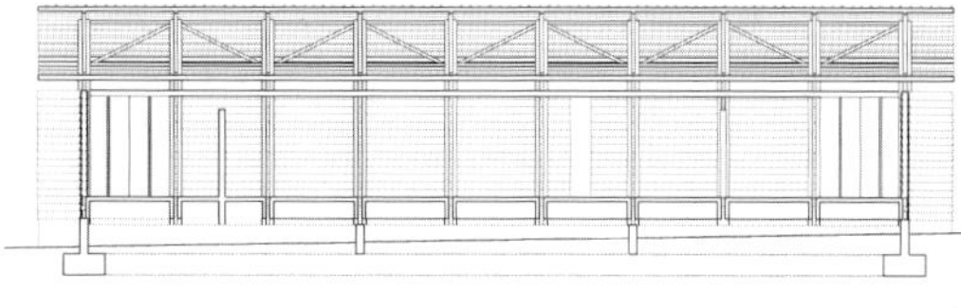

Section C-C'

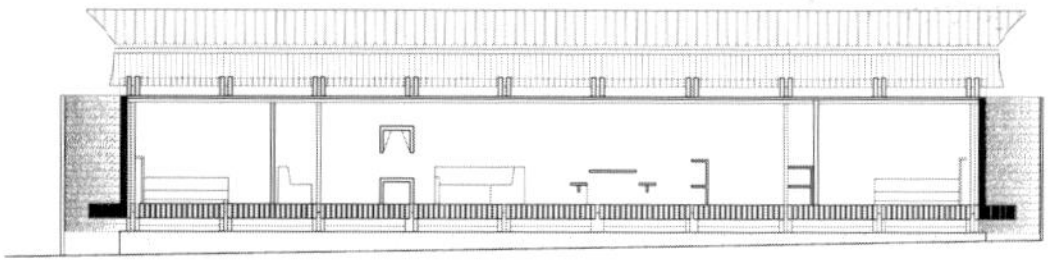

Section B-B'

HOUSE OF **STEEL AND WOOD**

ECOSISTEMA URBANO ARQUITECTOS
© Emilio P. Doiztua

This simple polygonal structure is a contemporary interpretation of vernacular architecture. More precisely, it utilizes formal and constructive typologies of traditional architecture in northern Spain. The exterior walls are a combination of two types of wood slats (North pine and Douglas Pine) of two different widths.

Cette structure polygonale simple est une interprétation contemporaine de l'architecture vernaculaire. Plus précisément, elle utilise les types de forme et de construction de l'architecture traditionnelle dans le nord de l'Espagne. L'extérieur des murs est une combinaison de deux types de latte de bois (pin du Nord et pin Douglas), avec deux largeurs différentes.

Die einfache polygonale Struktur stellt eine zeitgenössische Interpretation traditioneller Architektur dar. An diesem Projekt werden die für die traditionelle Architektur Nordspaniens charakteristische Form und Bauweise konkret angewandt. An den Außenwänden wurden zwei verschiedene Arten von Holzlatten (Kiefernholz aus dem Norden und Douglas-Kiefer), in zwei unterschiedlich breiten Abmessungen verwendet.

Deze eenvoudige veelhoekige constructie is een moderne interpretatie van traditionele architectuur. Ze sluit aan bij de manier van bouwen die in Noord-Spanje gebruikelijk is. De buitenwanden zijn vervaardigd van twee soorten hout, grove den en douglas. Er zijn latten van twee verschillende breedten gebruikt.

Esta sencilla estructura poligonal es una interpretación contemporánea de la arquitectura local, a saber: emplea tipologías formales y constructivas de la arquitectura tradicional del norte de España. En las paredes exteriores se mezclan armónicamente dos tipos de listones de madera (pino Norte y pino Douglas) con anchuras diferentes.

Questa semplice struttura poligonale è un'interpretazione contemporanea dello stile architettonico locale o, in altri termini, utilizza tipologie formali e costruttive dell'architettura tradizionale del nord della Spagna. Nelle pareti esterne si mescolano armoniosamente due tipi di listelli di legno (pino del nord e pino Douglas) con diverse larghezze.

Esta simples estrutura poligonal é uma interpretação contemporânea da arquitectura vernacular. Mais precisamente, utiliza tipologias formais e construtivas da arquitectura tradicional do norte de Espanha. As paredes exteriores são uma combinação de dois tipos de ripas de madeira (pinheiro do norte e pinheiro Douglas) com duas larguras diferentes.

Denna enkla polygonstruktur är en modern tolkning av inhemsk arkitektur. Mer exakt använder den formella och konstruktiva typologier i traditionell nordspansk arkitektur. Ytterväggarna är en kombination av två typer av träskivor (nordlig tall och Douglasgran) av två olika bredder.

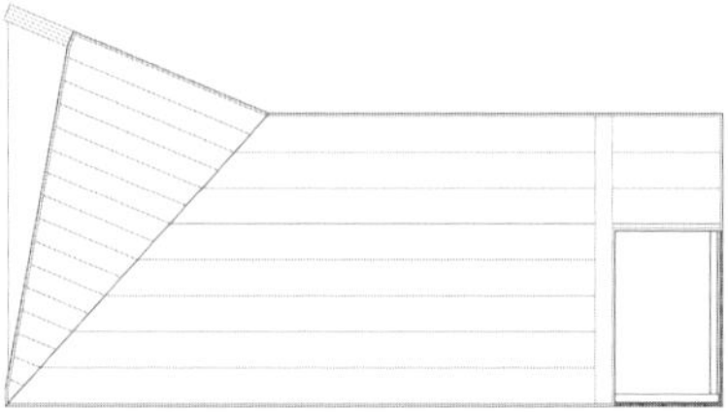

Roof

West elevation

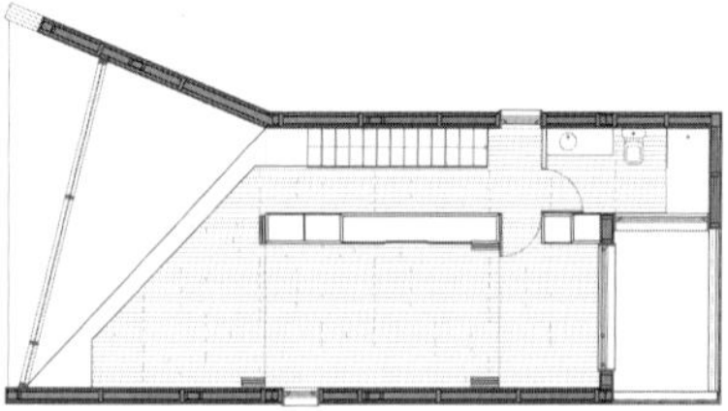

Second floor

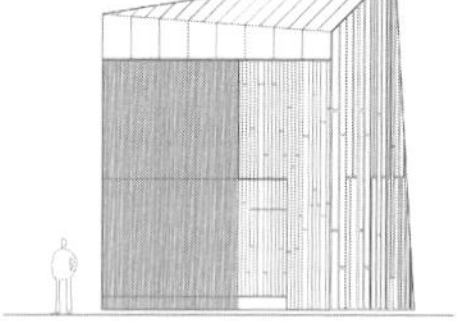

North elevation

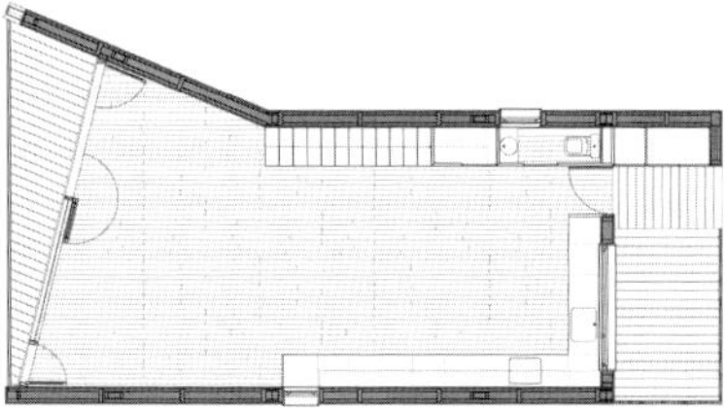

Ground floor

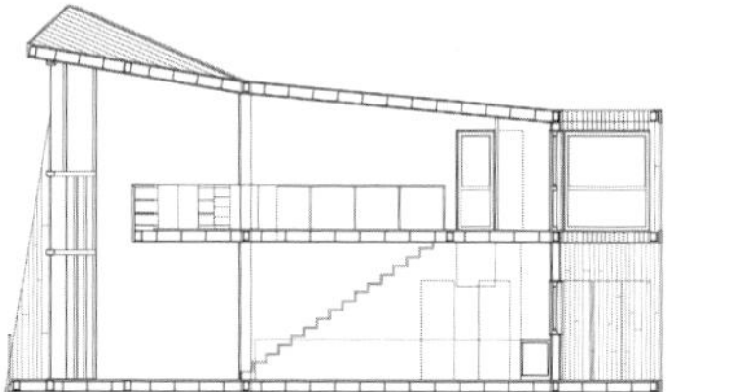

Longitudinal section

HOUSE OF **SILENCE**

CAZÚ ZEGERS

The use of rough-sawn wood on the exterior of most of the houses of the region of Kawelluco emphasizes the beauty of the wood in its natural state. The rustic appearance of the house becomes, at closer view, an elaborate and intricate work of carpentry visible in the casement of the windows, the louvers and the lattice work.

L'utilisation de bois brut de sciage pour le revêtement extérieur de la plupart des maisons, dans la région de Kawelluco, exalte la beauté du bois dans son état naturel. L'allure rustique de la maison dissimule un travail de charpente complexe et sophistiqué, bien visible dans le traitement des fenêtres, des persiennes et du travail de treillis.

Die Verwendung von grob geschnittenem Holz an der Außenfassade der Großzahl der Häuser in der Region von Kawelluco hebt die Schönheit von naturbelassenem Holz hervor. Bei näherer Betrachtung des zuerst rustikal anmutenden Hauses erkennt man die ausgeklügelte, aufwändige Zimmermannsarbeit, die an den Fensterflügeln, Jalousien und Spalieren sichtbar wird.

De meeste huizen in de omgeving van Kawelluco zijn vanbuiten afgewerkt met ruw gezaagd hout. Zo is te zien hoe mooi hout uitkomt in zijn natuurlijke staat. Het rustieke voorkomen van dit huis blijkt het resultaat van zorgvuldig uitgevoerd timmerwerk. De raamlijsten, jaloezieën en traliewerken zijn staaltjes van timmerkunst.

El empleo de la madera sin tratar en el exterior de la mayor parte de las viviendas de la región de Kawelluco acentúa la belleza de la madera en su estado natural. El aspecto rústico de la casa se convierte, al observarla de cerca, en un trabajo de carpintería muy elaborado y complejo, visible sobre todo en los marcos de las ventanas, los listones y en las rejas de las contraventanas.

L'uso del legno non trattato negli esterni della maggior parte delle abitazioni della Regione di Kawelluco dà enfasi alla bellezza del legno nel suo stato naturale. L'aspetto rustico della casa diviene, se si osserva più da vicino, un lavoro di falegnameria molto elaborato e complesso, visibile soprattutto negli stipiti delle finestre, nelle stecche e nelle grate delle imposte.

A utilização de madeira, cortada de forma grosseira, no exterior da maior parte das casas da região de Kawelluco salienta a beleza da madeira no seu estado natural. A aparência rústica da casa transforma-se, quando vista mais de perto, num elaborado e intrincado trabalho de carpintaria, bem visível nos caixilhos das janelas, nas venezianas e no trabalho das gelosias.

Användandet av grovsågat trä på utsidan av de flesta hus i Kawellucoregionen framhäver träets skönhet i dess naturliga form. Husets rustika framtoning blir vid en närmare titt ett avancerat och intrikat snickeriarbete som är synligt i fönstrens isättning, ventilationsgallren och spaljéerna.

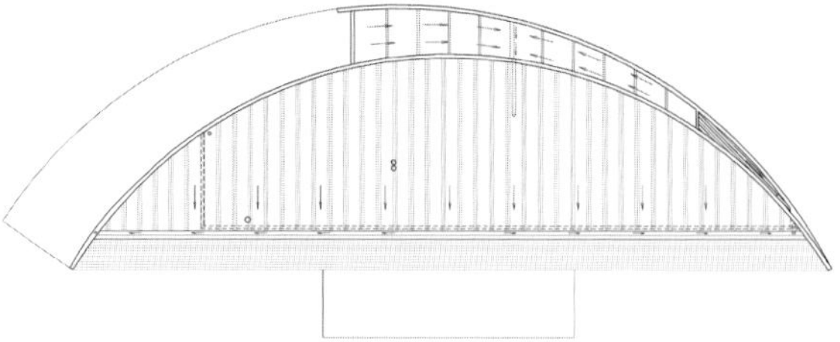

Roof

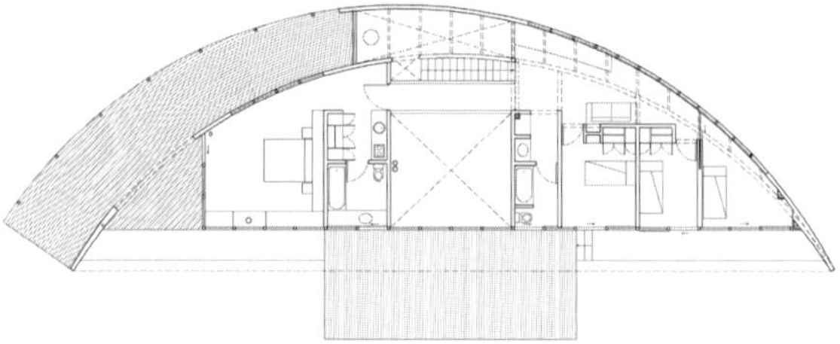

Second floor

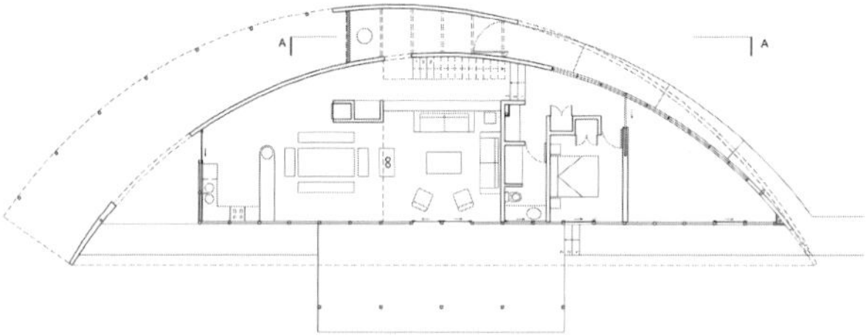

Ground floor

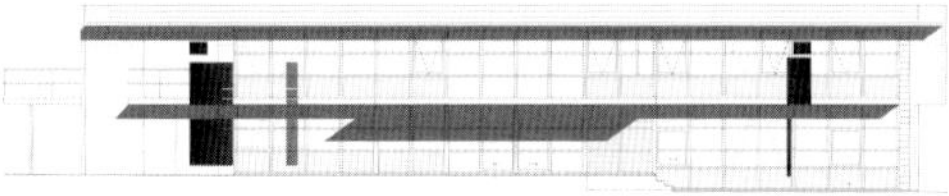

East elevation

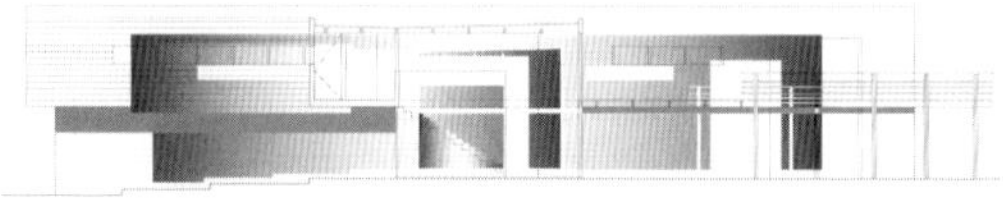

Section A-A

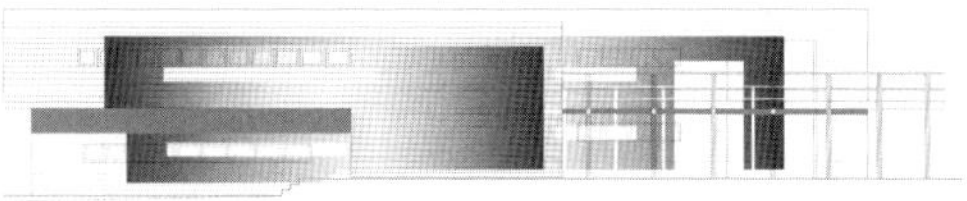

West elevation

SPLIT & ROTATE HOUSE

NICOS KALOGIROU
© Nicos Kalogirou

The general layout results from a split into two unequal parts: the main residence and the children's pavilion. The metal-framed structure with its exterior cladding of plywood was chosen for their low cost and rapid construction. The rough industrial materials of this prefabricated structure are left in their natural textures.

La disposition générale résulte de l'éclatement de l'ensemble en deux parties inégales : la résidence principale et le pavillon pour les enfants. La structure à ossature métallique et revêtement extérieur de contreplaqué a été choisie en raison de la modicité des coûts et de la rapidité de construction. Les matériaux industriels bruts de cette structure préfabriquée ont été laissés dans leur texture naturelle.

Der Grundriss des Projekts ergibt sich aus dessen Aufspaltung in zwei ungleiche Teile: das Hauptgebäude und den Pavillon für die Kinder. Die mit einem Metallrahmen umfasste Struktur mit einer Sperrholzverkleidung an der Außenfassade wurde aufgrund ihrer Wirtschaftlichkeit und der geringen Bauzeit gewählt. Die groben Industriematerialien dieses Fertigteilhauses wurden nicht nachbehandelt, sondern in ihrer natürlichen Textur belassen.

De vormgeving is het resultaat van de opsplitsing in twee ongelijke delen: de hoofdwoning en het verblijf voor de kinderen. Er is gekozen voor een met gelaagd hout bekleed metalen skelet vanwege de lage kosten en snelle constructie. De ruwe materialen van deze prefabwoning zijn in hun oorspronkelijke staat gelaten.

La distribución general es el resultado de una división en dos partes desiguales: la residencia principal y la caseta de los niños. Se eligió una estructura enmarcada en metal con un revestimiento exterior de contrachapado por su bajo coste y su rápida construcción. Los toscos materiales industriales de esta estructura prefabricada han conservado su textura natural.

La distribuzione generale è il risultato di una divisione in due parti diseguali: la residenza principale e dependance dei bambini. È stata scelta una struttura incorniciata di metallo con un rivestimento esterno di compensato per i suoi costi contenuti e la sua rapidità di montaggio. I materiali industriali impiegati in questa struttura prefabbricata hanno conservato la loro ruvida texture naturale.

O *layout* geral resulta de uma divisão em duas partes desiguais: a residência principal e o pavilhão das crianças. A estrutura de moldura metálica, com o seu revestimento exterior de contraplacado, foi escolhida pelo baixo preço e pela rápida construção. Foi mantida a textura original dos ásperos materiais industriais desta estrutura prefabricada.

Den generella layouten kommer från en delning i två asymmetriska delar: Det huvudsakliga residenset och barnens paviljong. Den metallramade strukturen klädd i plywood på utsidan valdes på grund av den låga kostnaden och den snabba konstruktionsmöjligheten. De grova industriella materialen i denna förkonstruerade strukturen har lämnats i sitt ursprungliga skick.

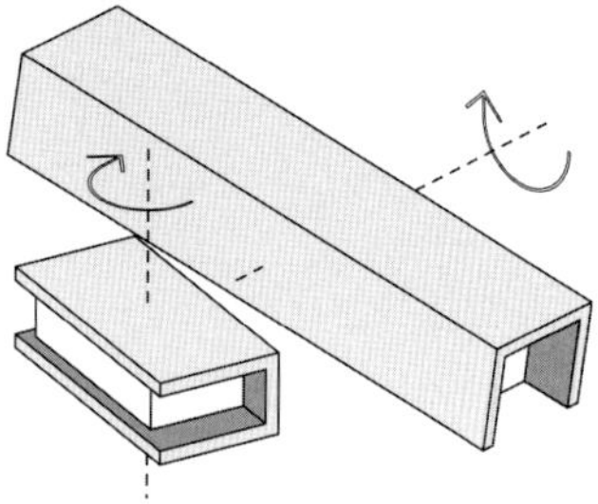

ROTATE ↻

Adaptation to site topography/views

1. Semi-open space
2. Master bedroom
3. Office
4. Bathroom
5. Kitchen/dining room
6. Living room
7. Children's bedroom

Floor plan

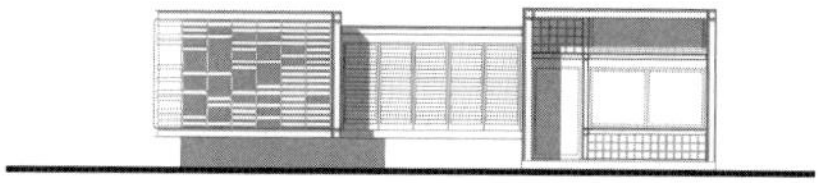

North-east elevation

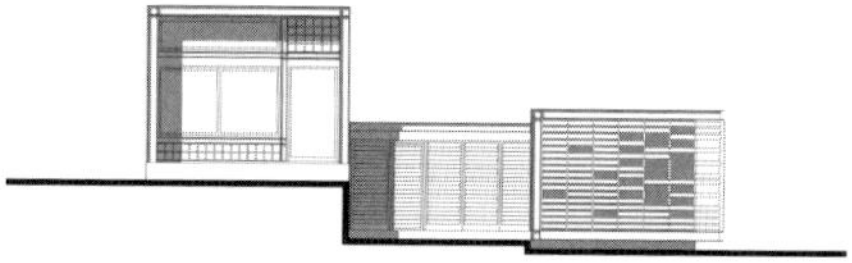

South-west elevation

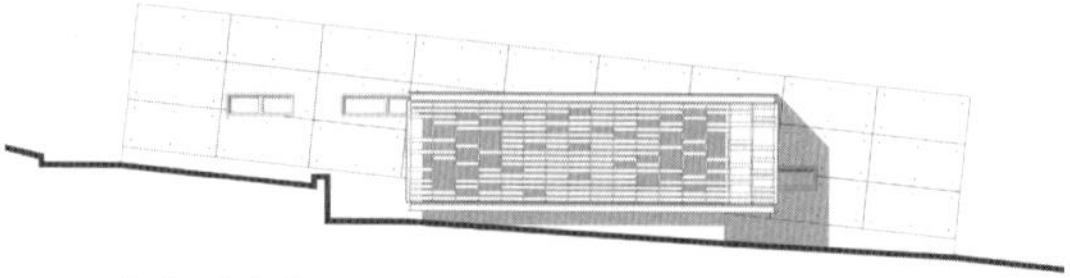

South-east elevation

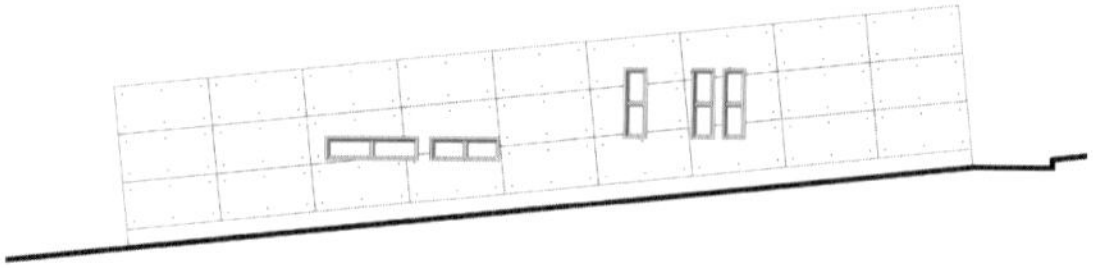

North-west elevation

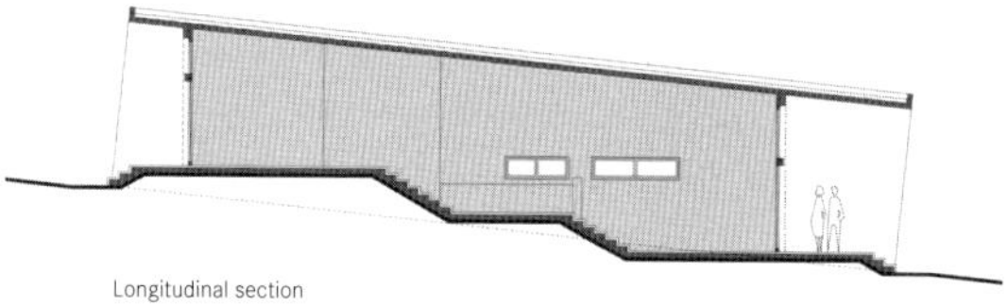

Longitudinal section

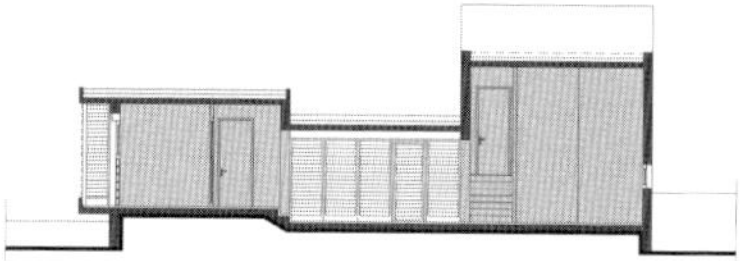

Cross section

HOUSE **NUMBER 19**

KORTEKNIE STUHLMACHER ARCHITECTEN, BIKVANDERPOL

This building served as accommodation for artists who had been invited to work in the framework of the municipal art organization "Beyond". The structure, made of solid, laminated panels of European softwood was stabilized by a steel frame. It is stable enough to be lifted and transported in one piece, and is environmentally sound.

Cette construction a servi de logement pour les artistes invités à travailler dans le cadre de la manifestation intitulée *Beyond* et organisée par la municipalité. La structure, faite de panneaux de contreplaqué plein en bois tendre d'Europe, est stabilisée par une ossature en acier : elle est assez solide pour être transportée d'un bloc, et sans impact négatif pour l'environnement.

Dieses Gebäude diente den Künstlern als Unterkunft, die man zur Mitarbeit in der städtischen Kunstorganisation „Beyond" eingeladen hatte. Die aus stabilen Brettschichtplatten europäischer Herkunft gefertigte Struktur wurde mithilfe eines Stahlrahmens fixiert. Die Konstruktion ist stabil genug, um im Ganzen hochgehoben und transportiert zu werden, und sie ist zudem auch noch umweltfreundlich.

Dit huis diende als tijdelijke woning voor kunstenaars die waren uitgenodigd voor Beyond, een door de gemeente georganiseerde manifestatie. Het is rond een stalen skelet opgetrokken van gelamineerde panelen van Europees naaldhout. Het milieuvriendelijke huis is stevig genoeg om opgetakeld en getransporteerd te worden.

Este edificio sirvió como alojamiento para los artistas invitados para participar en el marco de la organización artística municipal "Beyond". La estructura, levantada con sólidos paneles laminados de madera de conífera europea, fue estabilizada con un armazón de acero. Además de ser respetuosa con el medio ambiente, es lo suficientemente estable como para ser levantada y transportada en una sola pieza.

Questo edificio ha svolto la funzione di alloggio per gli artisti invitati nell'ambito dell'organizzazione artistica municipale "Beyond". La struttura, costruita con solidi pannelli di legno di conifera europea, è stata resa stabile mediante un telaio d'acciaio. Oltre a rispettare l'ambiente, è abbastanza stabile da poter essere sollevata e trasportata senza smontarla.

Este edifício servia para acomodar artistas convidados para colaborar com organização de arte municipal "Beyond". A estrutura, feita de painéis sólidos e laminados de macia madeira europeia, foi estabilizada por uma armação em aço. É suficientemente estável para ser levantada e transportada inteira, e é amiga do ambiente.

Denna byggnad tjänade som inackordering för artister som inbjudits till arbete i ramverket för den allmänna konstorganisationen "Beyond". Byggnaden som är gjord av solida laminerade paneler av tall stabiliserades av en stålram. Den är stabil nog för att lyftas och transporteras i ett stycke och är miljövänlig.

19

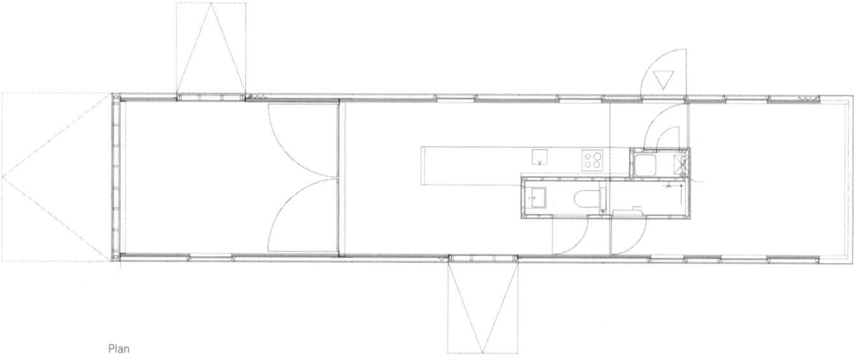

Plan

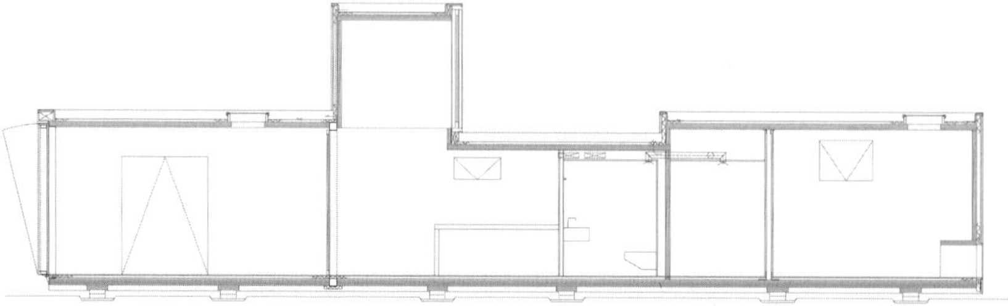

Longitudinal section

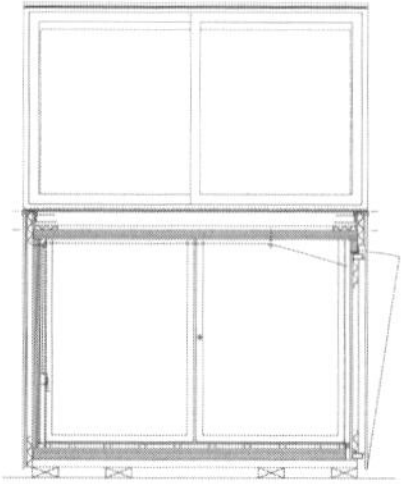

Cross-section

19

J-LOFT

PLYSTUDIO

All existing interior walls of this typical upper floor post war apartment were demolished. The plan is defined by a series of timber boxes arranged in a linear strip and housing storage, built-in seating, work surfaces and stairs. These boxes are constructed from 0.4 in plywood and clad in 0.1 in maple veneer.

Tous les murs intérieurs de cet appartement du dernier étage, typique de l'après-guerre, ont été abattus. Le plan est maintenant défini par une série de boîtes en bois disposées en ligne et contenant la réserve, les sièges incorporés, les plans de travail et les escaliers. Ces boîtes sont construites en contreplaqué de 12 mm et revêtues d'un placage d'érable de 3 mm.

Alle bestehenden Wände dieser für die Nachkriegszeit typischen Dachgeschosswohnung wurden niedergerissen. Das Projekt zeichnet sich durch streifenförmig angeordnete Holzboxen aus, die Speicherraum bieten, als Einbausitzmöbel und Arbeitsoberfläche dienen, und die Funktion von Stiegen erfüllen. Diese Boxen wurden aus 12 mm dickem Sperrholz und 3 mm dickem Ahornfurnier gefertigt.

De binnenmuren van deze bovenwoning werden allemaal afgebroken. Bepalend voor het ontwerp is een serie houten 'dozen', die in een rechte lijn zijn geplaatst en waarin opslagruimten, ingebouwde zitjes, werkruimten en trappen zijn ondergebracht. De dozen werden gemaakt van 12 mm dik multiplex met een 3 mm dikke fineerlaag van ahorn.

Para empezar, se demolieron todas las paredes de este típico piso superior de posguerra. El proyecto se define a partir de una serie de cajas de madera dispuestas en una franja lineal y de contenedores de almacén que componen soportes, superficies de trabajo y escaleras. Estas cajas están realizadas con madera contrachapada de 12 mm y revestidas con chapa de arce de 3 mm.

Per cominciare, sono state demolite le pareti di questo tipico appartamento della post-guerra. Il progetto prende forma mediante una serie di scatole di legno allineate e casse da magazzino, che formano supporti, piani da lavoro e scale. Queste casse sono di legno compensato di 12 mm e ricoperte da una lamina di acero di 3 mm.

Todas as paredes interiores deste típico apartamento no último andar de um edifício pós-guerra foram demolidas. A planta é definida por uma série de caixas de madeira organizadas numa faixa linear e que constituem os arrumos, assentos embutidos, superfícies de trabalho e escadas. Estas caixas foram construídas a partir de contraplacado de 12 mm e revestidas a folheado de ácer de 3 mm.

Alla existerande interiörväggar i denna typiska efterkrigslägenhet demolerades. Planlösningen definieras av en serie timmerlådor arrangerade i en rät linje för förvaring, inbyggda sittmöbler, arbetsytor och trappor. Dessa lådor är byggda av 12 mm plywood och är klädda i 3 mm lönnfanér.

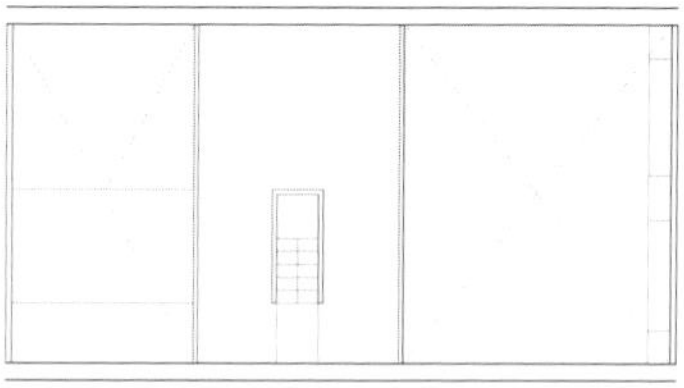

Upper floor plan

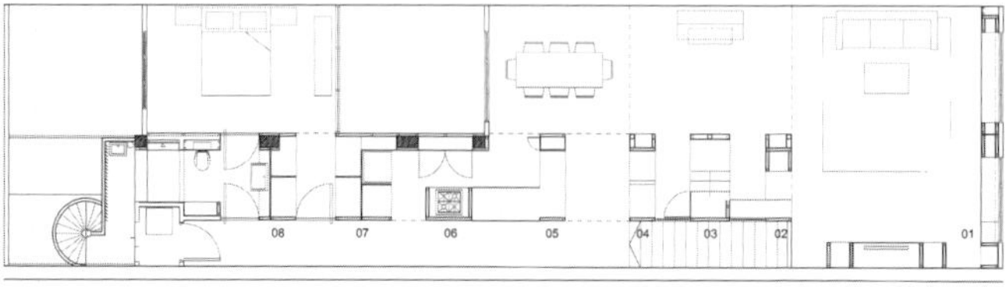

Lower floor plan

VIA APPIA HOUSE

MARIA CLAUDIA CLEMENTE, FRANCESCO ISIDORI, MARCO SARDELLA/LABICS
© Luigi Filetici

According to a specific spatial and functional sequence, vertical axes section the building into the main quarters, the service zones, the distribution areas, and outdoor spaces. The heart of the house is occupied by a broad, full-height vertical void clad on one side with wood slats that serves as a spatial membrane for circulation.

En application d'un ordonnancement spécifique d'espace et de fonction, des axes verticaux découpent le bâtiment en quartier d'habitation, zone de service, secteur de distribution et espaces extérieurs. Le cœur de la maison est occupé par un vaste vide vertical de toute hauteur, revêtu sur un côté de lattes de bois : il joue le rôle de membrane spatiale pour la circulation.

Gemäß der dem Gebäude eigenen räumlichen und funktionellen Unterteilung, trennen es die vertikalen Achsen in Hauptbereich, Servicebereich, Zugangsbereich und Außenbereich. Den Mittelpunkt des Gebäudes bildet ein Leerraum, der auf der einen Seiten mit Holzlatten verkleidet ist und als eine Art Membran die Erschließung ermöglicht.

Op grond van de diverse functies die het gebouw moet vervullen, is het door verticale assen ingedeeld in een hoofdgebouw, dienstvertrekken, distributieruimten en buitenruimten. Het hart van het huis is een vide, met aan één kant een bekleding van latten, als een ruimtelijk membraan waardoor de lucht kan circuleren.

De acuerdo con una secuencia espacial y funcional específica, los ejes verticales dividen el edificio en áreas principales, de servicios, de distribución y en espacios exteriores. El corazón de la casa está ocupado en uno de sus lados por una gran placa vertical de listones de madera que llega hasta el techo y sirve como membrana espacial para la circulación.

Secondo una specifica sequenza spaziale e funzionale, gli assi verticali dividono l'edificio in zone principali, di servizi, di distribuzione e spazi esterni. Il centro della casa ha uno dei lati occupato da un grande rivestimento verticale di listelli di legno che arriva fino al soffitto e serve da membrana per organizzare la circolazione negli spazi.

Respeitando uma sequência espacial e funcional específica, o edifício é dividido por eixos verticais, formando assim diferentes áreas: a parte principal, as zonas de serviço, as áreas de distribuição e os espaços exteriores. O centro da casa é ocupado por um amplo espaço vertical vazio, com a altura do edifício, revestido num dos lados por ripas de madeira que funcionam como uma membrana espacial destinada à circulação.

I enlighet med en specifik spatial och funktionell följd, delar vertikala axlar in byggnaden i huvudfjärdedelarna, servicezonerna, fördelningszonerna och utrymmena utomhus. Husets hjärta upptas av ett brett, vertikalt hål i fullhöjd, på ena sidan klätt med trälameller som fungerar som ett rumsmembran för cirkulation.

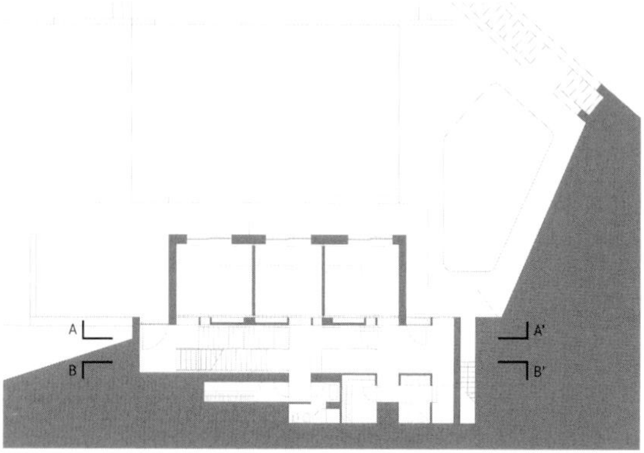

Ground floor plan

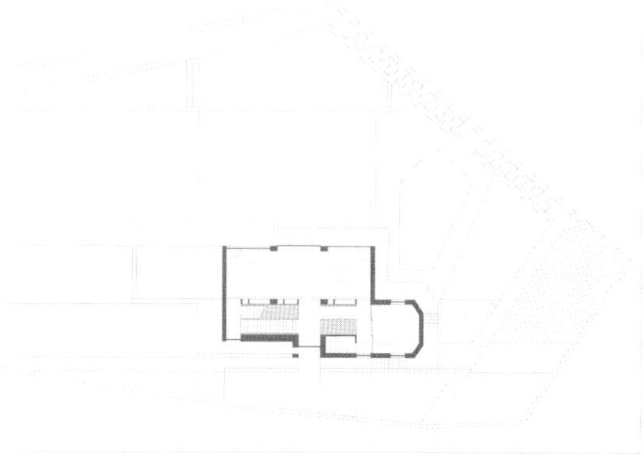

Second floor plan

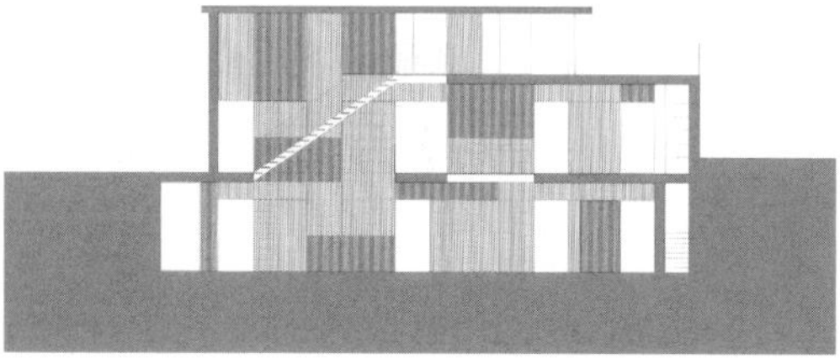

Section A-A'

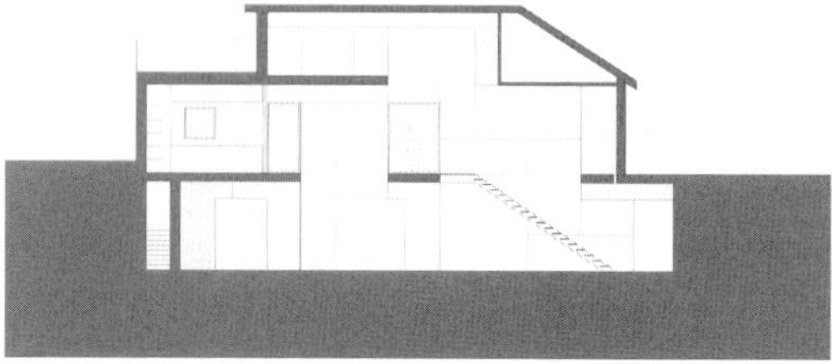

Section B-B'

Holz stellt aufgrund seiner Festigkeit, Wirtschaftlichkeit, Verarbeitbarkeit und Schönheit seit Anbeginn der Geschichte das Baumaterial par excellence dar. Von den Sauna-Hütten in Nordeuropa oder den hoch in den Bergen gelegenen Schutzhütten bis hin zu den modernen, ansprechenden Fertigteilhäusern – Holz hat bewiesen, dass es dem Wandel der Zeit standhalten kann.

Van oudsher is hout het bouwmateriaal bij uitstek. Het is sterk, goedkoop, makkelijk te bewerken en bezit een bijzondere schoonheid. Van de sauna's in Noord-Europa en de hutten hoog in de bergen tot de moderne, prefabwoningen aan toe heeft hout bewezen dat het van alle tijden is.

WOOD CONSTRUCTIONS

CONSTRUCTIONS EN BOIS

HOLZBAUTEN

BOUWEN MET HOUT

Throughout history, wood has been the construction material par excellence due to its strength, economy, workability, and beauty. From the saunas of northern Europe and the high mountain refuges through the modern and appealing prefabricated homes, wood construction has proven it can stand the test of time.

Tout au long de l'histoire, le bois a été le matériau de construction par excellence, en raison de sa solidité, de sa facilité de mise en œuvre et de sa beauté. Des saunas de l'Europe du Nord aux refuges de haute montagne et des cabanes en planches aux modernes maisons préfabriquées, le bois de construction a prouvé qu'il était à l'épreuve du temps.

A lo largo de la historia, la madera ha sido el material constructivo por excelencia debido a su resistencia, economía, docilidad y belleza. Desde las saunas del norte de Europa y los altos refugios de montaña hasta las atractivas y modernas casas prefabricadas, la construcción de madera ha demostrado que puede resistir el paso del tiempo.

Nel corso della storia, il legno è stato il materiale edile per eccellenza in virtù delle sue qualità di resistenza, economia, duttilità e bellezza. Dalle saune del nord Europa e dagli alti rifugi di montagna alle attraenti e moderne case prefabbricate, la costruzione di legno ha dimostrato che può resistere al trascorrere del tempo.

Ao longo da História, a madeira foi o material de construção de eleição, muito por causa da sua resistência, do seu baixo valor económico, da facilidade que oferece a quem o trabalha e da sua beleza. Das saunas do norte da Europa aos refúgios de alta montanha, e também nas modernas e apelativas casas pré-fabricadas, a construção em madeira provou resistir com sucesso à passagem do tempo.

Genom historien har trä varit byggmaterialet framför andra på grund av dess styrka, ekonomi, dess egenskap att låta sig arbetas och dess skönhet. Från norra Europas bastur och tillflyktsorter högt uppe i bergen, till de moderna och tilltalande prefabricerade husen, har träbyggnader bevisat att de kan bestå tidens prövningar.

CONSTRUCCIONES DE MADERA

COSTRUZIONI DI LEGNO

CONSTRUÇÕES EM MADEIRA

TRÄ-KONSTRUKTIONER

BPI COMPUTER OFFICE AND **SHOP**

ALBERTO MOZÓ LEVERINGTON

This office building appears to be slid between two existing houses on the site. The new three-story construction built on a podium, presents a single size of laminated pine timbers as the building's main structural system. This component used for all pillars, beams and a dramatic stair, provides the flexibility of dismantling and reassembling.

Cet immeuble de bureaux semble avoir été « glissé » entre deux maisons existant sur le site. La nouvelle construction à trois niveaux, montée sur un soubassement, offre une seule taille de poutres en pin lamellé-collé pour la structure principale du bâtiment. Ce matériau, utilisé pour tous les piliers, les solives et l'escalier - spectaculaire -, donne à l'ensemble une grande souplesse pour le démontage et le remontage.

Dieses Bürogebäude scheint zwischen zwei bereits existierende Häusern hineingerutscht zu sein. Gleich große Brettschichtholzlatten aus Lärche formen das strukturelle Grundgerüst dieses neuen dreigeschossigen, auf einem Podium errichteten Gebäudes. Durch den ausschließlichen Einsatz eines einzigen Bauelements für Stützen, Balken sowie eine dramatisch anmutende Stiege gestalten sich Errichtung und Demontage dieses Bauwerks sehr leicht.

Het is alsof dit gebouw tussen twee bestaande huizen is geschoven. Het nieuwe gebouw van drie verdiepingen staat op een platform. Het bestaat grotendeels uit even grote gelamineerde grenen delen. Alle zuilen en balken en ook de opvallende trap zijn ervan gemaakt. De delen zijn snel uit elkaar te halen en weer in elkaar te zetten.

Este edificio de oficinas parece estar deslizándose entre dos casas previamente construidas en el solar. La nueva construcción de tres pisos levantada sobre un podio presenta vigas laminadas de pino de tamaño único como sistema estructural principal del edificio. Estos elementos empleados tanto en los pilares como en las vigas y en las espectaculares escaleras tienen la ventaja de que pueden montarse y desmontarse según las necesidades.

Questo edificio per uffici sembra scivolare tra due case costruite in precedenza. La nuova costruzione di tre piani edificata su un basamento presenta grossi tronchi di pino laminato, di una sola misura, come sistema strutturale principale dell'edificio. Questi elementi, utilizzati sia per pilastri sia per travi nonché per le spettacolari scale, hanno il vantaggio che possono essere montati e smontati secondo le esigenze.

Este edifício de escritórios parece ter sido entalado entre duas casas já existentes no local. A nova construção de três andares, erguida num pódio, apresenta uma única medida de madeira de pinheiro laminada como principal sistema estrutural do edifício. Este componente, usado em todos os pilares, vigas e numa escadaria impressionante, garante a flexibilidade necessária para desmontar e voltar a montar.

Denna kontorsbyggnad ser ut att vara inskjuten mellan två redan existerande hus där det är byggt. Den nya trevåningskonstruktionen byggd på ett podium består av lika stora laminerade furustockar vilka agerar som byggnadens huvudsakliga strukturella system. Denna komponent används för alla pelare, balkar och en dramatisk trappa och bidrar till en hög grad av flexibilitet gällande isärplockande och hopsättande.

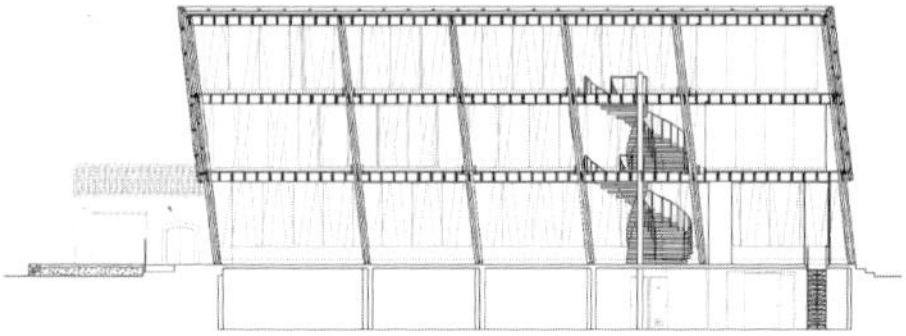

Longitudinal section

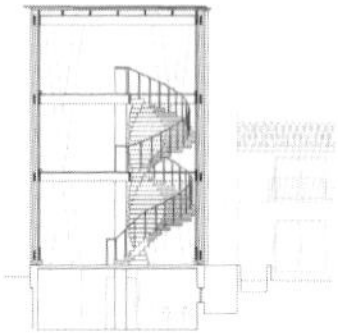

Cross-section

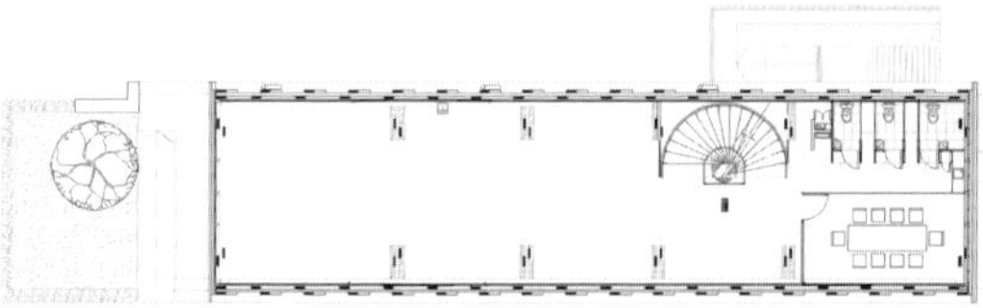

Second floor

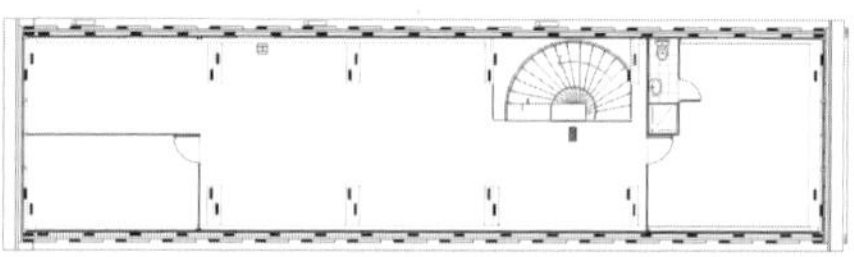

Third floor

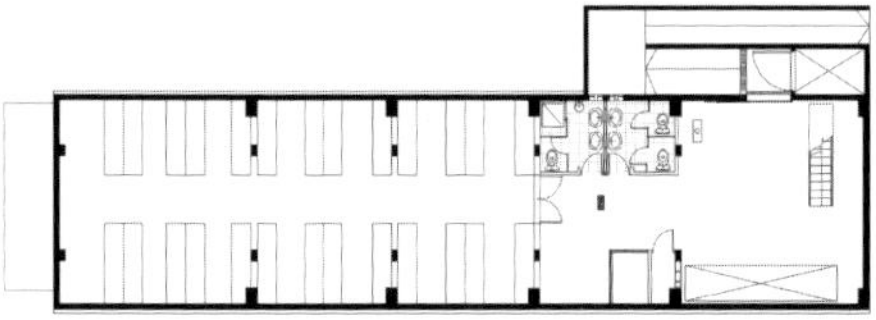

Basement

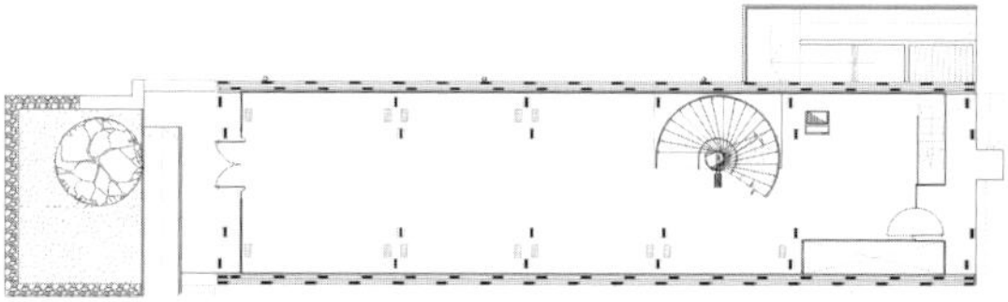

Ground floor

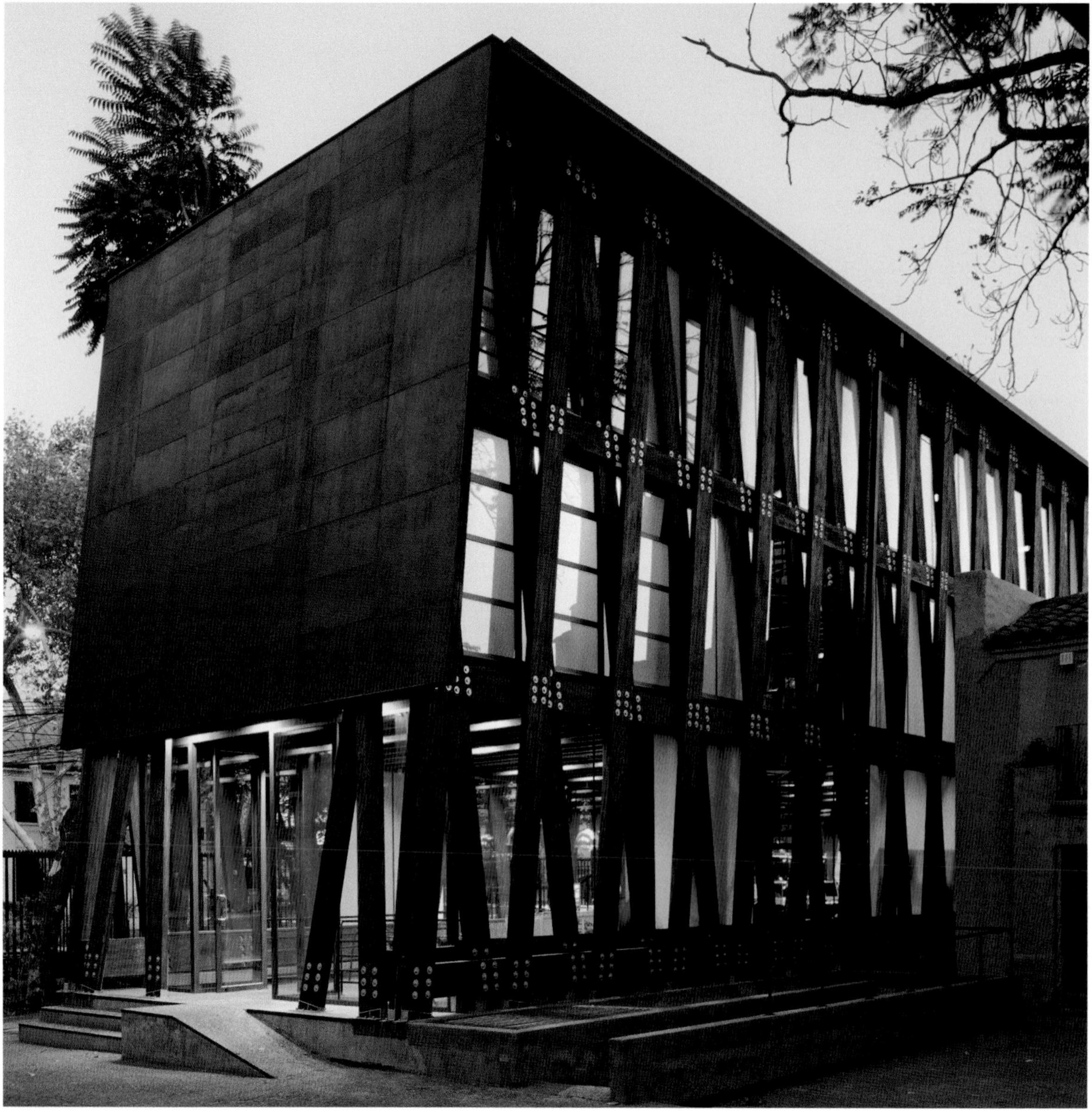

LIBRARY **IN THE GARDEN**

JORGE ARMANDO RODRÍGUEZ BELLO

The library is a wood structure set amongst trees and resting on pilotis that is conceived as an annex; isolated enough to encourage concentration but visually and formally connected to the house. The one-room space is characterized by overhead natural light while the curved walls are lined with rows of bookshelves.

Cette bibliothèque est une structure en bois aménagée parmi les arbres et reposant sur des pilotis. Elle a été conçue comme une annexe : assez à l'écart pour favoriser la concentration, mais visuellement et formellement rattachée à la maison. L'espace à pièce unique est caractérisé par son éclairage zénithal naturel ; les murs incurvés sont garnis de rayonnages pour les livres.

Die Bibliothek besteht aus einer hölzernen, inmitten der Bäume errichteten Struktur und wird von Pilotis (Stützen) getragen, die einen den Bau erweiternden Raum schaffen. Seine Abgeschlossenheit fördert die Konzentration, und doch ist er optisch und formell mit dem Haus verbunden. Das durch die Decke einfallende natürliche Licht beherrscht den als Einzelraum gestalteten Bereich, an dessen runden Wänden die Bücherregale hängen.

Dit houten bouwwerk is op palen tussen de bomen gezet. Het is ontworpen als bijgebouw. Visueel en formeel is het verbonden met het huis, maar het staat geïsoleerd genoeg om er ongestoord te kunnen werken. Het bestaat uit één ruimte, met van boven invallend daglicht. Langs de gebogen wanden zijn boekenplanken aangebracht.

Concebida como un anexo, esta biblioteca es una estructura de madera situada entre árboles y apoyada sobre unos pilotes; a pesar de haber sido aislada para estimular la concentración, no ha perdido por ellos el contacto visual y formal con la casa. El espacio de una sola habitación se caracteriza por una iluminación natural interior mientras que las paredes curvas están cubiertas de estantes con libros.

Concepita come un edificio annesso, questa biblioteca è una struttura di legno situata tra gli alberi e appoggiata su pali; sebbene sia stata costruita isolata per stimolare la concentrazione, non per questo ha perduto il contatto visivo e formale con la casa. Lo spazio costituito da una sola stanza è caratterizzato da un'illuminazione naturale interna mentre le pareti curve sono coperte da mensole con libri.

Esta biblioteca consiste numa estrutura de madeira, instalada entre árvores e assente sobre *pilotis*, que foi concebida como um anexo - suficientemente isolada para fomentar a concentração mas visual e formalmente ligada à casa. O espaço, com uma divisão apenas, caracteriza-se pela entrada de luz natural através do telhado, apresentando paredes curvas repletas de estantes de livros.

Biblioteket är en trästruktur placerad bland träd och som vilar på stöttor. Det utgör ett annex; tillräckligt isolerat för att uppmuntra koncentrationen, men visuellt och formellt sammanbundet med huset. Enrumsutrymmet karaktäriseras av naturligt ljus ovanifrån medan de kurviga väggarna är randade av rader med bokhyllor.

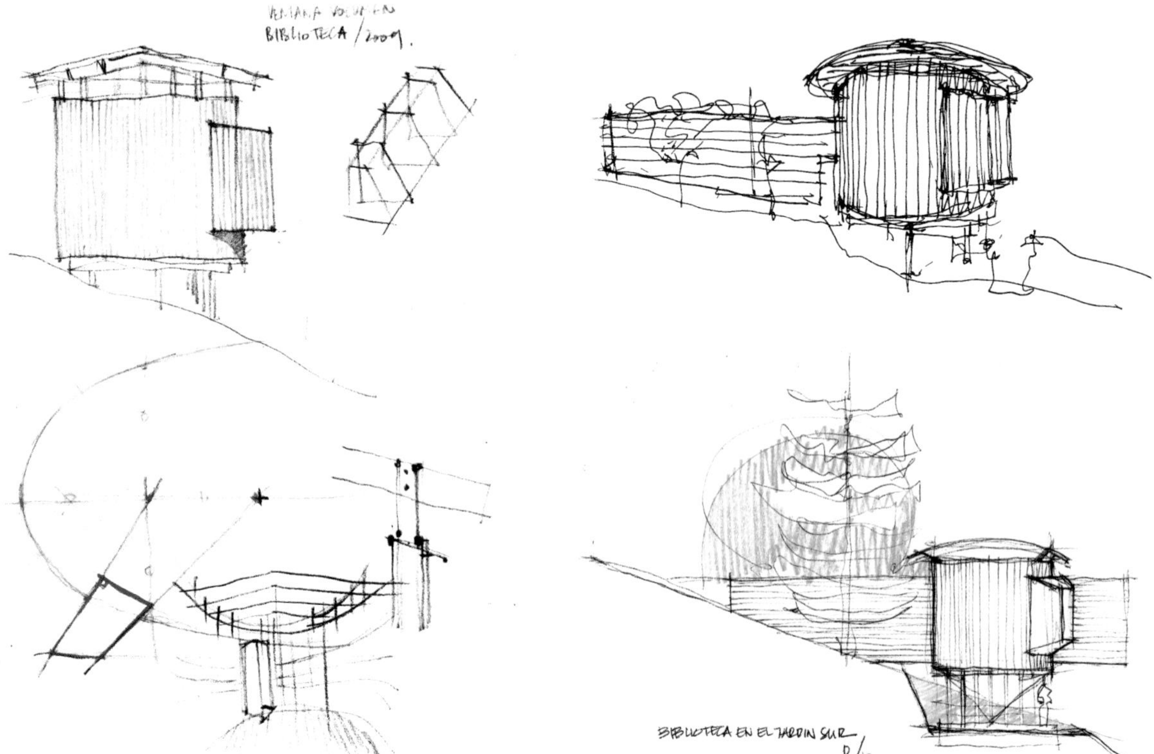

Design sketches

SCHWITZKASTEN SAUNA PAVILION

NAUMANN ARCHITEKTUR
© David Franck

This garden pavilion houses a sauna, a bathroom and storage space for garden tools. It consists of a cedar volume on top of a platform of the same material subdivided in three sections: two at each end are opaque, the third, in the middle is opened on two sides, but protected with glass sliding doors.

Ce pavillon de jardin abrite un sauna, une salle de bain et un espace de stockage pour les outils de jardinage. Il s'agit d'un volume de cèdre posé au sommet d'une plateforme du même matériau, divisée en trois sections : les deux de l'extrémité sont aveugles ; la troisième, au milieu, est ouverte sur deux côtés mais protégée par des portes en verre coulissantes.

Dieser Gartenpavillon beherbergt eine Sauna, ein Badezimmer und einen Speicherraum für Gartenwerkzeuge. Die Zedernholzkonstruktion wurde auf einer Plattform aus demselben Material errichtet, sie ist in drei Abschnitte geteilt: Die beiden Abschnitte an den Außenseiten sind undurchsichtig , wohingegen der in der Mitte gelegene Abschnitt auf beiden Seiten durchsichtig ist und durch Glaswände von der Außenwelt abgeschirmt wird.

Dit paviljoen herbergt een sauna, een badkamer en een opbergruimte voor tuingereedschap. Het is van cederhout en staat op een platform van hetzelfde materiaal. Het is in drieën verdeeld: twee dichte ruimten opzij met daartussen een ruimte die aan beide kanten open is, maar afgesloten kan worden met glazen schuifdeuren.

Este pabellón de jardín alberga una sauna, una cabina de ducha y aseo y un almacén para el equipamiento del jardín. Se trata de un prisma de madera de cedro de planta rectangular, dispuesto sobre una plataforma del mismo material y subdividido transversalmente en tres secciones: dos laterales compactas y una central abierta en dos de sus lados, pero protegida con puertas correderas de cristal transparente.

Questa padiglione da giardino contiene una sauna, una cabina per doccia e toilette e un ripostiglio per gli attrezzi da giardinaggio. Si tratta di un prisma di legno di cedro a pianta rettangolare, posto su una piattaforma dello stesso materiale e suddiviso trasversalmente in tre sezioni: due laterali compatte e una centrale con due lati aperti, ma protetta mediante porte scorrevoli di vetro trasparente.

Este pavilhão de jardim inclui uma sauna, uma casa de banho e um espaço de arrumos para as ferramentas de jardinagem. É constituído por um volume em cedro sobre uma plataforma do mesmo material subdividida em três secções: as duas da ponta são opacas, a terceira, no meio, é aberta para ambos os lados, mas protegida por portas deslizantes em vidro.

Denna trädgårdspaviljong hyser en bastu, ett badrum och ett förvaringsutrymme för trädgårdsredskap. Det består av en volym av ceder ovanpå en plattform av samma material, indelad i tre sektioner: två vid varje ände är opaka, den tredje i mitten är öppen på två sidor, men skyddas av skjutdörrar i glas.

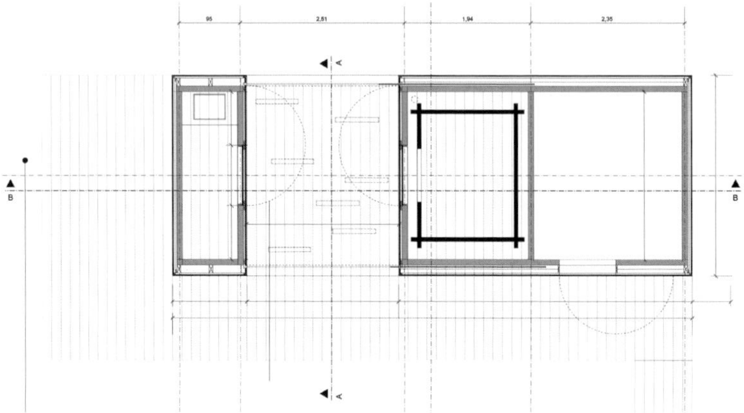

Floor plan

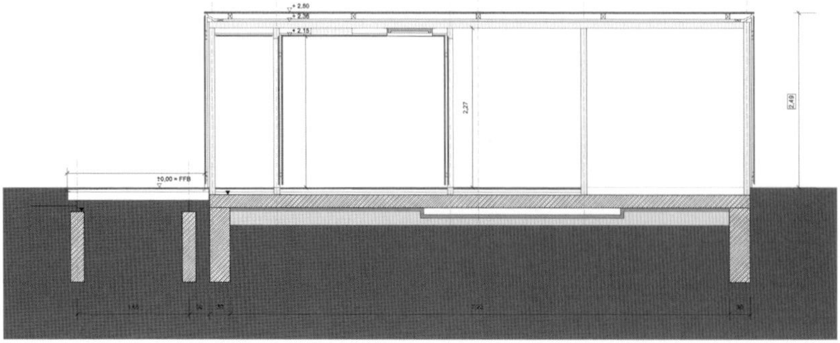

Section B-B

PATH **OF THE SENSES**

ARCHITEKTURBÜRO MATTHIAS LOEBERMANN

Path of the Senses is an exhibit space part in a larger building for Baufritz, a home building company specializing in the construction of ecologically friendly homes. The path is intended to show the costumers the sensual qualities of wood. Color, texture, sound and smell are elements that have generated the architecture of the space.

Path of the Senses est un espace d'exposition intégré à un bâtiment plus grand pour le compte de Baufritz GmbH, société bavaroise spécialisée dans la construction de maisons respectueuses de l'environnement. Le « passage » est destiné à montrer aux clients les qualités sensuelles du bois. Couleur, texture, son et odeur sont les éléments qui ont engendré l'architecture de cet espace.

Der Schauraum mit dem Namen „Weg der Sinne" befindet sich in einem größeren Gebäude für Baufritz, ein Wohnungsbau-unternehmen, das sich auf die Errichtung umweltfreundlicher Häuser spezialisiert hat. Der Weg soll dem Kunden die sinnlichen Qualitäten von Holz näher bringen. Die Architektur des Raums mit ihren Farben, Texturen, Klängen und Gerüchen regt unsere Sinne an.

Het 'Pad van de Zintuigen' is een expositieruimte in een groot gebouw voor Baufritz, een woningbouwbedrijf dat gespecialiseerd is in de bouw van milieuvriendelijke woningen. Het pad is bedoeld om de klanten te laten zien, horen, ruiken en voelen wat hout is. Kleur, structuur, geluid en geur waren bepalend voor de inrichting van de ruimte.

La Senda de los Sentidos es una parte de un espacio expositivo situada en el interior de un edificio más grande de Baufritz, una empresa constructora de viviendas especializada en la edificación de casas ecológicas. El camino ha sido concebido para mostrar a los clientes las cualidades sensuales de la madera. El color, la textura, el sonido y el olor son algunos de los elementos que han suscitado la arquitectura del espacio.

Il Percorso dei Sensi è parte di uno spazio espositivo situato all'interno di un edificio più grande di Baufritz, una ditta edile specializzata nella realizzazione di case ecologiche. Il percorso è stato concepito appositamente per mostrare ai clienti le qualità sensibili del legno. Il colore, la texture, il suono e l'odore sono alcuni degli elementi da cui è scaturito il progetto architettonico di questo spazio.

Path of Senses é um espaço expositivo integrado num edifício de grande escala da Baufritz, uma empresa especializada na construção de casas ecológicas. O percurso ("path") visa apresentar aos clientes as qualidades sensuais da madeira, tendo a cor, a textura, o som e os cheiros assumido um papel de destaque na arquitectura deste espaço.

Sinnenas Stig är ett utställningsutrymme i en del av en större byggnad till Baufritz, ett husbyggnadsföretag som är specialiserat på konstruktion av ekovänliga hem. Stigen är tänkt att visa kunderna träets sinnliga kvaliteter. Färg, struktur, ljud och doft är element som har gett upphov till utrymmets arkitektur.

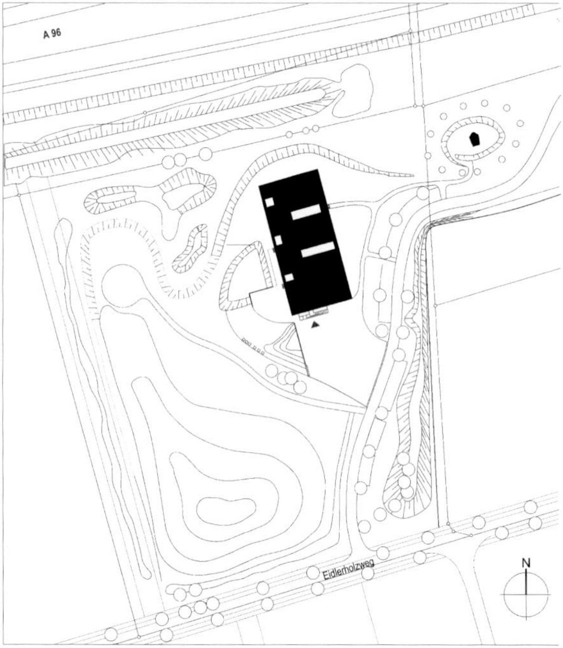

Site plan

1. Foyer
2. Reception
3. Office
4. Archive
5. Shop
6. Bar
7. Kitchen
8. Storage
9. Checkroom
10. Courtyard
11. Path of the Senses
12. Restrooms
13. Handicapped accessible restroom
14. Japanese garden
15. Conference room
16. Children's playroom
17. Relaxation room
18. "Welle"
19. Exhibition space
20. Science park
21. Information and equipment
22. Green courtyard

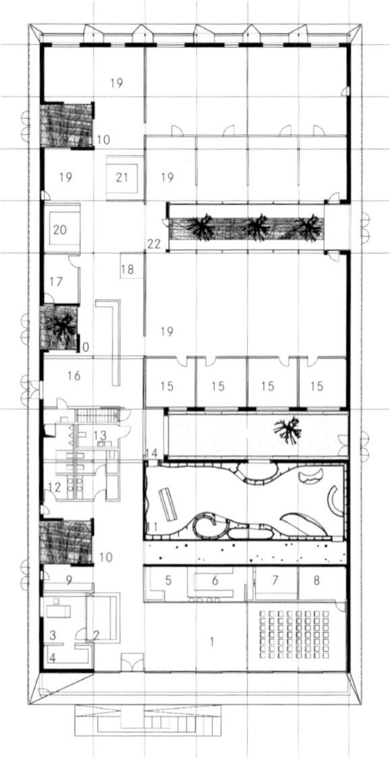

Floor plan

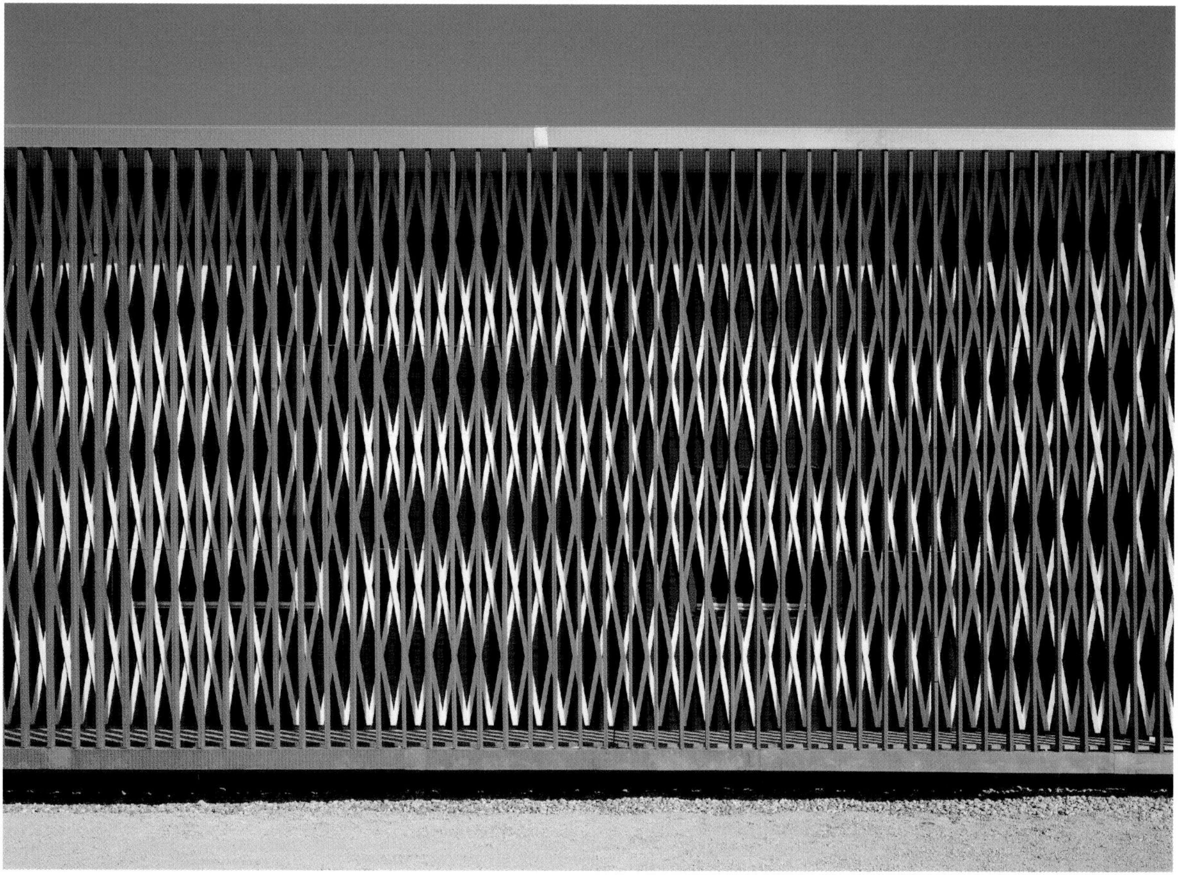

in Raum definiert sich
cht nur durch seine Geometrie
ondern durch das Lebensgefühl
as er uns vermittelt

REMODEL AND EXPANSION OF A SCHOOL

ZANDERROTH ARCHITEKTEN
© Andrea Kroth

The existing school consists of various detached buildings. The project expands the existing modular school rather than adding another separate structure in order to provide the existing building with an urban presence. A seamless curtain-wall facing made of wicker wraps the existing building and the two annexes to generate a unified exterior.

L'école existante avait un plan en H, avec deux cours. La proposition d'extension modulaire conçue par les architectes confère au bâtiment une stature urbaine. Une enveloppe continue autour des bâtiments préexistants et des deux nouvelles annexes crée une seule structure unifiée. Cette liaison est assurée par un mur-rideau en osier tressé.

Das ursprüngliche Schulgebäude war H-förmig und hatte zwei Innenhöfe. Der Entwurf des Architekten erweitert die modular aufgebaute, bestehende Schule und verleiht ihr so ein urbanes Erscheinungsbild. Eine nahtlose Verkleidung umhüllt die ursprünglich bestehenden Gebäude und die beiden Neubauten und lässt sie als eine Einheit erscheinen. Bei der Verkleidung handelt es sich um eine Vorhangfassade aus Weide.

De bestaande school was H-vormig en had twee binnenpleinen. In het uitbreidingsvoorstel van de architect kreeg het complex een steeds aanzien. Rondom de bestaande gebouwen en twee bijgebouwen werd een bekleding van vlechtwerk aangebracht, die het geheel als een gordijn omsluit en de eenheid ervan versterkt.

La escuela existente tenía forma de H y disponía de dos patios. La propuesta de los arquitectos para ampliar la escuela modular ya existente proporciona al edificio una presencia urbana. Gracias a un revestimiento continuo alrededor de los edificios ya existentes y dos nuevos anexos consiguieron crear una única estructura. El material de unión consiste en un muro-cortina de mimbre.

La vecchia scuola presentava una forma ad H e aveva due cortili. La proposta degli architetti per ampliare la preesistente scuola modulare conferisce all'edificio una presenza urbana. Grazie a un rivestimento continuo intorno ai volumi e a due nuove dipendenze, sono riusciti a creare una unica struttura. Il materiale utilizzato per la cortina che unisce il complesso è il vimini.

A escola existente tinha a forma de um H com dois pátios. A proposta do arquitecto para a expandir o edifício modular já existente confere-lhe uma presença urbana. O revestimento homogéneo em torno dos edifícios existentes e dos dois anexos cria uma estrutura única. O material de ligação consiste numa parede-cortina de trabalho em verga.

Den existerande skolan var formad som ett H med två gårdsplaner. Arkitekternas förslag att bygga ut den existerande modulärskolan förser byggnaden med en urban närvaro. En sömlös panel runt de existerande byggnaderna och två nya annex skapar en enda struktur. Länkningsmaterialet består av en gardinvägg byggd av vidjor.

Illustration of remodel and expansion process

Before the intervention

After the intervention

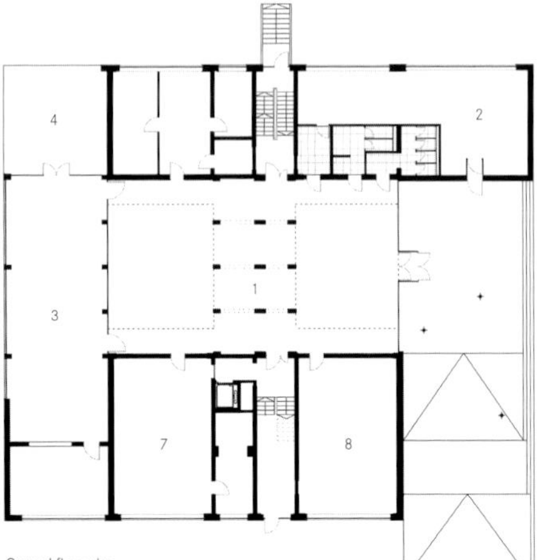

Ground floor plan

1. Foyer
2. Library
3. Cafeteria
4. Terrace
5. Atrium
6. Gallery
7. Classroom
8. Teachers' room

Second floor plan

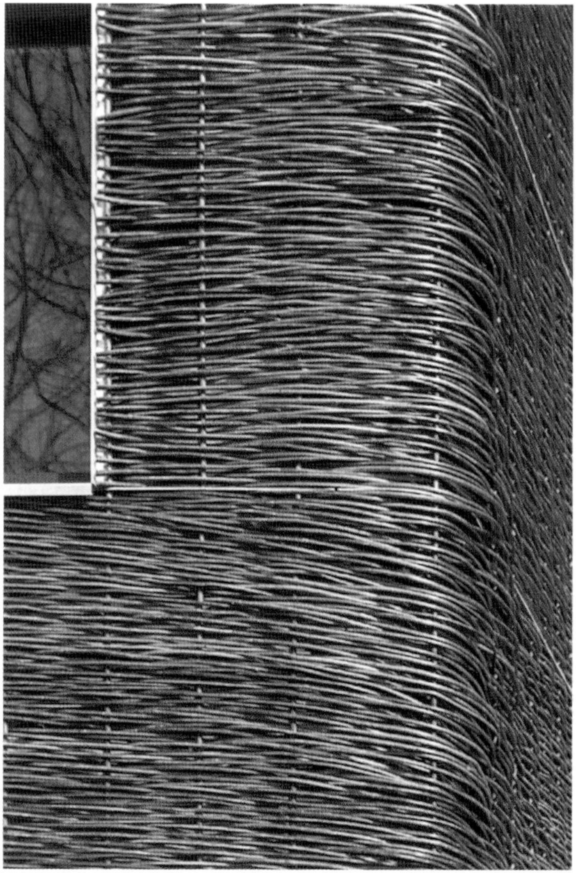

MARITIME YOUTH HOUSE

PLOT = BIG + JDS ARCHITECTS

Two different users had to share the facility: a sailing club and a youth center. The building consists of wood platform built high enough to allow for boat storage underneath while providing an undulating landscape for the kids to run and play above. The presence of hard surfaces used on the interior is meant to contrast with the wooden exterior.

Deux utilisateurs différents avaient à se partager les lieux : un club de voile et un centre de jeunes. Le bâtiment se compose d'une plateforme en bois construite assez haut pour permettre de ranger les bateaux au-dessous, tout en fournissant aux jeunes une aire de jeux et d'activités. La présence de surfaces en ciment à l'intérieur est destinée à créer un contraste avec l'extérieur en bois.

Das Gebäude wird von zwei Einrichtungen genutzt: einem Segelklub und einem Jugendzentrum. Das Bauwerk besteht aus einer hölzernen Plattform, die so hoch gebaut wurde, dass Boote darunter anlegen können, und die den Kindern außerdem eine wellenförmige Spielwiese zum Toben bietet. Die harten Oberflächen des Innenraums stellen einen bewussten Kontrast zu dem in Holz ausgeführten Außenraum dar.

Dit gebouw is een zeilclub en jeugdcentrum tegelijk. Er is een houten platform aangelegd, dat hoog genoeg is om de boten eronder te bergen en aan de bovenkant is omgetoverd tot een golvend landschap, waar kinderen kunnen spelen en rondrennen. Als contrast met de houten buitenkant bezit het interieur harde oppervlakken.

Dos tipos de usuarios diferentes iban a compartir la instalación: un club de vela y un centro juvenil. La construcción consiste en una plataforma de madera ondulante por donde los chavales puedan correr y jugar, levantada lo suficientemente arriba como para permitir el amarre de las embarcaciones. Las superficies duras empleadas en el interior de la instalación tienen como finalidad contrastar con la madera omnipresente en el exterior.

Questo impianto è stato pensato per due tipi differenti di utenti: un club di vela e un centro giovanile. L'edificio è formato da una piattaforma di legno "collinosa" su cui i bambini possono correre e giocare, posta a un'altezza sufficiente da permettere l'ormeggio delle imbarcazioni. La presenza di superfici dure all'interno del centro ha lo scopo di creare un contrasto con il legno onnipresente all'esterno.

As instalações destinavam-se a ser partilhadas por dois utilizadores diferentes: um clube de vela e um centro de juventude. O edifício consiste numa plataforma de madeira, construída a uma altura suficiente para permitir o armazenamento dos barcos no espaço inferior, criando, simultaneamente, uma paisagem ondulante, sobre a qual as crianças correm e brincam. A presença das superfícies duras usadas no interior tem como objectivo contrastar com o exterior em madeira.

Två olika användare var tvungna att dela på fastigheten: En seglingsklubb och ett ungdomscenter. Byggnaden består av en träplattform byggd hög nog för att tillåta båtförvaring på undersidan medan ett böljande landskap skapats på ovansidan där barnen kan springa och leka. Närvaron av hårda ytor använda till interiören är menade att kontrastera med träexteriören.

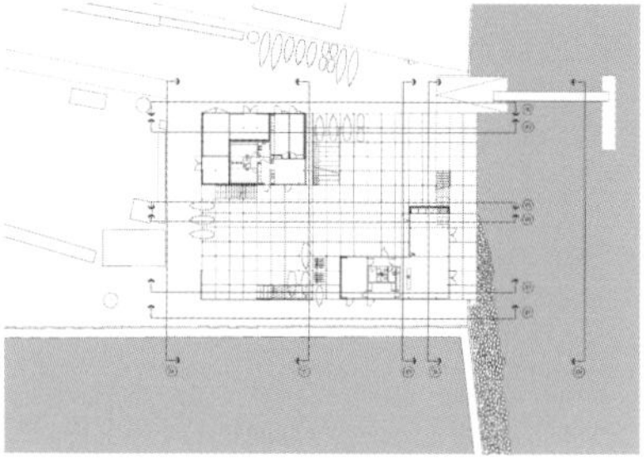

Floor plan

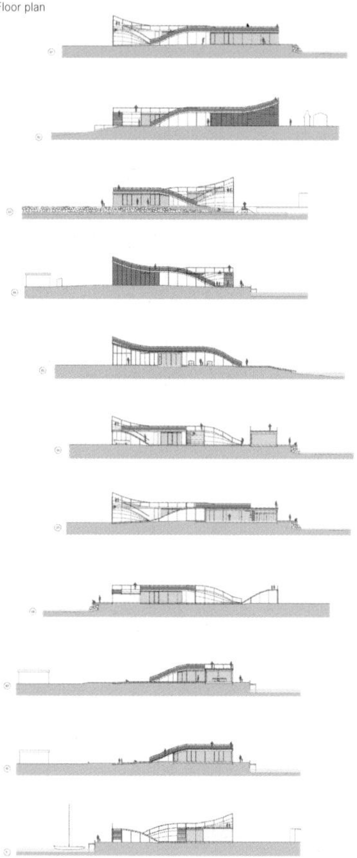

Sections

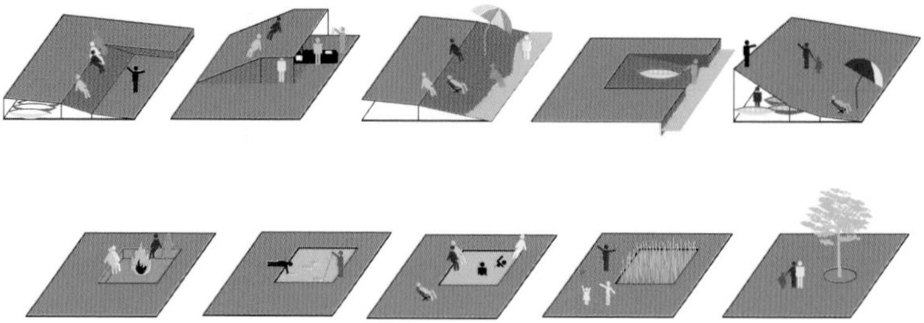

Diagrams of activities

Diagrams of design development

RUCKSACK HOUSE

STEFAN EBERSTADT

This temporary project is a cube suspended on the façade of any building by steel cables. The construction is made of steel clad in exterior grade plywood with an absorbent resin punctuated with Plexiglas inserts. The inside is clad with birch plywood and parts of the walls unfold to expose a desk, a bed and shelves.

Cette structure temporaire est un cube accrochable sur la façade de n'importe quel bâtiment, au moyen de câbles d'acier. La construction elle-même est en acier habillé extérieurement de contreplaqué de qualité, renforcé par une résine absorbante et ponctué d'inserts en plexiglas. L'intérieur est revêtu de contreplaqué de bouleau. Des portions de mur se déploient pour révéler un bureau, un lit et des étagères.

Der je nach Bedarf vor die Außenfassade eines beliebigen Gebäudes zu hängende Würfel wird von Stahlkabeln getragen. Die Stahlkonstruktion ist außenseitig mit qualitativ hochwertigem Sperrholz mit einer absorbierenden Harzbeschichtung ausgeführt und mit Plexiglaseinsätzen durchsetzt. Der Innenraum ist mit Birkensperrholz verkleidet. Teile der Wände lassen sich zu einem Bett, einem Tisch und Regalen auffalten.

Deze kubus kan met stalen kabels aan de gevel van een willekeurig gebouw worden gehangen. Het gelaagde hout aan de buitenkant van de stalen constructie is met hars behandeld. Er zitten ramen van plexiglas in. Van de met berkentriplex beklede binnenwand kunnen delen uitgeklapt worden tot een bureau, een bed en planken.

Este proyecto temporal consiste en un cubo suspendido sobre la fachada de cualquier edificio mediante unos cables de acero. La construcción está hecha de acero revestido externamente de madera contrachapada y una resina absorbente con insertos de plexiglas. El interior está revestido con madera contrachapada de abedul y algunas partes de las paredes se despliegan para poner al descubierto un escritorio, una cama y algunas estanterías.

Questo progetto effimero consiste in un cubo appeso sulla facciata di qualsiasi edificio mediante cavi d'acciaio. La costruzione è fatta d'acciaio ricoperto all'esterno di compensato con una resina assorbente costellata da inserti di Plexiglas. L'interno è foderato di legno compensato di betulla e alcune parti delle pareti si possono aprire per rivelare una scrivania, un letto e alcune mensole.

Este projecto temporário consiste num cubo que pode ser suspenso na fachada de um qualquer edifício por cabos de aço. A construção é feita de aço, revestido no exterior por contraplacado de qualidade coberto com resina absorvente e interrompido por inserções em Plexiglas. O interior é revestido de contraplacado de bétula e algumas partes das paredes abrem-se expondo uma secretária, uma cama e prateleiras.

Detta tillfälliga projekt är en kub upphängd på fasaden till vilken byggnad som helst med hjälp av stålkablar. Konstruktionen är gjord av stålpaneler och exteriörplywood med en absorberande resin punkterad av plexiglasinfattningar. Insidan är klädd med plywood i björk och delar av väggarna kan vikas ut för att användas som skrivbord, säng och hyllor.

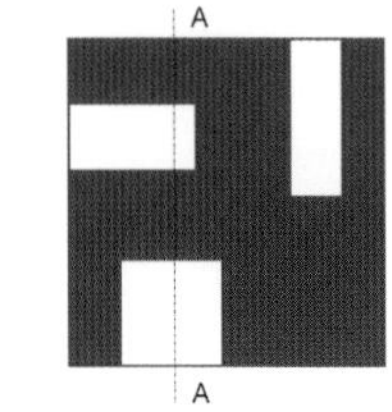

Front elevation

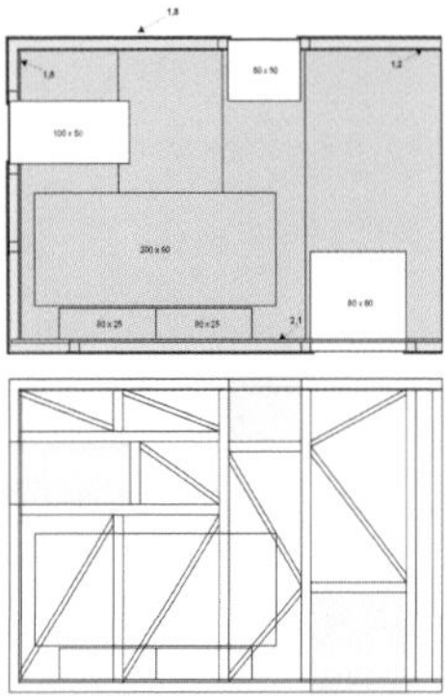

Vertical section A-A and framing plan

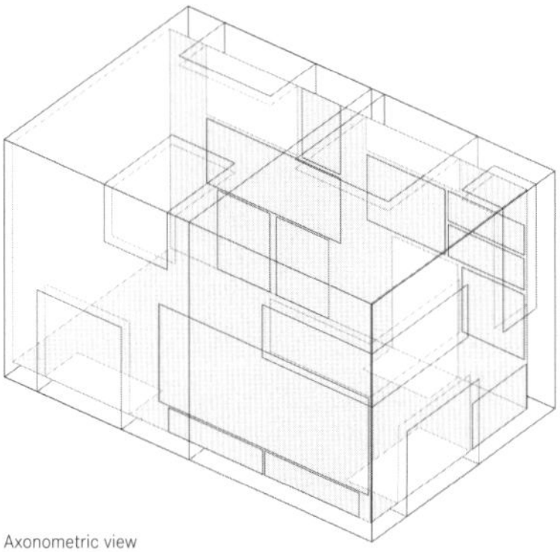

Axonometric view

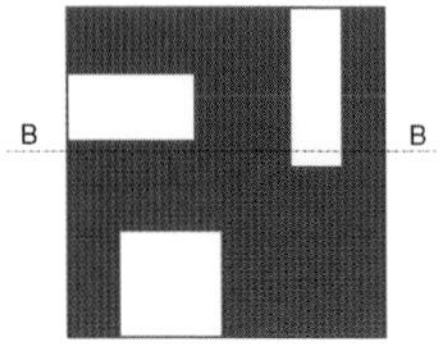

Front elevation

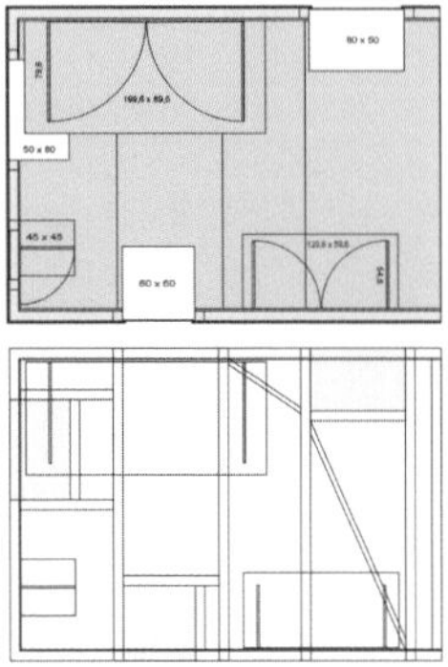

Horizontal section B-B and framing plan

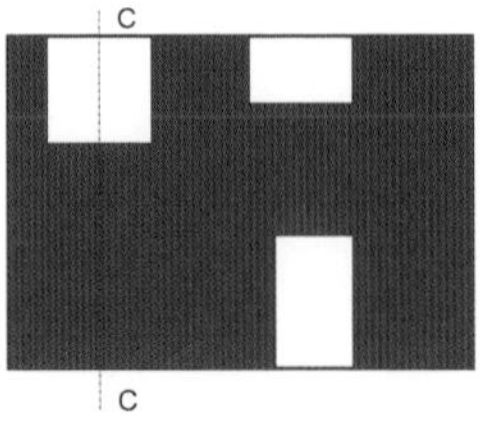

Side elevation

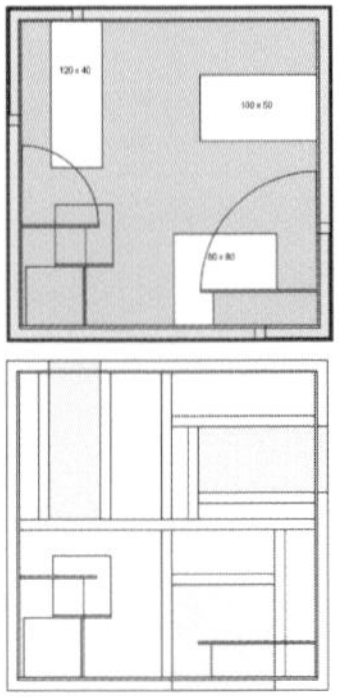

Vertical section C-C and framing plan

STABRAUM PAVILION

ARCHITEKTURBÜRO MATTHIAS LOEBERMANN

A path is proposed in the pavilion that plays with the idea of continuity and change. Continuity is achieved trough the material (40 × 80 mm wood slats) and the pathway itself. Change is experienced by the evolving geometry of the pavilion that sets up dualities such as order and disorder, light and shadow, movement and stability.

Un parcours est proposé dans ce pavillon conçu par Matthias Loebermann à Biberach (Allemagne), qui joue avec l'idée de continuité et de changement. La continuité est obtenue au moyen du matériau (des lattes de bois de 40 × 80 cm) et du parcours lui-même. On fait l'expérience du changement via l'évolution de la géométrie du pavillon, qui instaure des séries de contrastes tels qu'ordre et désordre, ombre et lumière, mouvement et stabilité, etc.

Der durch den Pavillon führende Weg weckt Gedanken an Kontinuität und Wandel. Die Kontinuität wird durch den Weg selbst und das verwendete Material (40 × 80 cm große Holzbretter) vermittelt, wohingegen der Wandel in der sich entfaltenden Geometrie des Pavillons zum Ausdruck kommt, die Gegensätze wie Ordnung und Chaos, Licht und Schatten, Bewegung und Stabilität widerspiegelt.

In het paviljoen moet een pad komen dat speelt met de begrippen continuïteit en verandering. Continuïteit wordt bereikt door het materiaal (houten latten van 40 × 80 cm) en het pad zelf. Verandering wordt ervaren door de wisselende geometrie van het paviljoen, dat licht en schaduw, beweging en stabiliteit tegenover elkaar stelt.

Con este proyecto se propone un recorrido que juega con la idea del cambio y la continuidad. Mientras la continuidad se logra a través del material (listones de madera de 40 × 80 cm de sección), las uniones y el recorrido mismo, el cambio se experimenta por medio de la geometría evolutiva del pabellón que crea dualidades como orden y desorden, luz y sombra, movimiento y estabilidad.

Con questo progetto si propone un tragitto che gioca con l'idea del cambiamento e della continuità. Se la continuità si ottiene mediante il materiale (listelli di legno di 40 × 80 mm), le unioni e il tragitto stesso, il cambiamento si sperimenta per mezzo della geometria evolutiva del padiglione che crea dualismi oppositivi come ordine e disordine, luce e ombra, movimento e stabilità.

Este pavilhão propõe um percurso que joga com as ideias opostas de continuidade e mudança. A continuidade é assegurada através do material (ripas de madeira com 40 × 80 cm) e do próprio caminho, enquanto a mudança se sente na geometria do pavilhão, em constante mutação, criando, assim, várias dualidades - ordem e desordem, luz e sombra, movimento e estabilidade.

En stig, som leker med idén om kontinuitet och förändring, är tänkt i paviljongen. Kontinuitet uppnås genom materialet (trälameller 40 × 80 mm) och genom själva stigen. Förändring upplevs genom paviljongens utvecklande geometri som ställer upp dualiteter som ordning och kaos, ljus och skugga och rörelse och stabilitet.

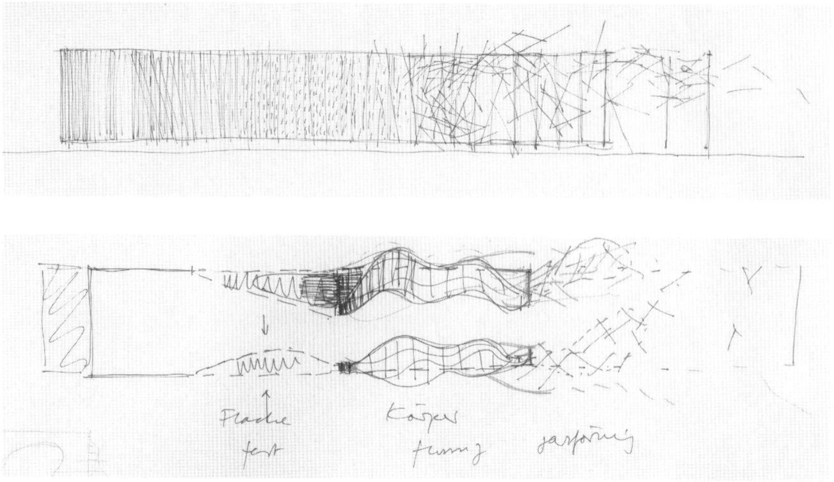

Sketches

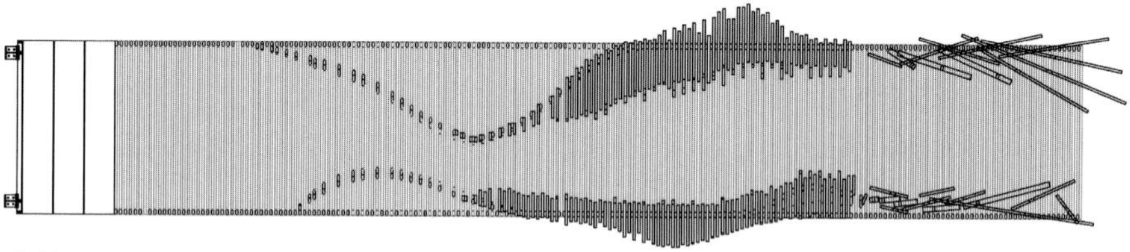

Roof plan

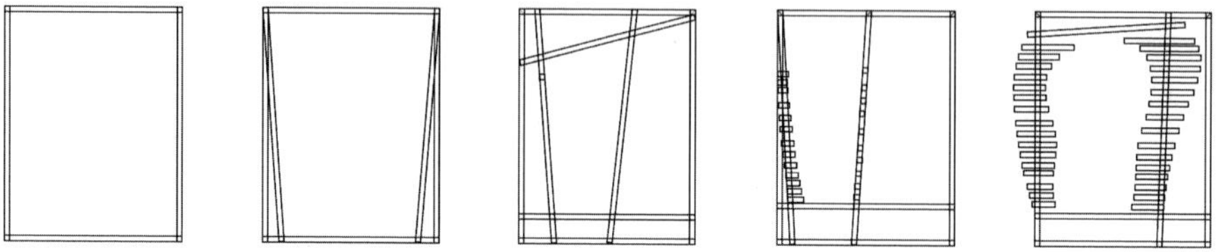

Cross-sections

PALLET PAVILION

ARCHITEKTURBÜRO MATTHIAS LOEBERMANN
© Landesbeirat Holz Bayern

The pavilion was designed as a meeting point for all the participants in the Ski World Cup in 2005. The organic shaped structure measured 6 m tall by 8 m wide and 18 m long and was composed of 1,300 recycled pallets. The structure was disassembled once the event was over and the pallets were available again for other uses.

Ce pavillon a également été conçu par Matthias Loebermann. Il a servi de lieu de rencontre aux participants à la Coupe mondiale de ski en 2005. La structure en bois seul mesurait 6 m de hauteur pour 8 m de largeur et 18 m de longueur ; elle était composée de 1300 palettes recyclables (qui donnaient leur nom au pavillon). Une fois l'événement terminé, la structure a été démontée et les palettes ont été récupérées pour d'autres usages.

Der Pavillon wurde als Treffpunkt für alle Teilnehmer des Ski World Cups 2005 konzipiert. Die organisch geformte Struktur ist sechs Meter hoch und acht Meter breit, bei einer Länge von 18 Metern. Sie wurde aus 1300 wiederverwerteten Paletten erbaut und nach Beendigung der Veranstaltung wieder demontiert, sodass die Paletten für andere Zwecke eingesetzt werden konnten.

Het paviljoen werd ontworpen als ontmoetingsplaats voor de deelnemers aan de Ski World Cup in 2005. Het organisch gevormde bouwwerk was 6 m hoog, 8 m breed en 18 m lang en bestond uit 1300 gerecyclede pallets. Na het evenement werd het paviljoen afgebroken en kwamen de pallets weer beschikbaar voor ander gebruik.

El pabellón se planeó como punto de encuentro para los participantes de la Copa del Mundo de Esquí en 2005. Compuesto por 1.300 pallets reciclados, representaba una forma orgánica de 6 metros de alto por 8 metros de ancho y 18 metros longitud. Una vez concluido el evento, se desmontó la estructura y los pallets se reciclaron para destinarlos a otros posibles usos.

Il padiglione venne concepito come un punto d'incontro per i partecipanti alla Coppa del Mondo di Sci nel 2005. Costruito mediante 1.300 pallet riciclati, era una forma organica di 6 metri d'altezza per 8 metri di larghezza e 18 metri di lunghezza. Una volta terminato l'evento, la struttura venne smontata e i pallet furono nuovamente riciclati per altri possibili usi.

Este pavilhão foi concebido como ponto de encontro dos participantes na Taça do Mundo de esqui alpino em 2005. A estrutura, que se distingue pela sua forma orgânica, apresentava 6 m de altura, 8 m de largura e 18 m de comprimento e era composta por 1300 paletes recicladas. No final do evento, a estrutura integral foi desmontada e as paletes voltaram a ser utilizadas para outros fins.

Paviljongen designades som en mötesplats för deltagarna i världscupen i skidor 2005. Den organiskt formade strukturen mätte 6 m på höjden, 8 m på bredden och 18 m på längden och var sammansatt av 1300 återvunna pallar. Strukturen togs isär när evenemanget var över och pallarna var åter tillgängliga för andra användningsområden.

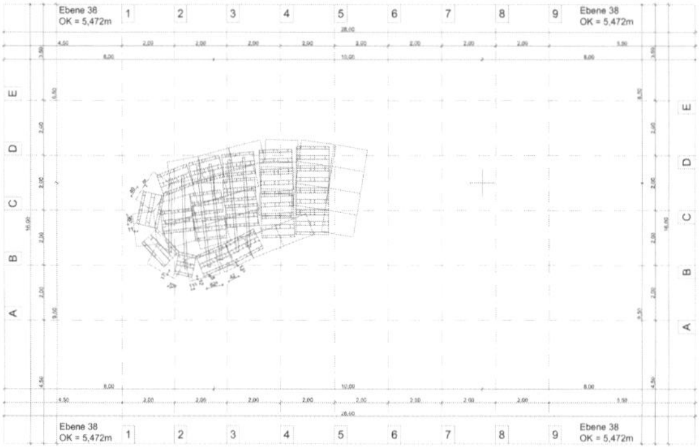

Location plan

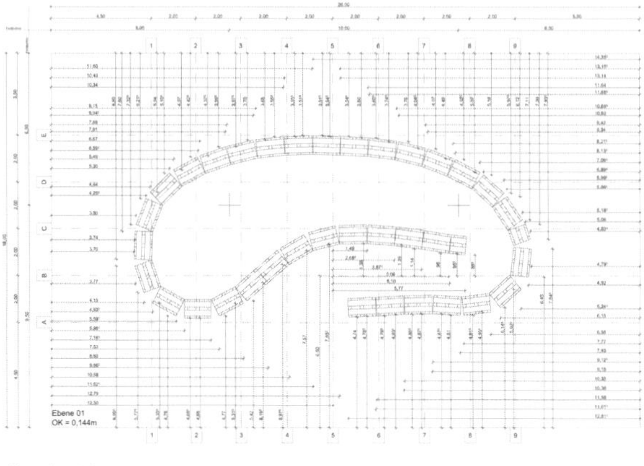

Dimensioned plan

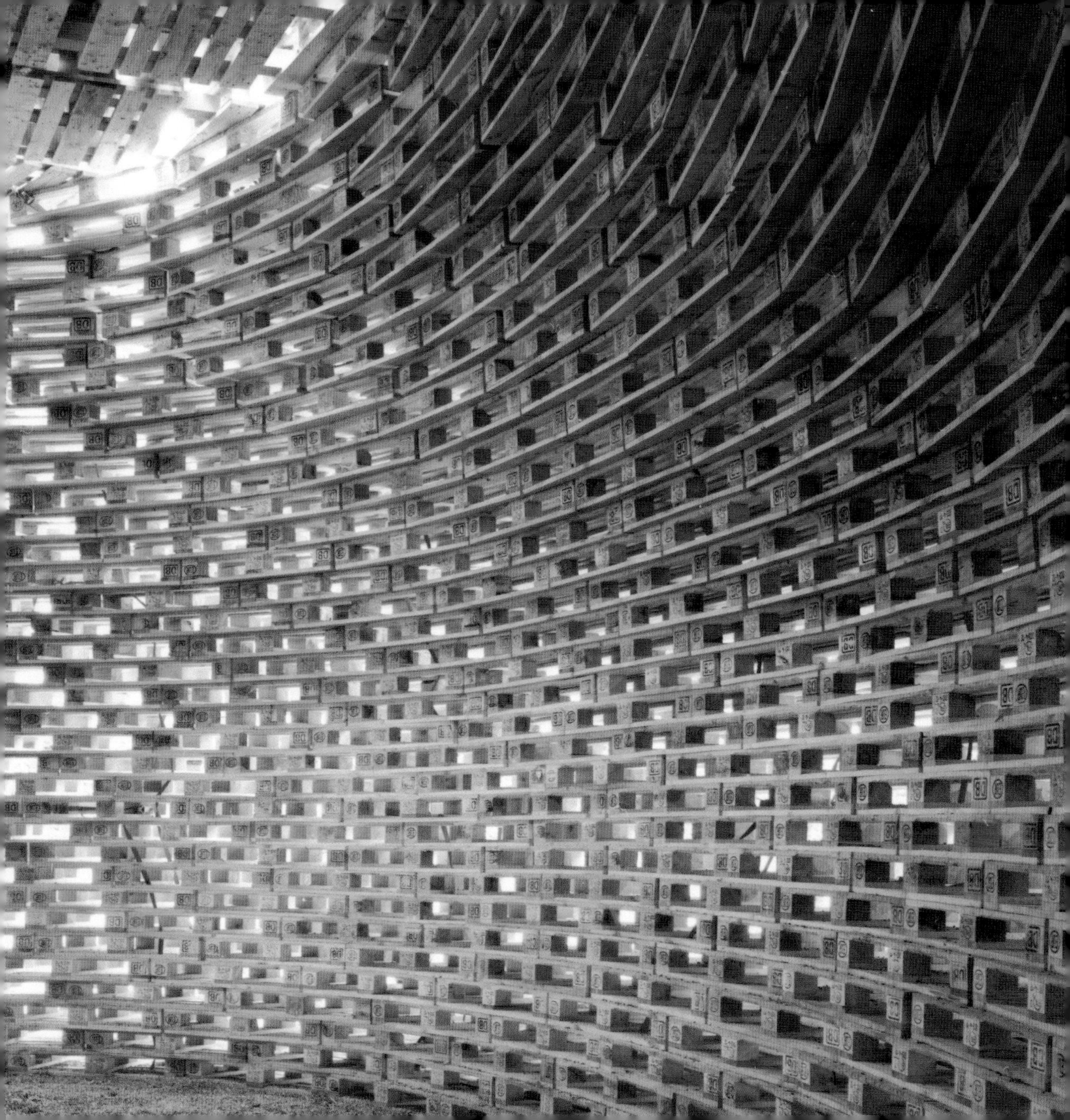

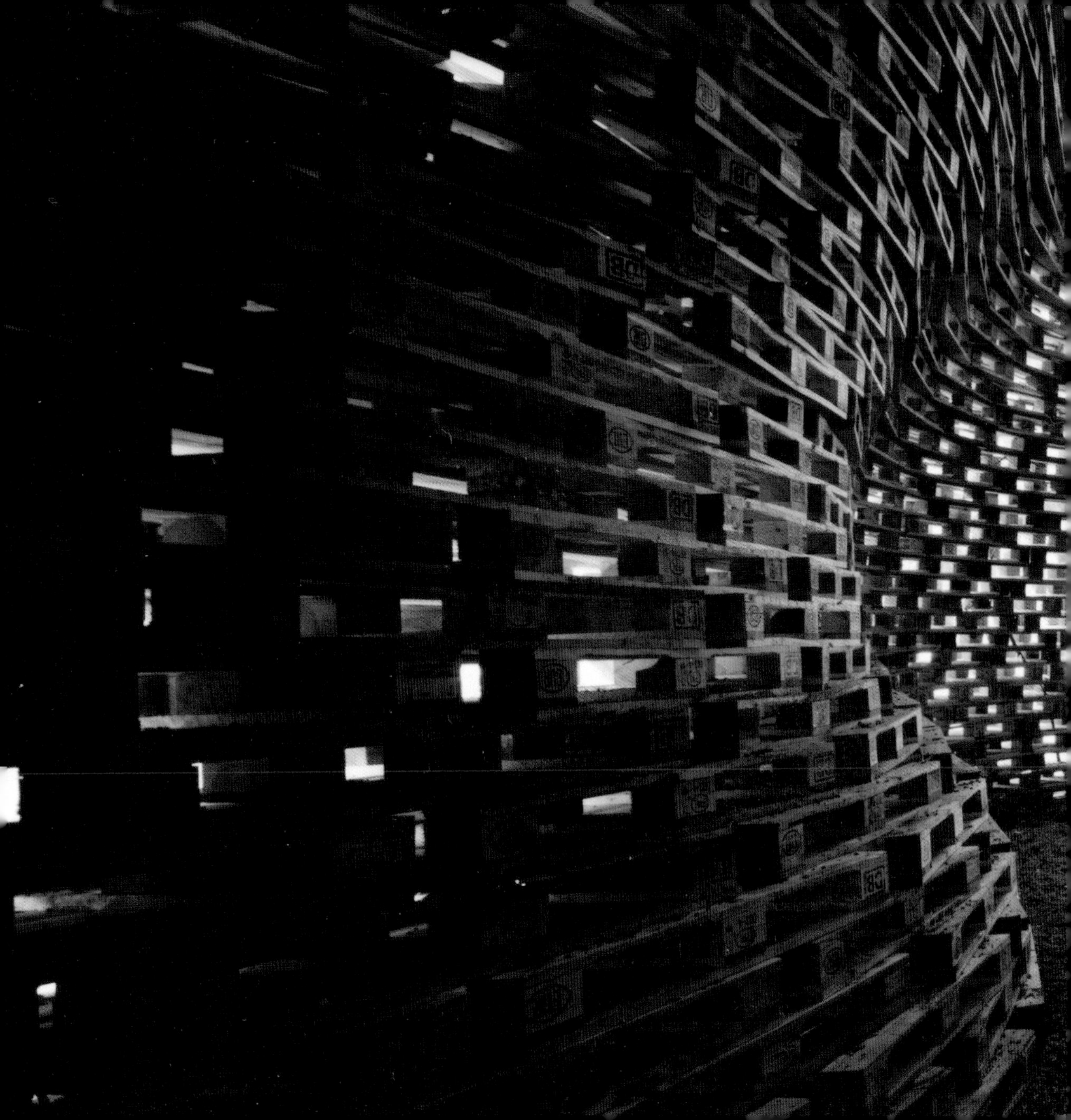

DESTINY OF TREES

ATELIER KLAUS BITTNER

This art project, located on a forest trail, consists of 205 × 205 × 230 cm lattice cage of steel filled with wood pieces. The art piece is based on a square module expressed both by the container (a large cubic cage and the formed by grids), and by the content (an arrangement of wood pieces).

Ce projet d'installation artistique, située sur un chemin forestier, consiste en une cage en treillis d'acier de 205 × 205 × 230 cm, remplie de morceaux de bois. L'œuvre d'art a pour base un module carré exprimé à la fois dans le contenant (une grande cage presque cubique et les petits carrés du treillis) et dans le contenu (un arrangement de morceaux de bois).

Dieses Kunstprojekt wurde auf einem Waldweg errichtet und besteht aus einem mit Holzstücken gefüllten Gitterkäfig aus Stahl mit den Maßen 205 × 205 × 230 cm. Das Kunstwerk zeichnet sich durch seine quadratische Form aus: Sowohl der Behälter (ein Gitterwürfel) als auch sein Inhalt (die Anordnung der Holzstücke) spiegeln diese Form wider.

Dit project is gesitueerd op een bospad. Het bestaat uit een stalen kooi van 205 × 205 × 230 cm die met stukken hout is gevuld. Het kunstwerk is gebaseerd op een vierkante modulus die zowel door het omhulsel (een kooi van traliewerk) als door de inhoud (gerangschikte stukken hout) tot uitdrukking wordt gebracht.

Este proyecto artístico, levantado en una pista forestal, consiste en un armazón de estructura reticular de 205 × 205 × 230 cm cm de acero rellenado con piezas de madera. Esta pieza artística se basa en un módulo cuadrado expresado tanto a través del continente (una gran jaula cúbica con enrejado), como por medio del contenido (una disposición de piezas de madera).

Questo progetto artistico, realizzato lungo una pista forestale, consiste in un telaio reticolare di 205 × 205 × 230 cm d'acciaio riempito di pezzi di legno. Questa pièce artistica si basa sulla forma di un modulo quadrato espresso sia mediante il contenitore (una grande gabbia cubica a griglie), sia attraverso il contenuto (una composizione di ciocchi di legno).

Este projecto artístico, situado num trilho florestal, é composto por uma gaiola de aço de 205 × 205 × 230 cm preenchida com troncos de madeira. A peça de arte está apoiada sobre um módulo quadrado, expresso tanto pelo contentor (uma grande gaiola cúbica) como pelo conteúdo (um conjunto de pedaços de madeira).

Detta är ett konstprojekt, beläget på en skogsled, som består av en 205 × 205 × 230 cm stor gallerbur av stål fylld med träbitar. Konstverket är baserat på en fyrkantig modul som uttrycks både genom behållaren (en stor fyrkantig bur och de därtill formade gallren) och genom innehållet (ett arrangemang av träbitar).

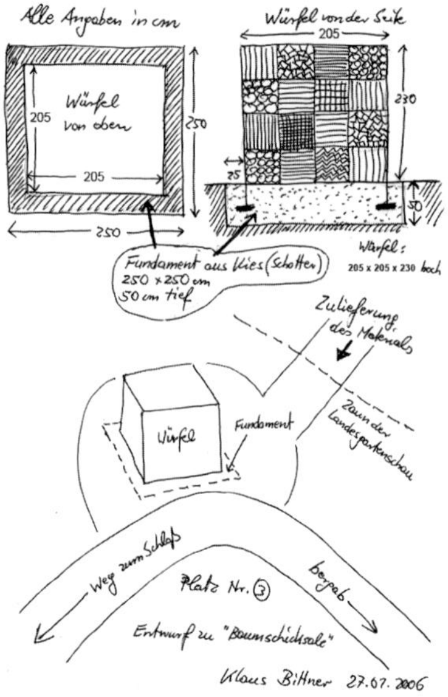

Verspannungen im Würfel jeweils oberhalb von Ebene 1, 2 und 3

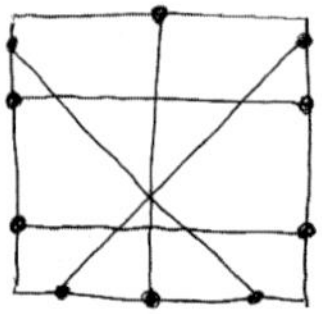

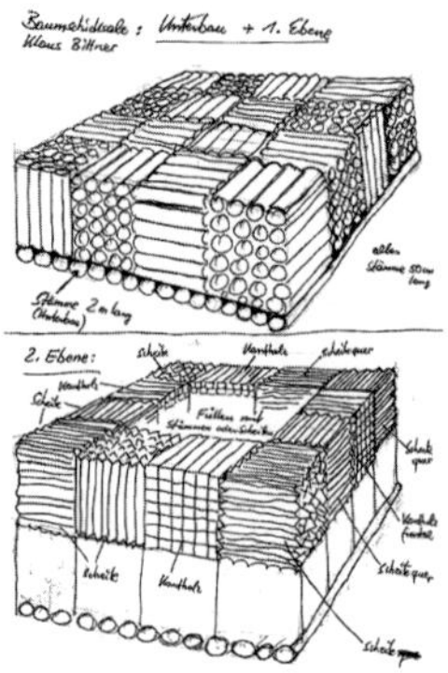

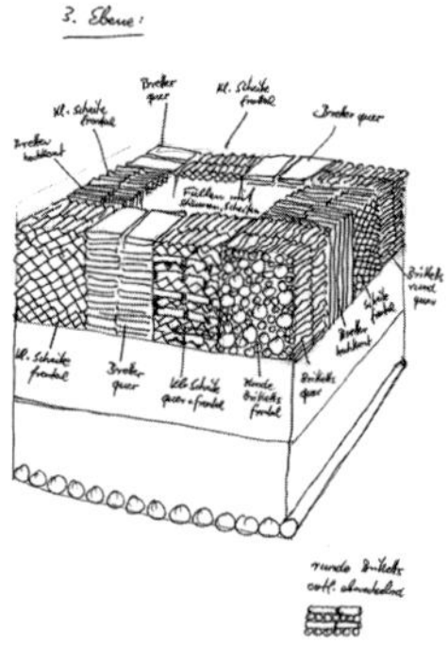

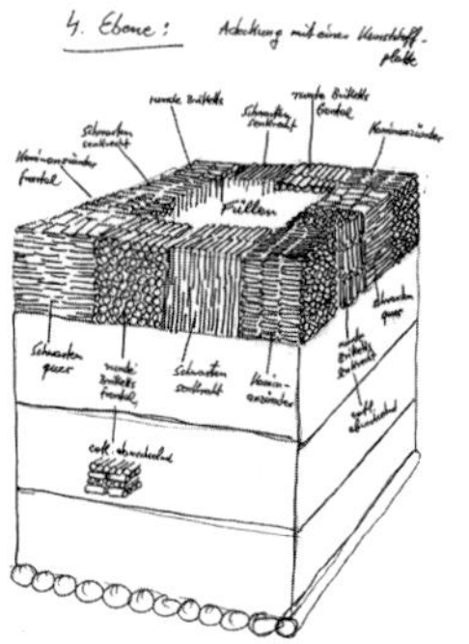

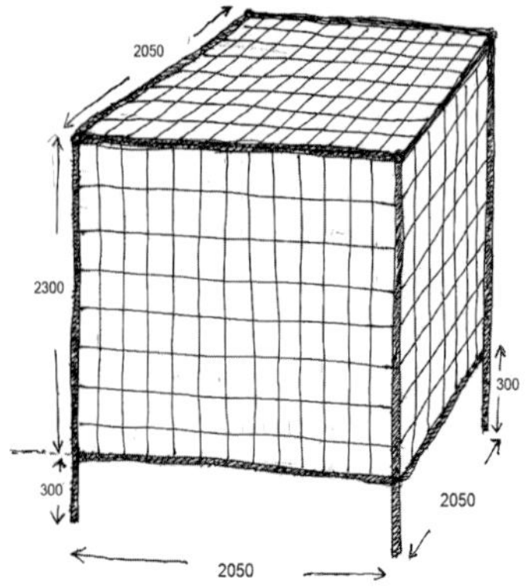

Vorstufen der Holzverarbeitung:

1 = Rundholz 200 cm (15 - 20 cm Durchm.) trunk wood with different diameters
2 = Rundholz 50 cm (10 - 15 cm Durchm.)
3 = Kantholz 50 cm (10 x 10 cm Durchm.) square timbers
4 = Bretter (50 x 25 x 2,4 cm) boards and planks
5 = Schwartenbretter (50 x 20 x 2,4 cm) slabs
6 = Stämme (bis 50 cm) trunk wood
7 = Buchenscheite (50 cm lang, dick) logs
8 = Kaminholz - Buchenscheite (25 cm lang) firewood
9 = Holzbriketts (rund, 25 cm lang) briquets
10 = Kaminanzünder (Buche)

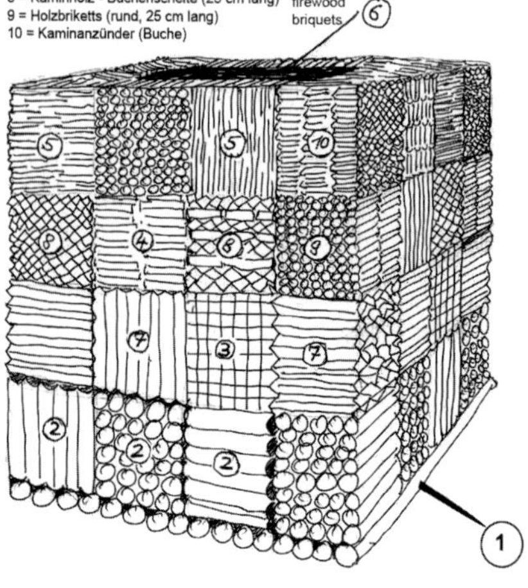

Wer hat nicht als Kind (oder sogar noch als Erwachsener) davon geträumt, in einem Baumhaus zu leben? Diese Projekte binden sich perfekt in die umliegende Landschaft und ihre natürlichen Gegebenheiten ein. Baumhäuser verbinden die Grundidee einer einfachen Holzstruktur im Baum mit weiterentwickelten Baumethoden, die an die spezifischen Wünsche des Kunden angepasst werden.

Wie heeft er als kind (of zelfs als volwassene) niet van gedroomd in een boomhut te wonen? De hier beschreven projecten zijn ingepast in de natuurlijke omgeving. Zonder de notie van een eenvoudig bouwsel los te laten, is er rekening gehouden met de laatste ontwikkelingen in bouwmethoden en de wensen van de cliënten.

TREE HOUSES

MAISONS DANS LES ARBRES

BAUMHÄUSER

BOOMHUIZEN

As a young child (or perhaps even an adult) who hasn't dreamed of living tree houses? These projects are successfully worked around the existing natural site conditions. Tree houses blend the notions of a simple wood structure in a tree with further developments of construction techniques customized to client wishes.

Qui n'a rêvé – enfant, ou encore peutetre à l'âge adulte – d'habiter une cabane aménagée dans un arbre ? Un tel projet est aujourd'hui accessible, en harmonie avec les conditions naturelles d'un site. Les « maisons dans les arbres » mêlent habilement la simplicité d'une structure de bois installée dans un arbre et les techniques de construction modernes, modulées selon les désirs du client.

De pequeños (o incluso de adultos), ¿quién no ha soñado alguna vez con vivir en una casa de árbol? Estos proyectos están funcionando satisfactoriamente en las condiciones de emplazamiento naturales existentes. Las casas de árbol mezclan las nociones de una estructura simple de madera con otros desarrollos de técnicas constructivas adaptadas a los deseos del cliente.

Da bambini (o perfino anche da adulti), chi non ha mai sognato di vivere in una casa su un albero? Questi progetti stanno funzionando in maniera soddisfacente nei contesti naturali in cui si trovano. Le case sugli alberi uniscono il concetto di una struttura semplice di legno con i progressi tecnici costruttivi adattati ai desideri del cliente.

Enquanto criança (e talvez já adulto), quem nunca sonhou viver numa casa no topo de uma árvore? Este tipo de projecto adapta-se exemplarmente às condições naturais oferecidas pela localização onde é construído. As casas nas árvores misturam na perfeição uma simples estrutura de madeira com técnicas de construção mais avançadas e que são desenvolvidas à medida das necessidades dos clientes.

Vem har inte som litet barn (eller kanske även som vuxen) dröm om att bo i trädhus? Dessa projekt är framgångsrikt byggda runt de existerande naturliga villkoren för omgivningen. Trädhus blandar föreställningar om en enkel trästruktur i ett träd med ytterligare utvecklingar av byggtekniker specialgjorda efter kundens önskningar.

LAS CASAS DE ÁRBOL

LE CASE SU ALBERI

CASAS NAS ÁRVORES

TRÄDHUS

NUT ROOM TREE HOUSE

ANDREAS WENNING/BAUMRAUM
© Andreas Wenning

This project, located in a private garden, was designed for a family with children. Shaped like a walnut, the tree house is supported by steel posts, and is equipped with a sleeping area and a bench with drawers. The curved steel frame is sided on the exterior with horizontal glazed oak lamellas, while the interior is finished with oak.

Ce projet – situé dans un jardin privé – a été conçu pour une famille avec enfants. Reprenant la forme d'une noisette, la cabane est soutenue par des pieux métalliques ; elle est aménagée avec un coin pour dormir et un banc muni de tiroirs. L'ossature d'acier cintrée est revêtue à l'extérieur de lamelles de chêne vernis, tandis que l'intérieur a reçu une finition en chêne naturel.

Dieses Projekt wurde in einem privaten Garten für eine Familie mit Kindern errichtet. Das walnussförmige Baumhaus wird von Stahlpfeilern getragen und ist mit einem Schlafbereich und einer Bank mit Schubladen ausgestattet. Der gebogene Stahlrahmen ist auf der Außenseite mit waagrecht verlaufenden, verglasten Eichenlamellen verkleidet. Auch für den Innenausbau wurde Eichenholz verwendet.

Dit huis werd ontworpen voor een gezin met kinderen en is in hun tuin gebouwd. Het heeft de vorm van een walnoot. Het steunt op stalen palen en heeft een slaapruimte en een bank met laden. Het geraamte van gebogen staal is vanbuiten bekleed met in eiken lamellen gevat glas. Het interieur is afgewerkt met eikenhout.

Este proyecto, situado en un jardín privado, fue diseñado para una familia con niños. Con forma de nuez, la casa del árbol se apoya en postes de acero y está equipada con una zona para el descanso y un banco con cajones. La estructura curva de acero está revestida con laminillas de roble horizontales vidriadas en el exterior, mientras el interior presenta acabados de roble.

Questo progetto, sito in un giardino privato, è stato realizzato per una famiglia con bambini. La casa sull'albero, la cui forma ricorda quella di una noce, poggia su pali d'acciaio e contiene una zona per il riposo e una panchina con cassetti. La struttura curva di acero è ricoperta all'esterno da listelli di quercia orizzontali e da una grande vetrata, mentre l'interno presenta rifiniture di quercia.

Este projecto, localizado num jardim privado, foi desenhado para uma família com crianças. Com a forma de uma noz, a casa da árvore é suportada por postes de aço e está equipada com uma área de dormir e um banco com gavetas. A estrutura curva, em aço, foi revestida pelo exterior com lamelas horizontais de carvalho vidrado, enquanto o interior recebeu acabamentos em carvalho.

Detta projekt, beläget i en privat trädgård, designades för en barnfamilj. Trädhuset som är format som en valnöt stöttas av stålstolpar och är utrustat med ett sovutrymme och en bänk med lådor. Den böjda stålramen är på utsidan klädd med horisontella, lackade eklameller, medan insidan har fått en yta av ek.

Elevation

WENCKE TREE HOUSE

ANDREAS WENNING/BAUMRAUM
© Alasdair Jardine

This tree house was built for a family with three children. Before construction started, the trees were inspected by a state certified tree expert, who determined the suitability of the trees to bear the weight of the larch-finished tree house. The large deck, partly roofed over and walled on one side appears as an extension of the cabin.

Cette *treehouse* a été construite pour une famille avec trois enfants. Avant le lancement de la construction, les arbres ont été inspectés par un expert d'État assermenté qui a déterminé la capacité des arbres à soutenir le poids de cette cabane revêtue de mélèze. La grande plateforme, partiellement couverte et close par un mur sur un côté, apparaît comme une extension de la cabane.

Das Baumhaus wurde für eine Familie mit drei Kindern errichtet. Vor Baubeginn wurden die Bäume von einem staatlich geprüften Baumexperten inspiziert, der bestätigte, dass die Bäume dafür geeignet waren, das Gewicht des in Lärchenholz ausgeführten Baumhauses zu tragen. Die teilweise überdachte Terrasse, die einseitig von einer Wand begrenzt wird, wirkt wie eine Verlängerung der Hütte.

Dit boomhuis werd gebouwd voor een gezin met drie kinderen. Van tevoren zijn de bomen onderzocht door een bevoegde expert, die concludeerde dat ze het gewicht van het met lariks afgewerkte boomhuis konden dragen. Het grote plankier, dat deels overdekt is en aan één kant van een wand is voorzien, sluit vloeiend aan op de cabine.

Esta casa de árbol fue construida para una familia con tres niños. Antes de que empezara la obra, un experto en árboles inspeccionó los árboles y determinó su idoneidad para soportar el peso de la casa de árbol con acabados de alerce. La gran terraza, parcialmente techada y tapiada en uno de sus lados, parece una extensión de la cabaña.

Questa casa sull'albero è stata costruita per una famiglia con tre bambini. Prima d'iniziare i lavori, un esperto di piante ha ispezionato gli alberi su cui avrebbe poggiato e ha decretato la loro idoneità a sostenere il peso della casa con rifiniture di larice. La grande terrazza, parzialmente coperta con una tettoia e riparata da una parete su un lato, sembra un'estensione stessa della casetta.

Esta casa da árvore foi construída para uma família com três crianças. Antes de iniciada a construção, as árvores foram inspeccionadas por um especialista certificado pelo estado que determinou a adequação das mesmas à sustentação do peso da casa da árvore, de acabamentos em lariço. A grande esplanada, parcialmente coberta e protegida de um dos lados, surge como uma extensão da cabine.

Detta trädhus byggdes för en familj med tre barn. Innan byggandet började inspekterades träden av en trädexpert, certifierad av staten, som fastslog trädens lämplighet att bära upp vikten av det lärkträklädda trädhuset. Det stora däcket, delvis taktäckt och med vägg på ena sidan framstår som en förlängning av stugan.

PEAR TREE HOUSE

ANDREAS WENNING/BAUMRAUM

The property is surrounded by orchards and vineyards. The design of the tree house is characterised by a dynamic vocabulary and a spiral-shaped arrangement around the old fruit tree. Two conical-shaped stabilisers secure the rear part of the tree house and ensure that the tree is not overloaded. The construction is made of indigenous larch.

La propriété des maîtres d'œuvre est entourée de vignobles et de vergers. La conception de cette cabane se caractérise par la dynamique du vocabulaire et par la disposition en spirale autour du vieil arbre fruitier. Deux stabilisateurs de forme conique assurent la partie arrière de la cabane, en épargnant toute surcharge au poirier. L'ensemble de la construction est en mélèze local.

Das Grundstück ist von Obst- und Weingärten umgeben. Charakteristisch für das Projekt sind die dynamischen Gestaltungselemente und seine spiralförmige Anordnung um den alten Obstbaum herum. Zwei konisch geformte Stützen stabilisieren den hinteren Teil des Hauses und verhindern eine Überbelastung des Baums. Das Bauwerk wurde aus einheimischen Lärchenholz gefertigt.

Het privédomein wordt omringd door wijn- en boomgaarden. Kenmerkend voor het ontwerp van het boomhuis is de dynamische opbouw in een spiraal rond de oude perelaar. Het achterste deel van het boomhuis rust op twee kegelvormige steunen, die voorkomen dat de boom te veel moet dragen. De constructie is van inheemse lariks.

La propiedad está rodeada de huertos y viñedos. El diseño de esta casa de árbol se caracteriza por un vocabulario dinámico y una disposición en forma de espiral alrededor del viejo árbol frutal. Dos estabilizadores con forma cónica afianzan la parte posterior de la casa de árbol y aseguran que éste no se sobrecargue. La construcción es de alerce autóctono.

Il progetto di questa casa sull'albero, che sorge in una proprietà circondata da orti e vigne, si distingue per l'uso di un vocabolario dinamico e per una disposizione a spirale intorno al vecchio albero da frutto. Due stabilizzatori a forma conica assicurano la parte posteriore della casa e impediscono che l'albero sopporti troppo peso. La costruzione è di larice autoctono.

A propriedade está rodeada de pomares e vinhas. O design da casa da árvore caracteriza-se por um aspecto dinâmico e um arranjo em espiral em torno da velha árvore de fruto. Dois estabilizadores de forma cónica sustentam a parte de trás da construção e garantem que a árvore não seja sobrecarregada. A construção foi concebida em lariço indígena.

Tomten är omgiven av frukträdgårdar och vingårdar. Trädhusets design karaktäriseras av en dynamisk vokabulär och ett spiralformat arrangemang runt det gamla fruktträdet. Två konformade stabilisatorer säkrar den bakre delen av trädhuset och ser till att trädet inte överbelastas. Konstruktionen är gjord i inhemskt lärkträ.

DJUREN TREE HOUSE

ANDREAS WENNING/BAUMRAUM
© Andreas Wenning

This tree house is constructed for a family with children. It is propped up by four posts on concrete foundations to lighten up the weight on the trees. The curved framework is sided with horizontal oak lamellas on the outside and the roof is covered with a zinc sheet. The spacious curved interior is finished in white and oak.

Cette maison perchée dans un arbre a été conçue pour une famille avec enfants. Elle est soutenue par quatre poteaux sur fondation de béton, afin de soulager le poids imposé aux arbres. L'ossature est revêtue à l'extérieur de lamelles de chêne horizontales ; le toit est recouvert d'une feuille de zinc. Les finitions du spacieux intérieur sont en blanc et en chêne naturel.

Dieses Holzhaus wurde für eine Familie mit Kindern entworfen. Es wird von vier in ein Betonfundament eingelassenen Pfosten gestützt, um die Bäume vom Gewicht zu entlasten. Die gebogene Rahmenstruktur ist außen mit waagrecht verlaufenden Eichenlamellen, das Dach mit einer Zinkplatte verkleidet. Der geräumige, gewölbte Innenraum ist mit Eichenholz ausgebaut und in Weiß gehalten.

Dit boomhuis werd gebouwd voor een gezin met kinderen. Het steunt op vier palen met een betonnen voet, zodat de bomen niet het volle gewicht hoeven te dragen. Het gebogen geraamte is vanbuiten bekleed met horizontale eiken lamellen en het dak is bedekt met een zinken plaat. Het ruime interieur is afgewerkt in wit en eiken.

Esta casa de árbol fue construida para una familia con niños. Está apuntalada con cuatro postes insertados en una base de hormigón para descargar el peso sobre los árboles. La estructura curvada está revestida con láminas horizontales de roble en el exterior y el tejado está cubierto con láminas de zinc. El espacioso interior curvado tiene acabados en blanco y madera de roble.

Questa casa sull'albero è stata costruita per una famiglia con bambini. È puntellata da quattro pali infilati in una base di calcestruzzo che servono per scaricare il peso che devono sostenere gli alberi. La struttura curvata è ricoperta da listelli orizzontali di legno di quercia all'esterno, mentre il tetto è rivestito da lamine di zinco. Gli spaziosi interni curvi presentano rifiniture bianche e quercia.

Esta casa da árvore foi construída para uma família com crianças. É sustentada por quatro postes sobre fundações de cimento, para aliviar o peso sobre as árvores. A estrutura curva foi revestida por lamelas horizontais de carvalho, pelo lado de fora, e o telhado foi coberto por folhas de zinco. O espaçoso interior curvo tem acabamentos a branco e carvalho.

Detta trädhus är konstruerat för en barnfamilj. Det har rests upp med hjälp av fyra stolpar på betongfundament för att göra vikten på träden lättare. Den böjda ramkonstruktionen är klädd med horisontella eklameller på utsidan och taket är täckt av ett lager zink. Den rymliga, svängda interiören har fått ytor i vitt och ek.

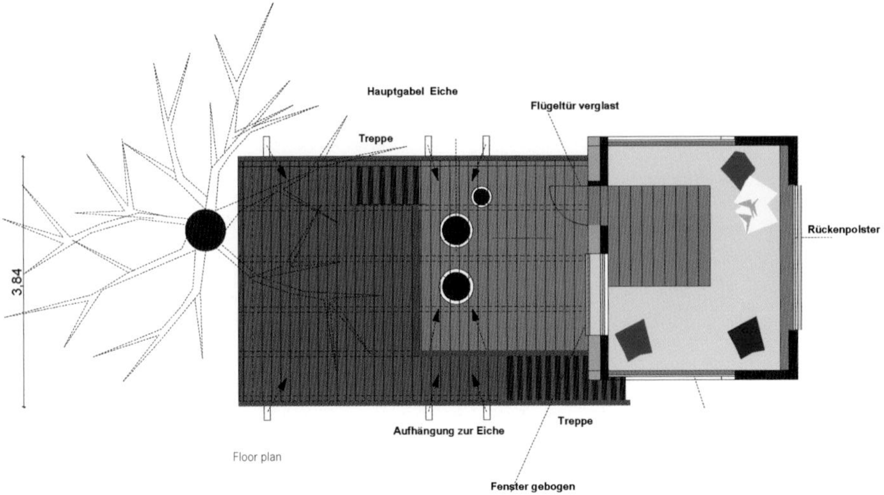

Floor plan

Back elevation

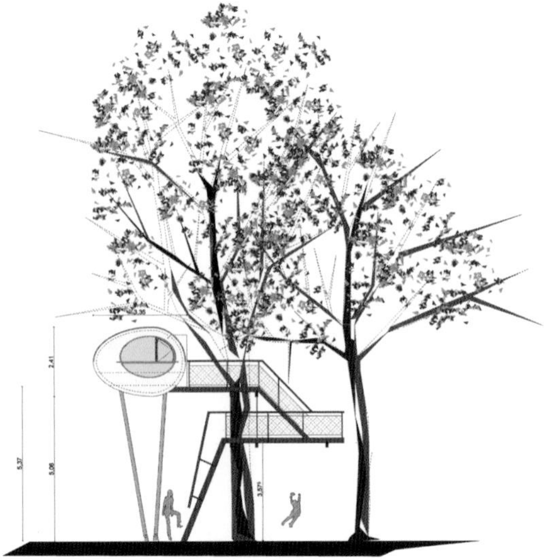

Side elevation

EILENRIEDE TREE HOUSE

ANDREAS WENNING/BAUMRAUM
© Alasdair Jardine

This tree house is built on private property adjacent to a public park for a family with three children. Entirely supported by the trees without additional support, it affords good views of the park, while protected from sight by the foliage. Wall construction consists of untreated larch boards on the outside, and bias-cut larch battens inside.

Cette cabane est construite sur la propriété privée d'une famille avec trois enfants, contiguë à un parc public. Entièrement soutenue par les arbres sans aucun support additionnel, elle procure de belles vues sur le parc, tout en étant protégée des regards par le feuillage. Les murs sont faits de planches de mélèze non traité à l'extérieur et de lattes de mélèze taillé dans le biais à l'intérieur.

Dieses Baumhaus steht auf einem neben einem öffentlichen Park gelegenem Privatgrund und wurde für eine Familie mit drei Kindern entworfen. Es wird allein von den Bäumen, ohne zusätzliche Stützen getragen und bietet einen herrlichen Ausblick über den Park, wobei das Blattwerk es vor fremden Blicken schützt. Die Wand besteht außenseitig aus unbehandelten Lärchenholzbrettern und ist innenseitig mit schräg geschnittenen Lärchendielen verkleidet.

Dit boomhuis werd voor een gezin met drie kinderen gebouwd in een tuin die aan een park grenst. De bomen dragen het volle gewicht van het huis, dat uitzicht op het park biedt en schuilgaat tussen het gebladerte. De wanden zijn vanbuiten bekleed met onbehandelde planken van larikshout en vanbinnen met schuine larikshouten latten.

Esta casa de árbol fue construida en una propiedad privada adyacente a un parque público para una familia con tres niños. Apoyada totalmente sobre tres árboles sin ningún soporte adicional, ofrece unas excelentes vistas del parque, a la vez que protege de las miradas ajenas gracias al tupido follaje. La construcción de las paredes consiste en tablas de alerce sin tratar en el exterior y listones de alerce cortados al bies en el interior.

Questa casa sull'albero è stata costruita in una proprietà privata adiacente a un parco pubblico per una famiglia con tre bambini. Completamente sostenuta da tre alberi senza alcun supporto in più, offre magnifiche viste del parco e, nel contempo, è protetta dagli sguardi indiscreti grazie folto fogliame. Le pareti sono fatte di assi di larice non trattato all'esterno e di listelli di larice tagliati di sbieco, all'interno.

Esta casa da árvore foi construída numa propriedade privada, adjacente a um parque público, para uma família com três crianças. Inteiramente suportada pelas árvores e sem apoio adicional, permite uma boa vista do parque, mantendo-se protegida dos olhares pela folhagem. As paredes foram construídas com tábuas de lariço não tratado, no lado de fora, e travessas de lariço cortadas na diagonal, no interior.

Detta trädhus är byggt på privat mark intill en allmän park åt en familj med tre barn. Huset är helt stöttat av träden och erbjuder fin utsikt över parken samtidigt som det är skyddat mot insyn av lövverket. Väggkonstruktionen består av obehandlat lärkträ på utsidan och diagonalt skurna balkar i lärkträ på insidan.

CLIFF TREE HOUSE

ANDREAS WENNING/BAUMRAUM
© Andreas Wenning

This tree house is built on a rocky hillside near the Hudson River on the property of a family with children. The tree house, designed to match the style of the main house, is accessed via a bridge from the top of the cliff. The framework is sided with oak boards on the inside and with horizontal rough-sawn larch boards on the exterior.

Cette maison perchée est construite sur une pente rocheuse, près de l'Hudson, sur la propriété d'une famille avec enfants. Conçue pour s'harmoniser avec le style de la résidence principale, la *tree house* est accessible par une passerelle depuis le sommet de la pente. L'ossature est habillée de planches de chêne à l'intérieur et de planches de mélèze brutes de sciage à l'extérieur.

Dieses Baumhaus wurde auf einem felsigen Hang in der Nähe des Hudsonflusses auf dem Grundstück einer Familie mit Kindern errichtet. Das Baumhaus wurde im Stil des Haupthauses entworfen und kann über eine an der Spitze des Felsvorsprungs ansetzende Brücke begangen werden. Das Rahmengerüst ist innenseitig mit Eichenbrettern ausgebaut und außenseitig mit waagrecht verlaufenden, grob gesägten Lärchenholzlatten verkleidet.

Op een rotsige helling bij de rivier de Hudson is dit boomhuis gebouwd. Het ontwerp past bij de stijl van de woning. Vanaf de top van de klip geeft een brug toegang tot het boomhuis. Het geraamte is vanbinnen bekleed met eiken planken en vanbuiten met ruw gezaagde planken van lariks, die horizontaal zijn aangebracht.

Esta casa de árbol se encuentra en una ladera rocosa cerca del Río Hudson dentro de la propiedad de una familia con niños. A la casa de árbol, diseñada siguiendo el estilo de la casa principal, se accede a través de un puente desde lo alto del risco. La estructura está revestida interiormente con tablas de roble y con tablas horizontales de alerce sin tratar en el exterior.

Questa casa sull'albero si trova lungo un pendio roccioso nei pressi del fiume Hudson all'interno della proprietà di una famiglia con bambini. Alla casa sull'albero, progettata rispettando lo stile della casa principale, si accede mediante un ponte dalla sommità della collina. La struttura è ricoperta all'interno con tavole di quercia e, all'esterno, con listelli orizzontali di larice no trattato.

Esta casa da árvore foi construída numa colina rochosa perto do rio Hudson, na propriedade de uma família com crianças. A casa da árvore, desenhada de forma a combinar com a casa principal, é acedida através de uma ponte no topo do penhasco. A estrutura foi revestida com tábuas de carvalho, por dentro, e com tábuas horizontais de lariço cortadas de forma irregular, por fora.

Detta trädhus är byggt på en klippig backsluttning nära Hudsonfloden på en barnfamiljs fastighet. Trädhuset, som är designat för att bostadshusets stil, nås via en bro från toppen av klippan. Ramverket är täckt av ekplattor på insidan och med horisontella, grovsågade plattor av lärkträ på utsidan.

MEDITATION TREE HOUSE

ANDREAS WENNING/BAUMRAUM

This tree house is constructed in a private park and serves as a room for meditation and relaxation. The tree carries the weight of the decks while the tree house is supported by two posts. The walls are clad with horizontal tatajuba boards on the exterior and painted white on the interior contrasting with the jatobâ flooring and sideboard.

Cette maison perchée dans un arbre est construite dans un parc privé et elle sert de lieu de retraite pour la méditation et la relaxation. L'arbre supporte le poids des plateformes, tandis que la cabane proprement dite est soutenue par deux poteaux. Les murs sont revêtus extérieurement de planches horizontales de tatajuba et peints intérieurement en blanc, contrastant avec le sol et le buffet en jatobá.

Dieses Baumhaus steht in einem Privatpark und dient als Raum zur Meditation und Entspannung. Der Baum trägt das Gewicht der Terrasse, während das Baumhaus selbst von zwei Pfosten gestützt wird. Die Wände sind außenseitig mit Tatajubaholz verkleidet, wodurch ein Kontrast zu dem Jatobaholzboden und der Anrichte geschaffen wird.

Dit boomhuis werd gebouwd in een besloten park en dient als ruimte voor meditatie en ontspanning. De boom draagt het gewicht van de plankieren. Het boomhuis zelf rust op twee palen. De wanden zijn vanbuiten bekleed met planken van tatajuba en vanbinnen wit geschilderd, als contrast met de vloer en het dressoir van jatoba.

Esta casa del árbol está construida en un parque privado y sirve como cuarto de meditación y relajación. El árbol sostiene el peso de las plataformas mientras la casa de árbol reposa sobre dos postes. En el exterior, las paredes están revestidas con tablones horizontales de tatajuba y en el interior están pintadas de blanco, contrastando así con el suelo y el aparador de jatoba.

Questa casa sull'albero sorge in un parco privato e funge da luogo di meditazione e rilassamento. L'albero sostiene il peso delle piattaforme, mentre la casa sull'albero poggia su due pali. All'esterno, le pareti sono ricoperte da tavole orizzontali di legno di tatajuba e all'interno sono dipinte di bianco, in contrasto con il pavimento e la credenza di jatoba.

Esta casa da árvore foi construída num parque privado e serve de sala de meditação e relaxamento. A árvore suporta o peso das esplanadas enquanto a casa é suportada por dois postes. As paredes foram revestidas por tábuas horizontais de tatajuba, pelo lado de fora, e pintadas de branco, pelo lado de dentro, contrastando com o chão e o aparador de jatobá.

Detta trädhus är konstruerat i en privat park och fungerar som ett rum för meditation och avslappning. Trädet bär upp däcken tyngd medan trädhuset stöttas av två stolpar. Väggarna är klädda med horisontella plattor av tatajubaträ på utsidan och målat vitt på insidan, vilket kontrasterar mot golvläggningen och sidorna i jatobâträ.

PLENDELHOF TREE HOUSE

ANDREAS WENNING/BAUMRAUM
© Andreas Wenning

The design consists of a small but comfortable tree house with a deck over the treetops facing south. The triangular frame is made of larch beams bolted together and sided with larch while spruce siding covers the boat-like interior. Larch has good weather resistant properties, which means the use of wood preservative could be avoided.

Cette maison perchée est petite mais confortable, dotée d'un toit au-dessus de la cime des arbres, face au sud. L'ossature triangulaire est faite de poutres de mélèze vissées ensemble ; elle est habillée extérieurement de mélèze, tandis que l'intérieur en forme de nacelle est revêtu d'épicéa. Le mélèze offre une bonne résistance aux intempéries, sans qu'il soit nécessaire d'employer de produit pour protéger le bois.

Der Entwurf besteht aus einem kleinen, aber komfortablen Baumhaus mit einer über den Baumkronen gelegenen Terrasse, die nach Süden gerichtet ist. Die dreieckige Form besteht aus miteinander verschraubten Lärchenholzbalken, deren Verkleidung ebenso aus Lärchenholz besteht, während der einem Boot ähnelnde Innenraum mit Fichtenholz ausgekleidet ist. Lärchenholz ist sehr wetterbeständig, daher konnte man auf Holzschutzmittel verzichten.

Het ontwerp voorzag in een klein, maar gerieflijk boomhuis met aan de zuidkant een plankier over de boomtoppen. Het driehoekige geraamte is gemaakt van lariksbalken, die met bouten aan elkaar zitten. Het interieur is afgewerkt met sparrenhout. De buitenkant is van lariks, dat weerbestendig is en niet geïmpregneerd hoeft te worden.

El diseño consiste en una pequeña pero cómoda casa de árbol con una plataforma sobre las copas de los árboles orientada hacia el sur. La estructura triangular está hecha de vigas de alerce sujetadas juntas y revestidas con alerce mientras que un revestimiento de pícea cubre el interior proyectado con forma de barco. La madera de alerce es muy resistente a los cambios climáticos, lo que implica que es posible evitar el uso de conservantes de la madera.

Il progetto consiste in una piccola, ma comoda casa sull'albero con una piattaforma posta sulle cime degli alberi e rivolta a sud. La struttura triangolare è stata realizzata con travi di larice fissate insieme e ricoperte di larice, mentre un rivestimento di abete rosso copre l'interno concepito a forma di barca. Il legno di larice è molto resistente alle variazioni del clima, permette quindi di evitare l'uso di conservanti del legno.

O *design* consiste numa pequena mas confortável casa da árvore com uma esplanada, sobre o topo das árvores, voltada para sul. A moldura triangular é feita de vigas de lariço aparafusadas e revestidas de lariço, enquanto um revestimento de espruce cobre o interior que faz lembrar um barco. O lariço tem boas propriedades resistentes à água, o que significa que pode ser evitado o uso de preservantes de madeira.

Designen består av ett litet men bekvämt trädhus med ett däck ovanför trädtopparna som vetter mot söder. Den triangelformade ramen är gjord av bjälkar i lärkträ som är sammanfogade och täckta med lärkträ, medan granbeklädnad täcker den båtlika interiören. Lärkträ har bra egenskaper för att stå emot vädret, vilket innebär att användning av träbehandling bör undvikas.

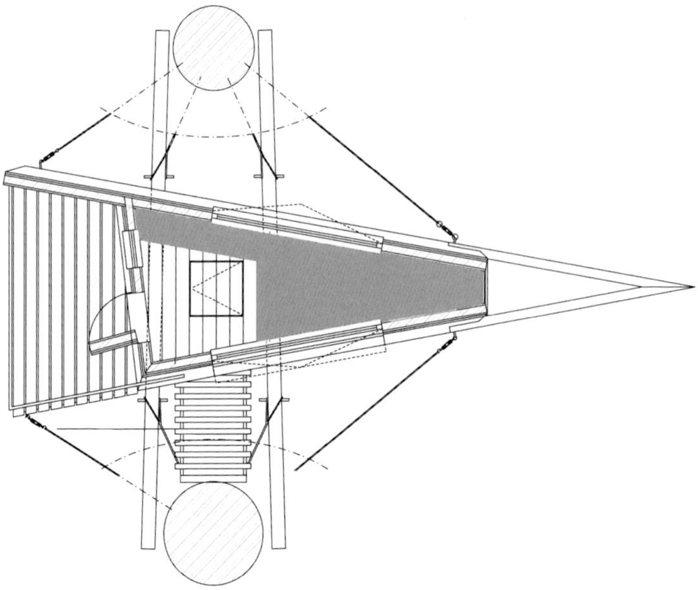

Floor plan

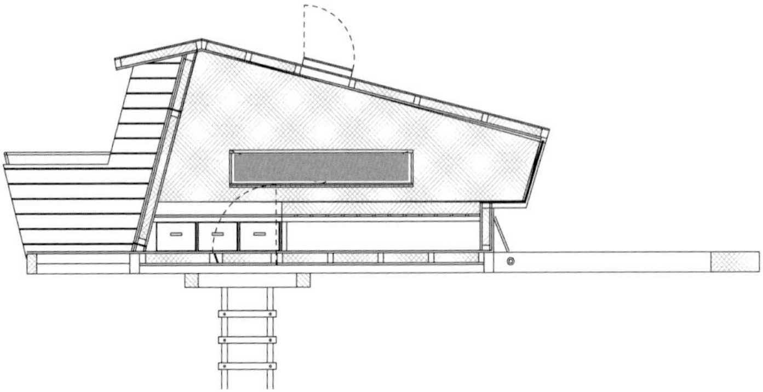

Section

APULIA TREE HOUSE

ANDREAS WENNING/BAUMRAUM

This project was designed for a family with children for their property by the sea as a summer vacation stay. The tree house is partly suspended from the pines by means of steel cables and straps and partly resting on two flexibly mounted stabiliser supports. The solid wood frame is sided both inside and out with larch boards.

Cette réalisation a été conçue pour une famille avec enfants, dans leur propriété de vacances au bord de la mer. La cabane est partiellement suspendue aux pins au moyen de câbles d'acier et de sangles, partiellement montée souplement sur deux supports de stabilisation. L'ossature en bois est habillée de planches de mélèze, à l'intérieur comme à l'extérieur.

Dieses Projekt wurde für eine Familie mit Kindern als Ferienaufenthaltsort für ihr an das Meer grenzende Grundstück entworfen. Das Gewicht des Baumhauses hängt zwar zum Teil an den Pinien, an denen es mithilfe von Stahlkabeln und Riemen befestigt wurde. Zusätzlich wird es jedoch von zwei beliebig aufstellbaren stabilisierenden Stützen getragen.

Dit ontwerp werd gemaakt als zomerverblijf voor een gezin met een huis aan zee. Het boomhuis hangt met riemen en stalen kabels aan de dennen en rust op twee flexibel gemonteerde steunen. Het stevige houten skelet is zowel aan de buitenkant als aan de binnenkant afgewerkt met planken van larikshout.

Una familia con hijos encargó este proyecto para su propiedad de estadía vacacional junto al mar. La casa del árbol cuelga parcialmente de los pinos por medio de cables y de correas de acero y se apoya también parcialmente sobre dos soportes estabilizadores fijados flexiblemente. La sólida estructura de madera está revestida con tablas de alerce tanto por dentro como por fuera.

Una famiglia con figli ha voluto questo progetto per la sua proprietà di vacanze accanto al mare. La casa sull'albero è parzialmente appesa ai peni mediante cavi d'acciaio e poggia anche, in parte, su due supporti stabilizzatori fissati in maniera flessibile. La solida struttura di legno è ricoperta da tavole di larice sia all'interno sia all'esterno.

Este projecto foi desenhado por uma família com crianças, para a sua propriedade junto ao mar, como retiro de Verão. A casa da árvore está parcialmente suspensa dos pinheiros por cabos de aço e presilhas, e parcialmente apoiada sobre apoios estabilizadores flexíveis. A sólida armação de madeira é revestida, tanto por dentro como por fora, por tábuas de lariço.

Detta projekt designades åt en barnfamilj för deras sjötomt som ett semesterhus. Trädhuset är delvis upphängt i tallarna med stålkablar och spännen och vilar delvis på två flexibelt monterade stabilisatorstöd. Den solida träramen är klädd i lärkträ både på in- och utsidan.

WORLD OF LIVING TREE HOUSE

YOUNG APPRENTICES OF WEBERHAUS IN COOPERATION WITH OTHER PARTNERS
© Alasdair Jardine

The tree house was built in the Weberhaus firm's World of Living Park to underline the innovative orientation of the company. It is fitted with glazing on all sides and is equipped with benches, drawers and small wooden tables on wheels. The interior of the curved walls and ceiling are covered with arboreal wallpaper.

Cette cabane perchée dans un arbre a été construite dans le *World of Living Park* de la société allemande WeberHaus, pour illustrer les tendances novatrices de cette entreprise. Elle est en bois vernis sur toutes ses faces, et dotée de bancs, de tiroirs et de petites tables en bois montées sur roues. L'intérieur des murs et du plafond courbes est revêtu de papier peint décoré d'arbres.

Dieses Baumhaus wurde im World of Living Park der Firma Weberhaus erbaut, um die Neuorientierung der Firma in Richtung innovativer Produkte zu unterstreichen. Es ist auf allen Seiten verglast und mit Bänken, Schubläden und kleinen Holztischen auf Rädern möbliert. Die Innenseiten der gewölbten Wände und der Decke sind mit einer Tapete mit Baummotiven ausgestattet.

Dit boomhuis werd gebouwd in het World of Living Park van Weberhaus om te laten zien hoe vernieuwend deze firma is. Het is rondom van glas voorzien en het meubilair bestaat uit banken, laden en houten tafeltjes op wieltjes. De gebogen wanden en het plafond zijn beplakt met behang waarop bomen zijn afgebeeld.

La casa de árbol se construyó en el Parque World of Living de la empresa Weberhaus para subrayar la orientación innovadora de la empresa. Dispone de cristales en todos sus lados y está equipada con bancos, cajones y pequeñas mesas de madera con ruedas. El interior curvado de las paredes y el techo está cubierto de papel pintado con motivos arbóreos.

Questa casa sull'albero è stata costruita nel parco World of Living della ditta Weberhaus per esprimere la tendenza innovatrice dell'azienda. Possiede vetri su tutti i lati ed è equipaggiata di panchine, cassetti e piccoli tavoli di legno con rotelle. L'interno ricurvo delle pareti e del soffitto, è coperto di carta da parati con motivi arborei.

A casa da árvore foi construída no parque World of Living da Weberhaus para salientar a orientação inovadora da empresa. Foram colocados vidros em todos lados e foi equipada com bancos, gavetas e pequenas mesas de madeira com rodas. O interior das paredes curvas e o tecto foram revestidos com papel de parede com motivos arbóreos.

Trädhuset byggdes i firman Weberhaus' World of Living-park för att understryka företagets innovativa inriktning. Det är lackat på alla sidor och utrustat med bänkar, lådor och små träbord på hjul. Insidan av de böjda väggarna och taket är täckt med trädmönstrad tapet.

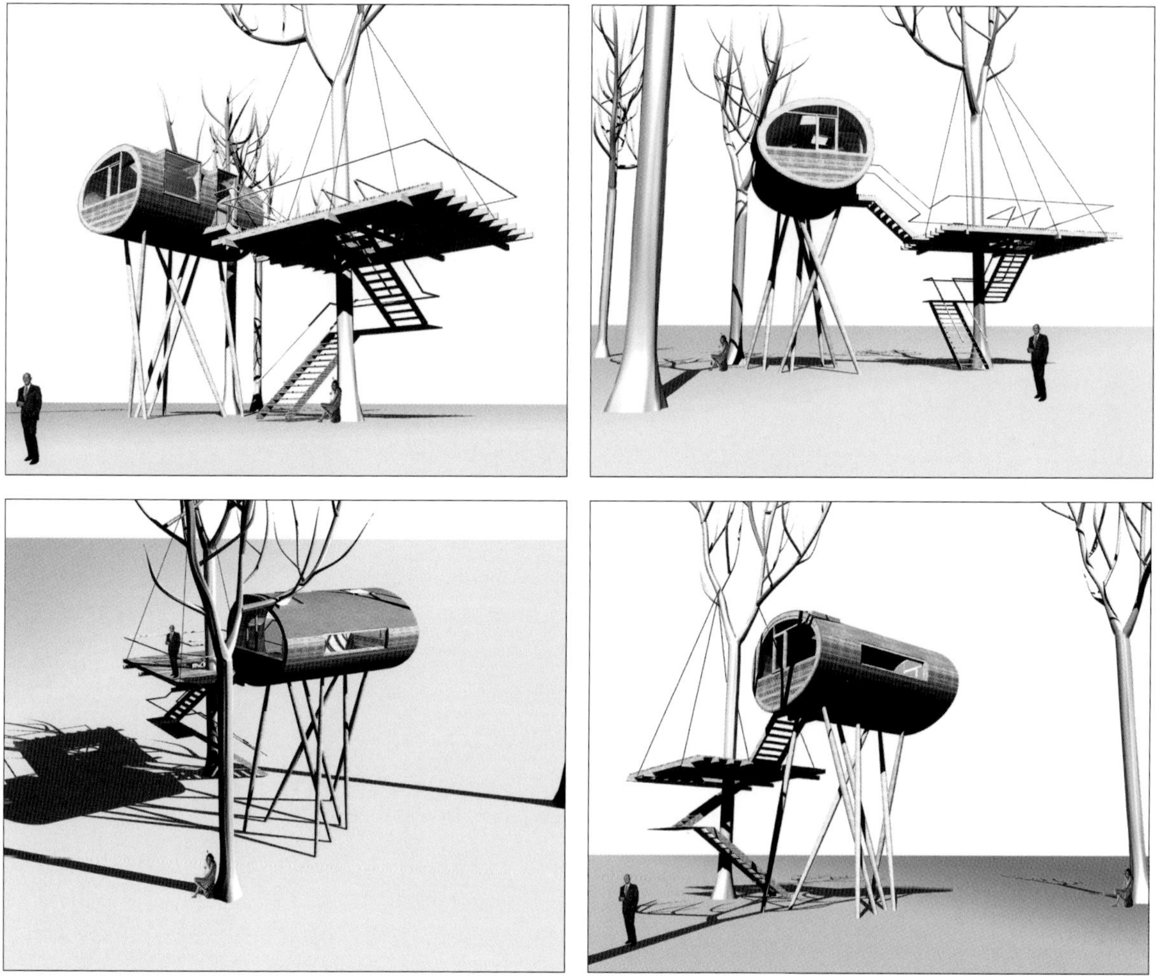

Computer generated renderings

le porte

GIRAFFE TREE HOUSE

ANDREAS WENNING/BAUMRAUM
© Andreas Wenning

A maple in the lawn area was chosen to have the tree house built for a family of four. The design consists of a terrace suspended in the tree and a freestanding cabin built on nine slender steel posts. The result makes one think of a giraffe. The exterior is finished with Ipé boards and the interior is clad with jatobá veneer on plywood.

Un érable du jardin a été choisi pour recevoir la *tree house* de cette famille de quatre personnes. L'ensemble se compose d'une terrasse suspendue dans l'arbre et d'une cabane indépendante juchée sur neuf poteaux d'acier élancés. Le résultat fait penser à la silhouette d'une girafe, d'où le nom. La finition extérieure est en planches d'ipé ; l'intérieur est revêtu d'un placage de jatobá sur un support de contreplaqué.

Die vierköpfige Familie wählte einen Ahornbaum im Garten für die Errichtung ihres Baumhauses. Der Entwurf besteht aus einer am Baum hängenden Terrasse und einer freistehenden Kabine, die von neun schmalen Stahlpfosten getragen wird. Das Erscheinungsbild erinnert an eine Giraffe. Während die Außenfassade mit Ipeholz verkleidet wurde, wurde für den Innenraum mit Jatobaholz furniertes Sperrholz verwendet.

Voor dit boomhuis, bestemd voor een gezin van vier personen, werd een esdoorn uitgekozen. Het girafachtige ontwerp voorzag in een in de boom gehangen terras en een vrijstaande hut op negen slanke stalen palen. De buitenkant is afgewerkt met Ipé-planken en het interieur is bekleed met fineer van jatoba op gelaagd hout.

Para construir esta casa de árbol que sería habitada por una familia de cuatro miembros, los arquitectos eligieron un arce en una zona de césped. El diseño consiste en una terraza suspendida en el árbol y una cabaña independiente levantada sobre nueve delgados postes de acero. El resultado recuerda a una jirafa. El exterior está acabado con tablas ipé y el interior está revestido con chapas de jatoba sobre contrachapado.

Per costruire questa casa sull'albero destinata a una famiglia di quattro persone, gli architetti hanno scelto un acero in una prato. Il progetto prevede una terrazza sospesa sull'albero e una casetta indipendente poggiante su nove sottili pali d'acciaio. Il risultato ricorda la forma di una giraffa. L'esterno è decorato con listelli di Ipè e l'interno è ricoperto da fogli di jatoba su compensato.

Um ácer existente no jardim relvado foi escolhido para acolher uma casa da árvore de uma família de quatro pessoas. O *design* consiste num terraço suspenso na árvore e de uma cabine independente construída sobre nove esguios postes de aço. O resultado faz pensar numa girafa. O exterior recebeu acabamentos em tábuas de ipê e o interior foi revestido por folheado de jobotá sobre contraplacado.

En lönn på gräsmattan valdes ut för bygget av detta trädhus åt en familj på fyra personer. Designen består av en terrass upphängd i trädet och en fristående stuga byggd på nio smala stålstolpar. Resultatet får en att tänka på en giraff. Exteriören är avslutad med ipe-skivor och interiören är klädd med jatoba-fanér på plywood.

BACHSTELZE TREE HOUSE

ANDREAS WENNING/BAUMRAUM
© Alasdair Jardine

This tree house is constructed on private property close to the main house along a creek. It is composed of a freestanding cabin on wood posts and a long deck on two stilts, which is attached to the trees with heavy-duty straps and steel ropes. The framework is finished with oak boards inside and Corten steel on the outside.

Cette maison perchée est construite sur une propriété privée, à proximité de la résidence principale, le long d'une rivière. Elle se compose d'une cabane indépendante sur poteaux de bois et d'une longue plateforme montée sur deux pilotis, attachée aux arbres par de puissantes sangles et de forts câbles d'acier. L'armature a reçu une finition intérieure en planches de bois et une finition extérieure en acier Corten.

Dieses Baumhaus steht auf einem Privatgrund in der Nähe des Hauptgebäudes an einem Bach. Es besteht aus einer freistehenden Hütte auf Holzpfosten und einer länglichen Terrasse auf zwei Pfeilern, die mithilfe von strapazierfähigen Bändern und Stahlseilen an dem Baum befestigt ist. Die Rahmenstruktur ist innenseitig mit Eichenbrettern und außenseitig mit Cortenstahl verkleidet.

Dit boomhuis is gebouwd op particulier terrein, aan een kreek naast de woning. Het bestaat uit een vrijstaande hut op houten palen en een lang plankier op twee pijlers, dat met sterke riemen en stalen kabels aan de bomen is bevestigd. Het geraamte is vanbinnen afgewerkt met eiken planken en met Cortenstaal aan de buitenkant.

Esta casa de árbol está situada en una propiedad privada cerca de la casa principal a orillas de riachuelo. Se compone de una cabina independiente levantada sobre postes de madera y de una larga plataforma soportada por dos pilares, ambas sujetas a los árboles con correas resistentes y sogas de acero. En el exterior, la estructura está acabada con tablas de roble y acero Corten.

Questa casa sull'albero sorge in una proprietà privata nei pressi della casa principale in riva a un ruscello. È composta da una cabina indipendente poggiante su pali di legno e da una lunga piattaforma sostenuta da due pilastri, entrambe sono assicurate agli alberi mediante cinghie robuste e cavi d'acciaio. All'interno, la struttura è rifinita con listelli di quercia e acciaio Corten.

Esta casa da árvore foi construída numa propriedade privada, perto da casa principal e junto a um rio. É composta por uma cabine independente, erguida sobre postes de madeira, e uma longa esplanada sobre duas andas, presa às árvores por correias resistentes e cordas de aço. A estrutura tem acabamentos de tábuas de carvalho, por dentro, e aço Corten, por fora.

Detta trädhus är konstruerat på en privat äga nära huvudfastigheten längs med en bäck. Det består av en fristående stuga på trästolpar och ett långt däck på två stöttor, som är fästade vid träden med remmar för tungt gods och stålvajrar. Ramverket har fått en yta av ekplattor på insidan och vittrat stål på utsidan.

LOUISA TREE HOUSE

ANDREAS WENNING/BAUMRAUM
© Andreas Wenning

A family with children commissioned the construction of a tree house in their garden full of magnificent trees. The design comprises a two-level terrace and an arched-shaped tree house. The construction consists of a curved steel frame with flanking wooden glulam arches sided with larch boards inside and larch shingles outside.

Une famille avec enfants a fait construire cette *tree house* dans son jardin rempli d'arbres magnifiques. La structure comporte une terrasse à deux niveaux et une cabane en forme d'arche. La construction consiste en une ossature d'acier cintré flanquée de nervures en glulam ; le revêtement est en planches de mélèze à l'intérieur, en bardeaux de mélèze à l'extérieur.

Eine Familie mit drei Kindern hat den Bau dieses Baumhaus für ihren mit wundervollen Bäumen bewachsenen Garten in Auftrag gegeben. Der Entwurf umfasst eine Terrasse mit zwei verschiedenen Ebenen und ein bogenförmiges Baumhaus. Die Konstruktion besteht aus Brettschichtholzbögen, die von einem gewölbten Stahlrahmen gehalten werden, außenseitig sind sie mit Schindeln verkleidet, der Innenraum ist mit Latten aus Lärchenholz vertäfelt.

Een gezin met kinderen wilde graag een huis in een van de majestueuze bomen in hun tuin. De architect ontwierp een terras met twee verdiepingen en een boogvormig boomhuis. De constructie bestaat uit een stalen frame, bogen van glulam en wanden van lariks - planken aan de binnenkant en latten aan de buitenkant.

Una familia con hijos encargó la construcción de una casa de árbol en su jardín repleto de espléndidos árboles. El diseño consta de una terraza de dos niveles y una casa de árbol de forma abovedada. La construcción consiste en una estructura curvada de acero flanqueada por arcos de madera laminada revestidos interiormente con tablas de alerce y de placas de alerce por fuera.

Una famiglia con figli ha incaricato la costruzione di una casa sull'albero nel suo giardino colmo di magnifiche piante. Il progetto prevede una terrazza su due livelli e una casa sull'albero a forma di volta. La costruzione consiste in una struttura curva d'acciaio affiancata da archi di legno laminato rivestiti all'interno da listelli di larice e da pannelli di larice all'esterno.

Uma família com crianças solicitou a construção de uma casa da árvore no seu jardim repleto de arvoredo magnificente. O *design* inclui um terraço com dois níveis e uma casa em forma de arco. A construção é composta por uma armação em aço curvo, flanqueada por arcos em Glulam, revestida por tábuas de lariço, pelo lado de dentro, e ripas de lariço, pelo lado de fora.

En barnfamilj beställde konstruktionen av ett trädhus i deras trädgård full av magnifika träd. Designen innefattar en tvåvånings-terrass och ett bågformat trädhus. Konstruktionen består av en böjd stålram med flankerande träbågar i glulam klädda med plankor i lärkträ och takplattor i lärkträ på utsidan.

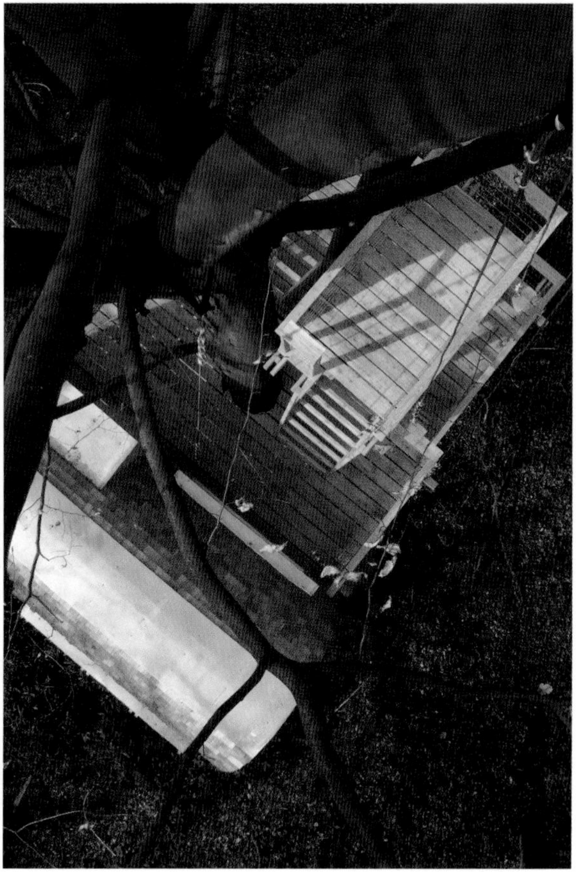

CONE TREE HOUSE

ANDREAS WENNING/BAUMRAUM
© Computer generated renderings

The design of this tree house is inspired by the shape of a pine cone. The tree house wraps the tree, which bears it without any additional support. Access is via a spiral staircase. The walls are finished in cedar shingles. The two-level interior is equipped with a living room with a cooking area and a sleeping area with a small toilet.

La conception de cette maison dans un arbre est inspirée de la forme d'une pomme de pin. La maison entoure l'arbre qui la porte sans aucun soutien additionnel. L'accès se fait par un escalier en spirale. La finition des murs est en bardeaux de cèdre. L'aménagement intérieur sur deux niveaux comprend un *living room* avec un coin cuisine et une chambre à coucher avec une petite toilette.

Das Design dieses Hauses inspiriert sich an der Form eines Tannenzapfens. Das Baumhaus wurde um den Baum herum gebaut, der es auch trägt, und ist über eine Wendeltreppe zu erreichen. Die Wände wurden mit Zedernschindeln verkleidet. Der zweigeschossige Innenraum umfasst ein Wohnzimmer, einen Küchenbereich, einen Schlafbereich und eine kleine Toilette.

Dit boomhuis is geïnspireerd op een dennenappel. Het is om de boom gewikkeld en steunt op niets anders. Een spiraalvormige trap geeft toegang tot het huis. De muren zijn afgewerkt met dakspanen van cederhout. De woning heeft twee verdiepingen en bezit een huiskamer met een keuken en een slaapvertrek met een kleine toiletruimte.

El diseño de esta casa de árbol encuentra inspiración en las formas de una piña. La construcción envuelve el mismo árbol que la sostiene sin ningún otro soporte adicional. A la vivienda se accede a través de una escalera de espiral. Las paredes están acabadas con tejas de madera de cedro. Los dos niveles interiores se componen de una sala de estar con cocina y de un área de descanso con un pequeño baño.

Il progetto di questa casa su un albero è ispirato alla forma di una pigna. La costruzione avvolge il tronco stesso dell'albero che la sostiene senza altro supporto addizionale. All'abitazione si ha accesso mediante una scala a chiocciola. Le pareti sono rifinite mediante scandole di legno di cedro. I due livelli interni sono composti da un soggiorno con cucina e una zona di riposo con un piccolo bagno.

O projecto para esta casa de árvore foi inspirado na forma de uma pinha. A casa envolve a árvore, que a suporta sem qualquer apoio adicional, e o seu acesso é feito através de uma escada em espiral. As paredes, por seu lado, apresentam acabamentos em ripas de cedro. No interior desta casa de dois pisos localiza-se uma sala de estar com uma área de cozinha e uma zona de dormir com uma pequena casa de banho.

Designen till detta trädhus är inspirerat av formen på en tallkotte. Trädhuset omlindar trädet, som bär upp det utan något ytterligare stöd. Tillgången sker via en spiraltrappa. Väggarna är avslutade med plattor av cederträ. Interiören i två nivåer är utrustad med ett vardagsrum med ett matlagningsutrymme och en sovavdelning med en liten toalett.

SLYNGENDE SLANGE TREE HOUSE

ANDREAS WENNING/BAUMRAUM
© Computer generated renderings

The giant Sequoia in the northern California coast is the setting of this tree house, which comprises a staircase winding up the tree and ending at a two-level cabin. Also a terrace is fixed to the tree with textile straps and cables. The weight of the construction is entirely borne by the tree known for its gigantic dimensions.

Un séquoia géant de la côte Nord de la Californie est le « cadre » naturel de cette maison perchée : un escalier s'enroule comme un serpent lové autour du tronc pour aboutir à une cabane sur deux niveaux. Une terrasse est également fixée à l'arbre par des câbles et des sangles de tissu. Le poids de la construction est entièrement supporté par l'arbre géant.

Ein Riesenmammutbaum an der nördlichen Küste Kaliforniens bietet diesem Baumhaus Halt. Die den Baum umschlingende Treppe führt in ein in zwei Etagen unterteiltes Haus. An den Baum ist außerdem eine Terrasse angebaut, die mithilfe von Stoffriemen und Kabeln befestigt wurde. Das gesamte Gewicht der Konstruktion wird vom Baum alleine getragen, der für seine riesigen Ausmaße bekannt ist.

Een reusachtige kustmammoetboom in het noorden van Californië beschermt dit boomhuis, dat bestaat uit een trap die zich om de boom slingert en uitloopt op een cabine met twee verdiepingen. Er is ook een terras aan de boom bevestigd, met kabels en repen stof. De gigantische boom draagt het volle gewicht van de constructie.

La secuoya gigante de la costa norte de California es el escenario de esta casa de árbol, que consta de una escalera que serpentea por el árbol y acaba en una cabaña distribuida en dos niveles. Dispone asimismo de una terraza fijada al árbol con correas y cables de tela. El peso de la construcción recae completamente sobre este magnífico árbol conocido por sus gigantescas dimensiones.

La sequoia gigante della costa settentrionale della California compone lo scenario di questa casa su albero, che è costituita da una scala che serpeggia lungo l'albero terminando in una capanna distribuita su due livelli. Possiede anche una terrazza fissata all'albero mediante cinghie e cavi di materiale tessile. Il peso della costruzione poggia completamente su questo straordinario albero noto per le sue gigantesche dimensioni.

Esta casa de árvore está instalada numa enorme sequóia na costa norte da Califórnia, apresentando uma escada em caracol que sobe pela árvore e termina numa cabina de dois pisos. Dispõe também de um terraço preso à árvore com correias e cabos têxteis. O peso integral desta construção é suportado pela árvore, que se distingue pela sua enorme dimensão.

Den enorma Sequoiaparken vid kusten i norra Kalifornien är platsen för detta trädhus, som består av en trappa som ringlar upp runt trädet och slutar i en stuga i två nivåer. Dessutom är en terrass fixerad vid trädet med textilremmar och kablar. Konstruktionens vikt bärs helt och hållet upp av trädet, som är känt för sina enorma dimensioner.

Holzmöbel strahlen Wärme und Behaglichkeit aus, und eignen sich für drinnen und draußen. Die rustikale Ästhetik handgefertigter Holzmöbel erfreut sich großer Beliebtheit, doch stehen dank innovativer Verfahrenstechniken vielfältige Möglichkeiten im Bereich des Möbeldesigns zur Verfügung, die allen Bedürfnissen und Geschmäckern gerecht werden.

Houten meubilair is warm en comfortabel en kan zowel binnen als buiten staan. Veel mensen geven de voorkeur aan rustieke, met de hand vervaardigde houten meubels, maar de technologie biedt meer mogelijkheden om meubels naar ieders smaak en behoefte te maken.

WOOD FURNITURE MOBILIER EN BOIS HOLZMÖBEL HOUTEN MEUBELS

Wood furniture is warm and comforting, and is available for outdoor or indoor applications. While many people prefer the rustic aesthetic of hand-crafted wooden furniture, technology offers greater possibilities for furniture design to suit every need and taste.

Un mobilier en bois est chaud et confortable, et l'on peut en utiliser à l'intérieur comme à l'extérieur d'une maison. Et si beaucoup préfèrent l'esthétique rustique d'un mobilier en bois fabriqué artisanalement, les techniques modernes offrent de grandes possibilités au design contemporain pour satisfaire tous les goûts et s'adapter à tous les besoins.

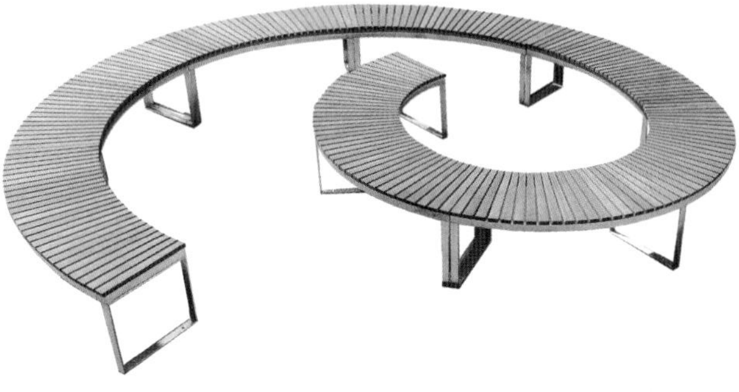

Además de ser cálidos y confortables, los muebles de madera son idóneos tanto en espacios exteriores como interiores. Si bien muchas personas prefieren una estética rústica, la tecnología ofrece grandes oportunidades al diseño contemporáneo de muebles gracias a las cuales puede adaptarse a las necesidades o los gustos del cliente.

Oltre a essere caldi e confortevoli, i mobili di legno sono idonei sia in spazi esterni sia in interni. Sebbene molte persone preferiscano un'estetica rustica, la tecnologia offre enormi opportunità al design contemporaneo di mobili, grazie alle quali è possibile adattarsi alle necessità o ai gusti del cliente.

O mobiliário em madeira é aconchegante e quente, e está disponível em soluções de interior e de exterior. E se muitos preferem os acabamentos rústicos do mobiliário em madeira trabalhado artesanalmente, a tecnologia actual tem para oferecer soluções infinitas e para todos os gostos no que diz respeito ao design de mobiliário.

Trämöbler är varma och behagliga och finns tillgängliga för bruk både utomhus och inomhus. Även om många människor föredrar det rustika utseendet hos handgjorda trämöbler erbjuder tekniken större möjligheter för möbeldesign att passa varje behov och smak.

MOBILIARIO DE MADERA

ARREDAMENTO DI LEGNO

MOBILIÁRIO EM MADEIRA

TRÄMÖBLER

IKEA PS SLINGRA
Ehlén Johansson
Solid birch, plywood and plastic

IKEA PS KARLJOHAN
Christian Halleröd
Solid birch

IKEA PS BRUSE
Christian Halleröd
Beech laminate and aluminum

Marcus Wespi & Gérôme de Meuron Architects
© Hannes Henz

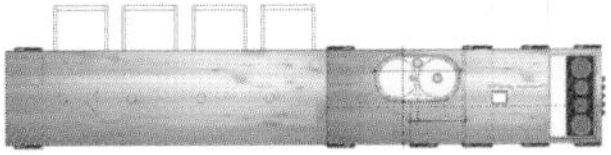

Bulthaup b3

Continua CH
© Binova

Coast GbR Architekten
Photograph: © David Frack

Samso + Associats
Photograph: © Jordi Miralles

Boston Curve Bench
© Beesawat
Teak

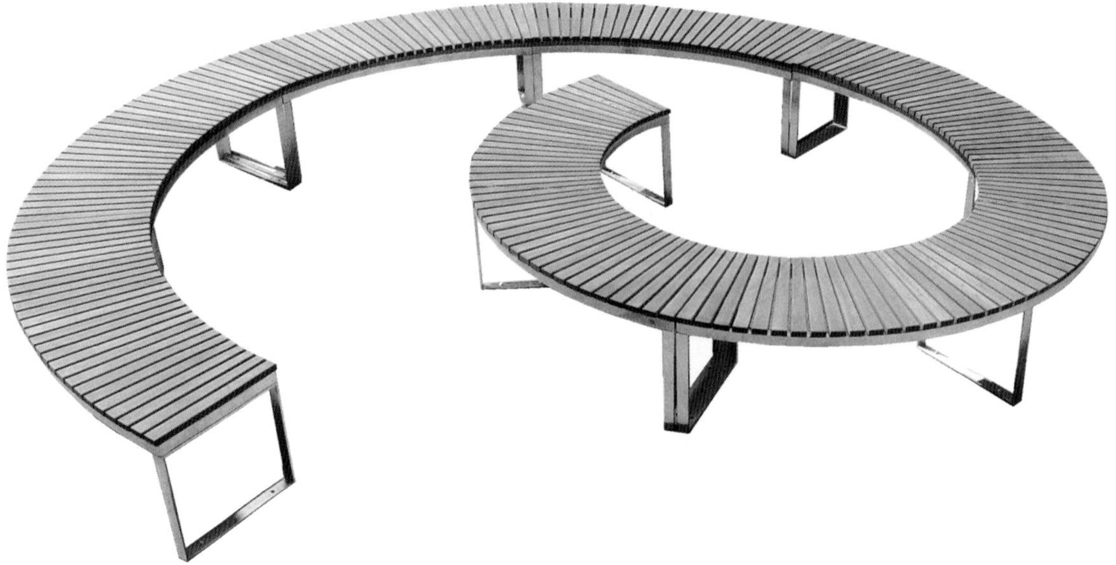

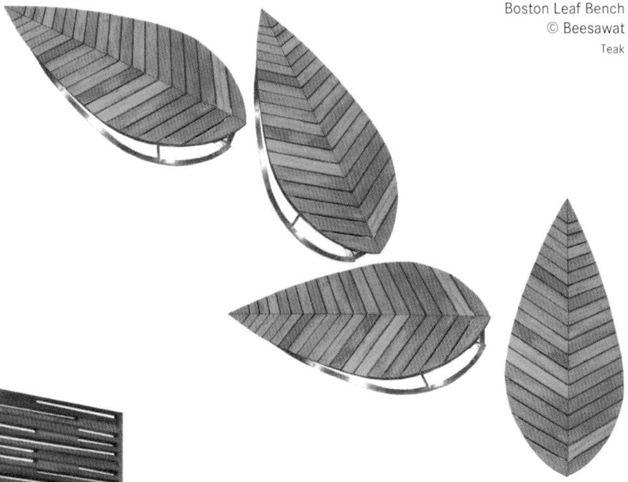

Boston Leaf Bench
© Beesawat
Teak

Noon Collection
© Beesawat
Teak

Cubic Collection
© Beesawat
Teak

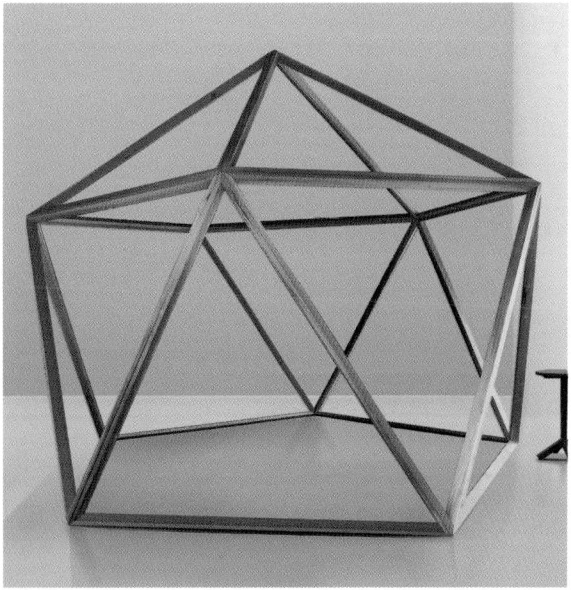

Dome
© Beesawat
Teak

Frankfurt Modular
© Beesawat
Teak

Frankfurt with Arm
© Beesawat
Teak

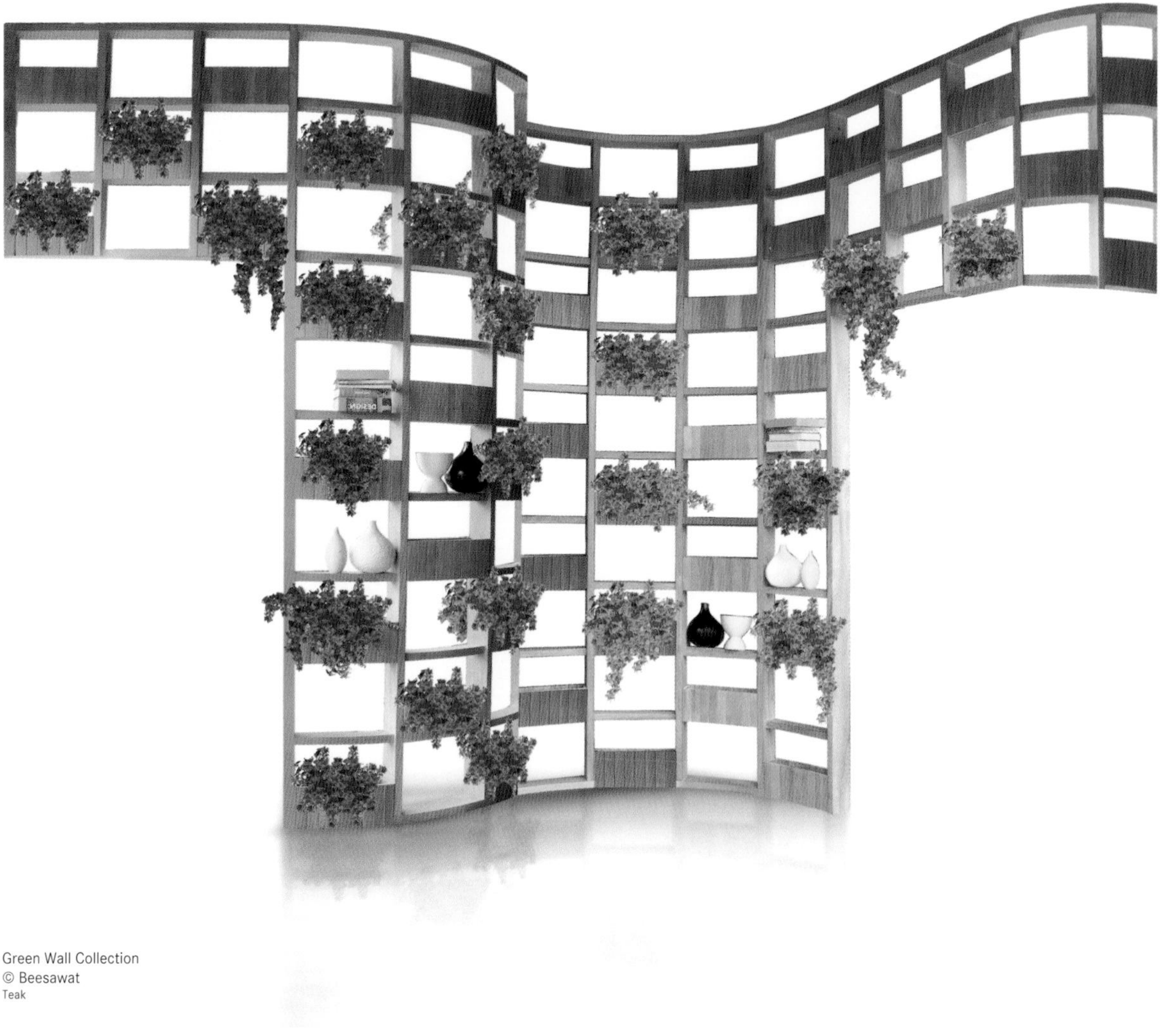

Green Wall Collection
© Beesawat
Teak

Noon Collection
© Beesawat
Teak

Stick Up Collection
© Beesawat
Teak

PHu Bench
© Beesawat
Teak

Riviera Collection
© Beesawat
Teak

Maritim Collection
© Beesawat
Teak

Summer Cabana Collection
© Beesawat
Teak

Summer Bed Collection
© Beesawat
Teak

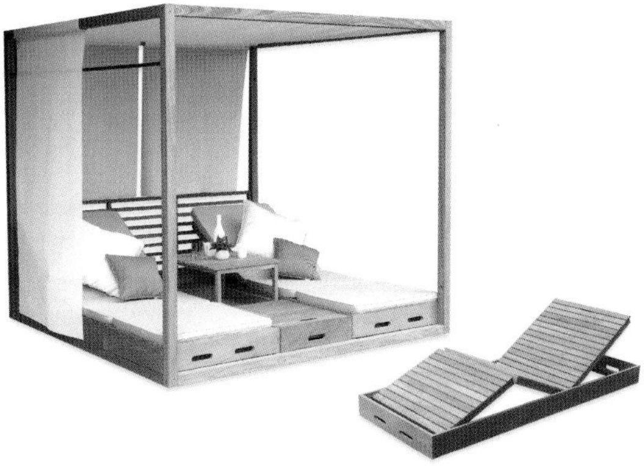

Tiera Bed
© Beesawat
Teak

Wave Collection
© Beesawat
Teak

Y Collection
© Beesawat
Teak

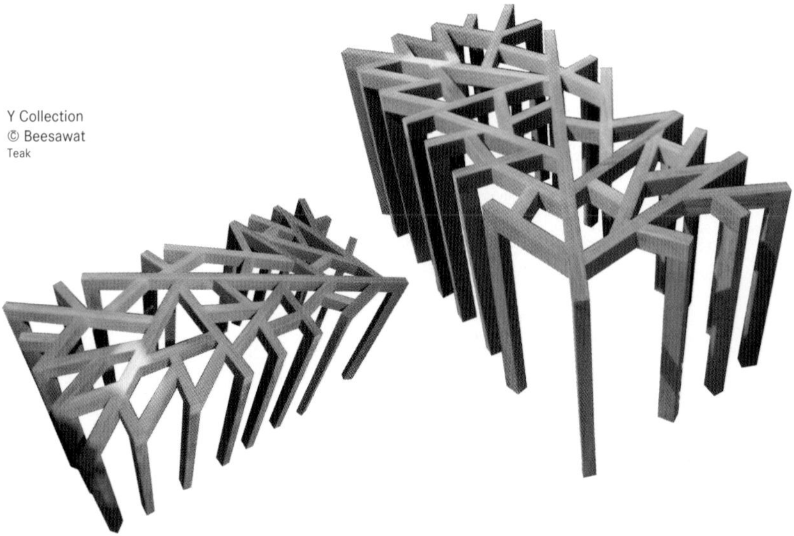

Kia Chair
Giuseppe Viganò
© Emmemobili
Wenge and oak plywood with natural or stained finish

Modular Chest
Ferrucio Laviani
© Emmemobili
Lacquered wood

Palermo Table
Ferrucio Laviani
© Emmemobili
Wenge and oak with natural or stained finish

Sorrento Chest
Alessandro Elli
© Emmemobili
Oak with natural or matte lacquer finish

Maison Chest
Ferrucio Laviani
© Emmemobili
Wood structure and plywood

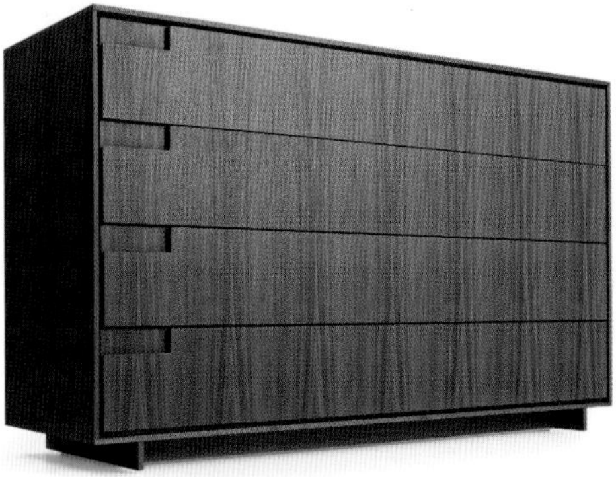

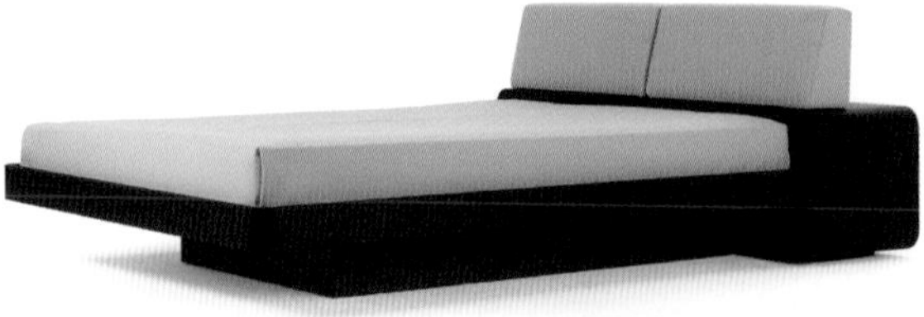

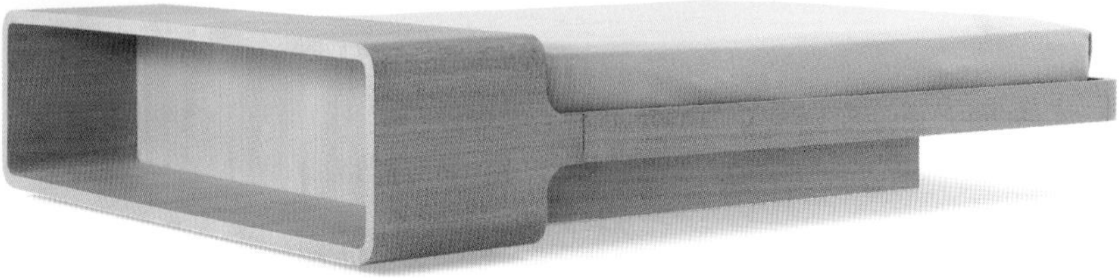

Coiba sofa bed
Balabio - Elli
© Emmemobili
Wenge and oak with natural or stained finish

Valentino sofa bed
Rodolfo Dordoni
© Emmemobili
Wenge and oak with natural or stained finish

Nassa Table
Ferruccio Laviani
© Emmemobili
Curved plywood elements

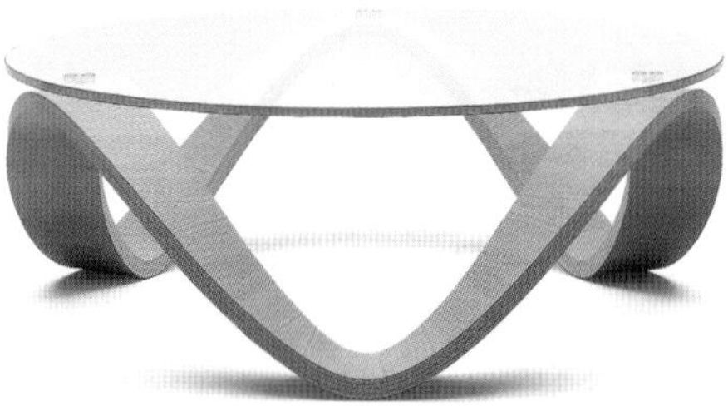

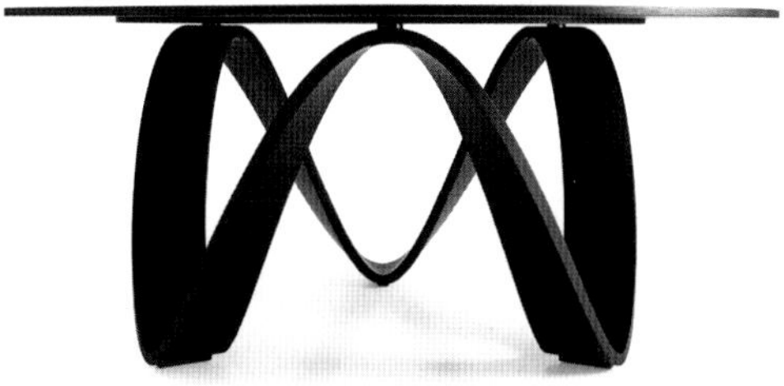

Sumo Table
Alessandro Pascolini
© Emmemobili
Curved plywood elements

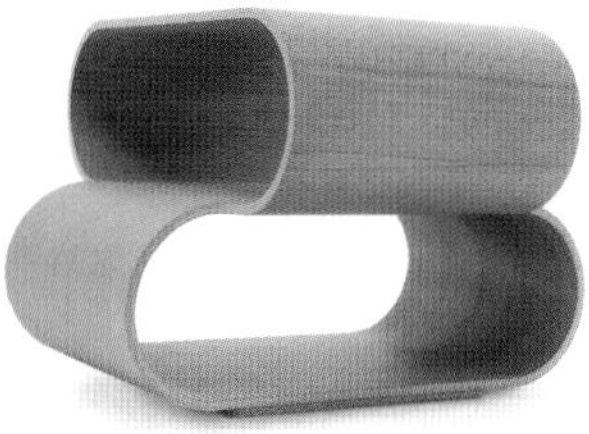

Escher Stackable Table
Ballabio - Elli
© Emmemobili
Wenge and oak with natural or stained finish

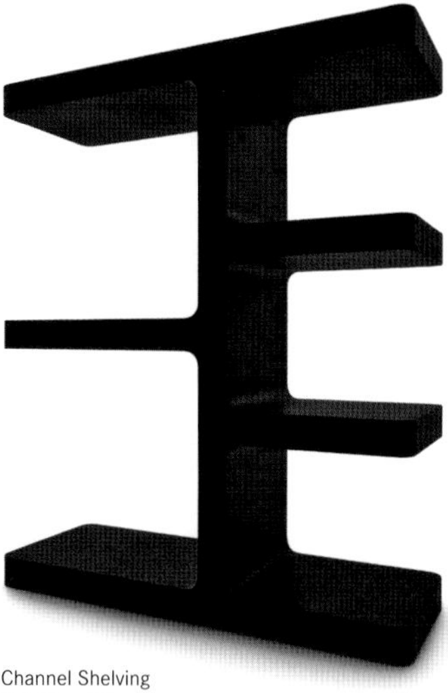

Channel Shelving
Ballabio - Elli
© Emmemobili
Wenge and oak with natural or stained finish

Nastro Chair
Geoffrey D. Harcourt
© Emmemobili
Oak plywood with natural or stained finish

VU.VU.VU Desk
Ballabio - Elli
© Emmemobili
Curved wenge and oak plywood with natural or stained finish

Waimea Chair
Ballabio - Elli
© Emmemobili
Oak plywood with natural or stained finish

Estantería Zero-Uno
Carlo Ballabio
© Emmemobili
Oak plywood with natural or stained finish, veneer or lacquered finish

Blabe Table
Carlo Ballabio
© Emmemobili
Ebony, wenge and oak with natural or stained finish

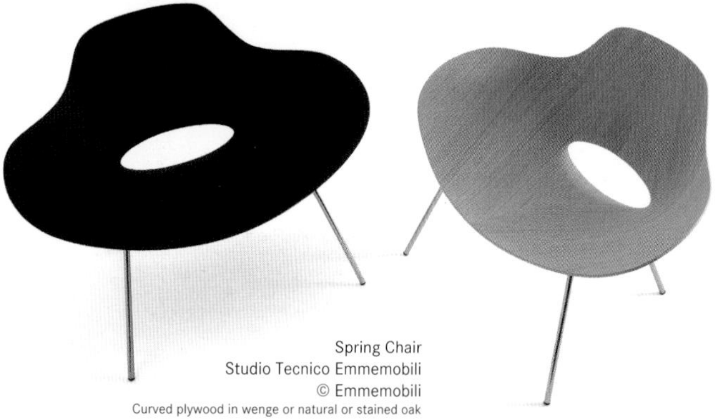

Spring Chair
Studio Tecnico Emmemobili
© Emmemobili
Curved plywood in wenge or natural or stained oak

Dogon Chair
Ferrucio Laviani
© Emmemobili
Curved plywood

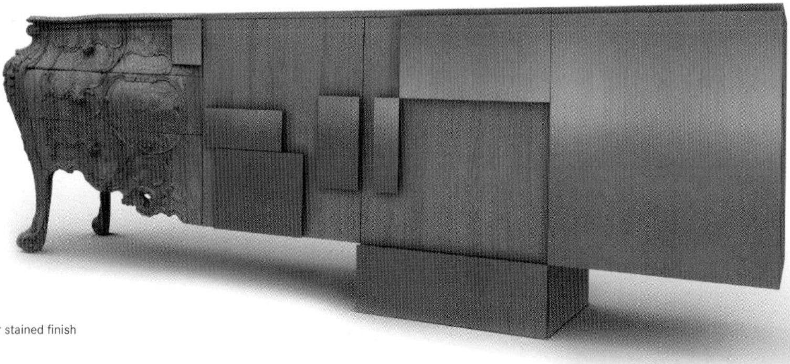

Evolution Chest
Ferrucion Laviani
© Emmemobili
Solid oak with natural or stained finish

Coupè S Chair
Carlo Colombo
© Emmemobili
Natural or stained curved oak plywood

DA.DO Wardrobe
Design D.T.
© Emmemobili
Natural or stained oak

Caos Shelving
Ferrucio Laviani
© Emmemobili
Stained oak

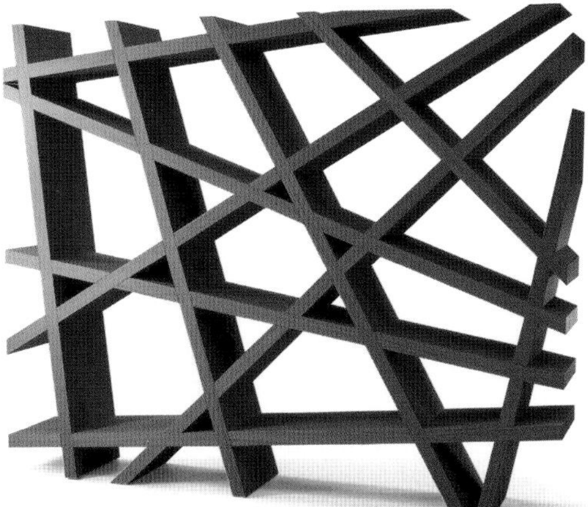

Rosa Shelving
Evgenij V. Poliantsev
© Emmemobili
Plywood structure

Pola Chair
Franco Poli
© Bernini
Curved plywood in Eucaluyptus or ash with natural or stained finish

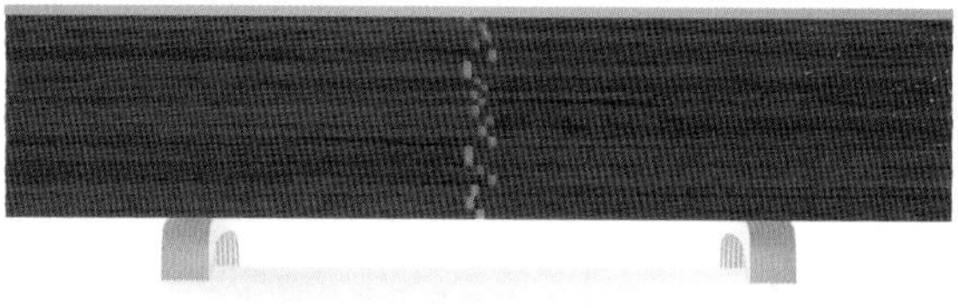

Frankie Chest
Franco Poli
© Bernini
Lacquered exterior with treated pine doors

Kave Sideboard
Karim Rashid
© Bernini
Lacquered exterior and Zebrano wood interior

Giorno/My Pil Magazine Rack
Carl Magnus Persson
© Villa Home Collection
Curved beech

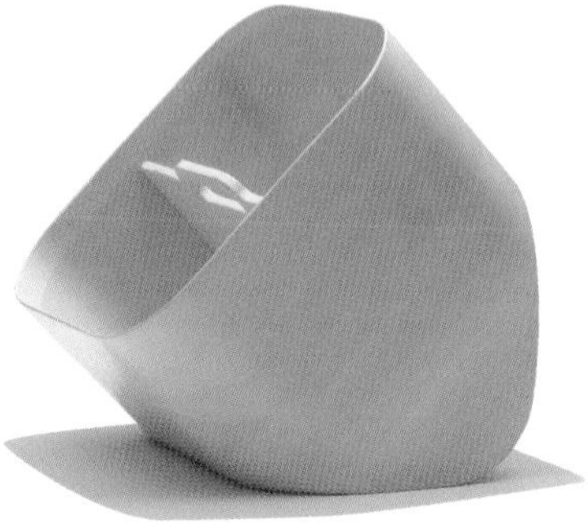

Giorno/Dedo Magazine Rack
Naoko Shintani
© Villa Home Collection
Curved ash

Giorno/Mole Magazine Rack
Naoko Shintani
© Villa Home Collection
Curved ash

Giorno/Pallet Shelving
M.G. Bonfiglio, S. Gabrielli
© Villa Home Collection
Birch plywood

Contenitori/Bellantonio Container
Luca Villa
© Villa Home Collection
Curved beech

Giorno/Nello Bottle Rack
Naoko Shintani
© Villa Home Collection
Curved beech

Giorno/Sollevante Table
M.G. Bonfiglio, S. Gabrielli
© Villa Home Collection
Beech

Notte/Tales Bed
M.G. Bonfiglio, S. Gabrielli
© Villa Home Collection
Beech

Notte/Macramé Bed
Naoko Shintani
© Villa Home Collection
Beech

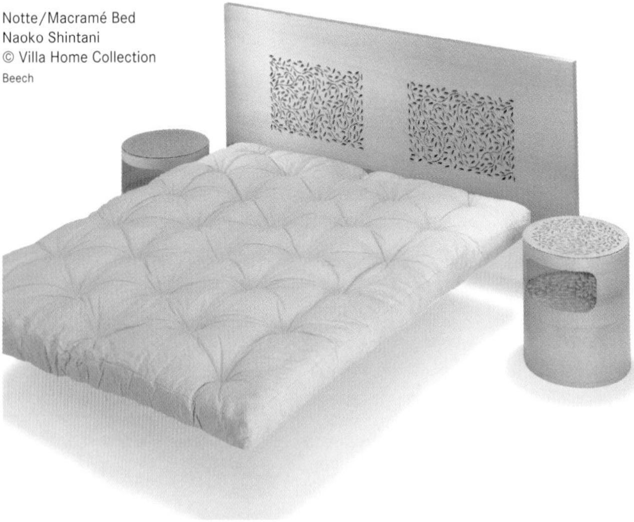

Notte/Macramé
& Oasi Night Table
Naoko Shintani
© Villa Home Collection
Curved beech

Luci/Akira Lamp
Takashi Kirimoto
© Villa Home Collection
Curved beech

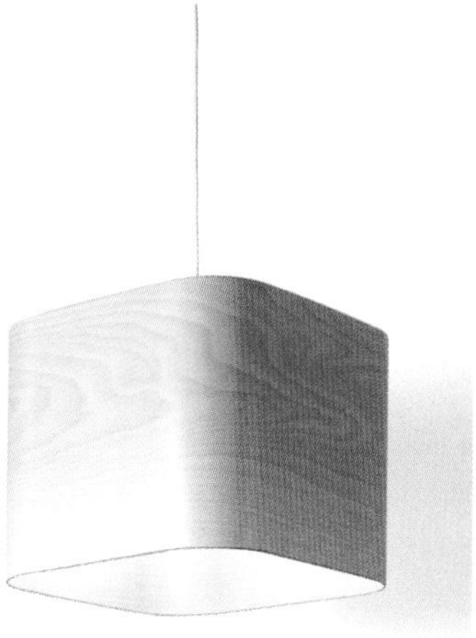

Luci/Lampadra Lamp
Takashi Kirimot
© Villa Home Collection
Curved ash

Luci/Orion Lamp
Marina Buchan
© Villa Home Collection
Curved beech

Luci/Lampura Light Appliqué
Takashi Kirimoto
© Villa Home Collection
Curved beech

Luci/Astra Lamp
Takashi Kirimoto
© Villa Home Collection
Curved ash

Klick Desk Children's Furniture
© Pkolino
Curved plywood

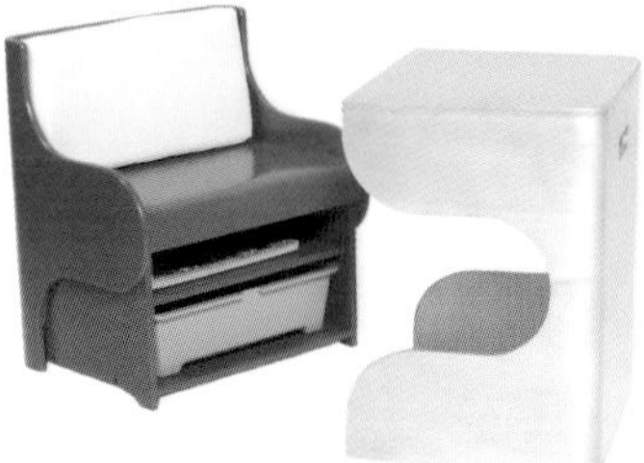

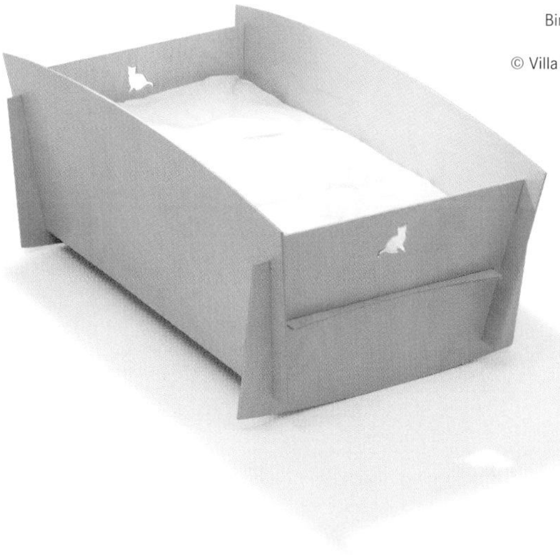

Bimbi/Gioculla Cot
Naoko Shintani
© Villa Home Collection
Silver-plated beech

Bimbi/Pupo Stackable Container
Naoko Shintani
© Villa Home Collection
Curved beech

Bimbi/Stool Container and Stool
Naoko Shintani
© Villa Home Collection
Beech

WOOD CATALOGUE

The following is an index for different types of wood in which the appearance, nomenclature, physical properties and uses are outlined.

Glossary

Alburnum (or sapwood): The part of the tree with living cells that transports or stores nutrients. It is a lighter color and more porous than the duramen, and can rot.
Duramen (or heartwood): The mature part of the wood that is the structural part of the tree. It is without living cells.

Microscopic Characteristics

Grain: The direction of the wood fibers in respect to the axis of the tree. Straight grain wood, parallel to the axis, is easy to work with. Wavy, curved, spiral or slanted grain is more difficult to work with, but aesthetically affords more possibilities.

Physical Characteristics

Density: The relationship between mass and volume with 12% humidity, which is expressed in kg/m³. In conifers it ranges from 400 (very light) to 700 (very heavy), and in broadleaves, from 500 to 950.
Hardness: Indicates the index of penetration of one material into another and specifies the resistance of the wood to abrasion or chipping.
Hygroscopicity: The capacity of the wood to absorb more or less moisture (water) from the atmosphere or from the medium that it is in.
Contraction: Shrinkage due to a loss of moisture.
Ratio of unit volume contraction: The change in volume that wood undergoes due to a 1% change in moisture. According to this ratio wood may have:

- slight density (0.15-0.40), ideal for the manufacture of furniture.
- fair density (0.35-0.49), good for carpentry.
- average density (0.40-0.55), good for construction.
- rather high density (0.55-0.75), good for radial construction.
- very high density (0.75-1), ideal for environments with perpetual moisture.

Mechanical characteristics

Cracking or splitting: It indicates the resistance to breakage if penetrated, nailed or screwed into.

Chemical characteristics

Workability: Woods with high resin, oil or wax contents are difficult to work with. Petro accumulation and mineral salts originating from the soil that crystallize in the wood, also hinder workability.
Natural durability: This is the resistance of the wood to attacks from destructive agents. This is important when the wood is to be found in conditions where there are changes to moisture that are superior to 18%. The agents can be fungi, xylophagous insects, (coleopterans and termites) and water xylophagous insects. Durability refers to the duramen (the alburnum is always vulnerable to attack) and is classified as durable, sensitive and non-durable.
Impregnability: Ease of treatment with liquids under pressure.
Average impregnability: Average penetration attained after 2 or 3 hours of treatment.
Low impregnability: Only superficial impregnation achieved after 3 or 4 hours.
Zero impregnability (or non-impregnability): It is practically impossible to impregnate.

LES DIFFÉRENTES ESSENCES DE BOIS

Caractéristiques générales

Alburnum (aubier) : désigne la partie de l'arbre dotée de cellules vivantes, qui véhicule ou stocke les nutriments de la plante. L'aubier est de couleur plus claire et il est plus poreux que le cœur du bois (ou *duramen*) et il peut pourrir.
Duramen (cœur du bois) : c'est la partie du bois arrivée à maturité et qui constitue la partie structurelle de l'arbre. Elle est dépourvue de cellules vivantes.

Caractéristiques microscopiques :

Fil : ce terme désigne la direction des fibres du bois par rapport à l'axe de l'arbre. Lorsque le fil est droit, c'est-à-dire parallèle à l'axe, le bois est facile à travailler. Si le fil est *ondé, incurvé, spiralé* ou *oblique,* le travail sera plus difficile, mais les possibilités esthétiques seront éventuellement plus grandes (figures).

Caractéristiques physiques :

Densité : ce terme désigne le rapport entre la masse et le volume, à 12 % d'humidité, exprimé en kg/m³. Il va, pour les conifères, de 400 (très léger) à 700 (très lourd) ; pour les feuillus, de 500 à 950.
Dureté : donne l'indice de pénétration d'un matériau dans un autre et spécifie aussi la résistance du bois à l'abrasion ou à l'écaillement.
Hygroscopicité : indique la capacité du bois à absorber plus ou moins d'humidité de l'atmosphère ou du milieu dans lequel il est plongé.
Retrait : rétrécissement dû à la perte d'humidité.
Coefficient de retrait volumique : indique le changement de volume que le bois subit pour 1 % de changement d'humidité. Selon ce coefficient, le bois peut avoir :

- une densité faible (0,15 à 0,40), idéale pour la fabrication de mobilier ;
- une densité légère (0,35 à 0,49), bonne pour le bois de charpente ;
- une densité moyenne (0,40 à 0,55), bonne pour le bois de construction ;
- une densité assez élevée (0,55 à 0,75), bonne pour la construction radiale ;
- une densité très élevée (0,75 à 1), idéale pour les conditions d'humidité permanente.

Caractéristiques mécaniques :

Éclatement ou fissurage : indique le degré de résistance en cas de pénétration, de clouage ou de vissage.

Caractéristiques chimiques :

Exploitabilité : les bois à forte teneur en résine, en huile ou en cire sont difficiles à travailler. L'accumulation de sels minéraux provenant du sol et qui cristallisent dans le bois diminue aussi l'exploitabilité de certaines essences.
Durabilité naturelle : ce terme désigne la capacité de résistance d'un bois aux agents de destruction naturels. Ce facteur est important si le bois doit se trouver dans des conditions où le pourcentage de changement dans l'humidité ambiante dépasse les 18 %. Ces agents destructeurs peuvent être des champignons, des insectes xylophages aériens (coléoptères et termites) ou aquatiques. L'indice de durabilité se réfère au duramen – l'aubier est toujours vulnérable aux attaques biologiques – qui peut être classé comme *durable, moyennement durable* ou *non durable.*
Imprégnabilité : désigne la facilité plus ou moins grande du traitement par liquides sous pression. L'imprégnabilité est dite *normale* si elle est obtenue après 2 à 3 heures de traitement ; *basse* si elle n'est que superficielle au bout de 3 à 4 heures de traitement ; *nulle,* si le bois est impossible à imprégner.

HOLZKATALOG

Im folgenden Inhaltsverzeichnis werden Erscheinungsbild, Nomenklatur, physikalische Eigenschaften und Nutzung der verschiedenen Holzarten erörtert.

Glossar

Alburnum (oder Splintholz): der lebende Teil des Baums, der Nährstoffe speichert oder transportiert. Splintholz weist eine hellere Farbe auf, ist poröser als das Duramen (Kernholz) und ist nicht faulbeständig.
Duramen (oder Kernholz): der reife Teil des Holzes, der den wesentlichen, strukturellen Teil des Baumes darstellt. Es enthält keine lebenden Zellen.

Mikroskopische Eigenschaften

Maserung: der Verlauf der Holzfasern im Bezug auf die Baumachse. Holz mit gerader, parallel zur Achse verlaufender Maserung lässt sich leicht bearbeiten, wohingegen ein welliger, spiralenförmiger oder schräger Faserverlauf die Bearbeitung erschwert, jedoch aufgrund seiner Ästhetik andere Verwendungsmöglichkeiten bietet.

Physikalische Eigenschaften

Dichte: das Verhältnis zwischen Masse und Volumen bei 12% Feuchtigkeit wird in kg/m³ ausgedrückt. Bei Nadelhölzern schwankt dieser Wert zwischen 400 (sehr leicht) und 700 (sehr schwer), bei Laubhölzern zwischen 500 und 950.
Härte: die Angabe der Härte bezieht sich auf den mechanischen Widerstand, den ein Körper dem Eindringen eines anderen Körpers entgegensetzt, und definiert die Abriebbeständigkeit des Holzes und seine Spaltfestigkeit.
Hygroskopie: die Eigenschaft von Holz, Feuchtigkeit aus der Luft oder aus einem anderen, es umgebenden Medium aufzusaugen, ist je nach Art unterschiedlich stark ausgeprägt.
Schrumpfung: Schwindung aufgrund von Feuchtigkeitsverlust.
Volumen-Schwindmaß: die Volumenabnahme eines Holzes bei Verlust von 1% Feuchtigkeit. Nach dieser Berechnung unterscheidet man zwischen:

- geringer Dichte (0.15-0.40), optimal für den Möbelbau.
- relativer Dichte (0.35-0.49), gut für Tischlerarbeiten.
- mittlerer Dichte (0.40-0.55), gut für den Bau.
- mittelhoher Dichte (0.55-0.75), gut für radiale Konstruktionen
- hoher Dichte (0.75-1), optimaler Einsatz in konstant feuchter Umgebung.

Mechanische Eigenschaften

Riss- oder Spaltfestigkeit: bezieht sich auf die Bruchbeständigkeit von Holz, wenn es durchsägt, genagelt oder gebohrt wird.

Chemische Eigenschaften

Verarbeitbarkeit: Holz mit hohem Harz-, Öl- oder Wachsgehalt ist schwer zu bearbeiten. Öl- und Mineralstoffansammlungen im Boden kristallisieren im Holz und erschweren ebenso seine Bearbeitung.
Natürliche Haltbarkeit: die Widerstandsfähigkeit von Holz gegenüber Schädlingen. Diese Eigenschaft

ist zu beachten, wenn das Holz Bedingungen ausgesetzt ist, in denen die Feuchtigkeitsveränderung über 18% liegt. Bei den Schädlingen kann es sich um Pilze, xylophage Insekten (Käfer und Termiten), und xylophage Wasserinsekten handeln. Die Haltbarkeit bezieht sich auf das Duramen (das Alburnum ist schädigenden Organismen gegenüber immer anfällig), man unterscheidet zwischen haltbarem, empfindlichem und nicht haltbarem Holz.
Imprägnierbarkeit: bezieht sich darauf, wie gut sich das Holz mit Flüssigkeiten druckbehandeln lässt.
Mittlere Imprägnierbarkeit: Mittelmäßige Durchtränkung des Holzes nach zwei- bis dreistündiger Behandlung.
Niedere Imprägnierbarkeit: Nach drei- bis vierstündiger Behandlung ist das Holz nur oberflächlich durchtränkt.
Keine Imprägnierbarkeit: Es ist praktisch unmöglich, das Holz zu imprägnieren.

OVERZICHT VAN HOUTSOORTEN

Hieronder vindt u een opsomming van diverse houtsoorten, waarin het uiterlijk, de naam, de fysieke kenmerken en de toepassingen worden omschreven.

Verklarende woordenlijst

Spinthout: het deel van de boom met levende cellen waarin voedingsstoffen worden getransporteerd of opgeslagen. Spinthout is lichter van kleur en poreuzer dan kernhout en kan gaan rotten.
Kernhout: het volgroeide deel van het hout dat de structuur van de boom bepaalt. Het bevat geen levende cellen.

Microscopische eigenschappen

Nerf: de richting waarin de houtvezels lopen ten opzichte van de as van de boom. Hout met een rechte nerf, d.w.z. evenwijdig aan de as, is gemakkelijk om mee te werken. Een golvende, gebogen, spiraalvormige of schuine nerf maakt de verwerking moeilijker, maar biedt in esthetische zin meer mogelijkheden.

Fysieke kenmerken

Dichtheid (soortelijk gewicht): de verhouding tussen massa en volume met 12% vocht, die wordt uitgedrukt in kg/m³. Bij naaldbomen varieert de dichtheid van 400 (heel licht) tot 700 (heel zwaar) en bij loofbomen van 500 tot 950.
Hardheid: maat voor de doordringbaarheid van het hout en de weerstand die het biedt aan bewerkingen als hakken, zagen en schaven.
Hygroscopiciteit: het vermogen van het hout om meer of minder vocht (water) op te nemen uit de lucht of het omringende materiaal.
Contractie: het krimpen van hout door vochtverlies.
Ratio van contractie per volume-eenheid: de verandering van volume die hout ondergaat bij een verandering van 1% in het vochtgehalte. Op grond van deze ratio heeft hout een:
- geringe dichtheid (0,15-0,40), ideaal voor de vervaardiging van meubels.
- redelijke dichtheid (0,35-0,49), goed voor timmerwerk.
- gemiddelde dichtheid (0,40-0,55), goed voor de bouw.
- vrij hoge dichtheid (0,55-0,75), goed voor radiale bouw.
- zeer hoge dichtheid (0,75-1), ideaal voor een omgeving waar het altijd vochtig is.

Mechanische eigenschappen

Weerstand tegen scheuren, splijten of breken als er in het hout wordt geboord, er spijkers in worden geslagen of schroeven in gedraaid.

Chemische eigenschappen

Hout met een hoog aandeel aan hars, olie of was is moeilijk te bewerken. Ook kiezelzuren en minerale zouten uit de bodem die kristalliseren in het hout, zijn hinderlijk voor de bewerking.
Natuurlijke duurzaamheid: de weerstand van het hout tegen schadelijke invloeden. Dit is belangrijk als het hout in omstandigheden zal verkeren waar de luchtvochtigheid hoger dan 18% zal zijn. Organismen die het hout bedreigen, zijn schimmels, zwammen en xylofage (houtetende) insecten, zoals termieten en een aantal keversoorten. De maat van duurzaamheid wordt gegeven voor het kernhout (het spinthout is altijd gevoelig voor aantasting).
Impregneerbaarheid: maat voor het succes van behandeling met een vloeistof onder druk.
- Gemiddeld: de vloeistof zal na 2 of 3 uur in het hout getrokken zijn.
- Laag: na 3 of 4 uur is er nog maar weinig ingetrokken.
- Nul: het is vrijwel onmogelijk het hout te impregneren.

CATÁLOGO DE MADERAS

A continuación se incluye un listado con diferentes tipos de madera y una explicación resumida sobre su aspecto, nomenclatura, propiedades físicas y usos.

Glosário

Albura (o madera de albura): la parte del árbol con células vivas que transporta o almacena nutrientes. Presenta un color más claro y es más porosa que el duramen; además, puede pudrirse.
Duramen (o madera enteriza): la parte madura de la madera que coincide con la parte estructural del árbol. No tiene células vivas.

Características microscópicas

Veta (hilo o grano): La dirección de las fibras de la madera con respecto al eje del árbol. La madera de fibra o veta recta, paralela al eje, es más fácil de trabajar; por el contrario, la madera con hilo curvado, ondulado, en espiral o inclinado, es más difícil de usar, pero ofrece mayores posibilidades desde un punto de vista estético.

Características físicas

Densidad: Se trata de la relación entre masa y volumen con una humedad del 12% expresada en kg/m³. En las coníferas oscila entre 400 (muy ligera) y 700 (muy consistente), y en árboles de hoja ancha, entre 500 y 950.
Dureza: Indica el índice de penetración de un material en otro y especifica la resistencia de la madera a la abrasión o al astillado.
Higroscopicidad: La capacidad de la madera para absorber la humedad atmosférica (agua) o del medio en que está inserta.
Contracción: Encogimiento o contracción debida a la pérdida de humedad.
Ratio de contracción volumétrica por unidad: El cambio en el volumen sufrido por la madera debido a una variación del 1% en la humedad. De acuerdo con esta ratio la madera puede tener:
- una baja densidad (0,15-0,40), ideal para la manufactura de muebles.
- una densidad razonable (0,35-0,49), buena para la carpintería.
- una densidad media (0,40-0,55), buena para la construcción.
- una densidad bastante alta (0,55-0,75), buena la construcción radial.
- una densidad muy alta (0,75-1), ideal para ambientes con una humedad constante.

Características mecánicas

Agrietamiento: Indica la resistencia a la rotura de la madera si es perforada o fijada con clavos.

Características químicas

Trabajabilidad: Las maderas con altos contenidos en resina, aceite o cera son difíciles para trabajar. La acumulación de petróleo y de sales minerales procedentes del suelo que cristaliza en la madera también dificulta el trabajo con la madera.
Durabilidad natural: Se trata de la resistencia de la madera a los ataques de agentes destructivos. Es una característica importante cuando la madera está en un ambiente en que se verifican cambios en la humedad superiores al 18%. Los agentes pueden ser hongos, insectos xilófagos (coleópteros y termitas) e insectos acuáticos xilófagos. La durabilidad hace referencia al duramen (la albura siempre es vulnerable al ataque), que se clasifica como durable, sensible y no durable.
Impregnabilidad: Facilidad de tratamiento con líquidos a presión.
- Impregnabilidad media: Penetración media obtenida tras 2 o 3 horas de tratamiento.
- Impregnabilidad baja: Impregnación superficial obtenida transcurridas 3 o 4 horas.
- Impregnabilidad cero: Imposibilidad de impregnación.

CATALOGO DELLE VARIETÀ DI LEGNO

Qui sotto riportiamo una lista con diversi tipi di legno e un breve riassunto esplicativo sul loro aspetto, la nomenclatura, le proprietà fisiche e gli usi.

Glossario

Alburno (o legno di alburno): la parte dell'albero con cellule vive che trasportano o contengono sostanze nutritive. Presenta un colore più chiaro ed è più poroso del durame; inoltre, può marcire.
Durame (o cuore del legno): la parte matura del legno coincidente con la porzione strutturale dell'albero. Non possiede cellule vive.

Caratteristiche microscopiche

Venatura: La direzione delle fibre del legno rispetto all'asse dell'albero. Il legno che presenta fibra o venatura retta, parallela all'asse, è più facile da lavorare; invece, il legno con venatura curva, ondulata, a spirale o inclinata, è meno duttile, ma offre maggiori vantaggi da un punto di vista estetico.

Caratteristiche fisiche

Densità: Si tratta del rapporto esistente tra massa e volume a un valore d'umidità del 12% espresso in kg/m³. Nelle conifere oscilla tra 400 (molto leggera) e 700 (molto

consistente), e negli alberi latifogli, si situa tra 500 e 950.
Durezza: Indica l'indice di penetrazione di un materiale in un altro e specifica il grado di resistenza del legno all'abrasione o alla truciolatura.
Igroscopicità: La maggiore o minore capacità che possiede il legno di assorbire l'umidità dall'atmosfera (acqua) o dall'ambiente in cui si trova.
Contrazione: Ritiro o contrazione a causa della perdita d'umidità.
Indice di contrazione volumetrica per unità: Il cambiamento di volume subito dal legno in seguito a una variazione dell'1% nell'umidità. In base a tale indice, il legno può avere:
- una bassa densità (0,15-0,40), ideale per la realizzazione di mobili.
- una densità sufficiente (0,35-0,49), buona per la carpenteria.
- una densità media (0,40-0,55), buona per l'edilizia.
- una densità abbastanza elevata (0,55-0,75), buona per l'edilizia radiale.
- una densità molto elevata (0,75-1), l'ideale per ambienti con un valore d'umidità costante.

Caratteristiche meccaniche

Spaccatura: Indica la resistenza del legno alla rottura quando viene perforata con chiodi o viti.

Caratteristiche chimiche

Duttilità: I legni con elevato contenuto di resina, olio o cera sono difficili da lavorare. Anche l'accumulazione di petrolio e di sali minerali provenienti dal suolo che cristallizzano nel legno rende il legno difficile da lavorare.
Durabilità naturale: Si tratta della resistenza del legno agli attacchi di agenti aggressivi. È una qualità importante quando il legno si trova in un ambiente caratterizzato da variazioni di umidità superiori al 18%. Gli agenti ostili possono essere funghi, insetti xilofagi (coleotteri e termiti) e insetti acquatici xilofagi. La durabilità fa riferimento al durame (l'alburno è sempre vulnerabile all'attacco), che viene classificato come durevole, sensibile e non durevole.
Impregnabilità: Facilità di trattamento con liquidi a pressione.
- Impregnabilità media: penetrazione media ottenuta in seguito a 2 o 3 ore di trattamento.
- Impregnabilità bassa: impregnazione superficiale ottenuta dopo 3 o 4 ore.
- Impregnabilità zero (o non-Impregnabilità): impossibilità d'impregnazione.

TIPOS DE MADEIRA

Seguidamente apresenta-se uma lista dos diferentes tipos de madeira, onde se destaca a sua aparência, a sua nomenclatura, as suas propriedades físicas e as suas aplicações.

Glossário

Alburno (ou borne): parte da árvore com células vivas capazes de transportar ou armazenar nutrientes. Tem uma cor mais clara e é mais porosa do que o cerne, e é passível de apodrecer.
Cerne: parte interior da madeira que forma a estrutura da árvore. Não contém células vivas.

Características microscópicas

Veio: direcção das fibras da madeira em relação ao eixo da árvore. Os veios paralelos ao eixo facilitam o trabalho com a madeira. Os demais tipos de veios, ondulados, curvados, espiralados ou retorcidos, implicam madeiras de mais difícil manuseamento, mas com um leque de possibilidades estéticas mais vasto.

Características físicas

Densidade: relação entre a massa e o volume com 12% de humidade, e que se expressa em kg/m³. Nas coníferas varia entre 400 (muito leve) e 700 (muito pesada), e nas árvores de folha larga varia entre 500 e 950.
Dureza: indica o índice de penetração de um material noutro, e especifica a resistência da madeira à fricção e ao cinzelamento.
Higroscopicidade: capacidade da madeira para absorver mais ou menos humidade (água) da atmosfera ou do meio onde se encontra.
Contracção: encolhimento devido a uma perda de humidade.
Rácio de unidade de volume de contracção: alteração do volume da madeira submetida a uma variação de 1% dos níveis de humidade. De acordo com este rácio, a madeira pode apresentar uma:
- densidade baixa (0.15-0.40), ideal para a fabricação de mobiliário.
- densidade razoável (0.35-0.49), boa para o trabalho de carpintaria.
- densidade média (0.40-0.55), boa para a construção.
- densidade alta (0.55-0.75), boa para a construção radial.
- muito alta densidade (0.75-1), ideal para ambientes permanentemente húmidos.

Características mecânicas

Estalamento e fissuração: indica a resistência à quebra quando penetrada, pregada ou aparafusada.

Características químicas

Capacidade para ser trabalhada: as madeiras com altos teores de resina, óleo ou cera são difíceis de ser trabalhadas. A acumulação de rochas e de sais minerais provenientes do solo e que cristalizam na madeira dificulta igualmente o trabalho com a madeira.
Durabilidade natural: resistência da madeira aos ataques de agentes destrutivos. Este factor é importante para as madeiras provenientes de locais com variações de humidade superiores a 18%. Os agentes podem ser fungos, insectos xilófagos, (coleópteros e térmitas) e insectos xilófagos aquáticos. A durabilidade da madeira reporta-se ao borne (o alburno é sempre vulnerável a ataques) e classifica-se como duradoura, sensível e pouco duradoura.
Impregnabilidade: facilidade de tratamento com líquidos sob pressão.
- Impregnabilidade média: penetração média atingida após 2 ou 3 horas de tratamento.
- Impregnabilidade baixa: impregnação superficial atingida ao fim de 3 ou 4 horas de tratamento.
- Impregnabilidade zero: é praticamente impossível impregnar.

TRÄKATALOG

Följande är ett index över olika trätyper där utseende, nomenklatur, fysiska egenskaper och användningsområden beskrivs.

Ordlista

Alburnum (eller vitved): Den del av träet med levande celler som transporterar eller lagrar näringsämnen. Det har en ljusare färg och är mer poröst än duramen och kan ruttna.
Duramen (eller kärnvirke): De mogna delarna av träet som är trädets strukturella del. Det saknar helt levande celler.

Mikroskopiska karaktäristika

Ådring: Träfibrernas riktning i förhållande till trädets axel. Rakådrat trä, parallellt med axeln, är lättarbetat. Vågigt, kurvigt, spiralformat eller snedådrat trä är mer svårarbetat, men erbjuder fler estetiska möjligheter.

Fysiska karaktäristika

Densitet: Förhållandet mellan massa och volym med 12 % fuktighet, vilket är uttryckt i kg/m³. Hos barrväxter varierar densiteten från 400 (lätt) till 700 (mycket hög), och hos lövträd från 500 till 950.
Hårdhet: Indikerar penetrationsindexet av ett material in i ett annat och specificerar träets motstånd mot skrapsår eller flisning.
Absorptionsförmåga: Träets kapacitet att absorbera mer eller mindre fukt (vatten) från atmosfären eller det medium det befinner sig i.
Sammandragning: Krympning på grund av fuktförlust.
Spännvidd över enhetlig volymsammandragning: Volymförändringen hos trä på grund av 1 % förändring i fuktnivå. Enligt denna spännvidd kan trä ha:
- lätt densitet (0.15-0.40), idealisk för möbeltillverkning.
- medeldensitet (0.35-0.49), bra till snickeri.
- normal densitet (0.40-0.55), bra till husbygge.
- relativt hög densitet (0.55-0.75), bra till radialkonstruktion.
- mycket hög densitet (0.75-1), idealisk för miljöer med konstant fukt.

Mekaniska karaktäristika

Sprickning eller delning: Indikerar träets sprickningsmotstånd om det penetreras, spikas eller skruvas i.

Kemiska karaktäristika

Grad av möjlig bearbetning: Trä med högt innehåll av resin, olja eller vax är svårt att jobba med. Petrifiering och mineralsalter från jorden som kristalliserar sig i träet försvårar också bearbetningen.
Naturlig hållbarhet: Detta är träets motståndskraft mot nedbrytande element. Detta är viktigt när träet skall befinna sig i situationer där fuktförändringar är högre än 18 %. De nedbrytande elementen kan vara svamp, träätande insekter (skalbaggar och termiter) och vattenlevande träätande insekter. Hållbarheten syftar på kärnvirket (kärnvirket är alltid sårbart mot attacker) och klassas som hållbart, känsligt och icke hållbart.
Impregneringsförmåga: Underlättande av behandling med hjälp av vätskor under högtryck.
- Genomsnittlig impregneringsförmåga: Genomgående impregnering uppnådd efter 2-3 timmars behandling.
- Låg impregneringsförmåga: Endast ytimpregnering uppnådd efter 3 eller 4 timmar.
- Noll impregneringsförmåga (eller icke-impregneringsförmåga): Det är praktiskt taget omöjligt att impregnera.

Pterocarpus soyauxii – **African Coralwood – Padouk d'Afrique – Afrikanisches Padouk – Afrikaans padoek**

Family: *Fabaceae*
Density: *0.65-0.85 g/cm³*
Zones of Production: *Cameroon, Guinea, Gabon, Congo*
Boles are 10 to 20 m (33 to 66 ft) tall and 60 to 100 cm (24 to 39 in) in diameter. African coralwood has straight to interlocked grain with a moderately coarse texture. Red at first, this very durable, hard and heavy wood becomes purplish-brown on exposure to light. Works well with hand and machine tools. It is however not suitable for steam bending. This wood is prized for high-end cabinetry, carving, veneer, flooring, and joinery.

Famille : *Fabacées*
Densité : *0,65-0,85 g/cm³*
Zones de production : *Cameroun, Guinée, Gabon et Congo*
Les troncs ont de 10 à 20 m de hauteur, pour 60 à 100 cm de diamètre. Le padouk d'Afrique possède un fil droit, parfois un contre-fil, un grain moyennement fin. D'abord rouge après la coupe, ce bois très stable, dur et dense, devient brun violacé lorsqu'il est exposé à la lumière. Il se travaille bien, manuellement comme à la machine-outil. Il est toutefois impossible de le cintrer à la vapeur. Ce bois est apprécié pour l'ébénisterie haut de gamme, la sculpture, le placage, le revêtement de sol et la menuiserie.

Familie: *Fabaceae*
Dichte: *0,65-0,85 g/cm³*
Vorkommen: *Kamerun, Guinea, Gabun, Congo*
Der Stamm ist 10 bis 20 m lang, bei einem Durchmesser von 60-100 cm. Die Maserung des afrikanischen Padouk ist gerade bis wechselwüchsig, seine Struktur ist mittelgrob. Das ausgesprochen haltbare, harte und schwere Holz ist von Natur aus rot und verfärbt sich bei Lichteinfall in ein leicht violettes Braun. Es kann gut von Hand und maschinell bearbeitet werden, ist jedoch für das Dampfbiegen nicht geeignet. Dieses Holz wird in der Möbeltischlerei, der Schnitzerei, als Furniermaterial, für den Fußbodenausbau und für Zimmerarbeiten verwendet.

Familie: *Fabaceae*
Dichtheid: *0,65-0,85 g/cm³*
Productiegebieden: *Kameroen, Guinee, Gabon, Congo*
De stam is 10 tot 20 meter lang en 60 tot 100 centimeter dik. Afrikaans padoek is recht- tot kruisdradig en matig grof van structuur. Dit zeer duurzame, harde en zware hout is eerst rood, maar kleurt paarsbruin bij blootstelling aan licht. Laat zich goed bewerken, zowel met handgereedschap als elektrisch. Het is echter niet geschikt om te buigen met stoom. Dit hout is geliefd voor kwaliteitskasten, houtsnijwerk, fineer, vloeren en schrijnwerk.

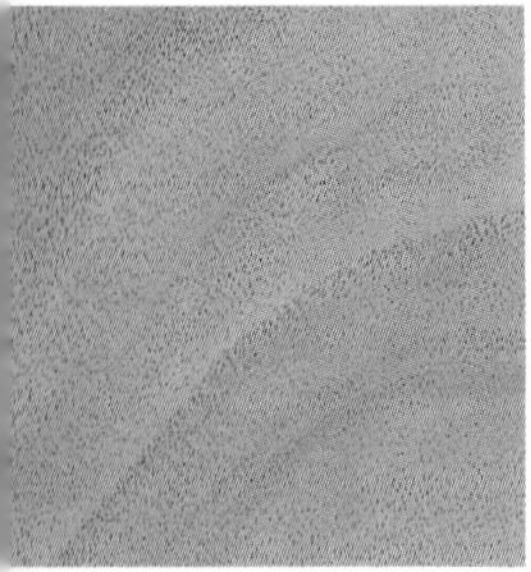

Khaya ivorensis – **African Mahogany – Acajou d'Afrique – Afrikanisches Mahagoni – Afrikaans mahonie**

Family: *Meliaceae*
Density: *0.45-0.60 g/cm³*
Zones of Production: *Ghana, Ivory Coast, Cameroon, Guinea, Gabon, Angola, Liberia, Nigeria*
Boles are 15 to 25 m (49 to 82 ft) tall. Diameter is 60 to 120 cm (24 to 47 in). African mahogany is a hardwood characterized by vertical bonds of varying luster and vessel markings. Very durable and stable, African mahogany is used for cabinet making, joinery, paneling, boat decking, veneer, and plywood. African mahogany can be stained and polished to an excellent finish.

Famille : *Méliacées*
Densité : *0,45-0,60 g/cm³*
Zones de production : *Ghana, Côte-d'Ivoire, Cameroun et Guinée, Gabon, Angola, Liberia et Nigeria*
Troncs de 15 à 25 m de hauteur, pour un diamètre de 60 à 120 cm. L'acajou d'Afrique est un bois dur caractérisé par ses bandes verticales au lustre changeant. Très résistant et très stable, l'acajou d'Afrique est utilisé en ébénisterie et en menuiserie, pour le lambrissage et les ponts de bateau, en placage et en contreplaqué. L'acajou d'Afrique peut être teinté et il est susceptible de recevoir un beau poli.

Familie: *Meliaceae*
Dichte: *0,45-0,60 g/cm³*
Vorkommen: *Ghana, Elfenbeinküste, Kamerun, Guinea, Gabun, Angola, Liberia, Nigeria*
Der Baumstamm ist 15-25 m lang, sein Durchmesser liegt zwischen 60 und 120 cm. Afrikanisches Mahagoni zeichnet sich durch eine senkrecht verlaufende Bänderung mit verschiedenen Glanzgraden und Gefäßmarkierungen aus. Es ist ausgesprochen haltbar und stabil und wird für den Schrankbau, in der Tischlerei, für Verkleidungen, Schiffsdeckbeläge, Furniere und Sperrholz verwendet.

Familie: *Meliaceae*
Dichtheid: *0,45-0,60 g/cm³*
Productiegebieden: *Ghana, Ivoorkust, Kameroen, Guinee, Gabon, Angola, Liberia, Nigeria*
De stam is 15 tot 25 meter lang en 60 tot 120 centimeter dik. Afrikaans mahonie is een hardhout dat gekenmerkt wordt door verticale banen van wisselende glans en tekenen van de houtvaten. Afrikaans mahonie is zeer duurzaam en stabiel en wordt gebruikt voor kasten, schrijnwerk, paneelwerk, scheepsdekken, fineer en multiplex. Afrikaans mahonie laat zich mooi beitsen en polijsten.

Lovoa trichilioides – **African Walnut – Dibétou – Afrikanischer Walnussbaum – Dibétou**

Family: *Meliaceae*
Density: *0.50-0.55 g/cm³*
Zones of Production: *Ivory Coast, Congo, Ghana, Nigeria, Cameroon, Guinea*
Boles are 15 to 20 m (49 to 66 ft) tall and 50 to 55 cm (19.6 to 21.6 in) in diameter. The wood is bronze-colored with irregular dark lines. It is extremely hard, heavy, close-grained, and resists water well. The wood is used in standard construction, to make pilings for bridges, railway ties, and in the production of charcoal. It is also used for furniture and cabinetry, veneers, paneling, fixtures and joinery.

Famille : *Méliacées*
Densité : *0,50-0,55 g/cm³*
Zones de production : *Côte-d'Ivoire, Congo, Ghana, Nigeria, Cameroun et Guinée*
Troncs de 15 à 20 m de hauteur, pour 50 à 55 cm de diamètre. Le bois est de couleur bronze, avec des lignes foncées irrégulières. Doté d'un fil serré, parfois d'un contre-fil, il est extrêmement dur et lourd, et résiste bien à l'eau. Ce bois est utilisé comme matériau de construction standard, pour les ponts, les traverses de chemin de fer et pour produire un excellent charbon de bois. On l'utilise aussi pour le mobilier et l'ébénisterie, le placage, le lambrissage et la menuiserie en général.

Familie: *Meliaceae*
Dichte: *0,50-0,55 g/cm³*
Vorkommen: *Elfenbeinküste, Kongo, Ghana, Nigeria, Kamerun, Guinea*
Der zwischen 50 und 55 cm starke Baumstamm ist 15-20 m lang. Das Holz weist eine bronzene Färbung und unregelmäßige schwarze Linien auf. Der Faserverlauf des ausgesprochen harten und schweren Holzes ist eng und es ist sehr wasserbeständig. Dieses Holz wird im herkömmlichen Bauwesen, für den Brückenbau, für Eisenbahnschwellen und für Holzkohle verwendet, aber auch für Möbel, Furniere, Verkleidungen, fest eingebaute Elemente und Zimmerarbeiten.

Familie: *Meiliaceae*
Dichtheid: *0,50-0,55 g/cm³*
Productiegebieden: *Ivoorkust, Congo, Ghana, Nigeria, Kameroen, Guinee*
De stam is 15 tot 20 meter lang en 50 tot 55 centimeter dik. Het hout is bronskleurig met onregelmatige donkere lijnen. Dit zware en extreem harde hout heeft een dichte nerf en is zeer waterbestendig. Het hout wordt gebruikt in de bouw voor brugpijlers en spoorbiels en bij de productie van houtskool. Het wordt ook gebruikt voor meubels en kasten, fineer, paneelwerk, diverse interieurelementen en schrijnwerk.

Coral africano o Palo rojo – Padauk africano – Padouk – Västafrikansk Padauk

Familia: *Fabáceas*
Densidad: *0,65-0,85 g/cm^3*
Zonas de producción: *Camerún, Guinea, Gabón, Congo*
Su tronco tiene entre 10 y 20 m de altura y un diámetro que oscila entre los 60 y 100 cm. El palo rojo o coral africano presenta una fibra alternada tirando a recta con una textura moderadamente gruesa. Su madera, fuerte y resistente, es roja, aunque adopta una tonalidad marrón violácea bajo la exposición a la luz. Si bien es fácil de trabajar tanto con herramientas manuales como mecánicas, no es apta para el curvado por vapor. Se trata de una madera muy preciada para la realización de muebles y armarios de gama alta, tallas, enchapados, revestimientos para suelos y obras de carpintería.

Famiglia: *Fabacee*
Densità: *0,65-0,85 g/cm^3*
Zone di produzione: *Camerun, Guinea, Gabon, Congo*
Il tronco ha un'altezza di 10-20 metri e un diametro che oscilla tra i 60 e i 100 centimetri. Il padauk africano presenta una fibra alternata tendenzialmente dritta, con una texture moderatamente spessa. Il suo legno, forte e resistente, è rosso, ma assume una tonalità marrone violacea quando è esposto alla luce. Benché sia facile da lavorare con strumenti sia manuali sia meccanici, non è adatto alla curvatura a vapore. Si tratta di un legno molto apprezzato nella realizzazione di mobili e armadi d'alto livello, lavori a intaglio, impiallacciatura, rivestimenti per pavimenti e lavori di falegnameria.

Família: *Fabaceae*
Densidade: *0,65-0,85 g/cm^3*
Zonas de Produção: *Camarões, Guiné, Gabão, Congo*
Os troncos medem 10 a 20 metros de altura e 60 a 100 centímetros de diâmetro. O padouk tem um grão direito a entrecruzado e uma textura moderadamente grosseira. Inicialmente vermelha, esta madeira, muito resistente, dura e pesada, torna-se castanha arroxeada com a exposição à luz. Trabalha-se bem com ferramentas manuais e eléctricas não sendo, contudo, apropriada para a moldagem a vapor. Esta madeira é apreciada para marcenaria de luxo, escultura, folheado, soalhos e carpintaria.

Familj: *Fabaceae*
Densitet: *0,65-0,85 g/cm^3*
Produktionsområden: *Kamerun, Guinea, Gabon, Kongo*
Trädstammarna är 10-20 meter höga och 60-100 cm i diameter. Västafrikansk padauk har raka till sammanhängande ådringar med en måttligt grov struktur. Detta mycket tåliga, hårda och tunga träslag är till en början rött för att bli lilabrunt när det utsätts för ljus. Arbetas bra med hand- eller maskinverktyg. Det är dock inte lämpligt som böjträ. Detta träslag är värderat till exklusivt möbelsnickeri, snideri, fanering, golvläggning och snickeri.

Caoba africana – Mogano bianco – Mogno africano – Khaya Mahogny

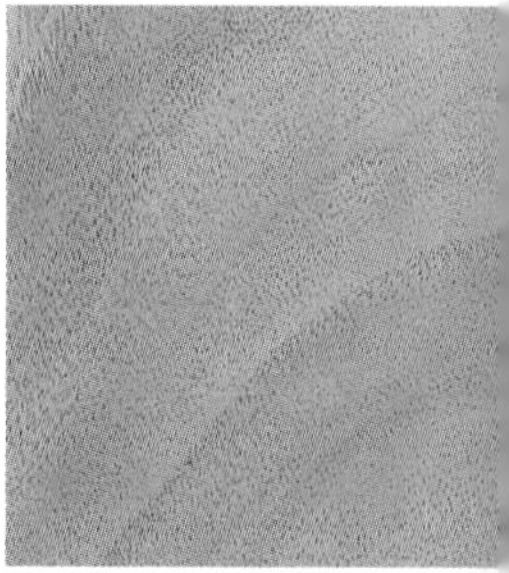

Familia: *Meliáceas*
Densidad: *0,45-0,60 g/cm^3*
Zonas de producción: *Ghana, Costa de Marfil, Camerún, Guinea, Gabón, Angola, Liberia, Nigeria*
Su tronco tiene entre 15 y 25 m de altura y un diámetro que oscila entre los 60 y 120 cm. La caoba africana es una madera noble caracterizada por uniones verticales de brillo variable y marcas de vasos xilemáticos. Muy duradera y sólida, la caoba africana se emplea para la fabricación de muebles, obras de carpintería, paneles, puentes de barcos, enchapados y contrachapados. La caoba Africana puede ser teñida y abrillantada a fin de obtener un excelente acabado.

Famiglia: *Meliacee*
Densità: *0,45-0,60 g/cm^3*
Zone di produzione: *Ghana, Costa d'Avorio, Camerun, Guinea, Gabon, Angola, Liberia, Nigeria*
Il tronco ha un'altezza di 15-25 metri e un diametro che oscilla tra i 60 e i 120 centimetri. Il mogano bianco è un legno nobile caratterizzato da unioni verticali di lucentezza variabile e segni dei vasi xilematici. Molto durevole e stabile, il mogano bianco si usa per la produzione di mobili, opere di falegnameria, falegnameria, ponti di barche, impiallacciatura e compensato. Il mogano bianco può essere tinteggiato e lucidato per ottenere un'eccellente rifinitura.

Família: *Meliaceae*
Densidade: *0,45-0,60 g/cm^3*
Zonas de Produção: *Gana, Costa do Marfim, Camarões, Guiné, Gabão, Angola, Libéria, Nigéria*
Os troncos medem 15 a 25 metros, o diâmetro é de 60 a 120 centímetros. O mogno africano é uma madeira dura, caracterizada por marcas de veios e linhas verticais de brilho variável.Muito resistente e estável, o mogno africano é usado em marcenaria, carpintaria, painéis, convés de navios, folheado e contraplacado. O mogno africano pode ser tingido e polido para um excelente acabamento.

Familj: *Meliaceae*
Densitet: *0,45-0,60 g/cm^3*
Produktionsområden: *Ghana, Elfenbenskusten, Kamerun, Guinea, Gabon, Angola, Liberia och Nigeria*
Trädstammarna är 15-20 meter höga. Diametern är mellan 60 och 120 centimeter. Khaya Mahogny är ett hårdträ som karaktäriseras av vertikala band med varierande lyster och kärlmarkeringar. Khaya Mahogny är mycket tåligt och stabilt och används till finsnickeri, snickeri, panel, båtdäck, fanering och plywood. Khaya Mahogny kan betsas och poleras till en utmärkt finish.

Embero o nogal africano – Dibetu – Nogueira africana – Afrikansk valnöt

Familia: *Meliáceas*
Densidad: *0,50-0,55 g/cm^3*
Zonas de producción: *Costa de Marfil, Congo, Ghana, Nigeria, Camerún, Guinea*
El tronco puede alcanzar una altura de entre 15 y 20 m y un diámetro de 50-55 cm. Su madera es de color bronce con líneas negras irregulares. Es dura, fuerte, de anillos apretados y muy resistente al agua.Se emplea en la construcción estándar para construir postes de puentes y traveseras de ferrocarril, y para la producción de carbón. También encuentra uso en la realización de muebles y armarios, enchapados, paneles, accesorios fijos y obras de carpintería.

Famiglia: *Meliacee*
Densità: *0,50-0,55 g/cm^3*
Zone di produzione: *Costa d'Avorio, Congo, Ghana, Nigeria, Camerun, Guinea*
Il tronco può raggiungere un'altezza di 15-20 metri e un diametro di 50-55 centimetri. Il suo legno è di color bronzo con linee nere irregolari. È estremamente duro, forte, ad anelli e molto resistente all'acqua. Si utilizza nell'edilizia in genere per costruire pali per ponti e traversine per ferrovie, oltre che nella produzione di carbone. Viene usato anche nella realizzazione di mobili e armadi, lavori d'impiallacciatura, falegnameria, infissi e opere di falegnameria.

Família: *Meliaceae*
Densidade: *0,50-0,55 g/cm^3*
Zonas de Produção: *Costa do Marfim, Congo, Gana, Nigéria, Camarões, Guiné*
Os troncos medem 15 a 20 metros de altura e 50 a 55 centímetros de diâmetro. A madeira é cor de bronze com linhas irregulares escuras. É extremamente dura, pesada, com anéis apertados, e resiste bem à água. É utilizada na construção, para fazer estacas para pontes, travessas de caminho de ferro e para a produção de carvão. É também utilizada para mobiliário e marcenaria, folheados, painéis, pré-fabricados e carpintaria.

Familj: *Meliaceae*
Densitet: *0,50-0,55 g/cm^3*
Produktionsområden: *Elfenbenskusten, Kongo, Ghana, Nigeria, Kamerun, Guinea*
Stammarna är 15-20 meter höga och 50-55 centimeter i diameter. Träet är bronsfärgat med oregelbundna mörka linjer. Det är extremt hårt, tungt, tätådrat och står emot vatten väl. Träet används i standarduppförande, för att göra pålverk till broar, järnvägsbalkar och i produktion av träkol. Det används också till möbler och finsnickeri, fanering, panel, inredning och snickeri.

Aningeria superba – **Anigre – Aniégré – Anegre – Anigré**

Family: *Sapotaceae*
Density: *0.50-0.60 g/cm^3*
Zones of Production: *Ivory Coast, Congo, Angola, Nigeria*
Boles are 12 to 20 m (39 to 66 ft) tall and 60 to 90 cm (25 to 35 in) in diameter. The heartwood is pale pink to reddish-brown, darkening upon exposure. The grain is usually straight but sometimes wavy. Lighter grades are medium to coarse textured while heavier grades are usually fine textured. The wood responds well to hand and machine tools.It is used in furniture, joinery, plywood, veneer, and bent shapes.

Famille : *Sapotacées*
Densité : *0,50-0,60 g/cm^3*
Zones de production : *Côte-d'Ivoire, Congo, Angola et Nigeria*
Troncs de 12 à 20 m de hauteur, pour un diamètre de 60 à 90 cm. Le cœur est rose pâle à brun rougeâtre, et fonce en étant exposé au jour. Le fil est habituellement droit, mais parfois aussi ondé. Les catégories plus légères ont un grain allant de grossier à moyen ; les catégories plus lourdes offrent habituellement un grain fin. L'essence se travaille bien, manuellement comme à la machine-outil. On l'utilise pour le mobilier, la menuiserie, le contreplaqué, le placage et les formes cintrées à la vapeur.

Familie: *Sapotaceae*
Dichte: *0,50-0,60 g/cm^3*
Vorkommen: *Elfenbeinküste, Kongo, Angola, Nigeria*
Die Länge der Stämme schwankt zwischen 12 und 20 m, der Durchmesser beträgt 60-90 cm. Das Kernholz ist blassrosa bis rötlich-braun und dunkelt bei Lichteinfall nach. Normalerweise ist sein Faserverlauf gerade, er kann aber auch wellig sein. Niedrige Güteklassen weisen eine mittelgrobe bis grobe Struktur auf, wohingegen hochwertige Güteklassen normalerweise eine fein gezeichnete Struktur besitzen. Das Holz kann gut manuell und maschinell bearbeitet werden. Es wird für den Möbelbau und in der Zimmerei, für Sperrholz, Furniere und gebogene Formen verwendet.

Familie: *Sapotaceae*
Dichtheid: *0,50-0,60 g/cm^3*
Productiegebieden: *Ivoorkust, Congo, Angola, Nigeria*
De stam is 12 tot 20 meter lang en 60 tot 90 centimeter dik. Het kernhout is bleekroze tot roodbruin en wordt donkerder bij blootstelling aan licht. De draad is meestal recht, maar soms golvend. Lichtere varianten van het hout zijn middelmatig grof tot grof van nerf, terwijl zwaardere meestal fijn van nerf zijn. Het hout laat zich goed bewerken met handgereedschap en elektrisch. Het wordt gebruikt voor meubels, schrijnwerk, multiplex, fineer en gebogen vormen.

Fraxinus excelsior – **Ash – Frêne – Esche – Essen**

Family: *Oleaceae*
Density: *0.65-0.80 g/cm^3*
Zones of Production: *France, United Kingdom, Germany, Italy*
Boles are 3 to 10 m (10 to 33 ft) tall and 30 to 100 cm (12 to 39 in) in diameter. The wood has a coarse and generally straight grain. Strong and stiff, it is noted for its excellent bending qualities. Ash is great for flooring but is also used for bent parts in boat building, plywood, furniture, joinery, paneling and veneer. Ash works well with hand and machine tools and can be brought to a fine surface finish.

Famille : *Oléacées*
Densité : *0,65-0,80 g/cm^3*
Zones de production : *France, Angleterre, Allemagne et Italie*
Troncs de 3 à 10 m de hauteur, pour un diamètre de 30 à 100 cm. Le fil est généralement droit, le grain grossier. Solide et résistant, ce bois est aussi connu pour son excellente aptitude au cintrage. Il est remarquable pour les revêtements de sol, mais on l'utilise aussi pour les pièces cintrées dans la construction navale, le contreplaqué, le mobilier, la menuiserie, les lambris et le placage. Le frêne se travaille très bien, manuellement comme avec des machines-outils, et il est susceptible de recevoir un beau poli de surface.

Familie: *Oleaceae*
Dichte: *0,65-0,80 g/cm^3*
Vorkommen: *Frankreich, Vereinigtes Königreich, Deutschland, Italien*
Der 30-100 cm dicke Stamm ist zwischen 3 und 10 m lang. Das Holz der Esche ist geradfaserig und von grober Textur. Dieses starke und steife Holz besitzt ausgezeichnete Biegeeigenschaften. Es eignet sich hervorragend für den Fußbodenausbau, wird aber auch im Schiffsbau, als Sperrholz, für den Möbelbau, für Zimmererarbeiten, als Verkleidungsmaterial und für Furniere verwendet. Eschenholz kann gut von Hand oder maschinell bearbeitet werden und eignet sich hervorragend für ein feines Oberflächenfinish.

Familie: *Oleaceae*
Dichtheid: *0,65-0,80 g/cm^3*
Productiegebieden: *Frankrijk, Verenigd Koninkrijk, Duitsland, Italië*
De stam is 3 tot 10 meter lang en 30 tot 100 centimeter dik. Het hout is grof van nerf en meestal rechtdradig.
Dit sterke en stijve hout staat bekend om zijn buigzaamheid. Es is erg geschikt voor vloeren, maar wordt ook gebruikt voor gebogen delen in de scheepsbouw en voor multiplex, meubels, schrijnwerk, paneelwerk en fineer. Essen is goed elektrisch en met handgereedschap te bewerken en laat zich mooi afwerken.

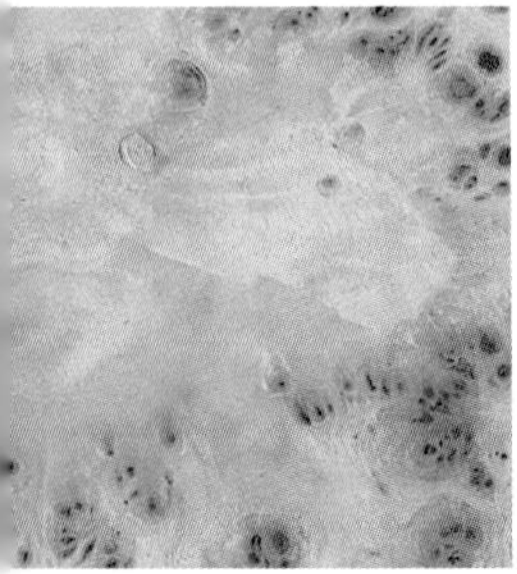

Populus tremula – **Aspen – Tremble – Espe, Zitterpappel – Ratelpopulier**

Family: *Salicaceae*
Density: *0.5 g/cm^3*
Zones of Production: *Alaska, Canada, northeastern and western United States*
Aspen can reach 48 m (157 ft) in height and up to 160 cm (63 in) in diameters. The bark is variable in color and in degree of furrowing. The wood of aspen has a uniform texture, straight grained, light, and soft. Aspen is easily worked with machines. Its pulp is used for newsprint and fine printing papers. Wood is used for sheathing, decking, pallets, furniture, lumber core, veneers, and paneling.

Famille : *Salicacées*
Densité : *0,5 g/cm^3*
Zones de production : *Alaska, Canada, ouest et nord-est des États-Unis*
Le tremble peut atteindre 48 m de hauteur et jusqu'à 160 cm de diamètre. Son écorce est de couleur variable, et plus ou moins crevassée. Le bois du tremble offre un grain uniforme, un fil droit ; il est léger et tendre. Le tremble se travaille facilement à la machine-outil. On utilise sa pulpe pour faire du papier journal, mais aussi des papiers d'impression de qualité supérieure. Le bois est utilisé pour les revêtements, les plateformes, les palettes, le mobilier, le bois d'œuvre, les placages et les lambris.

Familie: *Salicaceae*
Dichte: *0,5 g/cm^3*
Vorkommen: *Alaska, Kanada, Nordosten und Westen der USA*
Die Espe kann bis zu 48 Meter hoch werden und einen Durchmesser von 160 Zentimetern erreichen. Farbe und Furchen der Rinde variieren. Espenholz besitzt eine gleichmäßige Struktur und einen geradlinigen Faserverlauf, es ist leicht und weich. Espenholz ist gut maschinell bearbeitbar. Der Zellstoff der Espe wird für Zeitungs- und Feindruck verwendet, ihr Holz für Beschichtungen, Bodenbeläge, Paletten, Möbel, Tischlerplatten, Furniere und Verkleidungen.

Familie: *Salicaceae*
Dichtheid: *0,5 g/cm^3*
Productiegebieden: *Alaska, Canada, noordoosten en westen van de Verenigde Staten*
De ratelpopulier kan 48 meter hoog worden en tot 160 cm dik. De bast varieert in kleur en in de mate waarin hij gegroefd is. Het hout van de ratelpopulier heeft een uniforme structuur en is rechtdradig, licht en zacht. Ratelpopulier laat zich goed elektrisch bewerken. Het verpulpte hout wordt gebruikt voor krantenpapier en hoogwaardig drukpapier. Het hout wordt gebruikt voor beplanking, scheepsdekken, pallets, meubels, triplex, fineer en paneelwerk.

Aningre – Aningre – Anigre – Anegre

Familia: *Sapotáceas*
Densidad: *0,50-0,60 g/cm^3*
Zonas de producción: *Costa de Marfil, Congo, Angola, Nigeria*
El tronco puede alcanzar una altura de entre 12 y 20 m y un diámetro de 60-90 cm. El duramen es de color rosa pálido tirando a marrón rojizo y se oscurece con la exposición al sol. Aunque generalmente la fibra es recta, puede presentarse a veces ondulada. Las calidades más ligeras tienen una textura normal tirando a gruesa, mientras que las más pesadas tienen una estructura más fina. Esta madera es fácil de trabajar tanto con herramientas manuales como con máquinas-herramientas.Se emplea en la realización de muebles, obras de carpintería, contrachapados, enchapados y en elementos curvados.

Famiglia: *Sapotacee*
Densità: *0,50-0,60 g/cm^3*
Zone di produzione: *Costa d'Avorio, Congo, Angola, Nigeria*
Il tronco può raggiungere un'altezza di 12-20 metri e un diametro di 60-90 centimetri. Il durame è di color rosa pallido tendente al marrone rossastro e diviene più scuro se esposto al sole. Sebbene in genere la fibra sia dritta, a volte può presentarsi ondulata. Le qualità più leggere possiedono una texture normale tendente al ruvido, mentre quelle più pesanti hanno una struttura più fine. Questo legno è facile da lavorare sia con strumenti manuali sia con macchine utensili. Viene impiegato nella realizzazione di mobili, opere di falegnameria, compensato, lavori d'impiallacciatura e forme curve.

Família: *Sapotaceae*
Densidade: *0,50-0,60 g/cm^3*
Zonas de Produção: *Costa do Marfim, Congo, Angola, Nigéria*
Os troncos medem 12 a 20 metros de altura e 60 a 90 centímetros de diâmetro. O cerne da madeira é rosa claro a castanho avermelhado, escurecendo quando exposto. O grão é geralmente direito mas pode ser ondulado As qualidades mais leves têm uma textura média a grosseira, enquanto as mais pesadas têm geralmente uma textura fina. A madeira responde bem a ferramentas manuais e eléctricas. É utilizada em mobiliário, carpintaria, contraplacado, folheado e formas curvas.

Familj: *Sapotaceae*
Densitet: *0,50-0,60 g/cm^3*
Produktionsområden: *Elfenbenskusten, Kongo, Angola, Nigeria*
Stammarna är 12-20 meter höga och 60-90 centimeter i diameter. Kärnvirket är blekt rosa till rödbrunt och mörknar vid exponering. Ådringen är oftast rak men ibland vågig. Lättare kvaliteter har medel till grov struktur medan tyngre kvaliteter ofta har fin struktur. Träet svarar väl på hand- och maskinverktyg. Det används till möbler, snickeri, plywood, fanering och böjträ.

Fresno común – Frassino – Freixo – Ask

Familia: *Oleáceas*
Densidad: *0,65-0,80 g/cm^3*
Zonas de producción: *Francia, Reino Unido, Alemania e Italia*
El tronco puede alcanzar una altura máxima de 10 m y un diámetro de entre 30 y 100 cm. Este árbol tiene una veta recta y generalmente gruesa. Resistente y dura, esta madera es conocida por sus excelentes cualidades de plegado. Además de ser ideal para revestir suelos, se emplea también en la realización de partes curvadas en la construcción de barcos, contrachapados, muebles, obras de carpintería, paneles y enchapados. La madera de fresno funciona muy bien con herramientas manuales y con máquinas-herramientas y puede presentar una superficie mate excelente.

Famiglia: *Oleacee*
Densità: *0,65-0,80 g/cm^3*
Zone di produzione: *Francia, Inghilterra, Germania e Italia*
Il tronco può raggiungere un'altezza massima di 10 metri e un diametro compreso tra 30 e 100 centimetri. Questo albero presenta delle venature rette e generalmente ruvide. Resistente e duro, il suo legno è noto per le sue eccellenti attitudini alla piegatura. Oltre a essere l'ideale per ricoprire pavimenti, viene utilizzato anche per la costruzione di barche, compensato, mobili, opere di falegnameria, pannelli e impiallacciatura. Il legno di frassino funziona molto bene con strumenti manuali e con macchine utensili e può presentare un'eccellente superficie opaca.

Família: *Oleaceae*
Densidade: *0,65-0,80 g/cm^3*
Zonas de Produção: *França, Reino Unido, Alemanha, Itália*
Os troncos medem 3 a 10 metros de altura e 30 a 100 centímetros de diâmetro. A madeira tem um grão grosseiro e habitualmente direito. Forte e rígido, é conhecido pelas suas excelentes qualidades para encurvamento. O freixo é óptimo para soalhos mas também é utilizado para as peças curvas na construção naval, contraplacado, mobiliário, carpintaria, painéis e folheado. Trabalha-se bem com ferramentas manuais e eléctricas e permite um excelente acabamento da superfície.

Familj: *Oleaceae*
Densitet: *0,65-0,80 g/cm^3*
Produktionsområden: *Frankrike, Storbritannien, Tyskland, Italien*
Stammarna är 3-10 meter höga och 30-100 centimeter i diameter, träet har en grov och vanligen rak ådring.
Det är starkt och styvt och känt för sin utmärkta böjningsförmåga. Ask är suveränt till golvläggning men används också till böjda delar vid båtbyggande, plywood, möbler, snickeri, panel och fanering. Ask arbetas lätt med hand- och maskinverktyg och kan bringas till en fin ytfinish.

Álamo temblón – Pioppo tremulo – Choupo – Asp

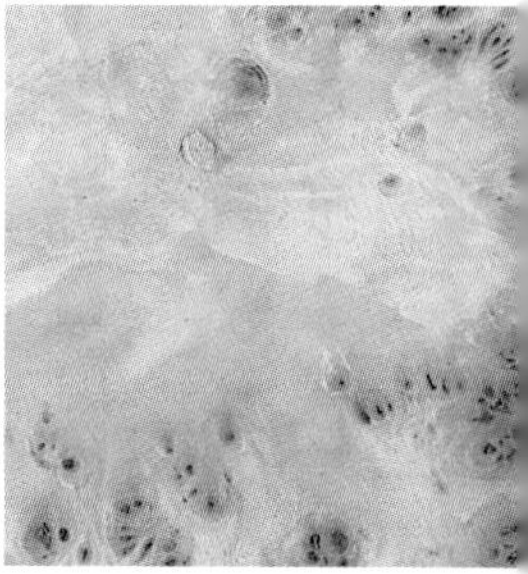

Familia: *Salicáceas*
Densidad: *0,5 g/cm^3*
Zonas de producción: *Alaska, Canadá, noreste y oeste de Estados Unidos*
El tronco del álamo temblón puede alcanzar los 48 m de altura y un diámetro de 160 cm. La corteza es variable por lo que se refiere al color y al grado de surcos. La madera del álamo posee una textura uniforme con una fibra recta, ligera y blanda. El álamo se trabaja fácilmente con máquinas. Su pasta se emplea en la fabricación del papel de prensa y de edición, y su madera en la realización de recubrimientos, plataformas, pallet, muebles, almas de madera, enchapados y paneles.

Famiglia: *Salicacee*
Densità: *0,5 g/cm^3*
Zone di produzione: *Alaska, Canada, Stati Uniti occidentali e nord-orientali*
Il tronco del pioppo tremulo può raggiungere i 48 metri d'altezza e un diametro di 160 centimetri. La corteccia è variabile in quanto al colore e al livello di solchi. Il legno del pioppo presenta una texture uniforme con una fibra dritta, leggera e dolce. Il pioppo si lavora facilmente con macchinari. La sua pasta è usata nella fabbricazione della carta per i giornali e per l'editoria, e il suo legno nella produzione di materiali da rivestimento, ponti e piattaforme, pallet, mobili, anime di legno, impiallacciatura e falegnameria.

Família: *Salicaceae*
Densidade: *0,5 g/cm^3*
Zonas de Produção: *Alasca, Canadá, nordeste e oeste dos Estados Unidos*
O choupo pode atingir os 48 metros de altura e ter até 160 cm de diâmetro. A casca varia em cor e em grau de sulcos. A madeira do choupo tem uma textura uniforme, de grão direito, leve e macia. Trabalha-se facilmente com máquinas. A polpa é utilizada para papel de jornal e para papel de impressão de qualidade. A madeira é utilizada para estruturas de cofragem, forros de tábuas, paletes, mobiliário, contraplacado tabuado, folheados, e painéis.

Familj: *Saliaceae*
Densitet: *0,5 g/cm^3*
Produktionsområden: *Alaska, Kanada, nordöstra och västra USA*
Asp kan nå en höjd av 48 meter och bli upp till 160 cm i diameter. Barken varierar i färg och räfflighet. Aspe har en enhetlig struktur, är rakådrat, lätt och mjukt. Asp arbetas lätt med maskiner. Dess massa används till tidningspapper och till fint skrivpapper. Trä används till brädbeklädnad, till däck, pallar, möbler, timmer, fanering och panel.

Fagus sylvatica - **Beech – Hêtre – Rotbuche – Beuk**

Family: *Fagaceae*
Density: *0.60-0.75 g/cm³*
Zones of Production: *France, United Kingdom, Germany*
Boles are 16 to 49 m (52 to 161 ft) tall and 40 to 90 cm (15 to 35 in) in diameter. The bark is smooth and light gray. This European species yields a utility timber that is tough but dimensionally unstable. It is widely used for furniture framing, carcass construction, flooring, engineering purposes, plywood and for household items like plates, but rarely as a decorative timber.

Famille : *Fagacées*
Densité : *0,60-0,75 g/cm³*
Zones de production : *France, Royaume-Uni et Allemagne*
Troncs de 5 à 15 m de hauteur, pour 40 à 90 cm de diamètre. L'écorce est lisse et gris clair. Cette essence typiquement européenne fournit un bois d'œuvre solide, malgré son instabilité dimensionnelle. On l'utilise largement pour les carcasses de mobilier, les ossatures de construction, le revêtement des sols, le contreplaqué et la fabrication d'ustensiles domestiques – mais rarement comme essence décorative.

Familie: *Fagaceae*
Dichte: *0,60-0,75 g/cm³*
Vorkommen: *Frankreich, Vereinigtes Königreich, Deutschland*
Der 40 bis 90 Zentimeter dicke Baumstamm ist 5 bis 15 Meter lang. Die Färbung der glatten Rinde ist hellgrau. Diese europäische Art liefert ein hartes Nutzholz, das aber nicht formstabil ist. Es wird häufig für Möbelrahmen, für den Gehäusebau und Fußbodenausbau, für technische Zwecke, Sperrholz und Haushaltsgegenstände wie zum Beispiel Teller verwendet, kommt jedoch selten für dekorative Zwecke zum Einsatz.

Familie: *Fagaceae*
Dichtheid: *0,60-0,75 g/cm³*
Productiegebieden: *Frankrijk, Verenigd Koninkrijk, Duitsland*
De stam is 5 tot 15 meter lang en 40 tot 90 centimeter dik. De bast is glad en lichtgrijs. Deze Europese soort levert een timmerhout dat vrij hard is, maar snel kromtrekt. Het wordt algemeen gebruikt voor meubelframes, skeletbouw, vloeren, werktuigen, multiplex en voor huishoudelijke artikelen als dienbladen, maar zelden als decoratief timmerhout.

Hibiscus tiliaceus - **Beach Hibiscus – Mahot – Lindenblättriger Eibisch – Waroeboom**

Family: *Malvaceae*
Density: *0.75 g/cm³*
Zones of Production: *Bahamas, Brazil, Cuba, Dominican Republic, Haiti, Jamaica, Peru, Puerto Rico*
The tree reaches a height of 18 to 21 m (59 to 69 ft) with a trunk diameter of 30 to 46 cm (12 to 18 in). The heartwood is grayish brown often mottled with purple shades. The grain is fairly straight and the texture is variable but often medium. It is used in boat construction, furniture, and cabinetry. Its tough bark can be made into durable rope and for sealing cracks in boats.

Famille : *Malvacées*
Densité : *0,75 g/cm³*
Zones de production : *Bahamas, Brésil, Cuba, République dominicaine, Haïti, Jamaïque, Pérou et Porto Rico*
L'arbre peut atteindre une hauteur de 18 à 21 m, avec un tronc de 30 à 46 cm de diamètre. Le cœur est brun grisâtre, souvent marbré de nuances pourpres. Le fil est très droit et le grain variable, mais fréquemment moyen. Le bois est utilisé pour la construction navale, le mobilier et l'ébénisterie. Son écorce solide peut être transformée en corde résistante, mais elle peut aussi servir à colmater les fissures dans les coques de bateau.

Familie: *Malvaceae*
Dichte: *0,75 g/cm³*
Vorkommen: *Bahamas, Brasilien, Kuba, Dominikanische Republik, Haiti, Jamaika, Peru, Puerto Rico*
Der Baum erreicht eine Höhe zwischen 18 und 21 Meter mit einem Stammdurchmesser zwischen 30 und 46 Zentimetern. Das Kernholz ist gräulich gefärbt und weist häufig eine violette Tönung auf. Der Faserverlauf ist geradlinig, die Textur variiert, ist jedoch meistens mittelgrob. Es wird im Schiffsbau, für den Möbelbau, und die Tischlerei verwendet. Seine zähe Rinde kann zu widerstandsfähigem Seilmaterial verarbeitet und zum Abdichten von Rissen in Booten verwendet werden.

Familie: *Malvaceae*
Dichtheid: *0,75 g/cm³*
Productiegebieden: *Bahama's, Brazilië, Cuba, Dominicaanse Republiek, Haïti, Jamaica, Peru, Puerto Rico*
De boom bereikt een hoogte van 18 tot 21 meter en wordt 30 tot 46 centimeter dik. Het kernhout is grijsbruin, vaak met paarse vlekken. De draad is vrij recht en de structuur varieert, maar is vaak matig grof. Het hout wordt gebruikt in de bootbouw en voor meubels en kasten. Met de taaie bast kan men duurzaam touw maken en scheuren in boten dichten.

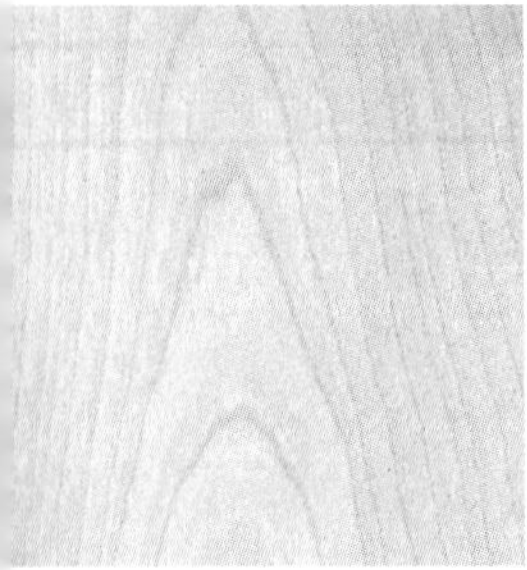

Betula alba - **Birch – Bouleau – Birke – Berk**

Family: *Betulaceae*
Density: *0.60-0.75 g/cm³*
Zones of Production: *Northern Europe, North America, Asia*
Boles are 13 to 33 m (43 to 108 ft) tall often tortuous with diameter between 30-60 cm (12-24 in). Birch wood is fine-grained and pale in color. Ripple figuring may occur, increasing the value of the timber for veneer and furniture-making. Birch wood is suitable for veneer. Birch ply is among the strongest and most dimensionally stable plywoods, although it is not suitable for exterior use.

Famille : *Bétulacées*
Densité : *0,60-0,75 g/cm³*
Zones de production : *Europe du Nord, Amérique du Nord et Asie*
Troncs souvent tortueux de 4 à 10 m de hauteur, pour un diamètre de 30 à 60 cm. Le bois de bouleau, de couleur pâle, possède un fil fin. On peut y trouver des figures, ce qui augmente la valeur du bois pour le placage et la fabrication du mobilier. Le bois de bouleau est très propre au placage. Le contreplaqué de bouleau est au nombre des plus solides et des plus stables pour ce qui est des dimensions – mais il ne convient pas pour l'usage extérieur.

Familie: *Betulaceae*
Dichte: *0,60-0,75 g/cm³*
Vorkommen: *Nordeuropa, Nordamerika, Asien*
Die häufig gewundenen Stämme werden 4–10 m lang, bei Durchmessern von 30–60 cm. Das Birkenholz weist eine fein gezeichnete Maserung und eine blasse Färbung auf. Wenn es eine gewellte Zeichnung aufweist, steigert sich sein Wert als Furnierholz oder Möbelholz. Das Birkenholz eignet sich gut für Furniere. Sperrholz aus Birke zählt zu den festesten und formstabilsten Sperrhölzern, doch ist es für die Verwendung im Freien ungeeignet.

Familie: *Betulaceae*
Dichtheid: *0,60-0,75 g/cm³*
Productiegebieden: *Noord-Europa, Noord-Amerika, Azië*
De vaak bochtige stam is 4 tot 10 meter lang en 30-60 centimeter dik. Berkenhout is fijn van nerf en bleek van kleur. Het patroon kan golvend zijn, wat het hout meer waarde geeft als fineer of meubelhout. Berkenhout is geschikt als fineer. Berkenmultiplex behoort tot de sterkste en stabielste soorten multiplex, al is het niet geschikt voor buitengebruik.

Haya – Faggio – Faia – Bok

Familia: *Fagáceas*
Densidad: *0,60-0,75 g/cm^3*
Zonas de producción: *Francia, Reino Unido, Alemania*
El tronco tiene entre 5 y 15 m de altura y un diámetro que oscila entre los 40 y los 90 cm. La corteza es homogénea y gris clara. La especie europea produce una madera funcional dura pero inestable en cuanto a las dimensiones. Se emplea ampliamente en la fabricación de armazones para muebles, carcasas, revestimientos de suelos, contrachapados y artículos para el hogar como bandejas, así como en proyectos de ingeniería, pero raramente con fines decorativos.

Famiglia: *Fagáceas*
Densità: *0,60-0,75 g/cm^3*
Zone di produzione: *Francia, Inghilterra, Germania*
Il tronco ha un'altezza di 5-15 metri e un diametro che oscilla tra i 40 e i 90 centimetri. La corteccia è omogenea e di colore grigio chiaro. La specie europea produce un legno funzionale duro, ma instabile per quanto riguarda le dimensioni. Si usa abbondantemente nella produzione di telai per mobili, ossature di costruzioni, pavimentazioni, progetti d'ingegneria, compensato e articoli per la casa come vassoi, ma raramente con finalità decorative.

Família: *Fagaceae*
Densidade: *0,60-0,75 g/cm^3*
Zonas de Produção: *França, Reino Unido, Alemanha*
Os troncos medem 5 a 15 metros de altura e 40 a 90 centímetros de diâmetro. A casca é macia e cinzenta clara. Esta espécie europeia produz uma madeira de construção dura mas dimensionalmente instável. É largamente utilizada para estruturas de mobiliário, estruturas de construção, soalhos, fins de engenharia, contraplacado e para objectos domésticos, como pratos, mas raramente como madeira decorativa.

Familj: *Fagaceae*
Densitet: *0,60-0,75 g/cm^3*
Produktionsområden: *Frankrike, Storbritannien, Tyskland*
Stammarna är 5-15 meter höga och 40-90 centimeter i diameter. Barken är slät och ljust grå. Denna europeiska art ger ett brukstimmer som är segt men dimensionellt instabilt. Det används flitigt till möbelstommar, byggnadsstommar, golvbeläggning, tekniska ändamål, plywood och till hushållsföremål som tallrikar, men sällan som dekorationsträ.

Hibisco marítimo – Hibiscus tiliaceus – Algodão da praia – Strandhibiskus

Familia: *Malváceas*
Densidad: *0,75 g/cm^3*
Zonas de producción: *Bahamas, Brasil, Cuba, República Dominicana, Haiti, Jamaica, Perú, Puerto Rico*
Este árbol puede alcanzar una altura máxima de 21 m y su tronco, un diámetro de entre 30-46 cm. El duramen es marrón grisáceo moteado a menudo con tonos violetas. La fibra es bastante recta y la textura suele ser variable, aunque suele presentar un grosor normal. La madera de hibisco se emplea en la construcción de barcos y en la realización de muebles y armarios. Su corteza, en cambio, es ideal para hacer cuerdas y para sellar grietas en los barcos.

Famiglia: *Malvacee*
Densità: *0,75 g/cm^3*
Zone di produzione: *Bahamas, Brasile, Cuba, Repubblica Dominicana, Haiti, Giamaica, Perù, Porto Rico*
Questo albero può raggiungere un'altezza massima di 21 metri e il suo tronco può avere un diametro di 30-46 centimetri. Il durame è marrone grigiastro, spesso screziato di tonalità porpora. La fibra è abbastanza dritta e la texture è in genere variabile, benché sia solita presentare una ruvidità normale. Il legno di ibisco è utilizzato nella costruzione di barche e nella realizzazione di mobili e armadi. La sua corteccia, invece, è l'ideale per preparare corde e per sigillare crepe negli scafi delle barche.

Família: *Malvaceae*
Densidade: *0,75 g/cm^3*
Zonas de Produção: *Bahamas, Brasil, Cuba, República Dominicana, Haiti, Jamaica, Peru, Porto Rico*
A árvore atinge 18 a 21 metros de altura e um diâmetro de tronco entre os 30 e os 46 centímetros. O cerne é castanho acinzentado, frequentemente matizado com sombras roxas. O grão é bastante direito e a textura é variável mas geralmente média. É utilizado na construção de barcos, mobiliário e marcenaria. A sua casca dura pode ser transformada em cabos resistentes e é utilizada para selar fendas em barcos.

Familj: *Malvaceae*
Densitet: *0,75 g/cm^3*
Produktionsområden: *Bahamas, Brasilien, Kuba, Dominikanska Republiken, Haiti, Jamaica, Peru, Puerto Rico*
Trädet når en höjd av mellan 18 och 21 meter med en diameter på stammen på mellan 30 och 46 centimeter. Kärnvirket är gråbrunt, ofta marmorerat med lila toner. Ådringen är ganska rak och strukturen varierar men är ofta medium. Det används till båtkonstruktion, möbler och möbelsnickeri. Dess sega bark kan användas till hållbara rep och till att laga sprickor i båtar.

Abedul – Betulla – Bétula – Björk

Familia: *Betuláceas*
Densidad: *0,60-0,75 g/cm^3*
Zonas de producción: *Europa del Norte, América del Norte, Asia*
El tronco, a veces tortuoso, tiene entre 4 y 10 m de altura y un diámetro que oscila entre los 30 y los 60 cm. La madera de abedul se caracteriza por los anillos apretados y el color pálido. Cuando presenta el veteado de caja violinera, su valor aumenta en la industria de los enchapados y de la fabricación de muebles. La madera de abedul es ideal para la realización de enchapados: con su chapa se fabrica uno de los contrachapados más fuertes y sólidos que se conocen. No es apta, en cambio, para usos exteriores.

Famiglia: *Betulacee*
Densità: *0,60-0,75 g/cm^3*
Zone di produzione: *Asia, Europa Settentrionale, America Settentrionale*
Il tronco, a volte tortuoso, ha un'altezza compresa tra 4 e 10 metri e un diametro che oscilla tra i 30 e i 60 centimetri. Il legno di betulla si distingue per le sue sottili venature e il colore pallido. Quando le venature sono ondulate, aumenta il suo valore come legname da impiallacciatura e per la fabbricazione di mobili. Il legno di betulla è ideale per i lavori di ebanista: con il suo foglio si ottiene uno dei compensati più forti e solidi che si conoscano. Non è invece un legno adatto a usi esterni.

Família: *Betulaceae*
Densidade: *0,60-0,75 g/cm^3*
Zonas de Produção: *norte da Europa, América do Norte, Ásia*
Os troncos, frequentemente tortos, medem 4 a 10 metros de altura e têm um diâmetro entre os 30-60 centímetros. A bétula tem um grão fino e uma cor clara. Podem surgir veios ondulados que aumentam o valor da madeira para folheados e para o fabrico de mobiliário. É apropriada para folheado; a folha de bétula é um dos contraplacados mais fortes e dimensionalmente mais estáveis, embora não seja apropriado para utilização no exterior.

Familj: *Betulaceae*
Densitet: *0,60-0,75 g/cm^3*
Produktionsområden: *Norra Europa, Nordamerika och Asien*
Stammarna är 4-10 meter höga och ofta krokiga med en diameter mellan 30 och 60 centimeter. Björkträ är finådrigt och blekt i färgen. Krusmönster kan förekomma och ökar värdet på virket för fanering och möbeltillverkning. Björkträ är lämpligt till fanering. Björkplywood är bland de starkaste och dimensionellt mest stabila plywoods, det är dock inte lämpligt för utomhusbruk.

Juglans nigra - **Black Walnut – Noyer noir – Schwarznuss – Zwarte Walnoot**

Family: *Juglandaceae*
Density: *0.50-0.60 g/cm³*
Zones of Production: *United States*
Boles are 8 to 15 m (26 to 49 ft) tall and the diameter ranges between 35 and 90 cm (13-35 in). The wood is strong and stable with a rich purplish-brown to a chocolate-brown tint. The texture is moderately coarse but uniform. Black Walnut works with ease in all hand tool and machine tool processes. It is the foremost wood for cabinetry, best used for veneers, turnery, joinery, musical instruments, and carving.

Famille : *Juglandacées*
Densité : *0,50-0,60 g/cm³*
Zones de production : *États-Unis*
Troncs de 8 à 15 m de hauteur, pour un diamètre de 35 à 90 cm. Le bois est solide et stable, avec une teinte allant du brun violacé au brun chocolat. Le grain est assez grossier, mais uniforme.Le noyer noir se travaille aisément, manuellement comme avec des machines-outils. C'est un bois de prédilection pour l'ébénisterie, au mieux pour le placage, le tournage, la facture d'instruments de musique, la sculpture – et la menuiserie en général.

Familie: *Juglandaceae*
Dichte: *0,50-0,60 g/cm³*
Vorkommen: *Vereinigte Staaten*
Die Länge des Baumstamms liegt zwischen 8 und 15 Metern, sein Durchmesser zwischen 35 und 90 Zentimetern. Das feste und solide Holz weist eine schokoladenbraune bis schwarzviolette Färbung auf. Die Textur ist mittelgrob aber gleichmäßig. Das Holz des Schwarznussbaums ist gut mit Handwerkzeugen und maschinell bearbeitbar. Es nimmt unter den für den Möbelbau verwendeten Hölzern die erste Stelle ein und eignet sich hervorragend für Furniere, Drechselarbeit, Zimmerei, Musikinstrumente und Schnitzereien.

Familie: *Juglandaceae*
Dichtheid: *0,50-0,60 g/cm³*
Productiegebieden: *Verenigde Staten*
De stam is 8 tot 15 meter lang en de dikte varieert van 35 tot 90 centimeter. Het hout is sterk en stabiel met een diepe paarsbruine tot chocoladebruine tint. De nerf is matig grof, maar wel homogeen. Zwarte walnoot laat zich prettig bewerken met alle elektrische en handgereedschappen. Het hout is eerste keus voor kasten, met name voor fineer, draaiwerk, schrijnwerk, muziekinstrumenten en houtsnijwerk.

Dalbergia nigra - **Brazilian Rosewood – Palissandre de Rio – Rio-Palisander – Rio-palissander**

Family: *Fabaceae*
Density: *0.80-1.10 g/cm³*
Zones of Production: *Brazil*
Boles are 3 to 12 m (10 to 39 ft) tall and 30 to 50 cm (12 to 20 in) in diameter. The heartwood is dark brown with noticeable black streaks. It is mostly straight-grained with medium to coarse texture, and a rose-like fragrance when worked. One of the most prized furniture of all times, Brazilian rosewood is now rare and tightly controlled on the world market. It is used for veneers, musical instrument, fine furniture, turnery, and marquetry.

Famille : *Fabacées*
Densité : *0,80-1,10 g/cm³*
Zones de production : *Brésil*
Troncs de 3 à 12 m de hauteur, pour un diamètre de 30 à 50 cm. Le cœur est brun foncé avec des veinures noires très visibles. Le fil est le plus souvent droit, pour un grain de moyen à grossier, et le bois dégage un parfum de rose quand on le travaille. Très prisé de tout temps pour le mobilier, le palissandre de Rio est devenu rare et il est sévèrement contrôlé sur le marché mondial. On l'utilise pour le placage, la facture d'instruments de musique, le mobilier de luxe, le tournage et la marqueterie.

Familie: *Fabaceae*
Dichte: *0,80-1,10 g/cm³*
Vorkommen: *Brasilien*
Der 30–50 cm dicke Stamm ist 3–12 m lang. Das Kernholz ist von einem satten Braun mit auffallenden schwarzen Streifen. Das Holz weist einen hauptsächlich geraden Faserwuchs und eine mittelgrobe bis grobe Textur auf, bei seiner Bearbeitung strömt es ein rosenähnliches Aroma aus. Jahrhundertelang zählte es zu den beliebtesten für den Möbelbau verwendeten Hölzern, mittlerweile ist es aber rar geworden und sein Verkauf auf dem internationalen Markt unterliegt strengen Kontrollen. Es wird für Furniere, Musikinstrumente, Ziermöbel, Drechsler- und Einlegearbeiten verwendet.

Familie: *Fabaceae*
Dichtheid: *0,80-1,10 g/cm³*
Productiegebieden: *Brazilië*
De stam is 3 tot 12 meter hoog en 30 tot 50 centimeter dik. Het kernhout is donkerbruin met opvallende zwarte strepen. Het is overwegend rechtdradig met een matig grove tot grove nerf en verspreidt bij bewerking een rozengeur. Rio-palissander, een van de geliefdste houtsoorten voor meubels aller tijden, is nu zeldzaam en streng gereguleerd op de wereldmarkt. Het wordt gebruikt voor fineer, muziekinstrumenten, kwaliteitsmeubilair, draaiwerk en marqueterie.

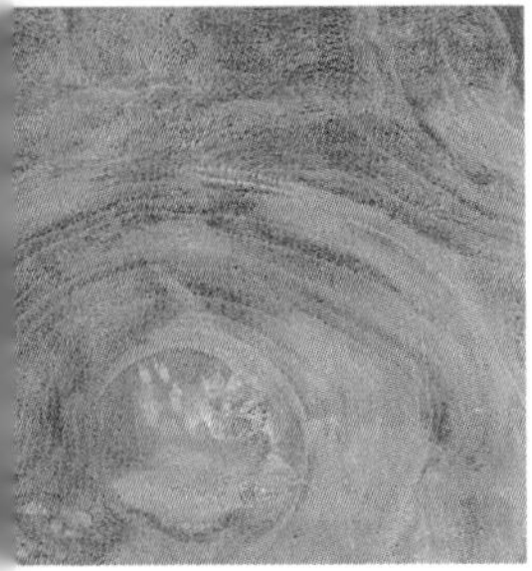

Phoebe porosa - **Brazilian Walnut – Imbuia – Imbuia – Imbuia**

Family: *Lauraceae*
Density: *0.96 g/cm³ approx*
Zones of Production: *Brazil, Argentina, Paraguay*
At their largest, the trees may reach 40 m (130 ft) in height and 1.8 m (6 ft) in trunk diameter. Brazilian walnut from South America has a deep dark brown colored wood with exceptionally fine graining. It is one of the densest woods available. The tree is a major commercial species in Brazil because of the value of its wood for high end furniture making. It is mostly used as a decorative veneer, and for flooring.

Famille : *Lauracées*
Densité : *0,96 g/cm³ approx.*
Zones de production : *Brésil, Argentine et Paraguay*
Les plus grands arbres peuvent atteindre 40 m de hauteur, pour un tronc de 180 cm de diamètre. L'imbuia d'Amérique du Sud a un bois de couleur brun foncé profond, avec un fil exceptionnellement fin. C'est l'un des bois les plus denses sur le marché. Ce bois est l'une des plus importantes essences commercialisées au Brésil, en raison de sa valeur pour la fabrication de mobilier haut de gamme. Il est essentiellement utilisé en placage décoratif, mais aussi pour les revêtements de sol.

Familie: *Lauraceae*
Dichte: *0,96 g/cm³ aprox.*
Vorkommen: *Brasilien, Argentinien, Paraguay*
Der ausgewachsene Baum erreicht eine Höhe von 40 m und einen Durchmesser von 180 cm. Imbuiaholz zeichnet sich durch eine satte dunkelbraune Färbung und einen ausgesprochen feinen Faserverlauf aus. Es zählt zu den dichtesten auf dem Markt erhältlichen Hölzern. Der Baum hat in Brasilien große kommerzielle Bedeutung wegen des Wertes seines Holzes für die Anfertigung von besonders hochwertigen Möbeln. Es wird hauptsächlich als Schmuckfurnier und für den Fußbodenausbau verwendet.

Familie: *Lauraceae*
Dichtheid: *ca. 0,96 g/cm³*
Productiegebieden: *Brazilië, Argentinië, Paraguay*
De boom kan 40 meter hoog en 1,8 meter dik worden. Het Zuid-Amerikaanse imbuia is diep donkerbruin van kleur en buitengewoon fijn van nerf. Weinig hout heeft zo'n hoge dichtheid als imbuia. Commercieel gezien is de boom in Brazilië van groot belang vanwege de waarde van het hout voor kwaliteitsmeubilair. Het wordt vooral gebruikt als decoratief fineer en voor vloeren.

Nogal negro – Noce nero – Nogueira preta – Svart valnöt

Familia: *Juglandáceas*
Densidad: *0,50-0,60 g/cm³*
Zonas de producción: *Estados Unidos*
Su tronco tiene entre los 8 y los 15 m de altura y un diámetro que oscila entre los 35 y los 90 cm. Esta fuerte y sólida madera es de color marrón violáceo tirando a chocolate. La textura es moderadamente gruesa pero uniforme. El nogal negro es fácil de trabajar tanto con herramientas de mano como con máquinas-herramientas. Se trata asimismo de la madera más utilizada en la fabricación de muebles y armarios, así como de enchapados, maderas torneadas, obras de carpintería, instrumentos musicales y tallas.

Famiglia: *Juglandacee*
Densità: *0,50-0,60 g/cm³*
Zone di produzione: *Stati Uniti*
Il suo tronco ha un'altezza compresa tra 8 e 15 metri e un diametro che oscilla tra i 35 e i 90 centimetri. Si tratta di un legno forte e solido, di color marrone violaceo tendente a toni cioccolato. La texture è moderatamente ruvida, ma uniforme. Il noce nero è facile da lavorare sia con strumenti a mano sia con macchine utensili. È, inoltre, il legno maggiormente impiegato nella produzione di mobili e armadi, nonché nell'impiallacciatura, in oggetti di legno tornito, in opere di falegnameria, per strumenti musicali e nell'intaglio.

Família: *Juglandaceae*
Densidade: *0,50-0,60 g/cm³*
Zonas de Produção: *Estados Unidos*
Os troncos medem 8 a 15 metros de altura e o diâmetro varia entre os 35 e os 90 centímetros. A madeira é forte e estável, de castanho purpúreo a cor de chocolate escuro. A textura é moderadamente grosseira mas uniforme. Trabalha-se bem com todas as ferramentas manuais e eléctricas. É a melhor madeira para marcenaria, indicada para folheados, torneados, carpintaria, instrumentos musicais e escultura.

Familj: *Juglandaceae*
Densitet: *0,50-0,60 g/cm³*
Produktionsområden: *USA*
Stammarna är 8-15 meter höga och diametern varierar mellan 35 och 90 centimeter. Träet är starkt och stabilt med en mustig lilabrun till chokladbrun nyans. Strukturen är lätt grov men enhetlig. Svart valnöt arbetas enkelt med alla handverktyg och maskinverktygsprocesser. Det är det främsta träet för möbelsnickeri, används bäst till fanering, svarvning, snickeri, musikinstrument och till snideri.

Palisandro de Brasil – Palissandro del Brasile – Pau-rosa – Rio-jakaranda

Familia: *Fabáceas*
Densidad: *0,80-1,10 g/cm³*
Zonas de producción: *Brasil*
La altura del tronco oscila entre los 3 y los 12 m y su diámetro entre los 30 y 50 cm. El duramen es marrón oscuro con vetas negras evidentes y bastante rectas y una textura media tirando a gruesa; además, al ser cortado, desprende un perfume como de rosas. Desde siempre, el palisandro ha sido una de las maderas más preciadas en la manufactura de muebles; sin embargo, hoy en día, debido a su escasez, está sometido a controles muy férreos en el mercado mundial. Se emplea para enchapados, instrumentos musicales, mobiliario elegante, madera torneada y marquetería.

Famiglia: *Fabacee*
Densità: *0,80-1,10 g/cm³*
Zone di produzione: *Brasile*
L'altezza del tronco oscilla tra i 3 e i 12 metri e il suo diametro va dai 30 ai 50 centimetri. Il durame è marrone scuro con venature nere evidenti e abbastanza dritte e una texture media tendente a ruvida; inoltre, quando viene tagliato, sprigiona un profumo che ricorda quello della rosa. Il legno del palissandro è sempre stato uno dei più pregiati nella manifattura di mobili; oggi, tuttavia, a causa della sua rarità, viene sottoposto a controlli molto ferrei nel mercato mondiale. Si usa per impiallacciatura, strumenti musicali, arredamento elegante, oggetti di legno tornito e intarsio.

Família: *Fabaceae*
Densidade: *0,80-1,10 g/cm³*
Zonas de Produção: *Brasil*
Os troncos medem 3 a 12 metros de altura e 30 a 50 centímetros de diâmetro. O cerne é castanho-escuro, com visíveis riscas pretas. Tem geralmente um grão direito com uma textura média a grosseira e, quando trabalhada, uma fragrância semelhante à da rosa. Um dos mais apreciados mobiliários de sempre, o pau-rosa é raro hoje em dia e severamente controlado no mercado mundial. É utilizado para folheados, instrumentos musicais, mobiliário de qualidade, torneados, e marchetados.

Familj: *Fabaceae*
Densitet: *0,80-1,10 g/cm³*
Produktionsområden: *Brasilien*
Stammarna är 3-12 meter höga och 30-50 cm i diameter. Kärnvirket är mörkbrunt med anmärkningsvärda svarta strimmor. Det är oftast rakådrat med medium till grov struktur och har en rosliknande doft när det arbetas. Ett av de högst värderade träslagen för möbler i alla tider, men idag är Rio-jakaranda sällsynt och hårt kontrollerat på världsmarknaden. Det används till fanering, musikinstrument, finmöbler, svarvning och intarsia.

Imbuia – Imbuia – Imbuia – Imbuia

Familia: *Lauráceas*
Densidad: *0,96 g/cm³ aprox.*
Zonas de producción: *Brasil, Argentina, Paraguay*
Esta especie puede alcanzar los 40 m de altura y su tronco, un diámetro de 1,8 m. La imbuia sudamericana es de color marrón oscuro con un veteado excepcionalmente fino, y una de las maderas con mayor densidad disponibles. Este árbol es una de las principales especies comerciales en Brasil debido al valor de su madera en la manufactura de muebles de gama alta. Se emplea principalmente en la realización de contrachapados decorativos y de revestimientos de suelos.

Famiglia: *Lauracee*
Densità: *0,96 g/cm³ circa*
Zone di produzione: *Brasile, Argentina, Paraguay*
Questa specie può raggiungere i 40 metri d'altezza e il suo tronco, un diametro di circa 1,8 metri. L'imbuia sudamericana è di color marrone scuro con venature eccezionalmente fini, e offre uno dei legni di maggiore densità disponibili nel mercato. Si tratta di una delle principali specie commerciali del Brasile, in virtù del suo valore nella manifattura di mobili d'alto livello. Si usa soprattutto nella realizzazione di compensati decorativi e nel rivestimento di pavimenti.

Família: *Lauraceae*
Densidade: *0,96 g/cm³ aprox.*
Zonas de Produção: *Brasil, Argentina, Paraguai*
No seu auge, as árvores podem atingir os 40 metros de altura e 1,8 metros de diâmetro de tronco. A imbuia da América do Sul tem uma madeira de cor castanha muito escura com um grão excepcionalmente fino. É uma das madeiras mais densas disponíveis. A árvore é uma das espécies com maior valor comercial no Brasil, devido ao valor da sua madeira para o fabrico de mobiliário de luxo. É utilizada sobretudo para folheado decorativo e para soalhos.

Familj: *Lauraceae*
Densitet: *0,96 g/cm³*
Produktionsområden: *Brasilien, Argentina, Paraguay*
Som störst kan träden nå en höjd av 40 meter och 1,8 meter i stamdiameter. Imbuia från Sydamerika har ett trä som är djupt mörkbrunt i färgen med exceptionellt fin ådring. Det är ett av de tätaste träslagen som finns tillgängligt. Trädet är en mycket stor handelsart i Brasilien på grund av träets värde till exklusiv möbeltillverkning. Det används mest till dekorationsfanering och till golvläggning.

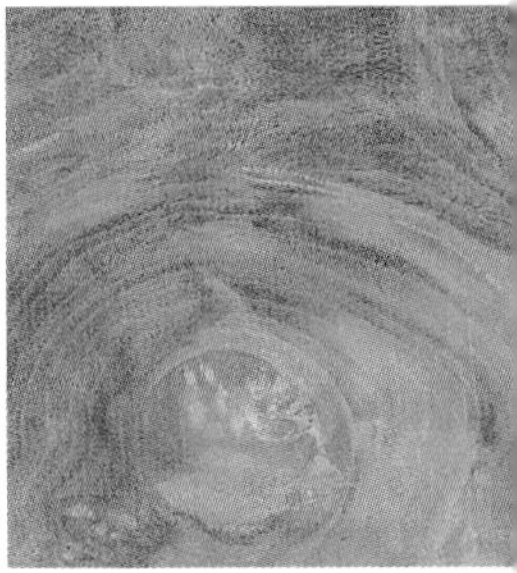

Guibourtia demeusei – **Bubinga – Bubinga – Bubinga – Bubinga**

Family: *Fabaceae*
Density: *0.80-0.95 g/cm³*
Zones of Production: *Cameroon, Gabon, Guinea, Congo*
Boles are 15 to 20 m (49 to 66 ft). Diameter is 80-150 cm (31-59 in). Bubinga is light brown through dark brown and red, some samples show as almost purple. This wood is commonly used for turned pieces, veneer, inlay work, high end furniture, and flooring. The wood can be worked with hand or power tools to a fine finish and takes a nice polish.

Famille : *Fabacées*
Densité : *0,80-0,95 g/cm³*
Zones de production : *Cameroun, Gabon, Guinée et Congo*
Troncs de 15 à 20 m de hauteur, pour un diamètre de 80 à 150 cm. Le bubinga est brun clair à brun foncé et rouge ; certains sujets vont presque jusqu'au pourpre. Cette essence est utilisée pour les pièces tournées, le placage, le travail d'incrustation, le mobilier haut de gamme et le revêtement de sol. Le bois se travaille aisément, manuellement comme avec des machines-outils. Il est susceptible d'acquérir un beau poli, en finition de luxe.

Familie: *Fabaceae*
Dichte: *0,80-0,95 g/cm³*
Vorkommen: *Kamerun, Gabun, Guinea, Kongo*
Der Baumstamm ist zwischen 15 und 20 Meter lang, sein Durchmesser liegt zwischen 80 und 150 Metern. Bubingaholz weist eine helle bis dunkelbraune, rötliche Färbung auf, in einigen Fällen ist es nahezu violett. Dieses Holz wird normalerweise für Drehteile, Furniere, Einlegearbeiten, Luxusmöbel und für Fußböden verwendet. Durch manuelle oder maschinelle Bearbeitung wird bei diesem Holz ein schöne Oberfläche erzielt, die sich gut polieren lässt.

Familie: *Fabaceae*
Dichtheid: *0,80-0,95 g/cm³*
Productiegebieden: *Kameroen, Gabon, Guinee, Congo*
De stam is 15 tot 20 meter lang. De dikte bedraagt 80-150 centimeter. Bubinga is lichtbruin tot donkerbruin en rood en soms haast paars. Dit hout wordt algemeen gebruikt voor draaiwerk, fineer, inlegwerk, kwaliteitsmeubilair en vloeren. Het hout is goed elektrisch of met handgereedschap te bewerken en laat zich mooi afwerken en polijsten.

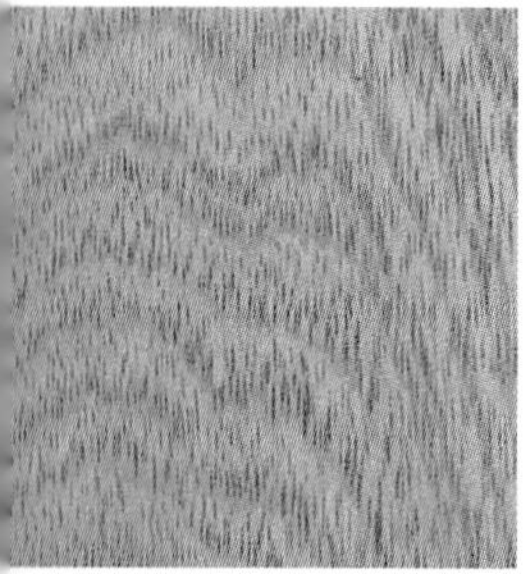

Cedrela odorata – **Cedar – Cèdre d'Amérique – Westindische Zeder – Ceder**

Family: *Meliaceae*
Density: *0.40-0.70 g/cm³*
Zones of Production: *Mexico, Suriname, Guyana, Nicaragua, Honduras, Brazil, Antilles*
Boles are 15 to 20 m (49 to 66 ft) tall and 50 to 110 cm 20 to 43 in in diameter. The trunk has a thick gray-brown colored bark, with longitudinal irregular grain. Known as Spanish-cedar in English commerce, the aromatic wood is in high demand in the American tropics because it is naturally termite and rot resistant. An attractive, moderately lightweight wood, its primary use is in household articles.

Famille : *Méliacées*
Densité : *0,40-0,70 g/cm³*
Zones de production : *Mexique, Surinam, Guyane, Nicaragua, Honduras, Brésil et Antilles*
Troncs de 15 à 20 m de hauteur, pour 50 à 110 cm de diamètre. Le tronc présente une épaisse écorce brun foncé, pour un bois à fil longitudinal irrégulier. Connue sous l'appellation de « cèdre espagnol » dans le commerce anglo-saxon, cette essence aromatique est très demandée dans l'Amérique tropicale parce qu'elle résiste naturellement aux termites et au pourrissement. C'est un bois attractif, de poids modéré, qui est surtout utilisé pour la fabrication d'articles domestiques.

Familie: *Meliaceae*
Dichte: *0,40-0,70 g/cm³*
Vorkommen: *Mexiko, Surinam, Guyana, Nicaragua, Honduras, Brasilien, Antillen*
Der Baumstamm ist zwischen 15 und 29 Meter lang und 50 bis 110 Zentimeter dick. Seine dicke Rinde weist eine graubraune Färbung und eine längsgerichtete, unregelmäßige Maserung auf. Auf dem deutschen Markt auch als Spanische Zeder bekannt, ist dieses aromatische Holz in den amerikanischen Tropen heiß begehrt, da es von Natur aus termiten- und faulbeständig ist. Dieses attraktive, mittelschwere bis leichte Holz wird vor allem für Haushaltsgegenstände verwendet.

Familie: Meliaceae
Dichtheid: 0,40-0,70 g/cm³
Productiegebieden: Mexico, Suriname, Guyana, Nicaragua, Honduras, Brazilië, Antillen
De stam is 15 tot 20 meter lang en 50 tot 110 centimeter dik. De stam heeft een dikke, grijsbruine bast met een onregelmatige draad in de lengte. Het aromatische hout is erg gewild in de Amerikaanse tropen omdat het van nature bestand is tegen termieten en rot. Dit aantrekkelijke en vrij lichte hout wordt hoofdzakelijk gebruikt voor huishoudelijke artikelen.

Chloroxylon swietenia – **Ceylon Satinwood – Citronnier de Ceylan – Westindisches Satinholz – Satijnhout**

Family: *Rutaceae*
Density: *0.85-0.95 g/cm³*
Zones of Production: *Sri Lanka, Pakistan, India*
Boles are 7 to 10 m (23 to 33 ft) tall and 30 to 60 cm (12 to 24 in) in diameter. The wood is often a golden color with a reflective sheen. The heartwood is light to golden yellow, darkening to a soft brown. It has an interlocked grain, sometimes having dark gum veins, which cause splits. This dense and hard wood turns, stains and polishes well. It is used for small luxury items, for furniture, joinery, and veneers.

Famille : *Rutacées*
Densité : *0,85-0,95 g/cm³*
Zones de production : *Sri Lanka, Pakistan et Inde*
Troncs de 7 à 10 m de hauteur, pour un diamètre de 30 à 60 cm. Le bois prend souvent une couleur dorée, avec un reflet poli. Le cœur est jaune clair à jaune d'or, et peut foncer jusqu'au brun clair. Le fil n'est pas homogène, avec parfois des veines résineuses sombres qui peuvent provoquer des fissures. Ce bois assez dense prend bien la teinture et il est susceptible d'un beau poli. On l'utilise pour de petits objets de luxe, le mobilier, les placages, et pour la menuiserie en général.

Familie: *Rutaceae*
Dichte: *0,85-0,95 g/cm³*
Vorkommen: *Sri Lanka, Pakistan, Indien*
Der Stamm ist 7 bis 10 Meter lang und 30 bis 60 Zentimeter dick. Das Holz glänzt häufig golden. Das Kernholz reift zu einem hellen bis goldenen Gelb, das zu einem hellen Braun nachdunkelt. Der Faserverlauf ist wechselwüchsig, charakteristisch für das Holz sind die dunklen Gummiadern, die Spaltungen verursachen. Dieses dichte und harte Holz lässt sich gut drehen, beizen und polieren. Es wird für kleinere Luxusgegenstände, Möbel, Zimmerarbeiten und Furniere benutzt.

Familie: *Rutaceae*
Dichtheid: *0,85-0,95 g/cm³*
Productiegebieden: *Sri Lanka, Pakistan, India*
De stam is 7 tot 10 meter lang en 30 tot 60 centimeter dik. Het hout is vaak goudachtig van kleur, met een weerschijnende glans. Het kernhout is licht- tot goudgeel en kleurt donkerder tot zachtbruin. Het is kruisdradig en heeft soms donkere gomaderen die het hout doen splijten. Dit dichte en harde hout laat zich goed draaien, beitsen en polijsten. Het wordt gebruikt voor kleine luxeartikelen, meubels, schrijnwerk en fineer.

Bubinga – Bubinga – Bubinga – Bubinga

Familia: *Fabáceas*
Densidad: *0,80-0,95 g/cm³*
Zonas de producción: *Camerún, Gabón, Guinea, Congo*
El tronco tiene entre 15 y 20 m de altura y un diámetro que oscila entre los 80 y los 150 cm. Su madera es marrón claro con reflejos rojos y marrones oscuro, en algunos casos casi violetas. Esta madera se emplea comúnmente en la realización de piezas torneadas, enchapados, incrustaciones, muebles de gama alta y revestimientos para suelos. Puede usarse con herramientas manuales y con máquinas-herramienta para obtener un buen acabado y un excelente pulido.

Famiglia: *Fabacee*
Densità: *0,80-0,95 g/cm³*
Zone di produzione: *Camerun, Gabon, Guinea, Congo*
Il tronco ha un'altezza di 15-20 metri e un diametro che oscilla tra i 80 e i 150 centimetri. Il suo legno è marrone chiaro con riflessi rossi e marroni scuri, a volte quasi viola. Questo legno si utilizza generalmente nella realizzazione di oggetti torniti, nell'impiallacciatura, nell'intarsio, nella produzione di mobili d'alto livello e nel rivestimento di pavimenti. Può essere lavorato con strumenti manuali e con macchine-utensili per ottenere una buona rifinitura e un'ottima lucidatura.

Família: *Fabaceae*
Densidade: *0,80-0,95 g/cm³*
Zonas de Produção: *Camarões, Gabão, Guiné, Congo*
Os troncos medem de 15 a 20 metros. O diâmetro é de 80-150 centímetros. A bubinga pode ser castanho-clara a castanho-escura e vermelha, algumas amostras são quase roxas. Esta madeira é normalmente utilizada para peças torneadas, folheado, incrustação, mobiliário de luxo e soalhos. Pode ser trabalhada com ferramentas manuais ou eléctricas para a obtenção de um bom acabamento e permite um bom polimento.

Familj: *Fabaceae*
Densitet: *0,80-0,95 g/cm³*
Produktionsområden: *Kamerun, Gabon, Guinea, Kongo*
Stammarna är 15-20 meter. Diametern är 80-150 centimeter. Bubinga är ljusbrun till mörkbrun och röd, vissa exemplar är nästan lila. Träet används ofta till svarvade föremål, fanering, intarsia, exklusiva möbler och golvläggning. Träet kan arbetas med hand- eller kraftverktyg till en fin finish och antar en fin glans.

Cedro americano – Cedro – Cedro – Västindisk ceder

Familia: *Meliáceas*
Densidad: *0,40-0,70 g/cm³*
Zonas de producción: *México, Surinam, Guyana, Nicaragua, Honduras, Brasil, Antillas*
El tronco tiene entre 15 y 20 m, un diámetro que oscila entre los 50 y los 110 cm y una gruesa corteza marrón grisácea, con una veta longitudinal irregular. Conocido como cedro español en el comercio inglés, este aromático árbol tiene una gran demanda en el trópico americano por su resistencia natural a las termitas y al deterioro. Esta atractiva y ligera madera se emplea principalmente en la fabricación de artículos para el hogar.

Famiglia: *Meliacee*
Densità: *0,40-0,70 g/cm³*
Zone di produzione: *Messico, Suriname, Guyana, Nicaragua, Honduras, Brasile, Antille*
Il tronco ha un'altezza di 15-20 metri, un diametro che oscilla tra i 50 e i 110 centimetri e una spessa corteccia marrone grigiastra, con venature longitudinali irregolari. Noto come cedro spagnolo nel mercato inglese, questo albero aromatico è molto richiesto nei tropici americani per la sua resistenza naturale alle termiti e al deterioramento. Questo legno bello e leggero si usa principalmente nella produzione di articoli per la casa.

Família: *Meliaceae*
Densidade: *0,40-0,70 g/cm³*
Zonas de Produção: *México, Suriname, Guiana, Nicarágua, Honduras, Brasil, Antilhas*
Os troncos medem 15 a 20 metros de altura e 50 a 110 centímetros de diâmetro. O tronco tem uma casca grossa de cor cinzenta acastanhada, com um grão irregular longitudinal. Conhecido como cedro espanhol no comércio inglês, a sua madeira aromática tem uma grande procura nos trópicos americanos porque é naturalmente resistente às térmitas e ao apodrecimento. Uma madeira atractiva, moderadamente leve, é principalmente utilizada em artigos para a casa.

Familj: *Meliaceae*
Densitet: *0,40-0,70 g/cm³*
Produktionsområden: *Mexico, Surinam, Guyana, Nicaragua, Honduras, Brasilien, Antillerna*
Stammarna är 15-20 meter höga och 50-110 centimeter i diameter. Stammen har en tjock gråbrun bark med longitudinell, oregelbunden ådring. Det aromatiska träet, känt som Spanskceder i engelsk handel, är mycket eftertraktat i de amerikanska tropikerna eftersom det är naturligt resistent mot termiter och röta. Ett attraktivt, relativt lätt trä vars främsta användningsområde är hushållsartiklar.

Limoncillo de Ceilán – Legno seta delle indie orientali – Pau-cetim – Sidenträ

Familia: *Rutáceas*
Densidad: *0,85-0,95 g/cm³*
Zonas de producción: *Sri Lanka, Pakistán, India*
El tronco tiene de 7 a 10 m de altura y un diámetro de 30 a 60 cm. La madera suele ser de color dorado con un brillo reflectante. El duramen es claro tirando al amarillo dorado y se oscurece hasta transformarse en marrón claro. Tiene una fibra alternada, a veces con vetas de resina oscuras que provocan grietas. Esta madera densa y dura es fácil de tornear, teñir y pulir. Se emplea para en la realización de pequeños artículos de lujo, muebles, obras de carpintería y contrachapados.

Famiglia: *Rutacee*
Densità: *0,85-0,95 g/cm³*
Zone di produzione: *Sri Lanka, Pakistan, India*
Il tronco ha un'altezza di 7-10 metri e un diametro di 30 a 60 centimetri. Il legno in genere si presenta di colore dorato luccicante. Il durame è chiaro tendente al giallo dorato e diviene scuro fino a trasformarsi in marrone chiaro. Possiede una fibra alternata, a volte con venature di resina scure che provocano spaccature. Questo legno denso e duro è facile da tornire, tingere e lucidare. Si usa per la realizzazione di piccoli articoli di lusso, mobili, opere di falegnameria e compensato.

Família: *Rutaceae*
Densidade: *0,85-0,95 g/cm³*
Zonas de Produção: *Sri Lanka, Paquistão, Índia*
Os troncos medem 7 a 10 metros de altura e 30 a 60 centímetros de diâmetro. A madeira é frequentemente dourada com um brilho reflector. O cerne é de amarelo claro a dourado, escurecendo para um castanho suave. Tem fibras entrecruzadas, por vezes com nervuras de resina escura que provocam rachas. A sua madeira densa e dura é facilmente transformada, tingida e polida. É utilizada para pequenos artigos de luxo, mobiliário, carpintaria e folheados.

Familj: *Rutaceae*
Densitet: *0,85-0,95 g/cm³*
Produktionsområden: *Sri Lanka, Pakistan, Indien*
Stammarna är 7-10 meter höga och 30-60 centimeter i diameter. Träet har ofta en gyllene färg med en reflekterande lyster. Kärnvirket är ljus-till gyllengult och mörknar till en lätt brun nyans. Det har en sammanflätad ådring, ibland har det mörka kådnerver som orsakar sprickor. Detta täta och hårda trä fungerar bra att svarva, betsa och polera. Det används till små lyxartiklar, till möbler, snickeri och fanering.

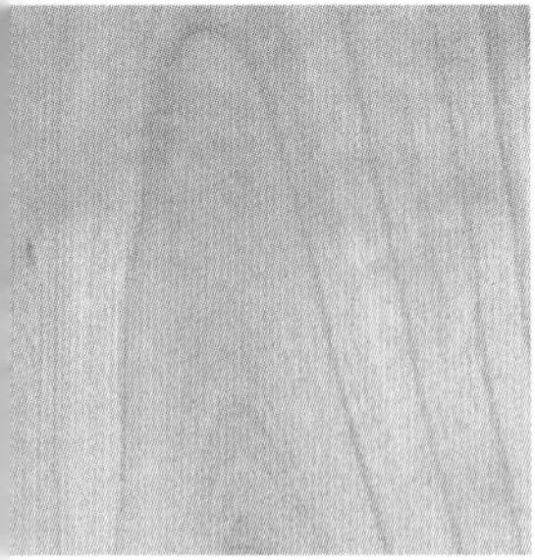

Prunus avium – **Cherry – Merisier – Kirschbaum – Kers**

Family: *Rosaceae*
Density: *0.60-0.70 g/cm³*
Zones of Production: *France, United Kingdom, Germany*
Boles are 3 to 12 m (10 to 39 ft) tall and 30 to 60 cm (12 to 24 in) in diameter. The heartwood is a medium red-brown. The grain is straight and finely textured. As one of the most sought after hardwoods, cherry is commonly used for the making of fine furniture, flooring, musical instruments, carving, turned pieces, joinery, veneers and plywood. Cherry works well, and takes all kinds of finishes excellently.

Famille : *Rosacées*
Densité : *0,60-0,70 g/cm³*
Zones de production : *France, Royaume-Uni et Allemagne*
Troncs de 3 à 12 m de hauteur, pour un diamètre de 30 à 60 cm. Le cœur est d'un brun-rouge moyen ; le fil est droit et le grain fin. Le merisier est l'un des bois durs les plus recherchés en ébénisterie. On l'utilise pour le mobilier haut de gamme, les revêtements de sol, la facture d'instruments de musique, la sculpture, les pièces tournées, les placages et le contreplaqué. Ce bois se travaille très bien et reçoit excellemment tous les types de finition.

Familie: *Rosaceae*
Dichte: *0,60-0,70 g/cm³*
Vorkommen: *Frankreich, Vereinigtes Königreich, Deutschland*
Der Baumstamm ist 3-12 m lang und 30-60 cm dick. Das Kernholz ist moderat rotbraun gefärbt. Der Faserverlauf ist gerade, die Textur fein. Als eines der begehrtesten Harthölzer wird die Kirsche normalerweise für die Herstellung von Ziermöbeln, für Fußböden, Musikinstrumente, Schnitzereien, Drehteile, Zimmerarbeiten, Furniere und Sperrholz benutzt. Kirschenholz lässt sich gut bearbeiten und eignet sich hervorragend für verschiedenste Oberflächenbehandlungen.

Familie: *Rosaceae*
Dichtheid: *0,60-0,70 g/cm³*
Productiegebieden: *Frankrijk, Verenigd Koninkrijk, Duitsland*
De stam is 3 tot 12 meter lang en 30 tot 60 centimeter dik. Het kernhout is licht roodbruin. Het hout is rechtdradig en fijn van nerf. Kersenhout, een van de meest gewilde hardhoutsoorten, wordt meestal gebruikt voor kwaliteitsmeubilair, vloeren, muziekinstrumenten, houtsnijwerk, draaiwerk, schrijnwerk, fineer en multiplex. Kersen is goed te bewerken en voortreffelijk af te werken met allerlei soorten lak.

Tieghemella heckelii – **Cherry Mahogany – Makoré – Makore – Makoré**

Family: *Sapotaceae*
Density: *0.67 g/cm³*
Zones of Production: *Sierra Leone, Cameroon, Gabon*
Boles are up to 30 m (98 ft) tall and generally 1 to 3 m (3 to 10 ft) in diameter. Heartwood is pink to red brown. Texture is fine to medium with grain generally straight, sometimes with an attractive moiré figure. The wood works well by hand or machine tools and finishes well. Its uses are in cabinetry, joinery, veneers, paneling, boat building, flooring, turned pieces, and plywood.

Famille : *Sapotacées*
Densité : *0,67 g/cm³*
Zones de production : *Sierra Leone, Cameroun, Gabon*
Troncs jusqu'à 30 m de hauteur, pour un diamètre de 100 à 300 cm. Le cœur est rose à rouge brun, avec un fil de moyen à fin. Le fil est droit et offre parfois des figures de moiré. Le makoré se travaille bien, manuellement comme à la machine-outil, et il est susceptible de belles finitions. On l'utilise en ébénisterie et en menuiserie, pour des placages, des lambris, des pièces tournées, des revêtements de sol et du contreplaqué ; parfois aussi pour la construction navale.

Familie: *Sapotaceae*
Dichte: *0,67 g/cm³*
Vorkommen: *Sierra Leone, Kamerun, Gabun*
Der Stamm wird bis zu 30 m hoch, sein Durchmesser liegt bei 1-3 m. Das Kernholz ist rosarot bis rötlichbraun gefärbt. Makoreholz besitzt eine feine bis mittelgrobe Textur mit einem meist geradlinigen Faserverlauf und gelegentlich einem reizvollen Moiré. Das Holz lässt sich gut von Hand oder maschinell bearbeiten und an der Oberfläche nachbehandeln. Es wird für Möbel, Zimmerarbeiten, Furniere, Verkleidungen, im Bootsbau, für Fußböden, Drehteile und Sperrholz verwendet.

Familie: *Sapotaceae*
Dichtheid: *0,67 g/cm³*
Productiegebieden: *Sierra Leone, Kameroen, Gabon*
De stam is tot 30 meter lang en meestal 1 tot 3 meter dik. Het kernhout is roze tot roodbruin. Makoré is fijn tot matig grof van nerf en overwegend rechtdradig, soms met een aantrekkelijke moirétekening. Het hout is goed te bewerken met de hand of machinaal en laat zich mooi afwerken. Het wordt gebruikt voor kasten, schrijnwerk, fineer, paneelwerk, bootbouw, vloeren, draaiwerk en multiplex.

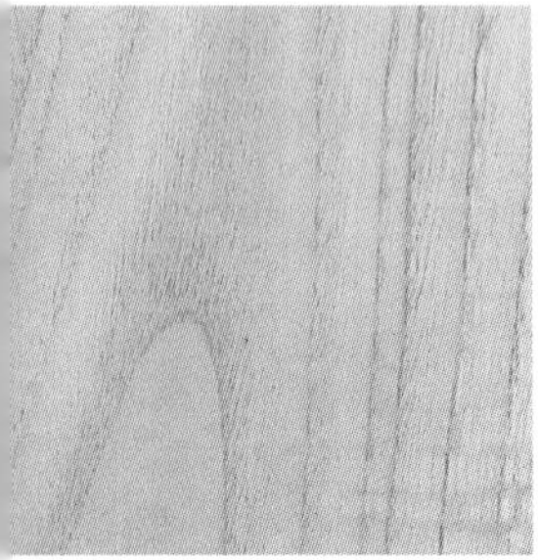

Castanea sativa – **Chestnut – Châtaignier – Kastanie, Edelkastanie – Kastanje**

Family: *Fagaceae*
Density: *0.60-0.70 g/cm³*
Zones of Production: *France, United Kingdom, Germany, Italy*
Boles are 3 to 8 m (10 to 26 ft) tall and 30 to 100 cm (12 to 40 in) in diameter. The wood is a light color, hard and strong. It is used to make furniture, barrels, and roof beams notably in southern Europe (for example in Alpujarra, Spain, or in southern France). Due to older wood's tendency to split and warp badly, and acquire certain brittleness, it is not frequently used in large pieces.

Famille : *Fagacées*
Densité : *0,60-0,70 g/cm³*
Zones de production : *France, Royaume-Uni, Allemagne et Italie*
Troncs de 3 à 8 m de hauteur, pour un diamètre de 30 à 100 cm. Le bois est de couleur claire ; il est dur et résistant. On utilise le châtaignier pour faire des meubles, des tonneaux et des poutres, notamment dans le sud de la France : le bois fait fuir les araignées. Le bois vieillissant ayant tendance à se fendre et à se voiler, on ne l'utilise guère pour les grandes pièces de mobilier.

Familie: *Fagaceae*
Dichte: *0,60-0,70 g/cm³*
Vorkommen: *Frankreich, Vereinigtes Königreich, Deutschland, Italien*
Der zwischen 30 und 100 Zentimetern dicke Baumstamm wird 3 bis 8 Meter lang. Das harte und feste Holz weist eine helle Färbung auf. Es wird als Möbelholz, für Fässer und, vor allem in Südeuropa (z.B. in Spanien in der Alpujarra oder in Südfrankreich), für Dachbalken verwendet. Das schwer spaltbare Holz besitzt geringe Biegefestigkeit und neigt zudem zu einer gewissen Sprödigkeit, daher wird es selten in großen Abmessungen verwendet.

Familie: *Fagaceae*
Dichtheid: *0,60-0,70 g/cm³*
Productiegebieden: *Frankrijk, Verenigd Koninkrijk, Duitsland, Italië*
De stam is 3 tot 8 meter lang en 30 tot 100 centimeter dik. Het hout is hard en sterk en licht van kleur. Het wordt gebruikt om meubels, tonnen en dakbalken te maken, met name in Zuid-Europa (bijvoorbeeld in de Spaanse Alpujarra en Zuid-Frankrijk). Omdat ouder hout nog wel eens splijt en erg krom kan trekken, en ook wat broos kan worden, werkt men meestal niet met grote stukken.

Cerezo – Ciliegio – Cerejeira – Körsbär

Familia: *Rosáceas*
Densidad: *0,60-0,70 g/cm^3*
Zonas de producción: *Francia, Reino Unido, Alemania*
El tronco tiene de 3 a 12 m de altura y un diámetro de 30 a 60 cm. El duramen es marrón rojizo medio, con vetas rectas y una textura fina. El cerezo, una de las maderas más buscadas después de las maderas nobles, se emplea comúnmente en la realización de muebles elegantes, revestimientos de suelos, instrumentos musicales, esculturas, piezas torneadas, obras de carpintería, enchapados y contrachapados. El cerezo es fácil de trabajar y apto para cualquier tipo de acabado.

Famiglia: *Rosacee*
Densità: *0,60-0,70 g/cm^3*
Zone di produzione: *Francia, Inghilterra, Germania*
Il tronco ha un'altezza che va da 3 a 12 metri e un diametro di 30-60 centimetri. Il durame è di marrone rossastro medio, con venature dritte e una texture fine. Il ciliegio, uno dei legni più ricercati dopo i legnami nobili, è generalmente impiegato nella realizzazione di mobili eleganti, di rivestimento per pavimenti, di strumenti musicali, sculture, oggetti torniti, opere di falegnameria, impiallacciatura e compensato. Si tratta di un legno facile da lavorare e adatto a qualsiasi tipo di rifinitura.

Família: *Rosaceae*
Densidade: *0,60-0,70 g/cm^3*
Zonas de Produção: *França, Reino Unido, Alemanha*
Os troncos medem 3 a 12 metros de altura e 30 a 60 centímetros de diâmetro. O cerne é de um castanho avermelhado médio. O grão é direito e a textura fina. Uma das madeiras mais procuradas a seguir às madeiras duras, a cerejeira é habitualmente utilizada para mobiliário de luxo, soalhos, instrumentos musicais, escultura, peças torneadas, carpintaria, folheados e contraplacado. Trabalha-se bem e permite, de uma forma excelente, todos os tipos de acabamentos.

Familj: *Rosaceae*
Densitet: *0,60-0,70 g/cm^3*
Produktionsområden: *Frankrike, Storbritannien, Tyskland*
Stammarna är 3-12 meter höga och 30-60 centimeter i diameter. Kärnvirket är mellanrödbrunt. Ådringen är rak och har fin struktur. Som en av de mest eftertraktade hårdträsorterna används körsbär ofta till möbeltillverkning, golvläggning, musikinstrument, sniderі, svarvade föremål, snickeri, fanering och plywood. Körsbär arbetas bra och tar utmärkt till sig alla typer av ytbehandlingar.

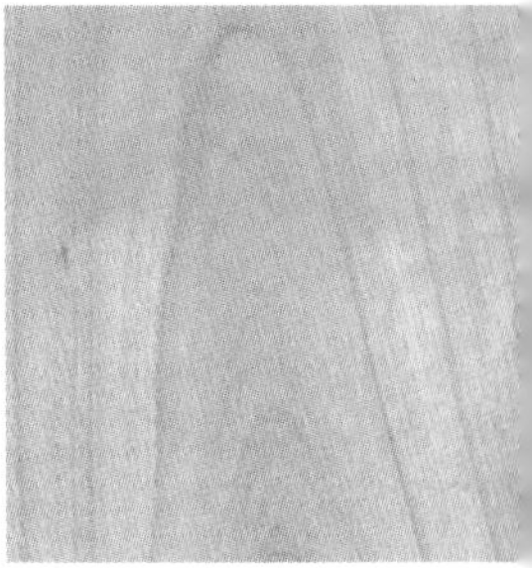

Makoré – Makoré – Macoré – Makore

Familia: *Sapotáceas*
Densidad: *0,67 g/cm^3*
Zonas de producción: *Sierra Leona, Camerún, Gabón*
El tronco puede alcanzar una altura máxima de 30 m y un diámetro de 1 a 3 m. El duramen es rosa tirando al marrón rojizo con una textura entre fina y media y una veta bastante recta, a veces describiendo una atractiva figura muaré. Esta madera es fácil de trabajar tanto con herramientas de mano como con máquinas-herramienta. Se emplea en la realización de armarios y muebles, en obras de carpintería, enchapados, paneles, revestimientos de suelos, piezas torneadas y contrachapados, así como en la construcción de barcos.

Famiglia: *Sapotacee*
Densità: *0,67 g/cm^3*
Zone di produzione: *Sierra Leone, Camerun, Gabon*
Il tronco può raggiungere un'altezza di 30 metri e un diametro di 1-3 metri. Il durame è rosa tendente al marrone rossastro con una texture tra fine e media e venature abbastanza dritte che, a volte, tracciano un'interessante figura marezzata. Questo legno è facile da lavorare sia con strumenti a mano sia con macchine-utensili. È impiegato nella realizzazione di armadi e mobili, in opere di falegnameria, impiallacciatura, rivestimenti a pannelli, pavimenti, oggetti torniti e compensato, oltre che nella costruzione di barche.

Família: *Sapotaceae*
Densidade: *0,67 g/cm^3*
Zonas de Produção: *Serra Leoa, Camarões, Gabão*
Os troncos podem medir até 30 metros de altura e habitualmente têm de 1 a 3 metros de diâmetro. O cerne é rosa a castanho avermelhado. A textura é fina a média, com um grão geralmente direito, por vezes com um atractivo veio ondulado. A madeira trabalha-se bem manualmente ou com ferramentas eléctricas e tem um bom acabamento. É utilizada em marcenaria, carpintaria, folheados, painéis, construção naval, soalhos, peças torneadas e contraplacado.

Familj: *Sapotaceae*
Densitet: *0,67 g/cm^3*
Produktionsområden: *Sierra Leone, Kamerun, Gabon*
Stammarna är upp till 30 meter höga och oftast 1-3 meter i diameter. Kärnvirket är rosa till rödbrunt. Strukturen är fin till medium med en vanligtvis rak ådring, ibland med ett mer attraktiv moirémönster. Träet arbetas lätt med hand- eller maskinverktyg och ytbehandlas enkelt. Dess användningsområden är möbelsnickeri, snickeri, fanering, panel, båtbyggnation, golvläggning, svarvade föremål och plywood.

Castaño – Castagno – Castanheiro – Kastanj

Familia: *Fagáceas*
Densidad: *0,60-0,70 g/cm^3*
Zonas de producción: *Francia, Reino Unido, Alemania, Italia*
El tronco tiene de 3 a 8 m de altura y un diámetro de 30 a 100 cm. La madera es dura, resistente y de color claro. Se emplea en la manufactura de muebles, barriles y vigas de tejados, sobre todo en el sur de Europa (por ejemplo, en la Alpujarra [España] o en el sur de Francia). Debido a la tendencia de los ejemplares más viejos a romperse, doblarse mal y debilitarse, esta madera no es apta para la realización de grandes piezas.

Famiglia: *Fagacee*
Densità: *0,60-0,70 g/cm^3*
Zone di produzione: *Francia, Inghilterra, Germania e Italia*
Il tronco ha un'altezza di 3-8 metri e un diametro che va da 30 a 100 centimetri. Il legno è duro, resistente e di colore chiaro. Si usa nella manifattura di mobili, botti e travi per tetti, soprattutto nell'Europa meridionale (per esempio, nell'Alpujarra, Spagna o nel sud della Francia). A causa della tendenza degli esemplari più vecchi di castagno a rompersi, piegarsi male e indebolirsi, non è adatto per la fabbricazione di grandi pezzi.

Família: *Fagaceae*
Densidade: *0,60-0,70 g/cm^3*
Zonas de Produção: *França, Reino Unido, Alemanha, Itália*
Os troncos medem 3 a 8 metros de altura e 30 a 100 centímetros de diâmetro. A madeira é clara, dura e forte. É utilizada para fazer mobiliário, barris e traves de telhado, especialmente na Europa Meridional (por exemplo, em Alpujarra, Espanha, e no sul de França). Devido á tendência da madeira mais velha para rachar e empenar bastante, tornando-se frágil, geralmente não é utilizada em peças grandes.

Familj: *Fagaceae*
Densitet: *0,60-0,70 g/cm^3*
Produktionsområden: *Frankrike, Storbritannien, Tyskland, Italien*
Stammarna är 3-8 meter höga och 30-100 centimeter i diameter. Träet är ljust i färgen, hårt och starkt. Det används till möbeltillverkning, tunnor och takbjälkar särskilt i södra Europa (till exempel i Alpujarra i Spanien eller i södra Frankrike). På grund av att äldre trä har en tendens att spricka och bli mycket skevt, och drabbas av viss skörhet, används det inte ofta till större saker.

Sequoia sempervirens - **Coast Redwood – Séquoia à feuilles d'if – Küstenmammutbaum – Kustmammoetboom**

Family: *Cuppressaceae*
Density: *0.40-0.50 g/cm³*
Zones of Production: *California*
Boles are up to 80 m (262 ft) in height and 8 m (26 ft) in diameter. The heartwood is a dark reddish brown and has straight grain, and high dimensional stability. Redwood works easily with both hand and machine tools. The wood is highly valued in building construction. It is commonly used for heavy beams, bridge timbers, planks, siding, doors, veneer, furniture, plywood, particle board, shingles, and posts.

Famille : *Cupressacées*
Densité : *0,40-0,50 g/cm³*
Zones de production : *Californie*
Les troncs peuvent atteindre 80 m de hauteur et 8 m de diamètre. Le cœur est d'un brun rougeâtre sombre, avec un fil droit et une grande stabilité dimensionnelle. Le coast redwood californien se travaille aisément, manuellement comme avec des machines-outils. Ce bois est extrêmement apprécié dans la construction. On l'utilise communément pour les grosses poutres, les ponts, les poteaux, les bardages, les portes et les panneaux de particules.

Familie: *Cuppressaceae*
Dichte: *0,40-0,50 g/cm³*
Vorkommen: *Kalifornien*
Der Stamm wird bis zu 30 Meter hoch und erreicht einen Durchmesser von bis zu 8 Metern. Das ausgesprochen formstabile Kernholz weist einen dunkelroten Braunton und einen geraden Faserverlauf auf. Mammutbaumholz lässt sich leicht von Hand und maschinell bearbeiten. Es wird im Bauwesen sehr geschätzt und meist für schwere Dachbalken, Brückenholz, Planken, Geleise, Türen, Furniere, Möbel, Sperrholz, Spanplatten, Schindeln und Pfosten verwendet.

Familie: *Cupressaceae*
Dichtheid: *0,40-0,50 g/cm³*
Productiegebieden: *Californië*
De stam is tot 80 meter lang en 8 meter dik. Het kernhout is donkerroodbruin en rechtdradig en zeer duurzaam. Dit hout is goed te bewerken, zowel met handgereedschap als elektrisch. Het hout is erg gewild in de bouw. Het wordt vaak gebruikt voor zware balken, brugbalken, planken, gevelbeplating, deuren, fineer, meubels, multiplex, spaanplaat, dakpannen en palen.

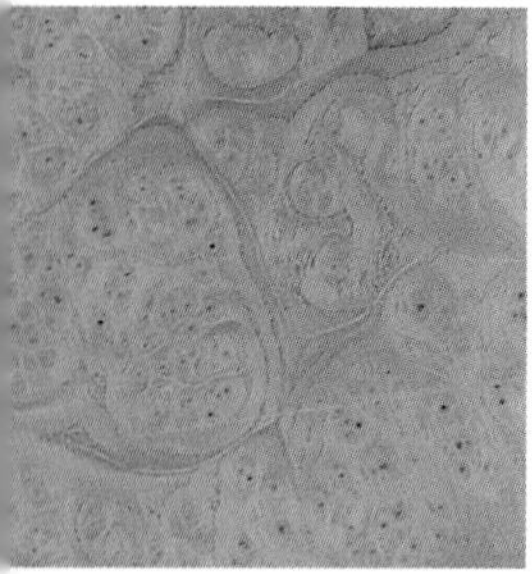

Ulmus minor - **Elm – Ormeau – Ulme – Iep**

Family: *Ulmaceae*
Density: *0.60-0.85 g/cm³*
Zones of Production: *France, United Kingdom, Germany*
Boles are 3 to 10 m (10 to 33 ft) tall and 40 to 130 cm (16 to 50 in) in diameter. The wood is a dull brown with a coarse texture. The grain is irregular, producing an attractive figure. The timber is difficult to work but has good steam-bending properties. It is commonly used in boat building, cabinetry, veneer, flooring, turnery, and furniture.

Famille : *Ulmacées*
Densité : *0,60-0,85 g/cm³*
Zones de production : *France, Royaume-Uni et Allemagne*
Troncs de 3 à 10 m de hauteur, pour un diamètre de 40 à 130 cm. Le bois est d'un brun terne, avec un grain grossier ; le fil est irrégulier et dessine parfois une figure intéressante. Le bois est difficile à travailler, mais il a de bonnes propriétés de cintrage à la vapeur. On l'utilise communément dans la construction navale, en ébénisterie, pour le placage, les revêtements de sols, le tournage et le mobilier.

Familie: *Ulmaceae*
Dichte: *0,60-0,85 g/cm³*
Vorkommen: *Frankreich, Vereinigtes Königreich, Deutschland*
Der 40 bis 130 Zentimeter dicke Baumstamm wird 3 bis 10 Meter lang. Das Holz besitzt eine dumpfe Brauntönung und eine grobe Textur. Der unregelmäßige Faserverlauf ergibt eine ansprechende Zeichnung. Es ist schwer zu bearbeiten, besitzt jedoch gute Dampfbiegequalitäten. Es wird im Bootsbau, in der Möbeltischlerei, für Furniere, für den Fußbodenausbau und für Drechselarbeiten verwendet.

Familie: *Ulmaceae*
Dichtheid: *0,60-0,85 g/cm³*
Productiegebieden: *Frankrijk, Verenigd Koninkrijk, Duitsland*
De stam is 3 tot meter lang en 40 tot 130 centimeter dik. Het hout is dofbruin en grof van nerf. De draad is onregelmatig, wat een fraaie tekening oplevert. Het hout laat zich moeilijk bewerken, maar is goed te buigen met stoom. Het wordt veel gebruikt voor boten, kasten, fineer, vloeren, draaiwerk en meubels.

Copaifera salikounda - **Etimoe – Étimoé – Etimoe – Etimoe**

Family: *Fabaceae*
Density: *0.65-0.75 g/cm³*
Zones of Production: *Ivory Coast, Cameroon, Gabon, Congo, Nigeria*
Etimoe is a West African hardwood with the greatest strength and hardness. Etimoe has enough of a resemblance to be used as a substitute for rosewood. It has a straight to interlocked grain with a fine, even texture, moderately rated for durability and steam bending. The trees possess a very high natural resistance to decay, which is why etimoe is used for boat building.

Famille : *Fabacées*
Densité : *0,65-0,75 g/cm³*
Zones de production : *Côte-d'Ivoire, Cameroun, Gabon, Congo et Nigeria*
L'étimoé est un bois dur d'Afrique occidentale très solide et très résistant. Il est assez ressemblant au palissandre pour qu'on l'utilise parfois à sa place. Le fil varie de droit à contre-fil, avec un grain fin et uniforme. Ses qualités de stabilité et de cintrage sont moyennes. Ce bois offre par contre une très grande résistance au pourrissement, ce qui le fait employer dans la construction navale.

Familie: *Fabaceae*
Dichte: *0,65-0,75 g/cm³*
Vorkommen: *Elfenbeinküste, Kamerun, Gabun, Kongo, Nigeria*
Etimoe ist ein westafrikanisches Hartholz von ausgesprochener Stärke und Härte. Es gleicht dem Palisanderholz so sehr, dass es als dessen Ersatz verwendet wird. Es weist eine gerade bis wechselwüchsige Maserung mit einer ebenmäßigen Textur auf, seine Haltbarkeit und seine Dampfbiegeeigenschaften sind als mittelmäßig einzustufen. Das Holz ist von Natur aus ausgesprochen verwitterungsbeständig und wird daher im Bootsbau eingesetzt.

Familie: *Fabaceae*
Dichtheid: *0,65-0,75 g/cm³*
Productiegebieden: *Ivoorkust, Kameroen, Gabon, Congo, Nigeria*
Etimoe is een West-Afrikaanse hardhoutsoort van buitengewone sterkte en hardheid. Etimoe lijkt genoeg op palissander om als vervanging te dienen. Het recht- tot kruisdradige hout is fijn en gelijkmatig van nerf en tamelijk geliefd omdat het duurzaam is en geschikt om te buigen met stoom. Omdat etimoe van nature zeer rotbestendig is, wordt het gebruikt om boten te bouwen.

Secuoya roja – Sequoia rossa – Sequóia sempre-verde – Amerikansk sekvoja

Familia: *Cupresáceas*
Densidad: *0,40-0,50 g/cm³*
Zonas de producción: *California*
El tronco puede alcanzar una altura máxima de 80 m y un diámetro de 8 m. El duramen es marrón rojizo oscuro, con vetas rectas y una elevada estabilidad por lo que se refiere a las dimensiones. La secuoya roja es fácil de trabajar tanto con herramientas manuales como con máquinas-herramienta. Esta madera es muy preciada en la construcción de edificios y se usa comúnmente en la fabricación de vigas resistentes, maderas para puentes, tablas, revestimientos exteriores, puertas, enchapados, muebles, contrachapados, tableros de partículas de madera, placas y postes.

Famiglia: *Cupressacee*
Densità: *0,40-0,50 g/cm³*
Zone di produzione: *California*
Il tronco può raggiungere un'altezza di 80 metri e un diametro di 8 metri. Il durame è marrone rossastro scuro, con venature dritte e un'elevata stabilità per quanto riguarda le dimensioni. La sequoia rossa è facile da lavorare sia con strumenti manuali sia con macchine-utensili. Questo legno è molto apprezzato nella costruzione di edifici e si usa in genere nella fabbricazione di travi resistenti, legname per ponti, assi, rivestimenti esterni, porte, impiallacciatura, mobili, compensato, pannelli di truciolato, scandole e tralicci.

Família: *Cuppressaceae*
Densidade: *0,40-0,50 g/cm³*
Zonas de Produção: *Califórnia*
Os troncos medem até 80 metros de altura e 8 metros de diâmetro. O cerne é de um castanho-escuro avermelhado e tem um grão direito, com grande estabilidade dimensional. A sequóia trabalha-se bem, quer com ferramentas manuais quer com ferramentas eléctricas. A madeira é muito apreciada na construção civil. É geralmente utilizada para vigas pesadas, madeira de construção, pranchas, resguardos, portas, folheado, mobiliário, contraplacado, aglomerados, telhas de madeira e postes.

Familj: *Cuppressaceae*
Densitet: *0,40-0,50 g/cm³*
Produktionsområden: *Kalifornien*
Stammarna är upp till 80 meter höga och 8 meter i diameter. Kärnvirket är mörkt rödbrunt och har en rak ådring och hög dimensionell stabilitet. Sekvoja arbetas lätt med både hand- och maskinverktyg. Träet är högt värderat inom byggnadskonstruktion. Det används ofta till tunga bjälkar, brotimmer, plank, fasad, dörrar, fanering, möbler, plywood, spånskiva, takspån och stolpar.

Olmo – Olmo – Olmo – Alm

Familia: *Ulmáceas*
Densidad: *0,60-0,85 g/cm³*
Zonas de producción: *Francia, Reino Unido, Alemania*
El tronco tiene de 3 a 10 m de altura y un diámetro de 40 a 130 cm. La madera es de color marrón apagado con una textura gruesa. La irregularidad de la veta crea una figura muy atractiva. La madera es difícil de trabajar pero tiene buenas propiedades para el curvado por vapor. Se emplea comúnmente en la construcción de barcos, en la realización de armarios y muebles, enchapados, revestimientos de suelos y tornería.

Famiglia: *Ulmacee*
Densità: *0,60-0,85 g/cm³*
Zone di produzione: *Francia, Inghilterra, Germania*
Il tronco ha un'altezza di 3-10 metri e un diametro di 40-130 centimetri. Il legno è di color marrone spento con una texture ruvida. L'irregolarità delle venature crea figure molto belle. Il legno è difficile da lavorare, ma possiede buone qualità per la curvatura a vapore. Si usa in genere nella costruzione di barche, nella realizzazione di armadi, nell'impiallacciatura, nel rivestimento di pavimenti, nella tornitura e nell'arredamento.

Família: *Ulmaceae*
Densidade: *0,60-0,85 g/cm³*
Zonas de Produção: *França, Reino Unido, Alemanha*
Os troncos medem 3 a 10 metros de altura e 40 a 130 centímetros de diâmetro. A madeira é castanha escura com uma textura grosseira. O grão é irregular, produzindo um veio atractivo. É uma madeira difícil de trabalhar mas possui boas qualidades para a moldagem a vapor. É geralmente utilizada para construção naval, marcenaria, folheado, soalhos, torneados e mobiliário.

Familj: *Ulmaceae*
Densitet: *0,60-0,85 g/cm³*
Produktionsområden: *Frankrike, Storbritannien, Tyskland*
Stammarna är 3-10 meter höga och 40-130 centimeter i diameter. Träet är mattbrunt med grov struktur. Ådringen är oregelbunden och bildar ett attraktivt mönster. Virket är svårarbetat men har goda böjträegenskaper. Det används ofta till båtbyggnation, möbelsnickeri, fanering, golvläggning, svarvning och möbler.

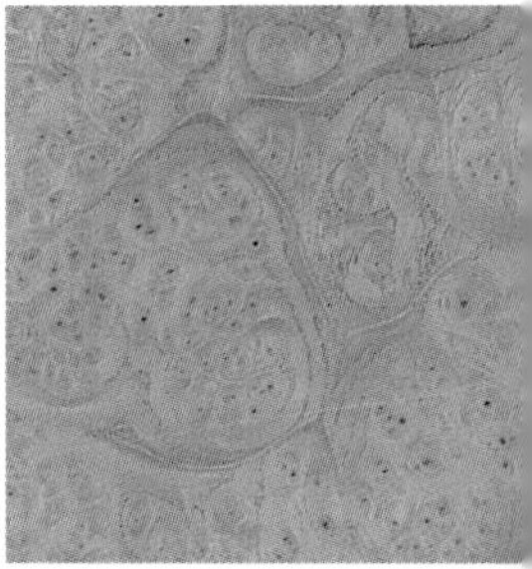

Etimoe – Etimoe – Etimoe – Etimoe

Familia: *Fabáceas*
Densidad: *0,65-0,75 g/cm³*
Zonas de producción: *Costa de Marfil, Camerún, Gabón, Congo, Nigeria*
El etimoe es una madera noble que se encuentra en África Occidental y se conoce por su gran resistencia y dureza. Se usa como sustituto del palisandro por su gran parecido. La fibra puede ser recta o ligeramente entrelazada y el grano entre fino y medio. Se trata de una madera durable y óptima para el curvado por vapor. Los árboles de esta especie poseen una resistencia natural al deterioro, por lo que su madera suele emplearse en la construcción de barcos.

Famiglia: *Fabacee*
Densità: *0,65-0,75 g/cm³*
Zone di produzione: *Costa d'Avorio, Camerun, Gabon, Congo, Nigeria*
L'etimoe è un legno nobile che si trova nell'Africa occidentale ed è conosciuto per la sua resistenza e la sua durezza. Si usa come sostituto del palissandro in virtù della grande somiglianza tra i due. La fibra può essere dritta o leggermente intrecciata e la texture è tra fine e media. Si tratta di un legno duraturo e ottimo per la curvatura a vapore. Gli alberi di questa specie presentano una resistenza naturale al deterioramento, per cui il suo legno si usa di solito nella costruzione di barche.

Família: *Fabaceae*
Densidade: *0,65-0,75 g/cm³*
Zonas de Produção: *Costa do Marfim, Camarões, Gabão, Congo, Nigéria*
O etimoe é uma das madeiras duras da África Ocidental com maior resistência e dureza. Tem bastante semelhança com o pau-santo, pelo que pode ser utilizada como seu substituto. Tem um grão direito a entrecruzado, com uma textura fina e uniforme, e é moderadamente apreciada pela resistência e pela moldagem a vapor. As árvores têm uma elevada resistência natural ao apodrecimento, razão porque o etimoe é utilizado na construção naval.

Familj: *Fabaceae*
Densitet: *0,65-0,75 g/cm³*
Produktionsområden: *Elfenbenskusten, Kamerun, Gabon, Kongo, Nigeria*
Etimoe är ett västafrikanskt hårdträ med största styrka och hårdhet. Etimoe är tillräckligt likt för att kunna användas som ersättning för jakaranda. Det har rak till sammanflätad ådring med en fin, jämn struktur, betraktas som måttligt hållbart och möjligt att böja. Träden besitter en mycket hög naturlig resistens mot förruttnelse, vilket är skälet till att etimoe används till båtbyggnation.

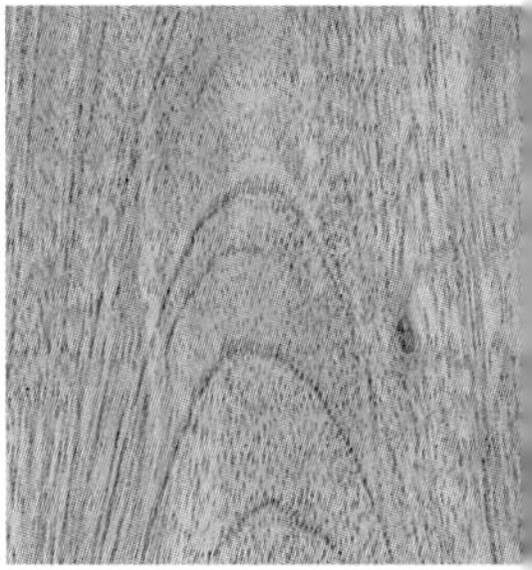

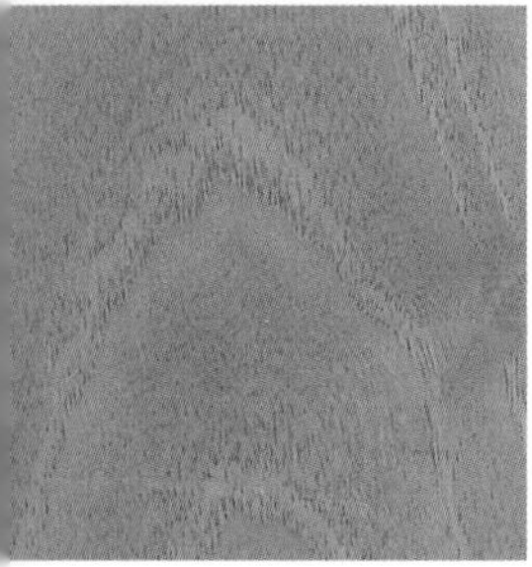

Juglans regia – **Persian Walnut – Noyer commun – Walnuss – Okkernoot**

Family: *Juglandaceae*
Density: *0.60-0.80 g/cm^3*
Zones of Production: *France, United Kingdom, Germany, Italy, Spain, Turkey, Iran, Kashmir*
Boles are 2 to 5 m (6.5 to 16 ft) tall and 40 and 80 cm (16 and 31 in) in diameter. The heartwood varies in color but it typically has a grayish-brown background with dark streaks. The wood is coarse textured with grain normally straight to wavy. Walnut has very good steam bending properties. While quite limited in availability, it is used in fine furniture, turned pieces, and veneer.

Famille : *Juglandacées*
Densité : *0,60-0,80 g/cm^3*
Zones de production : *France, Royaume-Uni, Allemagne, Italie, Espagne, Turquie, Iran et Cachemire*
Troncs de 2 à 5 m de hauteur, pour un diamètre de 40 à 80 cm. Le bois de cœur est de couleur variable, mais présente typiquement un fond brun-grisâtre avec des veines noires. Le bois a un grain grossier, avec un fil allant de droit à ondé. Le noyer a de bonnes qualités pour le cintrage à la vapeur. Devenu assez rare sur le marché, il reste employé pour les meubles de qualité, les pièces tournées et le placage.

Familie: *Juglandaceae*
Dichte: *0,60-0,80 g/cm^3*
Vorkommen: *Frankreich, Vereinigtes Königreich, Deutschland, Italien, Spanien, Türkei, Iran, Kaschmir*
Der Baumstamm ist zwischen 2 und 5 Meter hoch, sein Durchmesser beträgt 30 bis 80 Zentimeter. Das Kernholz kann verschiedene Farbtöne aufweisen, ist jedoch meist graubraun mit dunklen Streifen. Seine Faser ist gerade bis wellig mit einer groben Textur. Walnussholz besitzt ausgesprochen gute Dampfbiegeeigenschaften. Seine Verfügbarkeit ist begrenzt, es wird für Ziermöbel, Drehteile und Furniere verwendet.

Familie: *Juglandaceae*
Dichtheid: *0,60-0,80 g/cm^3*
Productiegebieden: *Frankrijk, Verenigd Koninkrijk, Duitsland, Italië, Spanje, Turkije, Iran, Kasjmir*
De stam is 2 tot 5 meter lang en 40 tot 80 centimeter dik. Het kernhout varieert in kleur, maar is doorgaans grijsbruin met donkere strepen. Het hout is grof van nerf en de draad is normaliter recht tot golvend. Notenhout is erg geschikt om te buigen met stoom. Dit vrij moeilijk verkrijgbare hout wordt gebruikt voor kwaliteitsmeubilair, draaiwerk en fineer.

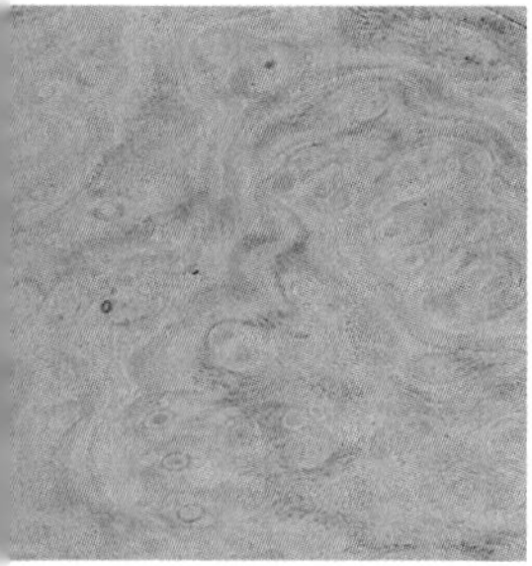

Terminalia bellirica – **Belleric – Myrobalan belleric – Baherabaum – Myrobalaan**

Family: *Combretaceae*
Density: *0.80-0.90 g/cm^3*
Zones of Production: *Burma, Cambodia, China, Laos, Thailand, Vietnam*
Boles are 10 to 20 m (33 to 66 ft) tall and 50 to 90 cm (20 to 35 in) in diameter. The wood is creamy yellow or yellowish gray occasionally with dark streaks. It turns brown with exposure. Texture is coarse and uneven. Grain is often straight. The wood responds well to hand and machine tools. It has such uses as beams, rafters, posts, boat building, furniture, paneling, turnery, and veneer.

Famille : *Combrétacées*
Densité : *0,80-0,90 g/cm^3*
Zones de production : *Birmanie, Cambodge, Chine, Laos, Thaïlande et Vietnam*
Des troncs de 10 à 20 m de hauteur, pour 50 à 90 cm de diamètre. Le bois est jaune crème à gris jaunâtre, avec parfois des stries foncées ; il devient brun à l'exposition. Son grain est grossier et non homogène. Le fil est souvent droit. Le bois se travaille bien, manuellement comme à la machine-outil. On l'utilise pour les poutres, les chevrons et les poteaux, la construction navale, mais aussi le mobilier, les lambris, le tournage et le placage.

Familie: *Combretaceae*
Dichte: *0,80-0,90 g/cm^3*
Vorkommen: *Burma, Kambodscha, China, Laos, Thailand, Vietnam*
Der zwischen 50 und 90 Zentimetern dicke Baumstamm ist 10 bis 20 Meter lang. Die Färbung des Holzes kann von einem cremefarbenen Gelb oder einem gelblichen Grau sein und gelegentlich dunkle Streifen aufweisen. Es dunkelt bei Lichteinfall zu einem Braunton nach. Die Textur des meist geradfaserigen Holzes ist grob und unregelmäßig. Es lässt sich gut von Hand oder maschinell bearbeiten. Es wird für Balken, Dachsparren, Pfosten, im Bootsbau, für Möbel, Verkleidungen, Drechselarbeiten und als Furnier genutzt.

Familie: *Combretaceae*
Dichtheid: *0,80-0,90 g/cm^3*
Productiegebieden: *Birma, Cambodja, China, Laos, Thailand, Vietnam*
De stam is 10 tot 20 meter lang en 50 tot 90 centimeter dik. Het hout is roomgeel of geelgrijs, soms met donkere strepen. Bij blootstelling aan licht kleurt het bruin. De nerf is grof en ongelijkmatig. De draad is vaak recht. Het hout laat zich goed bewerken met de hand en elektrisch. Het wordt onder meer gebruikt voor balken, daksparren, palen, boten, meubels, paneelwerk, draaiwerk en fineer.

Dalbergia latifolia – **Indian Rosewood – Palissandre des Indes – Schwarzes Rosenholz – Indisch palissander**

Family: *Fabaceae*
Density: *0.85-1.05 g/cm^3*
Zones of Production: *India, Indonesia, Malaysia, Nepal, Philippines, Vietnam*
Boles are 3 to 10 m (10 to 33 ft) tall and 50 and 100 cm (20 and 39 in) in diameter. The color ranges from rose to dark-brown with darker purple-black lines. The interlocked grain produces a ribbon figure on quarter-sawn surfaces. The texture is moderately coarse and uniform. The wood is commonly used in fine furniture, cabinetry, veneer, turned pieces, joinery, and musical instruments.

Famille : *Fabacées*
Densité : *0,85-1,05 g/cm^3*
Zones de production : *Madagascar, Inde, Indonésie, Malaisie, Népal, Philippines et Vietnam*
Des troncs de 3 à 10 m de hauteur, pour un diamètre de 50 à 100 cm. La couleur du bois de cœur va du rose au brun foncé, avec des lignes plus sombres, noir violacé. Le fil à contre-fil détermine des figures de ruban au sciage sur quartier. Le grain est relativement moyen et uniforme. Le palissandre des Indes est couramment utilisé pour le mobilier haut de gamme, en ébénisterie, en placage, pour les pièces tournées et la facture d'instruments de musique – et la menuiserie en général.

Familie: *Fabaceae*
Dichte: *0,85-1,05 g/cm^3*
Vorkommen: *Indien, Indonesien, Malaysia, Nepal, Philippinen, Vietnam*
Der 3 bis 10 Meter hohe Baumstamm hat einen Durchmesser zwischen 50 und 100 Zentimetern. Die Färbung ist rosarot bis dunkelbraun, mit dunkleren, schwarzvioletten Streifen. Der wechselwüchsige Faserverlauf ergibt auf radial geschnittenen Flächen eine gestreifte Zeichnung. Die Textur ist mittelgrob und gleichmäßig. Das Holz findet für Möbel, Furniere, Drehteile, Zimmereiarbeiten und Musikinstrumente Verwendung.

Familie: *Fabaceae*
Dichtheid: *0,85-1,05 g/cm^3*
Productiegebieden: *India, Indonesië, Maleisië, Nepal, Filippijnen, Vietnam*
De stam is 3 tot 10 meter lang en 50 tot 100 centimeter dik. De kleur varieert van roze tot donkerbruin met donkere paarszwarte lijnen. Door het kruisdraad verloopt de tekening op kwartiers gezaagde oppervlakken in smalle banen. De structuur is matig grof en uniform. Het hout wordt veel gebruikt voor kwaliteitsmeubels, kasten, fineer, draaiwerk, schrijnwerk en muziekinstrumenten.

Nogal común – Noce bianco – Nogueira-comum – Valnöt

Familia: *Juglandáceas*
Densidad: *0,60-0,80 g/cm³*
Zonas de producción: *Francia, Reino Unido, Alemania, Italia, España, Turquía, Irán, Kashmira.*
El tronco tiene de 2 a 5 m de altura y un diámetro de 40 a 80 cm. Aunque el duramen suele variar de color, por lo general presenta un fondo marrón ceniciento con rayas oscuras. La textura de la madera es gruesa con una veta entre recta y ondulada. El nogal se caracteriza por sus óptimas propiedades para el curvado por vapor. Hoy en día su disponibilidad es bastante limitada, por lo que se emplea principalmente en la realización de muebles de gama alta, piezas torneadas y enchapados.

Famiglia: *Juglandacee*
Densità: *0,60-0,80 g/cm³*
Zone di produzione: *Francia, Inghilterra, Germania, Italia, Spagna, Turchia, Iran, Kashmir*
Il tronco ha un'altezza che può variare tra 2 e 5 metri e un diametro che va da 40 a 80 centimetri. Sebbene il durame sia solito variare di colore, in genere presenta un fondo marrone cinerino con strisce scure. La texture del legno è ruvida con venature parzialmente dritte e ondulate. Il noce si distingue per le sue ottime qualità per la curvatura a vapore. Oggi la sua disponibilità è abbastanza ridotta, di conseguenza, è impiegato soprattutto nella realizzazione di mobili di alto livello, di pezzi torniti e impiallacciatura.

Família: *Juglandaceae*
Densidade: *0,60-0,80 g/cm³*
Zonas de Produção: *França, Reino Unido, Alemanha, Itália, Espanha, Turquia, Irão, Caxemira*
Os troncos medem 2 a 5 metros de altura e têm 40 a 80 centímetros de diâmetro. O cerne varia de cor mas tem tipicamente um fundo castanho acinzentado com veios escuros. A madeira tem uma textura grosseira com um grão habitualmente direito a ondulado. A nogueira tem muito boas propriedades para a moldagem a vapor. Embora muito limitada quanto à disponibilidade, é utilizada em mobiliário de luxo, peças torneadas e folheado.

Familj: *Juglandaceae*
Densitet: *0,60-0,80 g/cm³*
Produktionsområden: *Frankrike, Storbritannien, Tyskland, Italien, Spanien, Turkiet, Iran, Kashmir*
Stammarna är 2-5 meter höga och 40-80 centimeter i diameter. Kärnvirket varierar i färg men det typiska är en gråbrun bakgrund med mörka strimmor. Träet är grovt i strukturen med en ådring som normalt är rak till vågig. Valnöt har mycket bra böjträegenskaper. Eftersom det är ganska begränsad tillgång används träet till finmöbler, svarvade föremål och fanering.

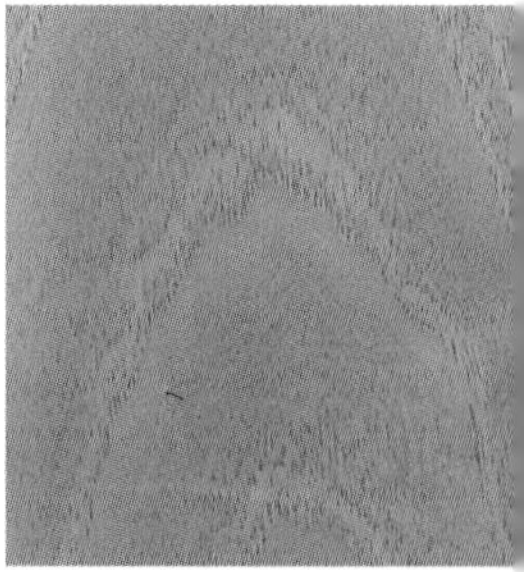

Belérico – Lauro indiano – Loureiro indiano – Bibhitaki

Familia: *Combretáceas*
Densidad: *0,80-0,90 g/cm³*
Zonas de producción: *Burma, Camboya, China, Laos, Tailandia, Vietnam*
El tronco puede alcanzar una altura de hasta 20 m y un diámetro de 50 a 90 cm. La madera posee un color amarillo cremoso o gris amarillento, a veces con rayas oscuras, que se vuelve marrón con la exposición a la luz. La textura es gruesa e irregular y la veta, generalmente recta. La madera no presenta dificultades ni con herramientas de mano ni con máquinas-herramienta. Se emplea en la realización de vigas, maderos, postes, muebles, paneles y enchapados, así como en la construcción de barcos y en tornería.

Famiglia: *Combretacee*
Densità: *0,80-0,90 g/cm³*
Zone di produzione: *Burma, Cambogia, Cina, Laos, Tailandia, Vietnam*
Il tronco può raggiungere un'altezza di 20 metri e un diametro di 50-90 centimetri. Il legno ha un colore giallo cremoso o grigio giallastro, a volte con strisce scure, che diventano marroni quando sono esposte alla luce. La texture è ruvida e irregolare e le venature, generalmente dritte. Il legno non presenta difficoltà di lavorazione né con strumenti a mano né con macchine-utensili. Si usa nella realizzazione di travi, puntoni, tralicci, barche, mobili, pannelli, oggetti torniti e impiallacciatura.

Família: *Combretaceae*
Densidade: *0,80-0,90 g/cm³*
Zonas de Produção: *Burma, Cambodja, China, Laos, Tailândia, Vietname*
Os troncos medem 10 a 20 metros de altura e 50 a 90 centímetros de diâmetro. A madeira é amarela cremosa ou cinzenta amarelada, por vezes com veios escuros, tornando-se castanha com a exposição. A textura é grosseira e irregular. O grão é frequentemente direito. A madeira responde bem às máquinas manuais e eléctricas. É utilizada para traves, vigas, postes, construção naval, mobiliário, painéis, torneados e folheado.

Familj: *Combretaceae*
Densitet: *0,80-0,90 g/cm³*
Produktionsområden: *Burma, Kambodja, Kina, Laos, Thailand, Vietnam*
Stammarna är 10-20 meter höga och 50-90 centimeter i diameter. Träet är krämgult eller gulaktigt grått, ibland med mörka strimmor. Det blir brunt vid exponering. Strukturen är grov och ojämn. Ådringen är ofta rak. Träet svarar väl på hand- och maskinverktyg. Dess användningsområden är som bjälkar, taksparrar, stolpar, båtbyggnation, panel, svarvning och fanering.

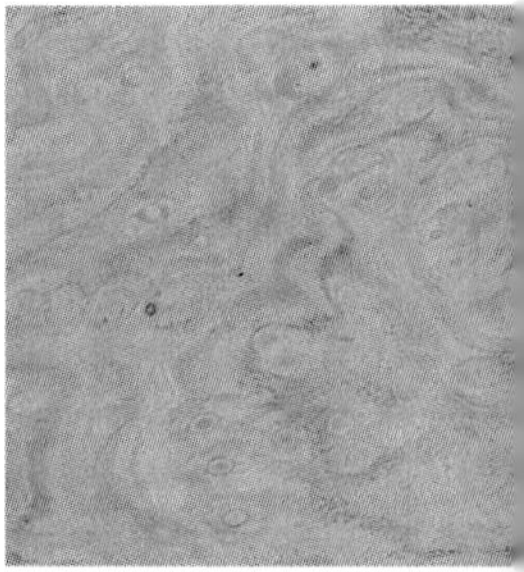

Palosanto de India – Palissandro delle Indie – Palissandro da Índia – Indisk palisander

Familia: *Fabáceas*
Densidad: *0,85-1,05 g/cm³*
Zonas de producción: *India, Indonesia, Malasia, Nepal, Filipinas, Vietnam*
El tronco tiene de 3 a 10 m de altura y un diámetro de 50 a 100 cm. El color de la madera va del rosa al marrón oscuro con líneas negras violáceas más oscuras. La fibra entrecruzada produce un veteado rayado en las superficies aserradas en cuartos. La textura es medianamente gruesa y uniforme. La madera de palosanto se emplea comúnmente en la realización de muebles de gama alta, armarios, contrachapados, piezas torneadas, obras de carpintería e instrumentos musicales.

Famiglia: *Fabacee*
Densità: *0,85-1,05 g/cm³*
Zone di produzione: *India, Indonesia, Malesia, Nepal, Filippine, Vietnam*
Il tronco può avere un'altezza di 3-10 metri e un diametro di 50-100 centimetri. Il colore del legno va dal rosa al marrone scuro con linee nere violacee più scure. La fibra intrecciata produce delle venature striate sulle superfici tagliate a quarti. La texture è di ruvidezza media e uniforme. Il legno di palissandro delle indie viene impiegato generalmente nella realizzazione di mobili l'alto livello, armadi, compensato, oggetti torniti, opere di falegnameria e strumenti musicali.

Família: *Fabaceae*
Densidade: *0,85-1,05 g/cm³*
Zonas de Produção: *Índia, Indonésia, Malásia, Nepal, Filipinas, Vietname*
Os troncos medem 3 a 10 metros de altura e 50 a 100 centímetros de diâmetro. A cor varia do rosa ao castanho-escuro com linhas mais escuras de um preto arroxeado. O grão entrecruzado produz um veio listado nas superfícies de corte radial. A textura é moderadamente grosseira e uniforme. A madeira é geralmente utilizada para mobiliário de luxo, marcenaria, folheado, peças torneadas, carpintaria e instrumentos musicais.

Familj: *Fabaceae*
Densitet: *0,85-1,05 g/cm³*
Produktionsområden: *Indien, Indonesien, Malaysia, Nepal, Filippinerna, Vietnam*
Stammarna är 3-10 meter höga och 50-100 centimeter i diameter. Färgen varierar från rosa till mörkbrunt med mörkare lilasvarta linjer. Den sammanflätade ådringen bildar ett rosettmönster på kantsågade ytor. Strukturen är måttligt grov och enhetlig. Träet används vanligen till finmöbler, möbelsnickeri, fanering, svarvade föremål, snickeri och musikinstrument.

Machaerium vergasii – **Jacaranda – Jacaranda – Jacaranda – Jacaranda**

Family: *Bignoniaceae*
Density: *0.09 g/cm^3*
Zones of Production: *South and Central America, the Caribbean, South Africa, Australia*
The attractive wood of the jacaranda exudes a pleasant aroma and is often used as veneer. This wood, much appreciated by furniture makers is frequently used to fabricate musical instruments.

Famille : *Bignoniacées*
Densité : *0,09 g/cm^3*
Zones de production : *Amérique centrale et du Sud, Caraïbes, Afrique du Sud, Madagascar et Australie*
Ce bois très attractif exhale un arôme agréable et on l'utilise souvent en placage. Très apprécié par les fabricants de meuble, il est également employé dans la facture des instruments de musique.

Familie: *Bignoniaceae*
Dichte: *0,09 g/cm^3*
Vorkommen: *Süd- und Zentralamerika, Karibik, Südafrika, Australien*
Das attraktive Jacarandaholz verströmt ein angenehmes Aroma und wird häufig für Furniere genutzt. Dieses von Möbeltischlern sehr geschätzte Holz wird auch häufig für Musikinstrumente verwendet.

Familie: *Bignoniaceae*
Dichtheid: *0,09 g/cm^3*
Productiegebieden: *Zuid- en Midden-Amerika, de Cariben, Zuid-Afrika, Australië*
Het fraaie hout van de jacaranda verspreidt een aangename geur en wordt vaak gebruikt als fineer. Dit hout, dat erg geliefd is bij meubelmakers, wordt vaak gebruikt om muziekinstrumenten te vervaardigen.

Diospyros celebica – **Makassar Ebony – Ébène de Macassar – Makassar-Ebenholz – Makassar Ebbenhout**

Family: *Ebaneceae*
Density: *1.10-1.20 g/cm^3*
Zones of Production: *Indonesia*
Boles are 26 to 33 m (85 to 108 ft) tall and 30 to 60 cm (12 to 24 in) in diameter. An exceptionally beautiful species, ebony has been much appreciated by woodworkers for the past two centuries and it has now become a very scarce and expensive timber. Rarely available amongst the market, Makassar ebony nowadays belongs to the highest priced species on the world while its region of growth is very restricted.

Famille : *Ebénacées*
Densité : *1,10-1,20 g/cm^3*
Zones de production : *Indonésie*
Des troncs de 8 à 10 m de hauteur, pour 30 à 60 cm de diamètre. Essence d'une beauté exceptionnelle, l'ébène a été très apprécié par les fabricants de meubles des deux derniers siècles. Il est devenu un bois rare et cher. Rarement disponible sur le marché, l'ébène de Macassar appartient aujourd'hui aux espèces les plus recherchées au monde, alors que sa région de production est très limitée.

Familie: *Ebaneceae*
Dichte: *1,10-1,20 g/cm^3*
Vorkommen: *Indonesien*
Der zwischen 8 und 10 Meter hohe Baumstamm ist 30 bis 60 Zentimeter dick. Diese außergewöhnlich ästhetische Holzart wurde in den letzten zwei Jahrhunderten intensiv genutzt und zählt mittlerweile zu den seltenen und teuren Hölzern. Makassar-Ebenholz ist heutzutage auf dem Markt kaum erhältlich und zählt weltweit zu den teuersten Holzarten, sein Vorkommen ist auf wenige Gegenden beschränkt.

Familie: *Ebaneceae*
Dichtheid: *1,10-1,20 g/cm^3*
Productiegebieden: *Indonesië*
De stam is 8 tot 10 meter lang en 30 tot 60 centimeter dik. Ebben, een uitzonderlijk mooie houtsoort, is al twee eeuwen erg geliefd bij houtwerkers en inmiddels zeer zeldzaam en duur. Ebbenhout is met zijn zeer kleine verspreidingsgebied moeilijk verkrijgbaar en een van de duurste houtsoorten ter wereld.

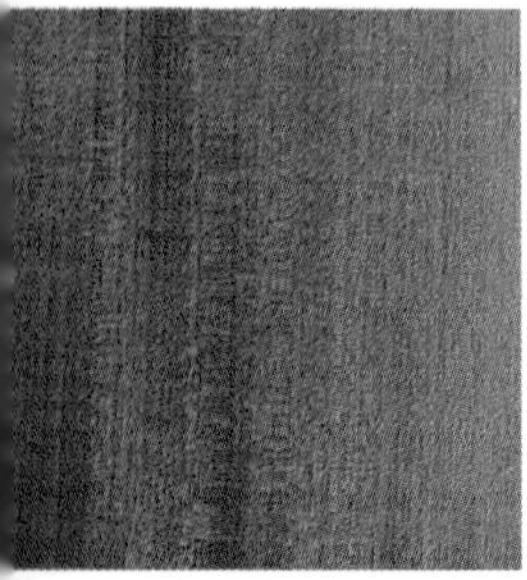

Mansonia altissima – **Mansonia – Bété – Mansonia – Mansonia**

Family: *Sterculiaceae*
Density: *0.66 g/cm^3*
Zones of Production: *Cameroon, Ivory Coast, Ghana, Nigeria*
Boles are up to 18 m (59 ft) in height and 90 cm (35 in) in diameter. The heartwood is yellow brown or dark gray brown. Texture is fine to medium and grain is generally straight. It works easily with hand or machine tools and has good steam-bending properties. As an alternate for walnut, the wood is often used in high quality cabinet and furniture work, joinery, turnery, and veneers.

Famille : *Sterculiacées*
Densité : *0,66 g/cm^3*
Zones de production : *Cameroun, Côte-d'Ivoire, Ghana et Nigeria*
Des troncs atteignant jusqu'à 18 m de hauteur et 90 cm de diamètre. Le cœur est brun jaune ou brun gris foncé. Le grain va de moyen à fin, pour un fil généralement droit. Le bété se travaille aisément, manuellement comme à la machine-outil, et il offre de bonnes possibilités de cintrage à la vapeur. Utilisé parfois à la place du noyer, il est employé en ébénisterie haut de gamme et en menuiserie, pour les pièces tournées et pour les placages.

Familie: *Sterculiaceae*
Dichte: *0,66 g/cm^3*
Vorkommen: *Kamerun, Elfenbeinküste, Ghana, Nigeria*
Der bis zu 18 m hohe Baumstamm erreicht Durchmesser bis 90 cm. Die Färbung des Kernholzes ist bräunlich-gelb oder von einem dunklem Graubraun. Es hat feine bis mittelgrobe Textur und ist für gewöhnlich geradfaserig. Es lässt sich gut von Hand und maschinell bearbeiten und besitzt gute Dampfbiegeeigenschaften. Als Alternative zum Walnussholz wird es häufig für hochwertigen Möbelbau, in der Zimmerei, für Drechselarbeiten und als Furnier verwendet.

Familie: *Sterculiaceae*
Dichtheid: *0,66 g/cm^3*
Productiegebieden: *Kameroen, Ivoorkust, Ghana, Nigeria*
De stam is tot 18 meter lang en 90 centimeter dik. Het kernhout is geelbruin of donkergrijsbruin. De nerf is fijn tot matig grof en de draad overwegend recht. Het hout is goed te bewerken met de hand of elektrisch en is geschikt om te buigen met stoom. Als alternatief voor notenhout wordt het vaak gebruikt om kasten en meubels van hoge kwaliteit te maken en voor schrijnwerk, draaiwerk en fineer.

Jacarandá – Palissandro del Brasile – Jacarandá – Jakaranda

Familia: *Bignoniáceas*
Densidad: *0,09 g/cm³*
Zonas de producción: *Sudamérica y Centroamérica, el Caribe, Sudáfrica, Australia*
La atractiva madera del jacarandá exuda un agradable aroma y se emplea habitualmente en la realización de contrachapados. Esta madera, muy apreciada por los fabricantes de muebles, es una de las más usadas en la manufactura de instrumentos musicales.

Famiglia: *Bignoniacee*
Densità: *0.09 g/cm³*
Zone di produzione: *America meridionale e centrale, Caraibi, Sudafrica, Australia*
Il bel legno di Jacaranda emana un gradevole profumo e si usa di solito nella realizzazione di compensato. Questo legno, molto apprezzato dai produttori di mobili, è uno dei più impiegati nella manifattura di strumenti musicali.

Família: *Bignoniaceae*
Densidade: *0,09 g/cm³*
Zonas de Produção: *América do Sul e Central, Caraíbas, África do Sul, Austrália*
A atraente madeira do jacarandá exala um aroma agradável e é frequentemente utilizada para folheado. Esta madeira, muito apreciada pelos fabricantes de mobiliário, é muitas vezes utilizada para fabricar instrumentos musicais.

Familj: *Bignoniaceae*
Densitet: *0,09 g/cm³*
Produktionsområden: *Syd- och Mellanamerika, Karibien, Sydafrika, Australien*
Det attraktiva jakarandaträet utsöndrar en angenäm doft och används ofta till fanering. Detta trä, som är mycket uppskattat av möbeltillverkare, används ofta till att tillverka musikinstrument.

Ébano de Macassar – Ebano di Macassar – Ébano de Makassar – Macassarebenholts

Familia: *Ebenáceas*
Densidad: *1,10-1,20 g/cm³*
Zonas de producción: *Indonesia*
El tronco puede alcanzar una altura de hasta 10 m y un diámetro de 30 a 60 cm. El ébano, una especie excepcionalmente bella, fue muy apreciado por los carpinteros durante los siglos pasados; hoy en día, por desgracia, es muy escaso y, por consiguiente, caro. Rara vez disponible en el mercado, el ébano de Macassar es una de las especies más preciadas del mundo en la actualidad, quizás porque su área de crecimiento es muy limitada.

Famiglia: *Ebenacee*
Densità: *1,10-1,20 g/cm³*
Zone di produzione: *Indonesia*
Il tronco può raggiungere un'altezza di 10 metri e un diametro di 30 a 60 centimetri. L'ebano, un legno eccezionalmente bello, è stato molto apprezzato dai falegnami nei secoli scorsi; oggi, purtroppo, la sua presenza è scarsa, quindi è anche molto caro. Difficilmente disponibile sul mercato, l'ebano di Macassar è una delle specie più pregiate del mondo, forse anche perché l'area in cui cresce è notevolmente ridotta.

Família: *Ebaneceae*
Densidade: *1,10-1,20 g/cm³*
Zonas de Produção: *Indonésia*
Os troncos medem 8 a 10 metros de altura e 30 a 60 centímetros de diâmetro. Uma espécie excepcionalmente bela, o ébano tem sido muito apreciado pelos artesãos de madeira nos últimos dois séculos e é hoje uma madeira muto escassa e dispendiosa. Raramente disponível no mercado, o ébano de Makassar é uma das espécies mais caras do mundo já que a região em que cresce é muito restrita.

Familj: *Ebaneceae*
Densitet: *1,10-1,20 g/cm³*
Produktionsområden: *Indonesien*
Stammarna är 8-10 meter höga och 30-60 centimeter i diameter. En exceptionellt vacker art, ebenholts har varit mycket uppskattat av träförädlare de senaste två seklerna och har nu blivit ett mycket sällsynt och dyrt virke. Det är sällan tillgängligt på marknaden. Macassar ebenholts tillhör idag de dyraste arterna i världen eftersom dess odlingsområde är mycket begränsat.

Mansonia – Mansonia – Mansonia – Mansonia

Familia: *Esterculiáceas*
Densidad: *0,66 g/cm³*
Zonas de producción: *Camerún, Costa de Marfil, Ghana, Nigeria*
El tronco puede alcanzar una altura de hasta 18 m y un diámetro máximo de 90 cm. El duramen es de color marrón amarillento o grisáceo oscuro con una textura entre fina y media y un grano generalmente recto. Es fácil de trabajar tanto con herramientas manuales como con máquinas-herramienta y posee óptimas propiedades para el curvado por vapor. Como alternativa al nogal, la mansonia se utiliza con frecuencia en la realización de armarios y de muebles de gama alta, así como en obras de carpintería, de tornería y para enchapados.

Famiglia: *Esterculiáceas*
Densità: *0,66 g/cm³*
Zone di produzione: *Camerun, Costa d'Avorio, Ghana, Nigeria*
Il tronco può raggiungere un'altezza di 18 metri e un diametro massimo di 90 centimetri. Il durame è di color marrone giallognolo o grigiastro scuro con una texture da fine a media e venature generalmente dritte. È facile da lavorare tanto con strumenti manuali quanto con macchine-utensili e possiede un'ottima propensione alla curvatura a vapore. Come alternativa al noce, la mansonia è frequentemente utilizzata nella realizzazione di armadi e di mobili di alto livello, nonché in opere di falegnameria, di tornitura e impiallacciatura.

Família: *Sterculiaceae*
Densidade: *0,66 g/cm³*
Zonas de Produção: *Camarões, Costa do Marfim, Gana, Nigéria*
Os troncos medem até 18 metros de altura e 90 centímetros de diâmetro. O cerne é amarelo, castanho ou cinzento-escuro acastanhado. A textura é fina a média e o grão é geralmente direito. Trabalha-se facilmente com ferramentas manuais ou eléctricas e tem boas propriedades para a moldagem a vapor. A madeira é frequentemente utilizada como alternativa à nogueira, para marcenaria e mobiliário de luxo, carpintaria, torneados e folheados.

Familj: *Sterculiaceae*
Densitet: *0,66 g/cm³*
Produktionsområden: *Kamerun, Elfenbenskusten, Ghana, Nigeria*
Stammarna är upp till 18 meter höga och 90 centimeter i diameter. Kärnvirket är gulbrunt eller mörkt gråbrunt. Strukturen är fin till medium och ådringen är i regel rak. Det arbetas lätt med hand- eller maskinverktyg och har goda böjträegenskaper. Som ett alternativ till valnöt används träet ofta i exklusivt möbelsnickeri, snickeri, svarvning och fanering.

Umbellularia californica - **Myrtle – Myrte – Myrte – Californische Mirte**

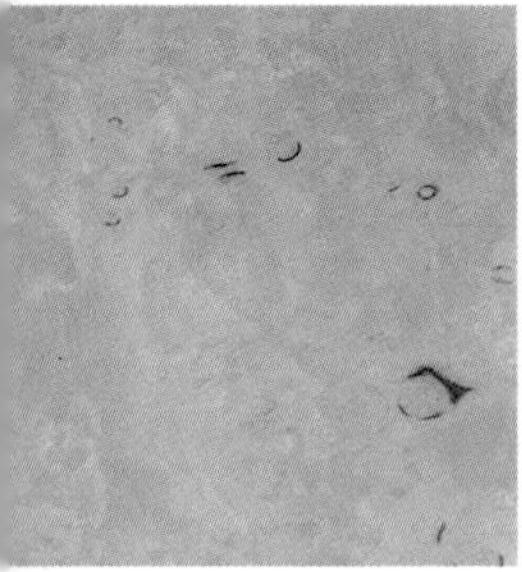

Family: *Myrtaceae*
Density: *0.62-0.86 g/cm³*
Zones of Production: *United States*
Boles are straight and clear to 9 m (30 ft) and about 50 to 80 cm (20 to 30 in) in diameter. The heartwood is rich golden brown to yellowish green. The grain is generally straight, but is often irregular or wavy. Texture is medium and firm. The wood is highly prized for its swirling burl wood and clusters. Wood is used in cabinetry, veneer, furniture, paneling, turned pieces, furniture, and bent shapes.

Famille : *Myrtacées*
Densité : *0,62-0,86 g/cm³*
Zones de production : *États-Unis*
Les troncs sont droits et nus jusqu'à 9 m de hauteur, pour un diamètre de 50 à 80 cm. Le cœur du bois est brun doré à vert jaunâtre. Le fil est généralement moyen, mais il est assez souvent irrégulier ou grossier. Le grain est moyen et stable. Le bois possède une bonne aptitude au cintrage à la vapeur. Extrêmement apprécié, le laurier de Californie (ou myrte) est employé en ébénisterie, en placage, pour le mobilier et le lambrissage, les pièces tournées.

Familie: *Myrtaceae*
Dichte: *0,62-0,86 g/cm³*
Vorkommen: *Vereinigte Staaten*
Der gerade gewachsene Baumstamm ist bis zu 9 Meter lang und zwischen 50 und 80 Zentimeter dick. Die Färbung des Kernholzes reicht von einem satten Goldbraun bis zu einem gelblichen Grün. Für gewöhnlich weist Myrtenholz eine gerade Maserung auf, sie kann aber auch unregelmäßig oder wellig sein. Seine Textur ist mittelgrob und fest. Es wird aufgrund des exklusiven Holzes seiner Wurzelmaser sehr geschätzt. Oftmals kommt es im Schrankbau zum Einsatz, für Furniere, Verkleidungen, Drehteile und für gebogene Formen.

Familie: *Myrtaceae*
Dichtheid: *0,62-0,86 g/cm³*
Productiegebieden: *Verenigde Staten*
De stam is recht en takvrij tot 9 meter en is zo'n 50 tot 80 centimeter dik. Het kernhout is diep goudbruin tot geelgroen. De draad is doorgaans recht, maar vaak ook onregelmatig of golvend. De structuur is matig grof en stevig. Het hout is erg geliefd om zijn kwasten met hun golvende tekening. Het wordt gebruikt voor kasten, fineer, meubels, paneelwerk, draaiwerk en gebogen vormen.

Thuja occidentalis - **White Cedar – Cèdre blanc – Lebensbaum – Westerse levensboom**

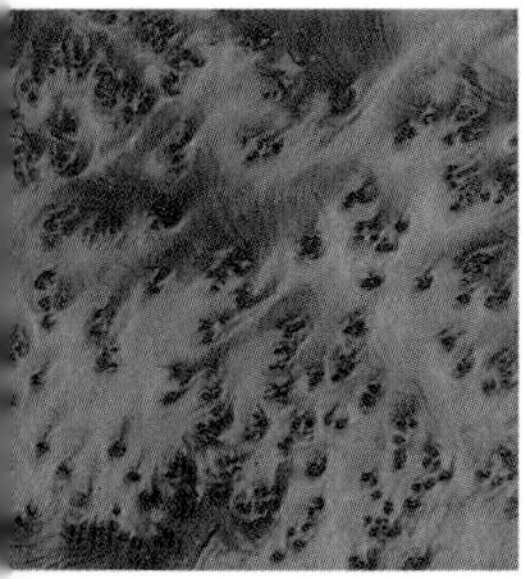

Family: *Cuppressaceae*
Density: *0.35-0.44 g/cm³*
Zones of Production: *Canada, United States*
White cedar heartwood is a light brown with an aromatic spicy odor. It has an even grain and a fine texture. The heartwood is resistant to decay and subterranean termites. White Cedar is easier to work with hand tools than with machines. The wood is used in rustic fencing and posts, lumber, poles, shingles, shipping containers, boat building, tanks, wooden wares and as pulp wood.

Famille : *Cupressacées*
Densité : *0,35-0,44 g/cm³*
Zones de production : *Canada, États-Unis*
Le cœur du bois est brun clair, avec une odeur aromatique légèrement épicée. Le fil est homogène et le grain est fin. Le bois est plus facile à travailler avec des outils manuels qu'avec des machines-outils. On l'utilise sur pied pour faire des haies rustiques. Après abattage et débitage, on en tirera des poteaux et du bois d'œuvre, des bardeaux, des caisses d'expédition et des ustensiles en bois. Il sert aussi en construction navale et pour faire de la pâte à papier.

Familie: *Cuppressaceae*
Dichte: *0,35-0,44 g/cm³*
Vorkommen: *Kanada, Vereinigte Staaten*
Das Kernholz des Lebensbaums besitzt eine helle Braunfärbung und ein würziges Aroma. Seine Maserung ist regelmäßig mit einer feinen Textur. Es ist verwitterungsfest und für unterirdische Termiten nicht anfällig. Der Lebensbaum lässt sich leichter von Hand als maschinell bearbeiten. Sein Holz wird häufig für rustikale Umzäunungen und Pfosten verwendet, als Bauholz, Pfahlholz, für Versandbehälter, Schindeln, Tanks, Holzwaren, Papier und im Bootsbau.

Dichtheid: *0,62-0,86 g/cm³*
Productiegebieden: *Canada, Verenigde Staten*
De Westerse levensboom is lichtbruin en verspreidt een gekruide, aromatische geur. De draad is gelijkmatig en de nerf fijn. Het kernhout is bestand tegen rot en ondergrondse termieten. Het hout laat zich beter handmatig dan elektrisch bewerken. Het wordt gebruikt voor hekken, palen, timmerhout, dakpannen, scheepscontainers, boten, reservoirs en houtwaren en als pulphout.

Quercus robur - **English Oak – Chêne pédonculé – Deutsche Eiche – Zomereik**

Family: *Fagaceae*
Density: *0.60-0.80 g/cm³*
Zones of Production: *Europe, Asia Minor and the north of Africa*
Boles are up to 20 m (66 ft) tall and 30 to 120 cm (12 to 47 in) in diameter. The wood is characterized by its distinct (often wide) dark and light brown growth rings. Oak has excellent steam-bending properties and produces long-lasting and durable heartwood, much in demand for interior and furniture work.

Famille : *Fagacées*
Densité : *0,60-0,80 g/cm³*
Zones de production : *Europe, Asie Mineure et nord de l'Afrique*
Les troncs peuvent atteindre 20 m de hauteur, pour un diamètre de 30 à 120 cm. Le bois est caractérisé par ses cercles de croissance, souvent larges, alternativement brun clair et brun foncé. Le chêne offre d'excellentes possibilités pour le cintrage à la vapeur et il donne un duramen solide et résistant, très demandé pour le mobilier et la décoration intérieure.

Familie: *Fagaceae*
Dichte: *0,60-0,80 g/cm³*
Vorkommen: *Europa, Kleinasien und Nordafrika.*
Der bis zu 20 Meter hohe Baumstamm besitzt einen Durchmesser zwischen 30 und 100 Zentimetern. Charakteristisch für das Holz sind seine ausgeprägten (oftmals breiten) Wachstumsringe in brauner und hellbrauner Farbe. Die Stieleiche besitzt hervorragende Dampfbiegeeigenschaften und ein langlebiges, haltbares Kernholz, das im Innenausbau und Möbelbau sehr gefragt ist.

Familie: *Fagaceae*
Dichtheid: *0,60-0,80 g/cm³*
Productiegebieden: *Europa, Klein-Azië en Noord-Afrika*
De stam is tot 20 meter lang en 30 tot 120 centimeter dik. Het hout wordt gekenmerkt door zijn opvallende (vaak brede) donker- en lichtbruine jaarringen. Eiken laat zich heel goed buigen met stoom en levert duurzaam kernhout dat erg gewild is voor interieur- en meubelwerk.

Laurel de California – Mirto – Loureiro da Califórnia – Kalifornisk lager

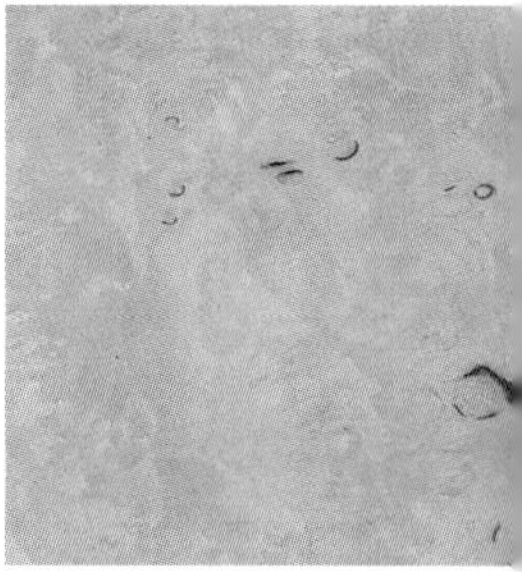

Familia: *Mirtáceas*
Densidad: *0,62-0,86 g/cm³*
Zonas de producción: *Estados Unidos*
El tronco es recto y puede alcanzar los 9 m de altura y un diámetro aproximado de 50 a 80 cm. El duramen es de color marrón dorado tirando al verde amarillento con un grano generalmente recto, aunque a veces puede presentarse irregularmente ondulado. La textura es media y sólida. La madera del laurel de california es muy apreciada por sus nudos en racimo y en espiral y se emplea en la realización de armarios, enchapados, muebles, paneles, piezas torneadas y formas curvadas.

Famiglia: *Mirtacee*
Densità: *0,62-0,86 g/cm³*
Zone di produzione: *Stati Uniti*
Il tronco è retto e può raggiungere i 9 metri d'altezza e ha un diametro di circa 50-80 centimetri. Il durame è marrone dorato tendente al verde giallognolo con venature generalmente dritte, sebbene a volte possa presentare onde irregolari. La texture è media e solida. Il legno del mirto è molto apprezzato per i suoi nodi a volute e a grappoli e si usa nella realizzazione di armadi e arredamento, nell'impiallacciatura, nella falegnameria, e per ottenere oggetti torniti e forme curve.

Família: *Myrtaceae*
Densidade: *0,62-0,86 g/cm³*
Zonas de Produção: *Estados Unidos*
Os troncos são direitos e sem ramos, têm até 9 metros e cerca de 50 a 80 centímetros de diâmetro. O cerne é de um bonito castanho dourado a um verde amarelado. O grão é usualmente direito, mas frequentemente irregular ou ondulado. A textura é média e firme. A madeira é muito apreciada pelos cachos e nós torcidos.
É utilizada em marcenaria, folheado, mobiliário, painéis, peças torneadas e formas curvas.

Familj: *Myrtaceae*
Densitet: *0,62-0,86 g/cm³*
Produktionsområden: *USA*
Stammarna är raka och fina upp till 9 meter och 50-80 centimeter i diameter. Kärnvirket är djupt gyllenbrunt till gulaktigt grönt. Ådringen är vanligen rak men är ofta oregelbunden eller vågig. Strukturen är medium och fast. Träet värderas högt för sitt slingrande knotträ och sina knippen. Trä används i möbelsnickeri, fanering, möbler, panel, svarvade föremål, möbler, och till böjda former.

Árbol de la vida – Albero della vita – Tuia – Tuja

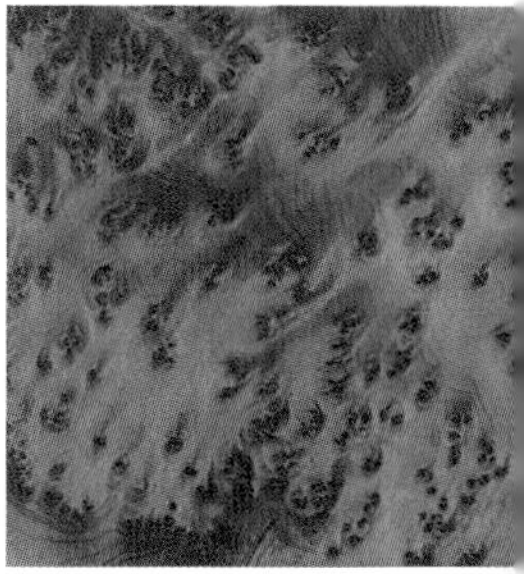

Familia: *Cupresáceas*
Densidad: *0,35-0,44 g/cm³*
Zonas de producción: *Canadá, Estados Unidos*
El duramen de la tuya occidental es marrón claro y desprende un perfume muy aromático y picante. Tiene un grano uniforme y una textura fina. El corazón es resistente al deterioro y a las termitas subterráneas. La tuya occidental es más fácil de trabajar con herramientas de mano que con máquinas-herramienta. La madera se emplea en la realización de cercas rústicas y postes, madera de construcción, tejas de madera, contenedores para el transporte, construcción de barcos, tanques, artículo varios y como pasta de madera.

Famiglia: *Cupressacee*
Densità: *0,35-0,44 g/cm³*
Zone di produzione: *Canada, Stati Uniti*
Il durame della tuia occidentale è marrone chiaro e sprigiona un profumo molto aromatico e aromatico. Presenta venature uniformi e una texture fine. Il cuore è resistente al deterioramento e alle termiti sotterranee. La tuia occidentale è più facile da lavorare con strumenti a mano che con macchine-utensili. Il legno viene utilizzato nella realizzazione di recinti rustici e pali, legname da costruzione, pertiche, scandole, container per trasporto marittimo, costruzione di barche, depositi, articoli vari e pasta di legno.

Família: *Cuppressaceae*
Densidade: *0,35-0,44 g/cm³*
Zonas de Produção: *Canadá, Estados Unidos da América*
O cerne da tuia é castanho claro e tem um aromático odor a especiarias, tem um grão uniforme e uma textura fina; é resistente ao apodrecimento e às térmitas subterrâneas. A tuia trabalha-se mais facilmente com ferramentas manuais do que com ferramentas eléctricas. A madeira é utilizada para vedações rústicas e postes, madeira de construção, estacas, telhas de madeira, contentores para navios, construção naval, tanques, produtos de madeira, e como pasta para papel.

Familj: *Cuppressaceae*
Densitet: *0,35-0,44 g/cm³*
Produktionsområden: *Kanada, USA*
Tujans kärnvirke är ljusbrunt med en aromatisk kryddig doft. Det har en jämn ådring med fin struktur. Tuja är lättare att arbeta med handverktyg än med maskiner. Träet används i rustika gärdsgårdar och stolpar, virke, pålar, takspån, fraktlårar, båtbyggnationer, reservoarer, trägods och som massaved.

Roble común – Farnia – Carvalho-roble – Ek

Familia: *Fagáceas*
Densidad: *0,60-0,80 g/cm³*
Zonas de producción: *Europa, Asia Menor, norte de África*
El tronco puede alcanzar una altura de hasta 20 m y un diámetro de 30 a 120 cm. El roble se caracteriza por sus definidos y amplios anillos de crecimiento de color marrón oscuro brillante. Su madera posee unas excelentes propiedades para el curvado por vapor y produce un corazón duradero, muy demando en los trabajos de carpintería interior y en la realización de muebles.

Famiglia: *Fagacee*
Densità: *0,60-0,80 g/cm³*
Zone di produzione: *Europa, Asia Minore, Africa del Nord*
Il tronco può raggiungere un'altezza di 20 metri e un diametro che va da 30 a 120 centimetri. La quercia si distingue per i suoi ben definiti e ampi anelli di crescita di colore marrone scuro e chiaro. Il suo legno possiede eccellenti proprietà per la curvatura a vapore e produce un cuore durevole, molto richiesto per lavori di falegnameria d'interni e nella realizzazione di mobili.

Família: *Fagaceae*
Densidade: *0,60-0,80 g/cm³*
Zonas de Produção: *Europa, Ásia Menor, norte de África*
Os troncos medem até 20 metros de altura e 30 a 120 centímetros de diâmetro. A madeira caracteriza-se pelos seus (frequentemente largos) nítidos anéis de crescimento, castanhos-escuros e claros. O carvalho tem excelentes propriedades para a moldagem a vapor e produz um cerne duradouro e resistente, muito procurado para interiores e mobiliário.

Familj: *Fagaceae*
Densitet: *0,60-0,80 g/cm³*
Produktionsområden: *Europa, Mindre Asien och Nordafrika*
Stammarna är upp till 20 meter höga och 30-120 centimeter i diameter. Träet karaktäriseras av dess distinkta (ofta breda) mörka och ljusa årsringar. Ek har utmärkta böjträegenskaper och bildar långvarigt och hållbart hjärtträ som är mycket eftertraktat till inredning och möbelarbeten.

Olea europaea - **Olive - Olivier - Ölbaum - Olijf**

Family: *Oleaceae*
Density: *0.75-0.90 g/cm^3*
Zones of Production: *Mediterranean Basin*
Boles are 2 to 3 m (6.5 to 10 ft) tall and their diameters range between 30 and 80 cm (12 and 30 in). This durable wood is hard, has an irregular grain and an oily touch. Mechanical properties: Gluing is difficult due to its oiliness. Drilling is required before nailing and screwing. It finishes well. Olive is used in interior carpentry (floors), decorative veneering and furniture.

Famille : *Oléacées*
Densité : *0,75-0,90 g/cm^3*
Zones de production : *bassin méditerranéen*
Des troncs de 2 à 3 m de hauteur, pour un diamètre allant de 30 à 80 cm. Ce bois résistant est dur, avec un fil irrégulier ; il est légèrement huileux au toucher. Propriétés mécaniques : ce bois est difficile à coller, en raison même de cette surface huileuse. Il faut le percer avant de le clouer ou de le visser. Il est susceptible de recevoir de belles finitions. L'olivier est utilisé en aménagement intérieur (pour les sols), en placage décoratif et pour le mobilier en général.

Familie: *Oleaceae*
Dichte: *0,75-0,90 g/cm^3*
Vorkommen: *Mittelmeerraum*
Der Durchmesser des 2-3 m langen Baumstamms liegt zwischen 30 und 80 cm. Dieses haltbare und harte Holz weist einen unregelmäßigen Faserverlauf auf, seine Oberfläche fühlt sich ölig an. Mechanische Eigenschaften: Das Verleimen gestaltet sich aufgrund seiner öligen Beschaffenheit schwierig. Es muss zum Nageln und Schrauben vorgebohrt werden. Seine Oberfläche lässt sich gut behandeln. Das Holz des Ölbaums wird im Innenausbau (Böden), für dekorative Furniere und für Möbel verwendet.

Familie: *Oleaceae*
Dichtheid: *0,75-0,90 g/cm^3*
Productiegebieden: *Middellandse Zeegebied*
De stam is 2 tot 3 meter lang en varieert in dikte van 30 tot 80 centimeter. Dit duurzame hout is hard, onregelmatig van draad en voelt olieachtig aan. Mechanische eigenschappen: lijmen is lastig vanwege het vettige oppervlak. Om spijkers en schroeven aan te brengen moet men eerst boren. Het hout laat zich mooi afwerken. Olijfhout wordt gebruikt voor vloeren, decoratief fineer en meubels.

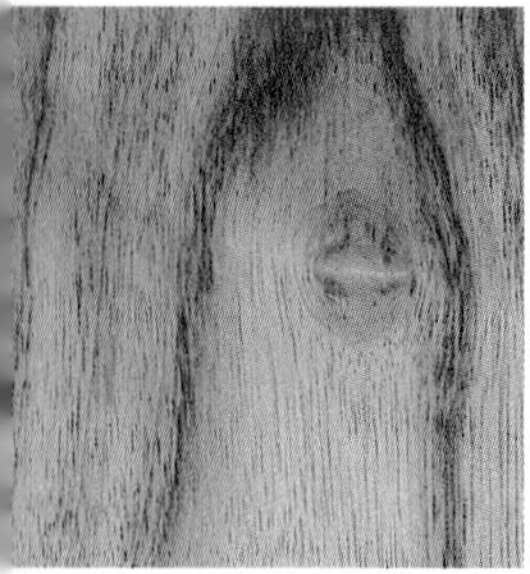

Guibourtia ehie - **Ovangkol - Ovangkol - Ovangkol - Ovangkol**

Family: *Fabaceae*
Density: *0.83 g/cm^3*
Zones of Production: *Gabon, Ghana, Ivory Coast, Nigeria*
The boles are often clear to about 20 m (70 ft) and 60 to 90 cm (23 to 35 in) in diameter. The heartwood is yellow brown to dark brown, with gray to almost black stripes. Texture is moderately coarse. Grain is straight to interlocked, and the wood exhibits an attractive figure. The timber works easily with hand tools. It is used in cabinetry, veneer, flooring, fine furniture, joinery, paneling, and turned pieces.

Famille : *Fabacées*
Densité : *0,83 g/cm^3*
Zones de production : *Gabon, Ghana, Côte-d'Ivoire et Nigeria*
Les troncs sont souvent nus jusqu'à environ 20 m du sol, avec un diamètre allant de 60 à 90¶cm. Le duramen est brun jaune à brun foncé, avec des stries grises à presque noires. Le grain est assez grossier. Le fil est droit, mais donne parfois au sciage des figures intéressantes. L'ovangkol se travaille aisément avec des outils manuels. On l'utilise en ébénisterie, pour le placage, le revêtement des sols ; en menuiserie, pour le lambrissage et les pièces tournées.

Familie: *Fabaceae*
Dichte: *0,83 g/cm^3*
Vorkommen: *Gabun, Ghana, Elfenbeinküste, Nigeria*
Der Stamm kann bis zu 20 m lang sein, der Durchmesser beträgt 60 bis 90 Zentimeter. Die Färbung des Kernholzes ist von einem gelben bis dunklen Braun, mit grauschwarzen Streifen. Die Textur ist mittelgrob. Aus dem geraden bis wechselwüchsigen Faserverlauf ergibt sich eine ansprechende Zeichnung. Das Holz ist leicht mit Handwerkzeugen zu bearbeiten. Es wird als Furnierholz, für Böden, edle Möbel, Zimmerarbeiten, Verkleidungen und Drehteile verwendet.

Familie: *Fabaceae*
Dichtheid: *0,83 g/cm^3*
Productiegebieden: *Gabon, Ghana, Ivoorkust, Nigeria*
De stam is vaak takvrij tot ca. 20 meter en 60 tot 90 centimeter dik. Het kernhout is geelbruin tot donkerbruin, met grijze tot bijna zwarte strepen. De nerf is matig grof. Het recht- tot kruisdradige hout vertoont een fraaie tekening en is goed te bewerken met handgereedschap. Het wordt gebruikt voor kasten, fineer, vloeren, kwaliteitsmeubilair, schrijnwerk, paneelwerk en draaiwerk.

Pyrus communis - **Pear Tree - Poirier - Birnbaum - Peerboom**

Family: *rosaceae*
Density: *0.70-0.85 g/cm^3*
Zones of Production: *France, United Kingdom, Germany, United States*
Boles are 2.5 to 4 m (8 to 13 ft) tall and 30 to 70 cm (12 to 28 in) in diameter. The wood is pinkish-brown, darker and more distinct in old trees, and has a very close and uniform texture. Grain is typically straight and quarter-sawn surfaces often show a large mottled figure. The wood is commonly used for veneers, engravings, musical instruments, tool handles, and turned pieces.

Famille : *Rosacées*
Densité : *0,70-0,85 g/cm^3*
Zones de production : *France, Royaume-Uni, Allemagne et États-Unis*
Des troncs de 2,5 à 4 m de hauteur, pour un diamètre de 30 à 70 cm. Le bois de cœur est brun rosé, plus nettement foncé chez les vieux arbres. Son grain est uniforme et très serré. Le fil est typiquement droit ; les surfaces sciées sur quartier présentent souvent une grande figure moirée. Le poirier est couramment utilisé pour le placage, la gravure, la facture d'instruments, la fabrication d'outils et les pièces tournées.

Familie: *rosaceae*
Dichte: *0,70-0,85 g/cm^3*
Vorkommen: *Frankreich, Vereinigtes Königreich, Deutschland, Vereinigte Staaten*
Der 30 bis 70 Zentimeter dicke Baumstamm ist 2,5 bis 4 Meter lang. Das Holz ist rosa-braun, mit einer dunkleren, stärker ausgeprägten Färbung bei alten Bäumen und einer sehr dichten, gleichmäßigen Textur. Der Faserverlauf ist meist gerade und ergibt im Radialschnitt häufig eine gesprenkelte Zeichnung. Es ist ein gängiges Holz für Furniere, Gravierungen, Musikinstrumente, Werkzeuggriffe und Drehteile.

Familie: *Rosaceae*
Dichtheid: *0,70-0,85 g/cm^3*
Productiegebieden: *Frankrijk, Verenigd Koninkrijk, Duitsland, Verenigde Staten*
De stam is 2,5 tot 4 meter lang en 30 tot 70 centimeter dik. Het hout is rozebruin, donkerder en markanter als het ouder is, en is zeer dicht en uniform van structuur. De draad is meestal recht en kwartiers gezaagde oppervlakken vertonen vaak een grote, gevlekte tekening. Het hout wordt meestal gebruikt voor fineer, gravures, muziekinstrumenten, handvatten van gereedschap en draaiwerk.

Olivo – Olivo – Oliveira – Olivträd

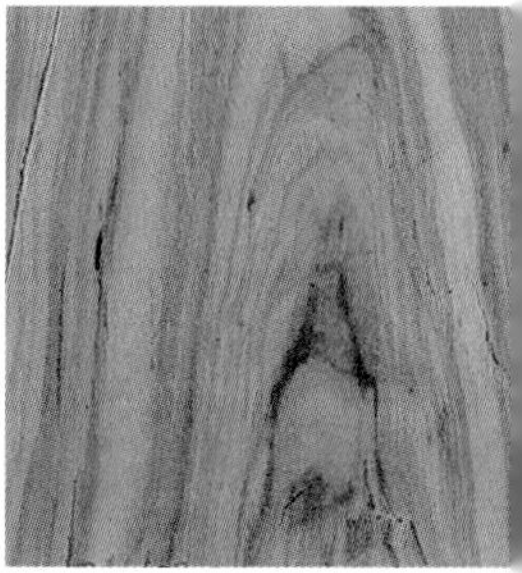

Familia: *Oleáceas*
Densidad: *0,75-0,90 g/cm³*
Zonas de producción: *Cuenca mediterránea*
El tronco puede alcanzar una altura de 2 a 3 m y un diámetro de 30 a 80 cm. Esta resistente y duradera madera tiene un grano irregular y es aceitosa al tacto. Por lo que se refiere a sus propiedades mecánicas, cabe decir que el encolado es difícil a causa de su oleaginosidad y que, antes de asegurarla con clavos y atornillarla, es necesario proceder a su perforación. Presenta un óptimo acabado. El olivo se emplea en la carpintería de interior (suelos) y en la realización de enchapados decorativos y de muebles.

Famiglia: *Oleacee*
Densità: *0,75-0,90 g/cm³*
Zone di produzione: *Bacino mediterraneo*
Il tronco può raggiungere un'altezza di 2 a 3 metri e un diametro di 30 a 80 centimetri. Questo legno resistente e duraturo presenta venature irregolari ed è oleoso al tatto. Per quanto riguarda le sue proprietà meccaniche, bisogna dire che l'incollatura è difficile a causa della sua oleosità e che, prima di piantarvi un chiodo o una vite, è necessario perforarla. Una volta rifinito ha un ottimo aspetto. L'olivo si usa nella falegnameria d'interni (pavimenti) e nella realizzazione di impiallacciature decorative e di mobili.

Família: *Oleaceae*
Densidade: *0,75-0,90 g/cm³*
Zonas de Produção: *Bacia do Mediterrâneo*
Os troncos medem 2 a 3 metros de altura e os diâmetros variam entre 30 e 80 centímetros. Esta madeira resistente é dura, com um grão irregular e um toque oleoso. Propriedades mecânicas: A colagem é difícil devido à sua oleosidade. Necessita ser perfurada antes da utilização de pregos e parafusos. Tem um bom acabamento. A oliveira é utilizada em carpintaria de interiores (soalhos), folheado decorativo e mobiliário.

Familj: *Oleaceae*
Densitet: *0,75-0,90 g/cm³*
Produktionsområden: *Medelhavsområdet*
Stammarna är 2-3 meter höga och deras diameter varierar mellan 30 och 80 centimeter. Detta tåliga trä är hårt, har en oregelbunden ådring och en oljig känsla. Mekaniska egenskaper: Svårt att limma på grund av dess oljighet. Förborrning krävs innan spikning och skruvning. Låter sig väl ytbehandlas. Olivträ används till inredningssnickerier (golv), dekorationsfanering och möbler.

Ovangkol – Ovangkol – Ovangkol – Ovangkol

Familia: *Fabáceas*
Densidad: *0,83 g/cm³*
Zonas de producción: *Gabón, Ghana, Costa de Marfil, Nigeria*
A veces su tronco puede alcanzar una altura de hasta 21 m y un diámetro de 60 a 90 cm. El duramen es marrón amarillento tirando a marrón oscuro, con rayas de color gris negruzco. La textura es moderadamente gruesa, con una veta entre recta y ondulada que describe atractivo dibujo. La madera es fácil de trabajar con herramientas manuales. Se usa en la realización de armarios, chapas decorativas, suelos, muebles de gama alta, obras de carpintería, paneles y piezas torneadas.

Famiglia: *Fabacee*
Densità: *0,83 g/cm³*
Zone di produzione: *Gabon, Ghana, Costa d'Avorio, Nigeria*
A volte il suo tronco può raggiungere un'altezza di 21 metri e un diametro di 60-90 centimetri. Il durame è marrone giallognolo tendente al marrone scuro, con strisce di color grigio quasi nero. La texture è moderatamente ruvida, con venature in parte dritte e in parte ondulate, che tracciano un affascinante disegno. Il legno è facile da lavorare con strumenti manuali. Si usa nella realizzazione di armadi, impiallacciatura, pavimenti, mobili di alto livello, opere di falegnameria, pannelli da rivestimenti e oggetti torniti.

Família: *Fabaceae*
Densidade: *0,83 g/cm³*
Zonas de Produção: *Gabão, Gana, Costa do Marfim, Nigéria*
Os troncos, frequentemente sem ramos, têm cerca de 21 metros de altura e 60 a 90 centímetros de diâmetro. O cerne é castanho amarelado a castanho-escuro, com riscas cinzentas a quase pretas. A textura é moderadamente grosseira. O grão é direito a entrecruzado e a madeira exibe um padrão atractivo. Esta madeira trabalha-se facilmente com ferramentas manuais. É utilizada em marcenaria, folheado, soalhos, mobiliário de luxo, carpintaria, painéis e peças torneadas.

Familj: *Fabaceae*
Densitet: *0,83 g/cm³*
Produktionsområden: *Gabon, Ghana, Elfenbenskusten, Nigeria*
Stammarna blir ofta runt 21 meter och 60-90 centimeter i diameter. Kärnvirket är gulbrunt till mörkbrunt med grå eller nästan svarta linjer. Strukturen är relativt grov. Ådringen är rak till sammanflätad och träet uppvisar ett attraktivt mönster. Virket arbetas lätt med handverktyg. Det används till finsnickeri, fanering, golvläggning, finmöbler, snickeri, panel och svarvade föremål.

Peral común – Pero comune – Pereira – Päronträ

Familia: *Rosáceas*
Densidad: *0,70-0,85 g/cm³*
Zonas de producción: *Francia, Reino Unido, Alemania, Estados Unidos*
El tronco tiene de 2,5 a 4 m de altura y un diámetro de entre 30 y 70 cm. La madera es marrón tirando a rosa -más oscuro y definido en los ejemplares viejos- y tiene una textura muy tupida y uniforme. El hilo o grano suele ser recto y las superficies aserradas en cuartos muestran frecuentemente un gran dibujo jaspeado. Su empleo más común lo encontramos en la realización de chapas decorativas, grabados, instrumentos musicales, mangos de herramientas y piezas torneadas.

Famiglia: *Rosacee*
Densità: *0,70-0,85 g/cm³*
Zone di produzione: *Francia, Inghilterra, Germania, Stati Uniti*
Il tronco ha un'altezza che va da 2,5 a 4 metri e un diametro tra i 30 e i 70 centimetri. Il legno è marrone tendente al rosa -più scuro e definito negli esemplari vecchi- e possiede una texture molto fitta e uniforme. Le venature sono di solito dritte e le superfici tagliate a quarti mostrano spesso un grande disegno screziato. L'uso più comune che gli viene dato è la realizzazione di lamine decorative, incisioni, strumenti musicali, manici di strumenti e oggetti torniti.

Família: *rosaceae*
Densidade: *0,70-0,85 g/cm³*
Zonas de Produção: *França, Reino Unido, Alemanha, Estados Unidos*
Os troncos medem 2,5 a 4 metros de altura e 30 a 70 centímetros de diâmetro. A madeira é castanha rosada, mais escura e mais nítida nas árvores velhas, tendo uma textura muito apertada e uniforme. O grão é tipicamente direito, e as superfícies de corte radial apresentam frequentemente um grande padrão sarapintado. É geralmente utilizada para folheados, gravuras, instrumentos musicais, cabos de ferramentas e peças torneadas.

Familj: *Rosaceae*
Densitet: *0,70-0,85 g/cm³*
Produktionsområden: *Frankrike, Storbritannien, Tyskland, USA*
Stammarna är 2,5-4 meter höga och 30-70 centimeter i diameter. Träet är rosabrunt, mörkare och mer distinkt hos äldre träd, och har en mycket tät och enhetlig struktur. Ådringen är typiskt rak och kantsågade ytor visar ofta ett stort fläckmönster. Träet används ofta till fanering, ingraveringar, musikinstrument, verktygshandtag och svarvade föremål.

Tabebuia impetiginosa - **Pink Lapacho – Ébène rose – Lapacho – Lapacho**

Family: *Bignoniaceae*
Density: *0.87-1.24* g/cm^3
Zones of Production: *Trinidad and Tobago, Mexico, Bolivia, Argentina*
The Pink Lapacho may reach 30 m (100 ft) in height and 80 cm (30 in) in diameter. The bark is brownish grey, tough and hard to peel. The wood is of a pleasant yellowish color, barely knotted, very tough, and heavy. Unfortunately, it is not very useful for furniture since it is so hard to work by hand. It can be found as beams or fulfilling other structural uses where needed outdoors.

Famille : *Bignoniacées*
Densité : *0.,87-1,24* g/cm^3
Zones de production : *Trinidad-et-Tobago, Mexique, Bolivie et Argentine*
L'arbre peut atteindre 30 m de hauteur et 80 cm de diamètre. L'écorce est gris brunâtre, résistante et dure à enlever. Le bois est d'une couleur jaunâtre assez plaisante, avec peu de nœuds, solide et dur. L'ébène rose n'est malheureusement pas très employé pour le mobilier, parce qu'il est très difficile à travailler manuellement. On l'utilise sous forme de poutres, ou comme bois d'œuvre en extérieur.

Familie: *Bignoniaceae*
Dichte: *0,87-1,24* g/cm^3
Vorkommen: *Trinidad und Tobago, Mexiko, Bolivien, Argentinien*
Der Lapachobaum kann bis zu 30 m hoch werden, sein Durchmesser beträgt bis zu 80 cm. Die bräunlichgraue Rinde ist hart und schwer zu schälen. Das astarme, zähe und schwere Holz weist eine ansprechende gelbliche Färbung auf. Leider ist es für den Möbelbau relativ ungeeignet, da es sehr schwer von Hand zu bearbeiten ist. Es wird oft für Balken oder als Trägerholz im Freien genutzt.

Familie: *Bignoniaceae*
Dichtheid: *0,87-1,24* g/cm^3
Productiegebieden: *Trinidad & Tobago, Mexico, Bolivia, Argentinië*
De lapacho kan 30 meter hoog en 80 centimeter dik worden. De bast is bruingrijs, taai en moeilijk af te halen. Het hout heeft een aangenaam gelige kleur, amper kwasten en is zeer taai en zwaar. Helaas is het niet erg geschikt voor meubels, omdat het zo moeilijk met de hand te bewerken is. Het wordt wel gebruikt voor balken of andere toepassingen buitenshuis.

Pterygota macrocarpa - **Pterygota – Koto – Pterygota – Pterygota**

Family: *Sterculiaceae*
Density: *0.56-0.68* g/cm^3
Zones of Production: *Cameroon, Ivory Coast, Ghana, Nigeria, Sierra Leone*
Boles are 12 to 24 m (40 to 80 ft) tall and 60 to 120 cm (24 to 48 in) in diameter. The wood is pale yellow to a creamy white. Its texture is rather coarse. The grain is straight to interlocked and often has small knot clusters. This wood is worked fairly easily with hand or machine tools. Pterygota is commonly used in furniture components, joinery, general carpentry, boxes, crates, and plywood.

Famille : *Sterculiacées*
Densité : *0,56-0,68* g/cm^3
Zones de production : *Cameroun, Côte-d'Ivoire, Ghana, Nigeria et Sierra Leone*
Des troncs de 12 à 24 m de hauteur, pour un diamètre de 60 à 120 cm. Le bois de cœur est de couleur jaune pâle à blanc crème. Le grain est assez grossier. Le fil est droit, parfois avec contre-fil, et présente souvent de petits groupes de nœuds. Le koto est très facile à travailler, manuellement comme à la machine-outil. Ce bois est communément utilisé pour des éléments de mobilier, en menuiserie et aussi comme bois de charpente. On en fait également des boîtes, des caisses et du contreplaqué.

Familie: *Sterculiaceae*
Dichte: *0,56-0,68* g/cm^3
Vorkommen: *Kamerun, Elfenbeinküste, Ghana, Nigeria, Sierra Leone*
Der Baumstamm ist 12 bis 24 Meter hoch und 60 Zentimeter bis 1,2 Meter dick. Das Holz ist blässlich gelb bis cremig weiß und von eher grober Textur. Die Maserung ist gerade bis wechselwüchsig und weist häufig kleine Astansammlungen auf. Das Holz lässt sich sehr leicht von Hand oder maschinell bearbeiten. Es wird für Möbelbauteile, in der Zimmerei und Tischlerei, für Schachteln, Kisten und als Sperrholz genutzt.

Familie: *Sterculiaceae*
Dichtheid: *0,56-0,68* g/cm^3
Productiegebieden: *Kameroen, Ivoorkust, Ghana, Nigeria en Sierra Leone*
De stam is 12 tot 24 meter lang en 60 tot 120 centimeter dik. Het hout is bleekgeel tot roomwit. De structuur is vrij grof. Het hout is recht- tot kruisdradig en heeft vaak kleine groepjes knoesten. Dit hout laat zich vrij goed elektrisch of met handgereedschap bewerken. Pterygota wordt veel gebruikt voor meubelonderdelen, schrijnwerk, algemeen timmerwerk, dozen, kisten en multiplex.

Aspidosperma polyneuron - **Peroba – Peroba – Peroba – Peroba**

Family: *Apocynaceae*
Density: *0.70-0.85* g/cm^3
Zones of Production: *Brazil, Suriname, Argentina*
Boles grow up to 20 m (66 ft) tall and 30 to 120 cm (12 to 48 in) in diameter. The heartwood is pink to rose red, with yellow or orange and purple streaks and patches. The grain is straight to irregular, and the texture is typically fine. Peroba wood is commonly used for building construction, cabinetry, veneers, furniture components, joinery, flooring, and boat building.

Famille : *Apocynacées*
Densité : *0,70-0,85* g/cm^3
Zones de production : *Brésil, Surinam et Argentine*
Les troncs peuvent atteindre 20 m de hauteur ; le diamètre va de 30 à 120 cm. Le bois de cœur est rose à rouge rose, avec des veines et des marbrures jaunes ou orange et pourpre. Le fil est droit à irrégulier ; le grain est d'une finesse typique. Le bois de peroba est couramment utilisé comme bois d'œuvre en construction, mais aussi en ébénisterie pour des placages et des éléments de mobilier, en menuiserie, en revêtement de sol et pour la construction navale.

Familie: *Apocynaceae*
Dichte: *0,70-0,85* g/cm^3
Vorkommen: *Brasilien, Suriname, Argentinien*
Der 30 bis 120 Zentimeter dicke Baumstamm wird bis zu 20 Meter hoch. Das Kernholz weist eine rosafarbene bis rosenrote Färbung mit gelben, orangenfarbenen oder violetten Streifen und Flecken auf. Das Holz dieses Baumes zeichnet sich durch eine gerade bis wechselwüchsige Maserung und eine feine Textur aus. Verbreitet ist der Gebrauch von Peroba im Bauwesen, Möbelbau, als Furnierholz, für Zimmereiarbeiten, für Fußböden und im Bootsbau.

Familie: *Apocynaceae*
Dichtheid: *0,70-0,85* g/cm^3
Productiegebieden: *Brazilië, Suriname, Argentinië*
De stam is tot 20 meter en 30 tot 120 centimeter dik. Het kernhout is roze tot rozerood, met gele of oranje en paarse strepen en plekken. De draad is recht tot onregelmatig en de nerf is doorgaans fijn. Perobahout wordt veel gebruikt in de bouw en voor kasten, fineer, meubelonderdelen, schrijnwerk, vloeren en boten.

Lapacho rosado – Lapacho rosa – Lapacho – Lapacho

Familia: *Bignoniáceas*
Densidad: *0,87-1,24 g/cm^3*
Zonas de producción: *Trinidad y Tobago, México, Bolivia, Argentina*
El lapacho rosado puede alcanzar los 30 m de altura y un diámetro de 80 cm. La corteza es de color gris pardo, resistente y difícil de despegar. La madera, dura y resistente, tiene un bonito color amarillento y pocos nudos. Por desgracia, no se emplea mucho en la realización de muebles debido a que es difícil de trabajar a mano. Es ideal para realizar vigas y en usos exteriores.

Famiglia: *Bignoniacee*
Densità: *0,87-1,24 g/cm^3*
Zone di produzione: *Trinidad e Tobago, Messico, Bolivia, Argentina*
Il lapacho rosa può raggiungere i 30 metri d'altezza e un diametro di 80 centimetri. La corteccia è di colore grigio brunastro, resistente e difficile da spelare. Il legno, duro e resistente, presenta un bel colore giallognolo e pochi nodi. Sfortunatamente non si utilizza molto nella produzione di mobili per il fatto che è difficile da lavorare a mano. È ideale per realizzare travi e in usi esterni.

Família: *Bignoniaceae*
Densidade: *0,87-1,24 g/cm^3*
Zonas de Produção: *Trindade e Tobago, México, Bolívia, Argentina*
O lapacho pode atingir 30 metros de altura e 80 centímetros de diâmetro. A casca é cinzenta acastanhada, rija e difícil de descascar. A madeira tem uma agradável cor amarelada, com poucos nós, muito dura e pesada. Infelizmente, não é muito adequada para mobiliário visto que é muito difícil de trabalhar manualmente. Pode ser encontrada em traves ou noutras utilizações estruturais necessárias em exteriores.

Familj: *Bignoniaceae*
Densitet: *0,87-1,24 g/cm^3*
Produktionsområden: *Trinidad och Tobago, Mexico, Bolivia, Argentina*
Lapacho kan nå en höjd av 30 meter och bli 80 centimeter i diameter. Barken är brunaktigt grå, seg och svår att skala av. Träet har en behaglig gulaktig färg, knappt knotigt, mycket segt och tungt. Tyvärr är det inte så användbart till möbler eftersom det är så svårt att arbeta för hand. Det kan hittas som bjälkar eller som fyllande andra strukturella användningsområden där det behövs utomhus.

Pterygota – Kotò – Pterygota – Pterygota

Familia: *Esterculiáceas*
Densidad: *0,56-0,68 g/cm^3*
Zonas de producción: *Camerún, Costa de Marfil, Ghana, Nigeria, Sierra Leona*
El tronco alcanza una altura de 12 a 24 m y un diámetro que oscila entre los 60 cm y los 1,2 m. La madera es de color amarillo pálido tirando a blanco cremoso. Su textura es más bien gruesa y muestra un veteado entre recto y rayado con nudos en racimos. Esta madera es bastante fácil de trabajar con herramientas manuales y con máquinas-herramienta. Pterygota se emplea comúnmente en la realización de componentes para el mobiliario y obras de carpintería, de cajas y jaulas de embalaje, contrachapados y en carpintería en general.

Famiglia: *Sterculiacee*
Densità: *0,56-0,68 g/cm^3*
Zone di produzione: *Camerun, Costa d'Avorio, Ghana, Nigeria, Sierra Leone*
Il tronco raggiunge un'altezza di 12-24 metri e un diametro che oscilla tra 60 e i 120 centimetri. Il legno è di colore giallo pallido tendente al bianco cremoso. La sua texture è più che altro ruvida e mostra venature dritte, che possono anche intrecciarsi, spesso con piccoli nodi a grappoli. Questo legno è abbastanza facile da lavorare con strumenti manuali e con macchine-utensili. Il kotò è usato in genere nella realizzazione di componenti per l'arredamento e lavori di falegnameria, di scatole e casse, compensato e falegnameria.

Família: *Sterculiaceae*
Densidade: *0,56-0,68 g/cm^3*
Zonas de Produção: *Camarões, Costa do Marfim, Gana, Nigéria e Serra Leoa*
Os troncos medem 12 a 24 metros de altura e 60 a 1,2 metros de diâmetro. A madeira é amarela pálida a branca cremosa. A sua textura é bastante grosseira. O grão é direito a entrecruzado e tem frequentemente pequenos grupos de nós. Esta madeira trabalha-se muito facilmente com ferramentas manuais ou eléctricas. A pterygota é geralmente utilizada para componentes de mobiliário, marcenaria, carpintaria em geral, caixas, caixotes e contraplacado.

Familj: *Sterculiaceae*
Densitet: *0,56-0,68 g/cm^3*
Produktionsområden: *Kamerun, Elfenbenskusten, Ghana, Nigeria och Sierra Leone*
Stammarna är 12-14 meter höga och 60-120 centimeter i diameter. Träet är blekgult till krämigt vitt. Dess struktur är relativt grovt. Ådringen är rak till sammanflätad och har ofta små knotiga ansamlingar. Träet arbetas relativt enkelt med hand- eller maskinverktyg. Pterygota är vanligt förekommande i möbeldelar, snickeri, vanligt snickeriarbete, boxar, packkorgar och plywood.

Peroba – Peroba – Peroba – Peroba

Familia: *Apocináceas*
Densidad: *0,70-0,85 g/cm^3*
Zonas de producción: *Brasil, Surinam, Argentina*
El tronco puede alcanzar una altura de 20 m y un diámetro de 30 a 120 cm. El duramen es rosa tirando a rojo, con rayas y manchas amarillas o naranjas y violetas. La fibra es recta tirando a irregular y la textura es generalmente fina. La madera de peroba se emplea comúnmente en la construcción de viviendas y de barcos, en la realización de armarios, enchapados, componentes para el mobiliario, obras de carpintería y revestimientos de suelos.

Famiglia: *Apocinacee*
Densità: *0,70-0,85 g/cm^3*
Zone di produzione: *Brasile, Suriname, Argentina*
Il tronco può raggiungere un'altezza di 20 metri e un diametro da 30 a 120 centimetri. Il durame è rosa tendente al rosso, con strisce e macchie gialle o arancione e viola. La fibra è dritta, ma tende a essere irregolare e la texture è generalmente fine. Il legno di peroba si usa nella costruzione di case e di barche, nella realizzazione di armadi, impiallacciatura, componenti per l'arredamento, lavori di falegnameria e rivestimento di pavimenti.

Família: *Apocynaceae*
Densidade: *0,70-0,85 g/cm^3*
Zonas de Produção: *Brasil, Suriname, Argentina*
Os troncos crescem até aos 20 metros de altura e 30 a 120 centímetros de diâmetro. O cerne é rosa a vermelho rosado, com listras e manchas amarelas ou laranja e roxas. O grão é direito a irregular e a textura é tipicamente fina. A peroba é geralmente utilizada para construção de edifícios, marcenaria, folheados, componentes de mobiliário, carpintaria, soalhos e construção naval.

Familj: *Apocynaceae*
Densitet: *0,70-0,85 g/cm^3*
Produktionsområden: *Brasilien, Surinam, Argentina*
Stammarna är upp till 20 meter höga och 30-120 centimeter i diameter. Kärnvirket är rosa till rosenrött med gula eller orange och lila strimmor och fläckar. Ådringen är rak till oregelbunden och strukturen är vanligen fin. Perobaträ är vanligt använt till byggnadskonstruktion, finsnickeri, fanering, möbelkomponenter, snickeri, golvläggning och båtbyggnation.

Entandrophragma cylindricum – **Sapele – Sapele – Sapeli – Sapeli**

Family: *Meliaceae*
Density: *0.60-0.75* g/cm^3
Zones of Production: *Ivory Coast, Nigeria, Cameroon, Congo*
Boles are 15 to 30 m (50 to 100 ft) tall and 60 to 140 cm (24 to 55 in) in diameter. The heartwood is red to dark reddish-brown. On quartered surfaces the wood shows a well defined ribbon striped figure. The grain is interlocked or wavy and the texture is fine. It works easily with both hand and power tools. This wood is commonly used in furniture, cabinetry, veneer, boat building, musical instruments, flooring and plywood.

Famille : *Méliacées*
Densité : *0,60-0,75* g/cm^3
Zones de production : *Côte-d'Ivoire, Nigeria, Cameroun et Congo*
Des troncs de 15 à 30 m de hauteur, pour un diamètre de 60 à 140 cm. Le bois de cœur est rouge à brun rougeâtre foncé. Les surfaces sciées sur quartier montrent des figures bien visibles en bandes rubanées. Le fil est à contre-fil, le grain fin. Ce bois se travaille facilement, manuellement comme à la machine-outil. Il est communément utilisé pour le mobilier et en ébénisterie, dans la construction navale et dans la facture des instruments de musique, en revêtement de sol et en contreplaqué.

Familie: *Meliaceae*
Dichte: *0,60-0,75* g/cm^3
Vorkommen: *Elfenbeinküste, Nigeria, Kamerun, Kongo*
Der 60 bis 140 Zentimeter dicke Baumstamm erreicht eine Höhe zwischen 15 und 30 Metern. Das Kernholz weist eine rötliche Färbung auf, die auch in ein dunkles Rotbraun übergehen kann. Im Radialschnitt weist das Holz eine gut definierte, gestreifte Zeichnung auf. Die Maserung ist wechselwüchsig oder wellig, mit einer feinen Textur. Es lässt sich gut von Hand und maschinell bearbeiten. Es wird für den Möbelbau, als Furnier, im Bootsbau, für Musikinstrumente, für Fußböden und als Sperrholz genutzt.

Familie: *Meliaceae*
Dichtheid: *0,60-0,75* g/cm^3
Productiegebieden: *Ivoorkust, Nigeria, Kameroen, Congo*
De stam is 15 tot 30 meter lang en 60 tot 140 centimeter dik. Het kernhout is rood tot donker roodbruin. Op kwartiers gezaagde oppervlakken verloopt de tekening in duidelijke smalle banen. Het hout heeft een golvende of kruisdraad en een fijne nerf. Het is zowel met de hand als elektrisch goed te bewerken. Dit hout wordt veel gebruikt voor meubels, kasten, fineer, boten, muziekinstrumenten, vloeren en mutliplex.

Diplotropis purpurea – **Sucupira – Cœurs dehors – Sucupira – Sucupira**

Family: *Papilionaceae*
Density: *0.80-1.10* g/cm^3
Zones of Production: *Guyana, Suriname, Venezuela, Brazil*
Boles are 8 to 15 m (25 to 50 ft) tall and 35 to 70 cm (14 to 28 in) in diameter. Freshly cut heartwood is generally chocolate brown turning to a lighter brown when dry. The texture is coarse and the grain is usually straight to slightly interlocked. The wood is moderately difficult to work.Sucupira wood is used in heavy construction work, boat building, flooring, furniture components, and turned pieces.

Famille : *Papilionacées*
Densité : *0,80-1,10* g/cm^3
Zones de production : *Guyane, Surinam, Venezuela et Brésil*
Des troncs de 8 à 15 m de hauteur, pour un diamètre de 35 à 70 cm. Fraîchement coupé, le bois de cœur est généralement brun chocolat, tournant au brun plus clair avec le séchage. Le grain est grossier, le fil droit ou avec léger contre-fil. Ce bois est moyennement difficile à travailler. On utilise le cœur-dehors pour les gros travaux de construction, la construction navale, le revêtement de sol, les éléments de mobilier et les pièces tournées.

Familie: *papilionaceae*
Dichte: *0,80-1,10* g/cm^3
Vorkommen: *Guyana, Suriname, Venezuela, Brasilien*
Der 35 bis 70 Zentimeter dicke Baumstamm erreicht eine Länge zwischen 8 und 15 Metern.Die schokoladenbraune Färbung des frisch geschnittenen Kernholzes hellt auf, wenn das Holz trocknet. Seine Textur ist grob, es ist geradfaserig bis leicht wechselwüchsig.Die Bearbeitung des Holzes gestaltet sich mittelmäßig schwer. Es wird für schwergewichtige Konstruktionen, im Bootsbau, für Böden, Möbel und Drehteile genutzt.

Familie: *Papilionaceae*
Dichtheid: *0,80-1,10* g/cm^3
Productiegebieden: *Guyana, Suriname, Venezuela, Brazilië*
De stam is 8 tot 15 meter lang en 35 tot 70 centimeter dik. Net gezaagd kernhout is doorgaans chocoladebruin en kleurt lichter bruin als het droog is. Het hout is grof van nerf en meestal recht- tot licht kruisdradig. Het hout is vrij lastig te bewerken. Sucupirahout wordt gebruikt voor zwaar constructiewerk, boten, vloeren, meubelonderdelen en draaiwerk.

Abies alba – **Silver Fir – Sapin gracieux – Weißtanne – Gewone zilverspar**

Family: *Pinaceae*
Density: *0.45-0.60* g/cm^3
Zones of Production: *France, Spain, Italy, Serbia*
This large evergreen coniferous tree grows to 30 to 45 m (100-150 ft) and has a trunk diameter of up to 1.2 m (4 ft). The wood is soft and not very strong; it is used for paper making, packing crates and other cheap construction work.

Famille : *Pinacées*
Densité : *0,45-0,60* g/cm^3
Zones de production : *France, Espagne, Italie et Serbie*
Ce grand conifère à feuilles persistantes peut atteindre 30 à 45 m de hauteur, avec un diamètre allant jusqu'à 120 cm. Son bois est tendre et peu solide : on l'utilise pour la pâte à papier, les cageots d'emballage et autres ustensiles peu coûteux.

Familie: *Pinaceae*
Dichte: *0,45-0,60* g/cm^3
Vorkommen: *Frankreich, Spanien, Italien, Serbien*
Dieser große, immergrüne, Zapfen tragende Baum wird 30 bis 45 Meter hoch und erreicht einen Durchmesser bis zu 1,2 Metern. Das Holz ist weich und nicht besonders fest, es wird für die Papierherstellung, für Verpackungskisten und andere preiswerte Bauarbeiten verwendet.

Familie: *Pinaceae*
Dichtheid: *0,45-0,60* g/cm^3
Productiegebieden: *Frankrijk, Spanje, Italië, Servië*
Deze grote groenblijvende naaldboom wordt 30-45 meter hoog en tot 1,2 meter dik. Het hout is zacht en niet erg sterk. Het wordt gebruikt om papier en kratten te maken en voor ander goedkoop constructiewerk.

Sapeli – Sapeli – Sapelli – Sapelli

Familia: *Meliáceas*
Densidad: *0,60-0,75 g/cm³*
Zonas de producción: *Costa de Marfil, Nigeria, Camerún, Congo*
El tronco tiene de 15 a 30 m y un diámetro de 60 a 140 cm. El duramen posee un color rojo tirando a marrón rojizo oscuro. En las superficies aserradas en cuartos, la madera muestra un veteado rayado muy definido. La fibra es alternada tirando a ondulada y la textura, fina. Se trabaja fácilmente tanto con herramientas manuales como con máquinas-herramienta. Esta madera se emplea comúnmente en la realización de muebles, armarios, enchapados, contrachapados e instrumentos musicales, así como en la construcción de barcos.

Famiglia: *Meliacee*
Densità: *0,60-0,75 g/cm³*
Zone di produzione: *Costa d'Avorio, Nigeria, Camerun, Congo*
Il tronco va dai 15 ai 30 metri e ha un diametro che varia tra 60 e 140 centimetri. Il durame possiede un colore rosso tendente al marrone rossastro scuro. Sulle superfici tagliate a quarti, il legno mostra venature striate ben definite. La fibra è alternata con tendenza a ondularsi e la texture fine. Si può lavorare con facilità tanto con strumenti manuali quanto con macchine-utensili. Questo legno è comunemente utilizzato nella realizzazione di mobili, armadi, impiallacciatura, compensato e strumenti musicali, nonché nella costruzione di barche.

Família: *Meliaceae*
Densidade: *0,60-0,75 g/cm³*
Zonas de Produção: *Costa do Marfim, Nigéria, Camarões, Congo*
Os troncos medem 15 a 30 metros de altura e 60 a 140 centímetros de diâmetro. O cerne é vermelho a castanho avermelhado escuro. Nas superfícies de corte radial exibe um padrão de fita riscada bem definido. O grão é entrecruzado ou ondulado e a textura é fina. Trabalha-se facilmente quer com ferramentas manuais quer com ferramentas eléctricas. Esta madeira é geralmente utilizada para mobiliário, marcenaria, folheado, construção naval, instrumentos musicais, soalhos e contraplacado.

Familj: *Meliaceae*
Densitet: *0,60-0,75 g/cm³*
Produktionsområden: *Elfenbenskusten, Nigeria, Kamerun, Kongo*
Stammarna är 15-30 meter höga och 60-140 centimeter i diameter. Kärnvirket är rött till mörkt rödbrunt. På kantsågade ytor uppvisar träet ett väldefinierat rosettrandigt mönster. Ådringen är sammanflätad eller vågig och strukturen är fin. Det arbetas lätt med både hand- och kraftverktyg. Detta trä används vanligen till möbler, finsnickeri, fanering, båtbyggnation, musikinstrument, golvläggning och plywood.

Sucupira – Sucupira – Sucupira – Sucupira

Familia: *Papilionáceas*
Densidad: *0,80-1,10 g/cm³*
Zonas de producción: *Guayana, Surinam, Venezuela, Brasil*
El tronco tiene de 8 a 15 m de altura y un diámetro que oscila entre los 35 y los 70 cm. Recién cortado, el duramen es de color marrón chocolate, pero, a medida que se seca, va aclarándose. La textura es gruesa y la veta recta tirando a alternada. La madera de sucupira plantea dificultades durante el mecanizado debido a su dureza. Suele emplearse en trabajos de construcción pesados, en construcción naval, tornería y carpintería interior (suelos), así como en la realización de componentes para muebles y piezas torneadas.

Famiglia: *Papilionacee*
Densità: *0,80-1,10 g/cm³*
Zone di produzione: *Guayana, Suriname, Venezuela, Brasile*
Il tronco ha un'altezza compresa tra 8 e 15 metri e un diametro che oscilla tra 35 e 70 centimetri. Quando è stato tagliato da poco, il durame è di colore marrone cioccolato, ma, mano a mano che si asciuga, si schiarisce. La texture è ruvida e la venature dritte tendente all'alternanza. Il legno di sucupira offre certa resistenza a essere lavorato. Si è soliti utilizzarlo in lavori di costruzione pesanti, nella costruzione navale, nella tornitura e nella falegnameria d'interni (pavimenti), nonché nella realizzazione di componenti per mobili e oggetti torniti.

Família: *papilionaceae*
Densidade: *0,80-1,10 g/cm³*
Zonas de Produção: *Guiana, Suriname, Venezuela, Brasil*
Os troncos medem 8 a 15 metros de altura e 35 a 70 centímetros de diâmetro. O cerne acabado de cortar é geralmente castanho chocolate, tornando-se castanho mais claro quando seco. A textura é grosseira e o grão é geralmente direito a ligeiramente entrecruzado. A madeira é moderadamente difícil de trabalhar. A madeira de sucupira é utilizada nos trabalhos pesados de construção, construção naval, soalhos, componentes de mobiliário e peças torneadas.

Familj: *Papilionaceae*
Densitet: *0,80-1,10 g/cm³*
Produktionsområden: *Guyana, Surinam, Venezuela, Brasilien*
Stammarna är 8-15 meter höga och 35-70 centimeter i diameter. Nyhugget kärnvirke är vanligen chokladbrunt och blir ljusare brunt när det torkar. Strukturen är grov och ådringen är vanligtvis rak till lätt sammanflätad. Träet är ganska svårarbetat. Sucupiraträ används i tungt konstruktionsarbete, båtbyggnation, golvläggning, möbeldelar och till svarvade föremål.

Abeto blanco – Abete bianco – Abeto-prateado – Silvergran

Familia: *Pináceas*
Densidad: *0,45-0,60 g/cm³*
Zonas de producción: *Francia, España, Italia, Serbia*
El tronco de esta gran conífera de hoja perenne tiene de 30 a 45 m de altura y un diámetro máximo de 1,2 m. La madera es blanda y no muy resistente y se emplea comúnmente en la elaboración de papel, cajas de embalaje y otros elementos funcionales y económicos para la construcción.

Famiglia: *Pinacee*
Densità: *0,45-0,60 g/cm³*
Zone di produzione: *Francia, Spagna, Italia, Serbia*
Il tronco di questa grande conifera sempreverde può avere un'altezza compresa tra 30 e 45 metri di altezza e un diametro massimo di 1,2 metri. Il legno è dolce e non molto resistente: viene impiegato comunemente nell'elaborazione della carta, di casse da imballaggio e altri elementi funzionali ed economici per l'edilizia.

Família: *Pinaceae*
Densidade: *0,45-0,60 g/cm³*
Zonas de Produção: *França, Espanha, Itália, Sérvia*
Esta grande árvore, conífera perene, cresce até aos 30-45 metros e tem um diâmetro de tronco até 1,2 metros. A madeira é macia e não muito forte; é utilizada para fabrico de papel, caixotes para embalagem e outros trabalhos vulgares de construção.

Familj: *Pinaceae*
Densitet: *0,45-0,60 g/cm³*
Produktionsområden: *Frankrike, Spanien, Italien, Serbien*
Detta stora städsegröna barrträd växer till en höjd av 30-45 meter och har en stamdiameter på upp till 1,2 meter. Träet är mjukt och inte särskilt starkt; det används till papperstillverkning, packlårar och annat billigt konstruktionsarbete.

Corymbia maculata – **Spotted Gum – Eucalyptus – Gesprenkelter Eukalyptus – Gomboom**

Family: *Myrtaceae*
Density: *0.75-0.85 g/cm^3*
Zones of Production: *Australia, Brazil, South Africa*
Boles are 30 to 45 m (100 to 150 ft) tall and 50 to 80 cm (20 to 30 in) in diameter. The wood is straight grained, coarse textured and moderately strong. This rapidly renewable lumber is both stable and beautiful. It is used for almost anything that most hardwoods are used for: exterior and interior furniture, joinery, paneling, boat building, flooring and veneer. This wood works well with machine and hand tools.

Famille : *Myrtacées*
Densité : *0,75-0,85 g/cm^3*
Zones de production : *Australie, Brésil et Afrique du Sud*
Des troncs de 30 à 45 m de hauteur, pour un diamètre de 50 à 80 cm. Le fil du bois est droit, le grain grossier : le bois est relativement solide. Rapidement renouvelable, c'est un bois d'œuvre à la fois stable et beau. Il se travaille bien, manuellement comme à la machine-outil. On l'utilise comme la plupart des autres bois durs : mobilier intérieur et extérieur, menuiserie, lambrissage, revêtement de sol et placage, mais aussi construction navale.

Familie: *Myrtaceae*
Dichte: *0,75-0,85 g/cm^3*
Vorkommen: *Australien, Brasilien, Südafrika*
Der 30 bis 45 Meter lange Baumstamm ist 50 bis 80 Zentimeter dick. Das Holz ist geradfaserig, von mittelgrober Textur und mittlerer Festigkeit. Dieses sich rasch erneuernde Nutzholz ist stabil und ästhetisch. Es kommt in nahezu allen für Hartholz typischen Bereichen zum Einsatz: für Innen- und Außenmöbel, in der Zimmerei, für Verkleidungen, im Bootsbau, für den Bodenausbau und als Furnierholz. Es lässt sich gut von Hand und maschinell bearbeiten.

Familie: *Myrtaceae*
Dichtheid: *0,75-0,85 g/cm^3*
Productiegebieden: *Australië, Brazilië, Zuid-Afrika*
De stam is 30 tot 45 meter lang en 50 tot 80 centimeter dik. Het hout is rechtdradig, grof van nerf en vrij sterk. Het hout van deze snelgroeiende boom is zowel stabiel als mooi. Het wordt gebruikt voor bijna alles waarvoor hardhoutsoorten gebruikt worden: meubels voor binnen en buiten, schrijnwerk, paneelwerk, boten, vloeren en fineer. Dit hout is goed met de hand en elektrisch te bewerken.

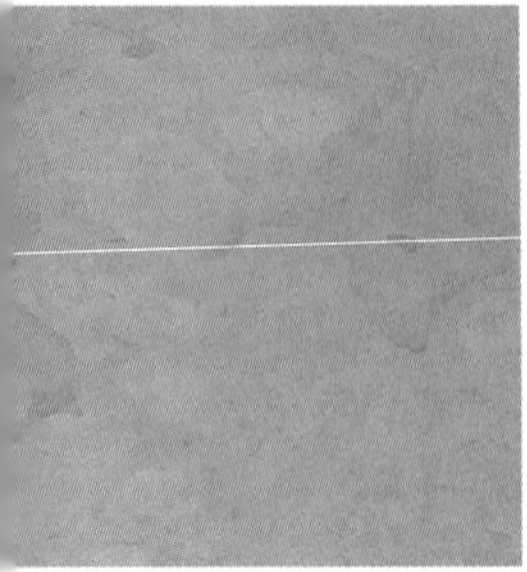

Arbutus unedo – **Strawberry tree – Arbousier – Erdbeerbaum – Aardbeiboom**

Family: *Ericaceae*
Zones of Production: *Mediterranean region, Western Europe north to Ireland*
The Strawberry Tree grows up to 10 m (33 ft) tall, with a trunk diameter of up to 80 cm (30 in). The timber of the strawberry tree is hard and dull brown with a fine pink grain. The bark has a dark reddish-brown color. It is a great fuel wood tree since it burns hot and long but it holds no value in the production of homes since it doesn't grow in straight timbers.

Famille : *Ericacées*
Zones de production : *région méditerranéenne, ouest de l'Europe et Irlande*
L'arbousier peut atteindre jusqu'à 10 m de hauteur, avec un tronc de 80 cm de diamètre. Son bois est dur et de couleur brun terne, avec un fil fin. L'écorce est de couleur brun rougeâtre. C'est un excellent bois de feu, car il tient longtemps en dégageant une grande chaleur. Il n'a par ailleurs aucune valeur, car il ne pousse pas droit.

Familie: *Ericaceae*
Vorkommen: *Mittelmeerraum, Westeuropa, Irland*
Der Erdbeerbaum erreicht eine Höhe bis zu 10 Metern und einen Durchmesser bis zu 80 Zentimetern. Sein hartes Holz weist eine dumpfe Braunfärbung mit einer fein gezeichneten rosafarbenen Maserung auf. Die Rinde hat einen dunklen, rötlich-braunen Farbton. Dieses Holz eignet sich hervorragend als Brennholz, da es intensiv und lange brennt und zudem für den Hausbau völlig wertlos ist, da es nicht gerade wächst.

Familie: *Ericaceae*
Productiegebieden: *Middellandse Zeegebied, West-Europa noordwaarts tot Ierland*
De aardbeiboom wordt tot 10 meter hoog en tot 80 centimeter dik. Het hout van de aardbeiboom is hard en dofbruin met een fijne roze draad. De bast is donker roodbruin. Het is goed brandhout, omdat het lang brandt en veel warmte afgeeft. Voor de woningbouw is de boom echter niet interessant, omdat hij geen rechte planken oplevert.

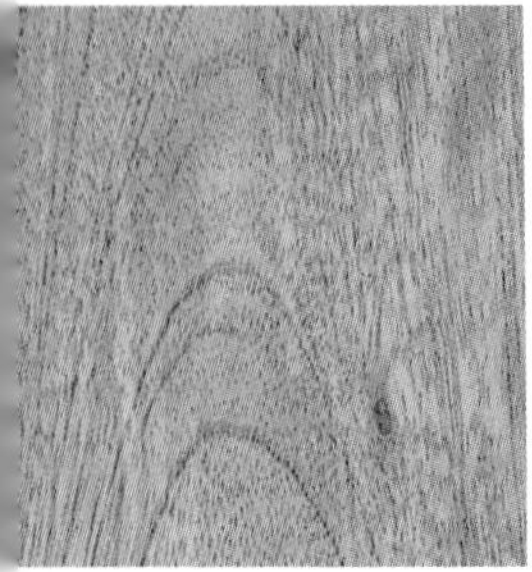

Acer saccharum – **Sugar Maple – Érable à sucre – Zuckerahorn – Suikeresdoorn**

Family: *Sapindaceae*
Density: *0.70-0.80 g/cm^3*
Zones of Production: *North America*
Boles are 4 to 10 m (13 to 33 ft) tall and 30 to 60 cm (12 to 24 in) in diameter. The trees have wavy wood grain, which can occur in much valued "birds eye maple" form. This wood is one of the hardest and densest of the maples. Bowling alleys and bowling pins are both commonly manufactured from sugar maple. It is also widely used in the manufacture of musical instruments, such as violins, guitars, and drums.

Famille : *Sapindacées*
Densité : *0,70-0,80 g/cm^3*
Zones de production : *Amérique du Nord*
Troncs de 4 à 10 m de hauteur, pour un diamètre de 30 à 60 cm. Les arbres ont un fil ondé que l'on peut retrouver dans l'érable à œil d'oiseau, espèce très recherchée. L'érable à sucre est l'un des plus durs et des plus denses parmi les érables. Les pistes et les quilles de bowling sont généralement faites avec ce bois. On l'utilise aussi beaucoup dans la facture des instruments de musique tels que violons, guitares et tambours.

Familie: *Sapindaceae*
Dichte: *0,70-0,80 g/cm^3*
Vorkommen: *Nordamerika*
Der 30–60 cm dicke Baumstamm erreicht eine Höhe von 4–10 m. Einen besonderen Marktwert besitzt die „Vogelaugenmaserung", die sich aus dem gewellten Faserverlauf des Holzes ergeben kann. Das Holz dieses Baumes zählt zu den härtesten und dichtesten unter der Ahornbäumen. Bowlingbahnen und -Pins werden normalerweise aus dem Holz des Zuckerahorns gefertigt. Sein Gebrauch für Musikinstrumente wie Geigen, Gitarren und Trommeln ist weit verbreitet.

Familie: *Sapindaceae*
Dichtheid: *0,75-0,85 g/cm^3*
Productiegebieden: *Noord-Amerika*
De stam is 4 tot 10 meter lang en 30 tot 60 centimeter dik. Het hout heeft een golvende draad, die zich kan voordoen in de zogenaamde 'bird's-eye'-vorm. Deze houtsoort behoort tot de hardste en dichtste van alle esdoorns. Bowlingbanen en kegels worden meestal van suikeresdoorn gemaakt. Het hout wordt ook veel gebruikt voor muziekinstrumenten, zoals violen, gitaren en drums.

Gomero manchado – Eucalipto – Eucalipto – Spotted Gum

Familia: *Mirtáceas*
Densidad: *0,75-0,85 g/cm^3*
Zonas de producción: *Australia, Brasil, Sudáfrica*
El tronco tiene de 30 a 45 m de altura y un diámetro de 50 a 80 cm. La madera presenta una veta recta y una textura gruesa moderadamente dura. Esta sólida y bella madera posee la gran cualidad de renovarse muy rápidamente. En cuanto al empleo, comparte prácticamente los mismos campos de aplicación que las maderas nobles o duras: muebles de exterior y de interior, obras de carpintería, paneles, construcción naval, revestimiento de suelos y enchapados. La madera de eucalipto es fácil de trabajar tanto con herramientas manuales como mecánicas.

Famiglia: *Mirtacee*
Densità: *0,75-0,85 g/cm^3*
Zone di produzione: *Australia, Brasile, Sudafrica*
Il tronco ha un'altezza di 30-45 metri e un diametro che può variare da 50 a 80 centimetri. Il legno presenta venature dritte e una texture ruvida moderatamente dura. Questo legno stabile e piacevole ha l'enorme vantaggio che si rinnova molto rapidamente. Per quanto riguarda l'uso che se ne fa, condivide quasi gli stessi campi d'applicazione dei legni nobili o duri: mobili per esterni e per interni, lavori di falegnameria, pannelli per rivestimenti, costruzione navale, pavimenti e impiallacciatura. Il legno di eucalipto è facile da lavorare con strumenti sia manuali sia meccanici.

Família: *Myrtaceae*
Densidade: *0,75-0,85 g/cm^3*
Zonas de Produção: *Austrália, Brasil, África do Sul*
Os troncos medem 30 a 45 metros de altura e 50 a 80 centímetros de diâmetro. A madeira tem um grão direito, uma textura grosseira e é moderadamente forte. Esta madeira rapidamente renovável é tanto estável como bonita. É utilizada praticamente para quase todos os fins para que são utilizadas as madeiras duras: mobiliário de exterior e interior, carpintaria, painéis, construção naval, soalhos e folheado. Trabalha-se bem com ferramentas manuais e eléctricas.

Familj: *Myrtaceae*
Densitet: *0,75-0,85 g/cm^3*
Produktionsområden: *Australien, Brasilien, Sydafrika*
Stammarna är 30-45 meter höga och 50-80 centimeter i diameter. Träet är rakådrat, har grovstruktur och är relativt starkt. Detta snabbt förnybara virke är både stabilt och vackert. Det används till nästan allt som de flesta hårda träslag används till: ute- och innemöbler, snickeri, panel, båtbyggnation, golvläggning och fanering. Detta trä arbetas enkelt med maskin- och handverktyg.

Madroño – Corbezzolom – Medronheiro – Smultronträd

Familia: *Ericáceas*
Zonas de producción: *Cuenca mediterránea, Oeste de Europa hasta Irlanda*
El madroño puede alcanzar una altura máxima de 10 m y su tronco un diámetro de 80 cm. La madera del madroño es dura y de color marrón apagado con una veta rosa fina. La corteza presenta una tonalidad marrón rojiza. Como leña es óptima ya que arde bien y prolongadamente, pero no tiene valor en la construcción de casas ya que su tronco y sus ramas crecen torcidos.

Famiglia: *Ericacee*
Zone di produzione: *Bacino mediterraneo, Europa occidentale tra Irlanda*
Il corbezzolo può raggiungere un'altezza massima di 10 metri e il suo tronco un diametro di 80 centimetri. Il legno del corbezzolo è duro e di color marrone spento con venature fini di tonalità rosa. La corteccia presenta sfumature marrone rossiccio. Come legna da ardere è ottima giacché brucia bene e lentamente, tuttavia, non ha alcun impiego nella costruzione di case poiché il suo tronco e i suoi rami crescono storti.

Família: *Ericaceae*
Zonas de Produção: *região do Mediterrâneo, Europa Ocidental até a Irlanda*
O medronheiro cresce até aos 10 metros de altura, podendo o diâmetro do tronco atingir os 80 centímetros. A madeira do medronheiro é dura, castanho-escura, com um fino grão rosa. A casca tem uma cor castanha avermelhada escura. É uma óptima madeira combustível, já que arde bem e durante muito tempo, mas não tem valor para a construção de casas pois não produz tábuas direitas.

Familj: *Ericaceae*
Produktionsområden: *Medelhavsområdet, Västeuropa norra till Irland*
Smultronträdet växer upp till 10 meters höjd med en stamdiameter på upp till 80 centimeter. Smultronträdets virke är hårt och dovt brunt med en fin rosa ådring. Barken har en mörk rödbrun färg. Det är ett mycket bra vedträ eftersom det bränner hett och länge men inte är värdefullt vid husbyggnation eftersom det inte växer rakt.

Arce azucarero – Acero zuccherino – Bordo-açucareiro – Sockerlönn

Familia: *Sapindáceas*
Densidad: *0,70-0,80 g/cm^3*
Zonas de producción: *América del Norte*
El tronco tiene de 4 a 10 m de altura y un diámetro de 30 a 60 cm. El arce presenta una veta ondulada que puede darse en muchos tipos preciados de arce de ojo de pájaro. Esta madera es una de las más duras y densas de entre todas las variedades de la familia. El arce azucarero suele emplearse en la fabricación de las pistas de las boleras y también de sus bolos. También se usa ampliamente en la realización de instrumentos musicales, como violines, guitarras y tambores.

Famiglia: *Sapindacee*
Densità: *0,70-0,80 g/cm^3*
Zone di produzione: *America settentrionale*
Il tronco ha 4-10 metri d'altezza e un diametro che va da 30 a 60 centimetri. Presenta venature ondulate che possono apparire in molti tipi pregiati di "acero a occhio d'uccello". Questo legno è uno dei più duri e densi tra tutte le varietà d'acero. L'acero zuccherino di solito viene impiegato nella produzione di campi e birilli da bowling. Si usa ampiamente però anche nella realizzazione di strumenti musicali, come violini, chitarre e tamburi.

Família: *Sapindaceae*
Densidade: *0,70-0,80 g/cm^3*
Zonas de Produção: *América do Norte*
Os troncos medem 4 a 10 metros de altura e 30 a 60 centímetros de diâmetro. As árvores têm um grão ondulado que pode aparecer sob a forma do muito apreciado "ácer olho-de-pássaro". Esta madeira é uma das mais duras e densas dos áceres. As pistas e os pinos de "bowling" são geralmente feitos de ácer-do-açúcar. É também largamente utilizado na manufactura de instrumentos musicais, tais como violinos, guitarras e tambores.

Familj: *Sapindaceae*
Densitet: *0,70-0,80 g/cm^3*
Produktionsområden: *Nordamerika*
Stammarna är 4-10 meter höga och 30-60 centimeter i diameter. Träden har vågig trääådring som kan uppstå i den högt värderade "fågelögonlönn"-formen. Detta trä är en av de hårdaste och tätaste av lönnträsorterna. Bowlingbanor och bowlingkäglor tillverkas vanligen av sockerlönn. Detta används och mycket till tillverkning av musikinstrument, såsom fioler, gitarrer och trummor.

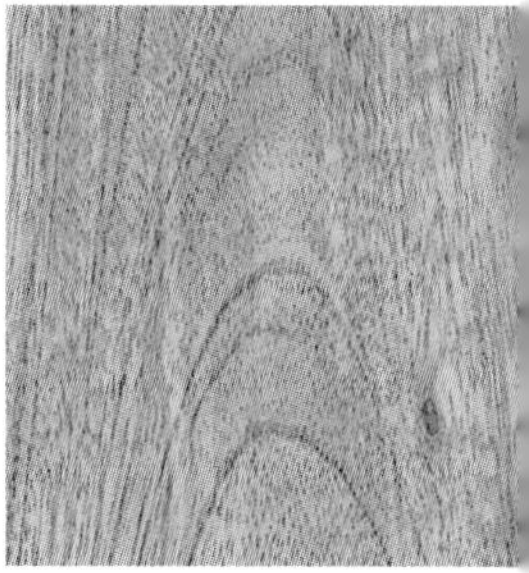

Tectona grandis - **Teak – Teck – Teak – Teak**

Family: *Lamiaceae*
Density: *0.60-0.80 g/cm^3*
Zones of Production: *Indies*
Boles are 8 to 15 m (25 to 50 ft) tall and 40 to 80 cm (15 to 30 in) in diameter. True teak of Burma is a hardwood with a golden-brown color, straight to wavy grain, and a coarse and oily texture. It also has excellent strength properties. Teak works well although it is hard on tools. Teak is best used for ship building, decking, furniture, paneling, carvings, turned shapes, joinery, veneer, and plywood.

Famille : *Lamiacées*
Densité : *0,60-0,80 g/cm^3*
Zones de production : *Asie du Sud et du Sud-Est*
Troncs de 8 à 15 m de hauteur, pour un diamètre de 40 à 80 cm. Le véritable teck de Birmanie est un bois dur de couleur brun doré, avec un fil droit ou ondé, et un grain grossier et huileux. Il a d'excellentes qualités de solidité, de résistance et de stabilité. Le bois se travaille bien, mais il est très dur pour les outils. On l'utilise pour la construction de bateaux et de plateformes, mais aussi pour la fabrication de meubles, le lambrissage, la sculpture, le tournage, le placage et la menuiserie.

Familie: *Lamiaceae*
Dichte: *0,60-0,80 g/cm^3*
Vorkommen: *Süd- und Südostasien*
Der Baumstamm ist 8-15 m lang, sein Durchmesser beträgt 40-80 cm. Beim echten Teakholz aus Burma handelt es sich um ein goldgelb-bräunliches Hartholz mit geradem bis welligem Faserverlauf und grober, öliger Textur. Es besitzt hervorragende Festigkeitseigenschaften. Das Holz lässt sich gut bearbeiten, es beansprucht die Werkzeuge jedoch sehr stark. Teakholz ist am besten für den Schiffsbau, für Bohlen, als Möbelholz, für Verkleidungen, Schnitzereien, Drehformen, Zimmerarbeiten, Furniere und Sperrholz geeignet.

Familie: *Lamiaceae*
Dichtheid: *0,60-0,80 g/cm^3*
Productiegebieden: *Zuid- en Zuidoost-Azië*
De stam is 80 tot 15 meter lang en 40 tot 80 centimeter dik. Echte teak uit Birma is een hardhout met een goudbruine kleur, een rechte tot golvende draad en een grove en vettige structuur. Het is ook erg sterk. Teak laat zich goed bewerken, hoewel het veel van gereedschap vraagt. Teak is het geschiktst voor schepen, scheepsdekken, meubels, paneelwerk, gravures, draaiwerk, schrijnwerk, fineer en multiplex.

Dalbergia decipularis - **Brazilian Tulipwood – Bois de rose – Bahia-Rosenholz – Bahia rozenhout**

Family: *Fabaceae*
Density: *0.70-0.90 g/cm^3*
Zones of Production: *Guyana, Brazil, Colombia, Venezuela*
Boles are often tortuous, 2 to 10 m (6.5 to 30 ft) in height and 15 to 25 cm (6 to 10 in) in diameter. Heartwood is cream colored dominated by red-purplish stripes. Grain is straight to wavy. It is very hard, heavy and strong, difficult to work with. Because of the small size and very high cost it is generally found today only in inlays, marquetry, turnery, and other small decorative fancy goods.

Famille : *Fabacées*
Densité : *0,70-0,90 g/cm^3*
Zones de production : *Guyane, Brésil, Colombie et Venezuela*
Les troncs – souvent tortueux – ont de 2 à 10 m de hauteur, pour un diamètre de 15 à 25 cm. Le bois de cœur est de couleur crème, avec des bandes rouge violacé marquées. Le fil varie de droit à ondé. Le bois est très dur, lourd et dense, et très difficile à travailler. En raison de la petite taille des pièces obtenues à partir des grumes et de leur prix très élevé, on ne l'emploie aujourd'hui qu'en marqueterie pour des incrustations et de petits éléments tournés, et autres babioles aussi décoratives que coûteuses.

Familie: *Fabaceae*
Dichte: *0,70-0,90 g/cm^3*
Vorkommen: *Guyana, Brasilien, Kolumbien, Venezuela*
Der oft gewundene Baumstamm ist 2-10 m lang, sein Durchmesser liegt zwischen 15 und 25 cm. Das cremefarbene Kernholz weist ausgeprägte rot-violette Streifen auf. Die Maserung ist gerade bis wellig. Die Verarbeitung dieses harten, schweren und festen Holzes gestaltet sich schwierig. Aufgrund seines geringen Durchmessers und hohen Preises wird es meist nur für Intarsien, Drechselarbeiten und andere kleine dekorative Liebhaberprodukte verwendet.

Familie: *Fabaceae*
Dichtheid: *0,70-0,90 g/cm^3*
Productiegebieden: *Guyana, Brazilië, Colombia, Venezuela*
De stam is vaak kronkelig, 2 tot 10 meter lang en 15 tot 25 centimeter dik. Het kernhout is roomwit met veel paarsrode strepen. De draad is recht tot golvend. Het hout is erg hard, zwaar en sterk en moeilijk om mee te werken. Omdat de boom maar klein en het hout erg duur is, komt men het tegenwoordig bijna alleen tegen in inlegwerk, marqueterie, draaiwerk en andere kleine decoratieve voorwerpen.

Entandrophragma utile - **Utile – Assié – Sipo – Sipo**

Family: *Meliaceae*
Density: *0.55-0.70 g/cm^3*
Zones of Production: *Ivory Coast, Ghana, Cameroon, Gabon, Congo*
Boles are 15 to 25 m (50 to 80 ft) tall and 60 to 130 cm (24 to 70 in) in diameter. Heartwood is fairly uniform red or purple brown. It has an interlocked, medium grained texture that is rather irregular. It has a faint cedar-like scent. The wood is used for furniture and cabinet work, joinery, decorative veneers, plywood, and boat construction.

Famille : *Méliacées*
Densité : *0,55-0,70 g/cm^3*
Zones de production : *Côte-d'Ivoire, Ghana, Cameroun, Gabon et Congo*
Des troncs de 15 à 25 m de hauteur, pour un diamètre de 60 à 130 cm. Le bois de cœur est très uniformément rouge ou brun pourpre. Son fil est à contre-fil, son grain plutôt irrégulier. Il dégage une faible odeur, similaire à celle du cèdre. L'assié est utilisé en ébénisterie comme en menuiserie, en placage décoratif et en contreplaqué, mais aussi dans la construction navale.

Familie: *Meliaceae*
Dichte: *0,55-0,70 g/cm^3*
Vorkommen: *Elfenbeinküste, Ghana, Kamerun, Gabun, Kongo*
Der 60 bis 130 cm dicke Baumstamm wird 15 bis 25 Meter hoch. Das Kernholz ist gleichmäßige rot oder violett-braun gefärbt. Seine Faser ist wechseldrehwüchsig, seine mittelgrobe Textur neigt zur Unregelmäßigkeit. Es strömt einen milden, zedernähnlichen Geruch aus. Das Holz wird für den Möbelbau, für Zimmerarbeiten, dekorative Furniere, Sperrholz und im Bootsbau verwendet.

Familie: *Meliaceae*
Dichtheid: *0,55-0,70 g/cm^3*
Productiegebieden: *Ivoorkust, Ghana, Kameroen, Gabon, Congo*
De stam is 15 tot 25 meter lang en 60 tot 130 centimeter dik. Het kernhout is vrij homogeen rood- of paarsbruin. Het heeft een matig grove, kruisdradige structuur die vrij onregelmatig is. Het verspreidt een lichte cederachtige geur. Het hout wordt gebruikt voor meubels en kasten, schrijnwerk, decoratief fineer, multiplex en boten.

Teca – Tek – Teca – Teak

Familia: *Lamiáceas*
Densidad: *0,60-0,80 g/cm^3*
Zonas de producción: *India, Asia Sudoriental*
El tronco tiene de 8 a 15 m y un diámetro de entre 40 y 80 cm. La verdadera teca de Burma se caracteriza por un duramen de color marrón dorado con una fibra recta tirando a ondulada y una textura oleaginosa y gruesa. Posee asimismo unas excelentes propiedades de resistencia. La madera de teca es fácil de trabajar aunque puede estropear las máquinas. Se emplea comúnmente en la construcción naval y en la realización de tablones, muebles, paneles, tallas, piezas torneadas, obras de carpintería, enchapados y contrachapados.

Famiglia: *Lamiacee*
Densità: *0,60-0,80 g/cm^3*
Zone di produzione: *India, Asia sudorientale*
Il tronco ha un'altezza che va dagli 8 ai 15 metri e un diametro compreso tra 40 e 80 centimetri. Il vero tek di Burma si distingue per un durame di color marrone dorato con una fibra dritta tendente ondularsi e una texture oleaginosa e ruvida. Possiede inoltre eccellenti qualità di resistenza. Il legno di tek è facile da lavorare sebbene possa rompere le macchine. Si usa soprattutto nella costruzione navale e nella realizzazione di ponti e pedane, mobili, pannelli da rivestimento, lavori a intaglio, oggetti torniti, lavori di falegnameria, impiallacciatura e compensato.

Família: *Lamiaceae*
Densidade: *0,60-0,80 g/cm^3*
Zonas de Produção: *Índias, Sudeste Asiático*
Os troncos medem 8 a 15 metros de altura e 40 a 80 centímetros de diâmetro. A verdadeira teca de Burma é uma madeira dura com uma cor castanha dourada, um grão direito a ondulado e uma textura grosseira e oleosa. Tem também excelentes qualidades de resistência. Trabalha-se bem, embora seja rija para as ferramentas. A teca é utilizada preferencialmente para construção naval, forros de tábuas, mobiliário, painéis, esculturas, formas curvas, carpintaria, folheado e contraplacado.

Familj: *Lamiaceae*
Densitet: *0,60-0,80 g/cm^3*
Produktionsområden: *Indien, Sydostasien*
Stammarna är 8-15 meter höga och 40-80 centimeter i diameter. Äkta teak från Burma är ett hårdträ med en gyllenbrun färg, rakt till vågigt ådrat och med en grov och oljig struktur. Det har också utmärkta styrkeegenskaper. Teak arbetas enkelt med verktyg trots att det är hårt. Teak är bäst lämpat till båtbyggnation, båtdäck, möbler, panel, sniderier, svarvade former, snickeri, fanering och plywood.

Tulipero – Bois de rose – Pau-de-fuso – Brasiliansk tulipwood

Familia: *Fabáceas*
Densidad: *0,70-0,90 g/cm^3*
Zonas de producción: *Guayana, Brasil, Colombia, Venezuela*
Con frecuencia tortuoso, el tronco mide entre 2 y 10 m de altura y tiene un diámetro que oscila entre los 15 y los 25 cm. El duramen es de color crema con rayas rojizas con una veta recta tirando a ondulada. Es una madera muy dura y resistente, difícil de trabajar. Debido a su pequeño tamaño y su elevado coste, actualmente solo se emplea en ebanistería, marquetería, tornería y en la realización de pequeños y lujosos artículos decorativos.

Famiglia: *Fabacee*
Densità: *0,70-0,90 g/cm^3*
Zone di produzione: *Guayana, Brasile, Colombia, Venezuela*
Spesso di aspetto tortuoso, il tronco misura tra 2 e 10 metri d'altezza e ha un diametro che oscilla tra i 15 e i 25 centimetri. Il durame è di color crema con striature rossastre e venature dritte tendenti a ondularsi. È un legno molto duro e resistente, difficile da lavorare. A causa delle sue piccole dimensioni e del suo prezzo elevato, si usa oggi solo nei lavori d'intarsio, di tornitura e nella realizzazione di piccoli e lussuosi articoli decorativi.

Família: *Fabaceae*
Densidade: *0,70-0,90 g/cm^3*
Zonas de Produção: *Guiana, Brasil, Colômbia, Venezuela*
Os troncos são frequentemente tortos, com 2 a 10 metros de altura e 15 a 25 centímetros de diâmetro. O cerne é creme, dominado por riscas vermelho-púrpura. O grão é direito a ondulado. É uma madeira muito dura, pesada e forte, difícil de trabalhar. Devido ao seu pequeno tamanho e alto preço, hoje em dia geralmente só se encontra em embutidos, marchetados, torneados, e outros pequenos e dispendiosos objectos decorativos.

Familj: *Fabaceae*
Densitet: *0,70-0,90 g/cm^3*
Prduktionsområden: *Guyana, Brasilien, Colombia, Venezuela*
Stammarna är ofta krokiga, 2-10 meter höga och 15-25 centimeter i diameter. Kärnvirket är krämfärgat dominerat av rödlila ränder. Ådringen är rak till vågig. Det är mycket hårt, tungt och starkt, svårt att arbeta med. På grund av den lilla storleken och den mycket höga kostnaden återfinns det idag oftast enbart i inläggningar, intarsia, svarvning och andra små dekorativa flotta föremål.

Sipo – Sipo – Sipo – Sipo

Familia: *Meliáceas*
Densidad: *0,55-0,70 g/cm^3*
Zonas de producción: *Costa de Marfil, Ghana, Camerún, Gabón, Congo*
El tronco tiene de 15 a 25 m de altura y un diámetro de 60-130 cm. El duramen es de color rojo uniforme o marrón morado con una fibra alternada media bastante irregular. Exhala un suave aroma que recuerda al cedro. La madera se emplea en la realización de muebles y de armarios, obras de carpintería, enchapados decorativos, contrachapados y en la construcción naval.

Famiglia: *Meliacee*
Densità: *0,55-0,70 g/cm^3*
Zone di produzione: *Costa d'Avorio, Ghana, Camerun, Gabon, Congo*
Il tronco ha un'altezza di 15-25 metri e un diametro di 60-130 centimetri. Il durame è di color rosso uniforme o marrone violaceo con una fibra alternata media abbastanza irregolare. Sprigiona un piacevole profumo che ricorda il cedro. Il legno s'impiega nella realizzazione di mobili e armadi, di lavori di falegnameria, impiallacciatura decorativa, compensato e nella costruzione navale.

Família: *Meliaceae*
Densidade: *0,55-0,70 g/cm^3*
Zonas de Produção: *Costa do Marfim, Gana, Camarões, Gabão, Congo*
Os troncos medem 15 a 25 metros de altura e 60 a 130 centímetros de diâmetro. O cerne é de um vermelho bastante uniforme ou castanho púrpura. Tem uma textura de grão entrecruzado médio, bastante irregular. Tem um aroma ligeiro, parecido com o do cedro. A madeira é utilizada para mobiliário e trabalhos de marcenaria, carpintaria, folheados decorativos, contraplacado e construção naval.

Familj: *Meliaceae*
Densitet: *0,55-0,70g/cm^3*
Produktionsområden: *Elfenbenskusten, Ghana, Kamerun, Gabon, Kongo*
Stammarna är 15-20 meter höga och 60-130 centimeter i diameter. Kärnvirket är ljust enhetligt rött eller lilabrunt. Det har en sammanflätad, medelådrig struktur som är ganska oregelbunden. Det har en svag cederliknande doft. Träet används till möbler och finsnickeri, snickeri, dekorationsfanering, plywood och båtkonstruktion.

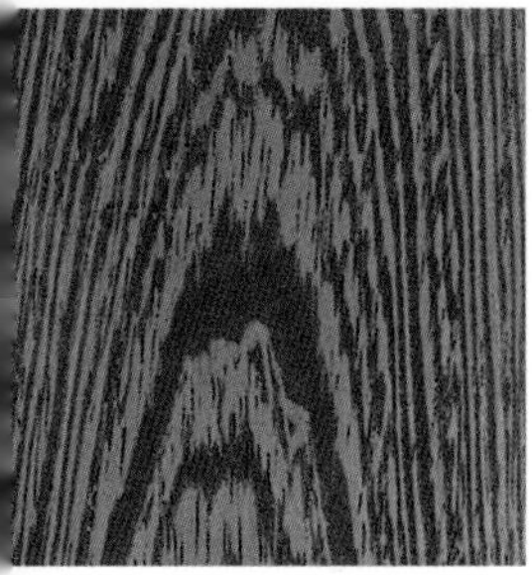

Millettia laurentii - **Wenge – Wenge – Wenge – Wengé**

Family: *Papilionaceae*
Density: *0.80-0.95 g/cm³*
Zones of Production: *Cameroon, Congo, East Africa*
Boles are 8 to 15 m (25 to 50 ft) tall and 50 to 100 cm (20 to 40 in) in diameter. Wenge is an exotic dark brown hardwood with very close, fine, almost black veins. The texture is coarse and the grain is straight to slightly wavy. Wenge is used for flooring, joinery, turned shapes, veneer, cabinets, and carving. It works well with power tools and when filled, it can be brought to a nice finish.

Famille : *Papilionacées*
Densité : *0,80-0,95 g/cm³*
Zones de production : *Cameroun, Congo, Afrique de l'Est*
Des troncs de 8 à 15 m de hauteur, pour un diamètre de 50 à 100 cm. Le wenge est un bois dur exotique brun sombre, avec des veines très serrées, fines et presque noires. Le grain est grossier et le fil varie de droit à légèrement ondé. Ce bois se travaille bien à la machine-outil. Il est susceptible de recevoir une belle finition. On utilise le wenge pour les revêtements de sol et les formes tournées, la menuiserie et l'ébénisterie, ainsi que la sculpture.

Familie: *Papilionaceae*
Dichte: *0,80-0,95 g/cm³*
Vorkommen: *Kamerun, Kongo, Ostafrika*
Der 50 bis 100 Zentimeter dicke Baumstamm ist 8 bis 15 Meter lang. Wenge ist ein exotisches dunkelbraunes Hartholz mit dichten, fein gezeichneten, nahezu schwarzen Adern. Seine Maserung ist gerade bis leicht wellig bei mittelgrober Textur. Es lässt sich gut mit Maschinenwerkzeugen bearbeiten und seine Oberfläche lässt sich sehr schön gestalten.

Familie: *Papilionaceae*
Dichtheid: *0,80-0,95 g/cm³*
Productiegebieden: *Kameroen, Congo, Oost-Afrika*
De stam is 8 tot 15 meter lang en 50 tot 100 centimeter dik. Wengé is een exotisch, donkerbruin hardhout met zeer dichte, fijne, haast zwarte aderen. De nerf is grof en de draad recht tot licht golvend. Wengé wordt gebruikt voor vloeren, schrijnwerk, draaiwerk, fineer, kasten en gravures. Het is goed elektrisch te bewerken, en als het gevuld is, laat het zich mooi afwerken.

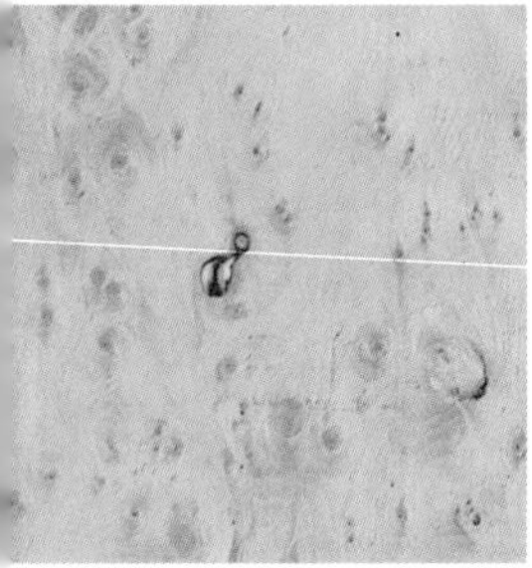

Taxus baccata - **Yew – If – Eibe – Venijnboom**

Family: *Taxaceae*
Density: *0.70-0.85 g/cm³*
Zones of Production: *France, United Kingdom*
Boles are knotty and reach 15 m (50 ft) in height. Diameters range between 20 to 100 cm (8 to 40 in). Bark thin, reddish brown and flaky, sometimes deeply fissured in very old trees.
In coarse-grained yew, the wood is yellow and may have flecks. In fine-grained yew wood is pink to red. Yew is legendary in bow-crafting circles.

Famille : *Taxacées*
Densité : *0,70-0,85 g/cm³*
Zones de production : *France et Royaume-Uni*
Les troncs – noueux – ont de 1 à 15 m de hauteur, pour un diamètre de 20 à 100 cm. L'écorce brun rougeâtre est fine et écailleuse, parfois profondément crevassée sur les très vieux arbres. Dans l'if à grain grossier, le bois de cœur est jaune et peut présenter plusieurs taches ; dans l'if à grain fin, il est rose à rouge. L'if est un bois légendaire pour les passionnés d'archerie.

Familie: *Taxaceae*
Dichte: *0,70-0,85 g/cm³*
Vorkommen: *Frankreich, Vereinigtes Königreich*
Der astreiche Baumstamm erreicht eine Höhe bis zu 15 Metern. Sein Durchmesser liegt zwischen 20 und 100 cm. Die dünne, schuppige Rinde ist rötlich-braun und zeigt bei sehr alten Bäumen häufig tiefe Risse. Das Holz der grobfaserigen Eibe ist gelb und kann Flecken aufweisen. Das feinfaserige Eibenholz ist rosa bis rot gefärbt. Die Eibe ist besonders für die Bogenherstellung beliebt.

Familie: *Taxaceae*
Dichtheid: *0,70-0,85 g/cm³*
Productiegebieden: *Frankrijk, Verenigd Koninkrijk*
De stam is knoestig en wordt tot 15 meter lang. De dikte varieert van 20 tot 100 centimeter. De dunne bast is roodbruin en schilferig, bij zeer oude bomen soms diep gespleten. Bij grofnervige venijnbomen is het hout geel en kan het vlekken vertonen.
Bij fijnnervige is het hout roze tot rood. Het hout is legendarisch in boogmakerskringen.

Microberlinia brazzavillensis - **Zebrawood – Zingana – Zebrano – Zebrano**

Family: *Fabaceae*
Density: *0.70-0.85 g/cm³*
Zones of Production: *Cameroon, Guinea, Gabon*
Boles are 10 to 20 m (33 to 66 ft) tall and 60 to 100 cm (24 to 40 in) in diameter. This exotic hardwood is pale golden brown to pinkish-brown with pronounced dark brown streaks giving the quartered surfaces a zebra-stripe appearance. This wood has a coarse texture and lustrous surface. Zebrawood is used for cabinet work, inlay, flooring, joinery and turnings. The wood works easily with hand and power tools.

Famille : *Fabacées*
Densité : *0,70-0,85 g/cm³*
Zones de production : *Cameroun, Guinée et Gabon*
Des troncs de 10 à 20 m de hauteur, pour un diamètre de 60 à 100 cm. Ce bois dur exotique est de couleur brun doré pâle à brun rosé, avec des veines marquées brun foncé, qui prennent des allures de zébrure sur les surfaces sciées sur quartier. Le grain est grossier, la surface est lustrée. Le zingana se travaille aisément, manuellement ou à la machine-outil. On l'utilise en ébénisterie comme en menuiserie, pour le tournage et pour les revêtements de sol, mais aussi en incrustation.

Familie: *Fabaceae*
Dichte: *0,70-0,85 g/cm³*
Vorkommen: *Kamerun, Guinea, Gabun*
Der 60 bis 100 Zentimeter dicke Baumstamm erreicht eine Höhe von 10 bis 20 Metern. Dieses exotische Hartholz ist blass goldbraun bis blassrosa braun, mit ausgeprägten dunkelbraunen Linien, die im Radialschnitt eine zebraähnliche Streifung ergeben. Das Holz mit grober Textur weist eine glänzende Oberfläche auf. Zebrano wird für Schränke, Einlegearbeiten, für Fußböden, in der Zimmerei und für Drehformen verwendet. Es lässt sich gut von Hand und maschinell bearbeiten.

Familie: *Fabaceae*
Dichtheid: *0,70-0,85 g/cm³*
Productiegebieden: *Kameroen, Guinea, Gabon*
De stam is 10 tot 20 meter lang en 60 tot 100 centimeter dik. Dit exotische hardhout is licht goudbruin tot rozebruin en heeft duidelijke donkerbruine strepen die kwartiers gezaagde oppervlakken een zebra-uiterlijk geven. Het heeft een grove structuur en een glanzend oppervlak. Zebrano wordt gebruikt voor kasten, inlegwerk, vloeren, schrijnwerk en draaiwerk. Het hout is goed elektrisch en met de hand te bewerken.

Wengué – Wengé – Wengé – Wenge

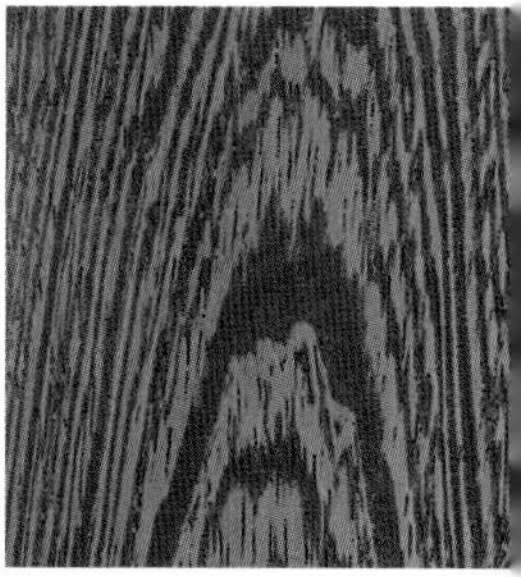

Familia: *Papilionáceas*
Densidad: *0,80-0,95 g/cm³*
Zonas de producción: *Camerún, Congo, África Oriental*
El tronco tiene de 8 a 15 m de altura y un diámetro de 50 a 100 cm. El wengué se caracteriza por un exótico duramen de color marrón oscuro con venas muy tupidas y finas casi negras. La textura es gruesa y el hilo es recto tirando a ondulado. La madera se emplea para revestir suelos, en obras de carpintería, piezas torneadas, enchapados, armarios y tallas. Funciona bien con herramientas para mecanizado y, una vez pulida, presenta un óptimo acabado.

Famiglia: *Papilionacee*
Densità: *0.80-0.95 g/cm³*
Zone di produzione: *Camerun, Congo, Africa orientale*
Il tronco ha da 8 a 15 metri d'altezza e un diametro di 50-100 centimetri. Il wengé si distingue per un esotico durame di color marrone scuro con vene molto ravvicinate e fini quasi nere. La texture è ruvida e il filo è retto, ma tendente a ondularsi. Il legno si usa per ricoprire pavimenti, in lavori di falegnameria, oggetti torniti, impiallacciatura, armadi e lavori a intaglio. Funziona bene con macchine utensili e, una volta levigato, presenta un'ottima rifinitura.

Família: *Papilionaceae*
Densidade: *0,80-0,95 g/cm³*
Zonas de Produção: *Camarões, Congo, África Oriental*
Os troncos medem 8 a 15 metros de altura e 50 a 100 centímetros de diâmetro. O wengé é uma madeira exótica dura, castanho escura, com veios muito juntos, finos e quase pretos. A textura é grosseira e o grão é direito a ligeiramente ondulado. É utilizado para soalhos, carpintaria, formas curvas, folheado, armários e escultura. Trabalha-se bem com ferramentas eléctricas e quando moldado permite um excelente acabamento.

Familj: *Papilionaceae*
Densitet: *0,80-, 095 g/cm³*
Produktionsområden: *Kamerun, Kongo, Östafrika*
Stammarna är 8-15 meter höga och 50-100 centimeter i diameter. Wenge är ett exotiskt mörkbrunt hårdträ med mycket täta, fina, nästan svarta ådror. Strukturen är grov och ådringen är rakt till något vågig. Wenge används till golvläggning, snickeri, svarvade former, fanering, möbler och sniderі. Det arbetas lätt med kraftverktyg och om det mättas kan det ges en fin ytbehandling.

Tejo común – Tasso – Teixo – Idegran

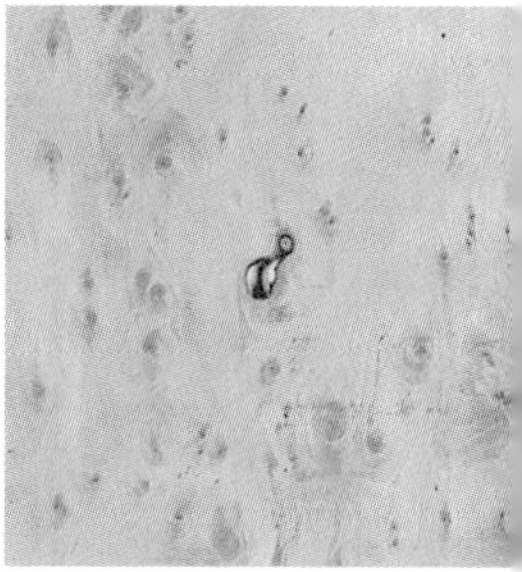

Familia: *Taxáceas*
Densidad: *0,70-0,85 g/cm³*
Zonas de producción: *Francia, Reino Unido*
El tronco es nudoso y puede alcanzar una altura de 15 m y un diámetro de 20 a 100 cm. La corteza es delgada, laminada y de color marrón rojizo. En los ejemplares más viejos, suelen aparecer muchas fisuras. La madera de los tejos de veta gruesa es amarilla y puede presentar motas; por el contrario, la de los tejos de veta fina es rosa tirando a rojo. El tejo es legendario en el sector dedicado a la manufactura de arcos.

Famiglia: *Taxacee*
Densità: *0,70-0,85 g/cm³*
Zone di produzione: *Francia, Inghilterra*
Il tronco è nodoso e può raggiungere un'altezza di 15 metri e un diametro da 20 a 100 centimetri. La corteccia è sottile, scagliosa e di color marrone rossastro. Negli esemplari più vecchi, appaiono di solito molte fessure. Il legno del tasso che presenta venature ruvide è giallo e può avere macchie; invece, il tasso dalle venature fini ha un legno rosa tendente al rosso. Quello del tasso è un legno leggendario negli ambienti dediti alla costruzione di archi.

Família: *Taxaceae*
Densidade: *0,70-0,85 g/cm³*
Zonas de Produção: *França, Reino Unido*
Os troncos são nodosos e atingem 15 metros de altura. Os diâmetros variam entre os 20 e os 100 centímetros. A casca é fina, castanha avermelhada e escamosa, por vezes profundamente fendida em árvores muito velhas. No teixo de grão grosseiro a madeira é amarela e pode ter manchas. No teixo de grão fino a madeira é cor-de-rosa a vermelha. O teixo é lendário entre os artesãos de arcos.

Familj: *Taxaceae*
Densitet: *0,70-0,85 g/cm³*
Produktionsområden: *Frankrike, Storbritannien*
Stammarna är knotiga och når 15 meters höjd. Diametern varierar mellan 20 och 100 centimeter. Barken är tunn, rödbrun och flagig, ibland djupt fårad hos mycket gamla träd. Hos grovådrad idegran är träet gult och kan ha fläckar. Hos finådrad idegran är träet rosa till rött. Idegran är legendariskt i pilbågskretsar.

Zebrano – Zebrano – Zingana – Zebrano

Familia: *Fabáceas*
Densidad: *0,70-0,85 g/cm³*
Zonas de producción: *Camerún, Guinea, Gabón*
El tronco tiene de 10 a 20 m de altura y un diámetro de 60 a 100 cm. Esta exótica madera noble es de color marrón dorado pálido tirando a marrón rosáceo con rayas marrón oscuro muy pronunciadas, algo que en las superficies serradas en cuartos nos recuerda al pelaje de las cebras. Se caracteriza asimismo por una textura gruesa y una superficie brillante. El zebrano se emplea en la realización de armarios, incrustaciones, revestimientos para suelos, obras de carpintería y en tornería. Se trabaja bien tanto con herramientas manuales como con máquinas-herramienta.

Famiglia: *Fabacee*
Densità: *0,70-0,85 g/cm³*
Zone di produzione: *Camerun, Guinea, Gabon*
Il tronco ha un'altezza di 10-20 metri e un diametro tra i 60 e i 100 centimetri. Questo esotico legno nobile è di color marrone dorato pallido tendente a marrone rosaceo con striature marrone scuro molto pronunciate, una caratteristica che sulle superfici tagliate ricorda il manto delle zebre. Si distingue inoltre per una texture ruvida e una superficie lucida. Lo zebrano si usa nella realizzazione di armadi, nell'intarsio, nel parquet, in lavori di falegnameria e in tornitura. Si lavora bene sia con strumenti manuali sia con macchine-utensili.

Família: *Fabaceae*
Densidade: *0,70-0,85 g/cm³*
Zonas de Produção: *Camarões, Guiné, Gabão*
Os troncos medem 10 a 20 metros de altura e 60 a 100 centímetros de diâmetro. Esta exótica madeira dura é castanha dourada clara a castanha rosada, com acentuadas listas castanho escuras que dão às superfícies cortadas radialmente uma aparência de riscas de zebra. Esta madeira tem uma textura grosseira e uma superfície brilhante. A zingana é utilizada em trabalhos de marcenaria, embutidos, soalhos, carpintaria e torneados. Trabalha-se bem com ferramentas manuais e eléctricas.

Familj: *Fabaceae*
Densitet: *0,70-0,85 g/cm³*
Produktionsområden: *Kamerun, Guinea, Gabon*
Stammarna är 10-20 meter höga och 60-100 centimeter i diameter. Det exotiska hårdträet är blekt gyllenbrunt till rosabrunt med framträdande mörkbruna strimmor som ger de kantsågade ytorna ett zebrarandigt utseende. Detta trä har en grov struktur och en glänsande yta. Zebranoträ används till möbeltillverkning, inläggningar, golvläggning, snickeri och svarvning. Träet arbetas enkelt med hand- eller kraftverktyg.

DIRECTORY

3LHD Architects
Zagreb, Croatia
www.3lhd.com
Collaborators: Paula Kukuljica, Lucija Staničić, Marija Babojelić
Structural engineer: Ivan Palijan
House J2

Alberto Mozó Leverington
Santiago de Chile, Chile
alberto@mozo.cl
Collaborators: Francisca Cifuentes, Mauricio Leal, Luis Fernández
Contractors: Estructura Madera Arauco, Constructora Las Torcasas
BPI Computer Office and Shop

Andreas Wenning/Baumraum
Bremen, Germany
www.baumraum.de
All Tree House Projects

Arbau Studio
Treviso, Italy
www.arbau.org
Collaborators: Francesca Toppazzini, Monica Martini
Ghaus

Architekturbüro Matthias Loebermann
Nuremberg, Germany
www.aml-partner.de
Collaborators: Berit Richter, students at the University of Biberach
Path of the Senses
Stabraum Pavilion
Pallet Pavilion

Atelier Klaus Bittner
Frankfurt, Germany
www.atelier-bittner.de
Destiny of Trees

Bernard Quirot Architecte et Associés
Pesmes, France
www.quirotassocies.com
Convercey House

Bevk Perovič Architekti
Ljubljana, Slovenia
www.bevkperovic.com
House R

Casanova & Hernandez Architecten
Rotterdam, The Netherlands
www.casanova-hernandez.com
Contractor: BAM Wilma
Structural engineer: Dijkhuis
Services engineer: Van der Weele
Patio Villas

Cazú Zegers/Aira Arquitectos
Santiago de Chile, Chile
www.cazuzegers.cl
Granary House
Tent House
Shell House
House of Silence

Counson Architectes
Vielsalm, Belgium
www.counson-architecte.net
POB 62: Prototype of Precast Wooden House

Cukrowicz Nachbaur Architekten
Bregenz, Austria
www.cn-architekten.at
House for a Carpenter

Despang Architekten
Hannover, Germany
www.despangarchitekten.de
Structural engineer: Drewes & Speth
TMT wood and glass facçades: Branning
Farm House Voges Redux

Ecosistema Urbano Arquitectos
Madrid, Spain
www.ecosistemaurbano.com
House of Steel and Wood

Foreign Office Architects
London, United Kingdom
www.f-o-a.net
Contractor: Acciona
Structural engineers: Jesús Hierro, JHS Proyecto de Estructuras y Arquitectura
Quantity surveyor: Alfonso Cuenca Sánchez
Electrical engineer: Faseven
Mechanical engineer: Asetecnic
Telecommunication engineers: Raúl Heranz, SDC
Carabanchel Social Housing

Jorge Armando Rodríguez Bello
Chia, Colombia
rodriguezbello2000@yahoo.com
Library in the Garden

Juan Pablo Corvalán/Supersudaka
www.supersudaka.cl
Engineer: Cesar Moreira/Sigma Ingenieros
Kiltro House

Kimmo Friman/Friman Laaksonen Arkkitehdit
Helsinki, Finland
www.fl-a.fi
Interior design: Jouko Järvisalo (kitchen)
Construction engineers: Tero Aaltonen, Stefan Forstén/Innostructura; Yrjo Kinnunen/Peruskonsultit
HPAC engineer: Jukka Penttinen/BSC Busecon
Electrical engineer: Antti Syrjänen
Carpenters: Risto Niilimäki, Mikko Immonen (house); Saara ja Vesa Isola/Heikkisen Haka (sauna)
The Humlegård House and Logsauna

Korteknie Stuhlmacher Architecten
Rotterdam, The Netherlands
www.kortekniestuhlmacher.nl
Collaborator: Bikvander Pol
House Number 19

Marco Casagrande, Frank Chen/C-Laboratorio
Inkoo, Finland
www.clab.fi
Chen House

Maria Claudia Clemente, Francesco Isidori, Marco Sardella/Labics
Rome, Italy
www.labics.it
Structural engineer: Studio 3S
Via Appia House

Markus Wespi & Jérôme de Meuron
Caviano, Switzerland
www.wespidemeuron.ch
Wood House in Caviano

Naumann Architektur
Stuttgart, Germany
www.fnp-architekten.de
Schwitzkasten Sauna Pavilion

Nicos Kalogirou
Thessaloniki, Greece
nkalogir@arch.auth.gr
Collaborators: Telis & Prodromos Vassiliadis, Artemis Kalogirou, Evangelos Kotsioris
Split & Rotate House